Touring
Swedish
America

New Sweden Evangelical Lutheran Church, Manor, Texas

Touring Swedish America

Where to Go and What to See

Alan H. Winquist and Jessica Rousselow-Winquist

Minnesota Historical Society Press

Published in cooperation with the Swedish Council of America.

Updated and expanded edition of *Swedish-American Landmarks—Where to go and what to see* by Alan H. Winquist, © 1995 by the Swedish Council of America.

Design by Dennis Anderson; maps by Cartographics.

Text photographs: Alan Winquist and Jessica Rousselow-Winquist Collection

www.mhspress.org

The Minnesota Historical Society Press is a member of the Association of American University Presses.

Manufactured in the United States of America

10 9 8 7 6 5 4 3 2 1

♾ The paper used in this publication meets the minimum requirements of the American National Standard for Information Sciences— Permanence for Printed Library Materials, ANSI Z39.48-1992.

International Standard Book Number-13: 978-0-87351-559-7
International Standard Book Number-10: 0-87351-559-5

Library of Congress Cataloging-in-Publication Data:

Winquist, Alan H.
    Touring Swedish America : where to go and what to see / Alan H. Winquist and Jessica Rousselow-Winquist.
    p. cm.
Rev. ed of: Swedish-American landmarks, ©1995.
Includes index.
ISBN-13: 978-0-87351-559-7 (pbk. : alk. paper)
ISBN-10: 0-87351-559-5 (pbk. : alk. paper)
1. Swedish Americans—History. 2. Swedish Americans—Monuments—Guidebooks.
3. Historic sites—United States—Guidebooks. 4. United States—Guidebooks. I. Rousselow-Winquist, Jessica. II. Winquist, Alan H. Swedish-American landmarks. III. Title.
E184.S23W53 2006
973'.04397—dc22   2005036352

Contents

Acknowledgments

Writing this book required a great amount of research. We would not have been able to complete it without the help of many friends and acquaintances who acted as readers and fact checkers. The list of people who deserve our grateful appreciation is long. Birger Jansson, former chair of the Committee for Cultural Affairs of the Swedish Council of America, deserves special recognition. He was the driving force in achieving publication of the first edition. We regret he did not live to see the publication of this new edition.

We wish to give special thanks to Susan Larson, former executive director of the Swedish Council, and other members of this organization for their vision for this second edition. The authors greatly appreciate the assistance and support of the Minnesota Historical Society Press, particularly Gregory M. Britton, director, and his able staff, especially Marilyn Ziebarth, editor, and Helen S. Newlin. Also, thank you to Kerry Porter and Monica Rusu, who helped with the indexing.

In the Northeast, people who were especially helpful include Richard Waldron, Margaretha Talerman, and Christy Schneider of Philadelphia; Carol Firenj of Upland, Pennsylvania; Rebecca Ross and Christine Almerico of Elverson, Pennsylvania; Alicia Bjornson of Hancock's Bridge, New Jersey; Ray Nickels, Barbara Mayers, and Marianne Mackenzie of Wilmington, Delaware; Harry Rink of Gibbstown, New Jersey; Nancy Jackson of Mauricetown, New Jersey; Father Samuel Hartman of North East, Maryland; Reverend Timothy Alleman of Mount Jewett, Pennsylvania; Mabel Todd of New Sweden, Maine; Ingrid Ogren of Rockport, Massachusetts; Reverend Paul Lindstrom and Carol Davis of Worcester, Massachusetts; Irene Wheeler, Bob Anderson, and Mark Parker of Woodstock, Connecticut; Karen Livsey, Kathy Ziebert, and Beth Johnson of Jamestown, New York.

We wish to acknowledge Kai Swanson, Dag Blanck, and Anne Jenner of Rock Island, Illinois; William Glendon of East Moline, Illinois; Barbara and Richard Lunde, Leah M. Nelson, Dan Bartlett, and William C. Mohr of Rockford, Illinois; John Norton and Richard Horngren of Bishop Hill, Illinois; Harold Smith of Galva, Illinois; Charles Peterson, Charlene Sandberg, Steve Elde, and James Saiki of Chicago; Sharon Wold of Eau Claire, Wisconsin; and Reverend Sean Nemecek of Tustin, Michigan, who aided us on our chapter about the eastern Midwest.

For the western Midwest chapter, we especially want to thank A. John Pearson, as well as Irene L. Nielsen, Kathi Patterson, Charlotte Thernstrom, and Becky Anderson of Lindsborg, Kansas; Louise Unkrich and Jane Wickham of

Swedesburg, Iowa; Don Peterson of Stanton, Iowa; Gloria and Wilma Jackson of Lansing, Iowa; Carol and Wayne Larson and Keith Carlson of Stratford, Iowa; Anne Anderson and Merle Block of Gothenburg, Nebraska; Maxine Bridgman Isackson of Brady, Nebraska; Janet Benson of Ong, Nebraska; William Bina of Axtell, Nebraska; Carroll and Leona Falk of Wilcox, Nebraska; Sandra Anderson of Oakland, Nebraska; Shirley and Dick Carter of Omaha, Nebraska; Virginia Johnson of Vermillion, South Dakota; Reverend Daryl Runion of Alcester, South Dakota; Lois and Ralph Hansen of Beaver Creek, Minnesota; Ken and Bea Johnson of Grafton, North Dakota; and John Parrish of Norman, Oklahoma.

In Minnesota, fact checkers and important resource people include acting executive director Elise Peters and project manager Holly Johnson of the Swedish Council of America, Minneapolis; William Beyer and Mariann Tiblin of Minneapolis; James Spickelmier and Diana Magnuson of St. Paul; Reverend Arden Haug of Marine on St. Croix; Jeanne Kehn of Harris; Reverend Jonathan Larson and Dorothy Nelson of Cambridge; Steve Waldhauser of St. Peter; David and Linda Rousselow of Mankato; Bernard Anderson and Wallace Gardiner Jr. of Vasa; Neil Brodin and Danielle Rodgers of Litchfield; Helen Fosso of Pennock; Richard Carlson of Nisswa; and James Kaplan of Morehead.

We are grateful to these people in the South: Curtis Peterson and Amy Oliver of Newport News, Virginia; Karen Jacobs and Alicia Clarke of Sanford, Florida; James and Joy Forsman of Shalimar, Florida; Ted Forsman and Dixie White of Silverhill, Alabama; and in Texas, Annette Bethke, Dan Utley, Egina G. Reyes, and Michelle M. Mears of Austin; Marilyn Murray, Reverend Elroy Havelah, Grace Telander, and Liz Duke of Round Rock; Marilynn Guard of Georgetown; Lamar Lentz and Richard R. Royall of Round Top; Joshua Rousselow of San Antonio; Amber Puckett of Corpus Christi; Dwight and Lynne Lind of McAllen; Cynthia Quinn and Mr. and Mrs. David Dahlberg of Brady; and Yvonne Hansen of Avoca.

In the West special thanks goes to Byron Magnusson of Fox Island, Washington; Reverend J. Murray and Mrs. Nancy Marshall of Seattle; Ross Fogelquist and Mary Sicilia of Portland, Oregon; California's Aina Abrahamson and Mr. and Mrs. Richard Lundgren of Thousand Oaks, Reverend Janice Nairn of Templeton, Stephen A. Wilson of Los Gatos, Astrid Olson of San Francisco, and June Olson Hess and Ronald Bergman of Kingsburg; Colorado's Annely Peterson of Longmont, Malcolm G. Stevenson of Littleton, Michelle Zupan of Golden, and Robert Beer of Telluride; John Chilcote of Clayton, New Mexico; and Kathrine Neilsen of Willcox, Arizona.

Finally, we would like to thank Taylor University for sabbatical leaves to rewrite the book, especially Dwight Jessup, former provost and academic dean, and his wife, Karin, for their wise counsel, and members of the history and communication departments for their support.

Touring
Swedish
America

Water tower, Stanton, Iowa

Introduction

Nearly thirty years ago, a student of Swedish ancestry inquired whether a guidebook had ever been written that described existing historic landmarks—pioneer homes, churches, schools, hospitals, monuments, and plaques—relating to Swedish immigrants in the United States. The answer was no, and the plan for such a book began to develop.

During the course of three summers and the fall of 1982, Alan Winquist traveled from the northeast corner of Maine to San Diego, California, and from Seattle, Washington, to Silverhill, Alabama, searching for noteworthy Swedish American historic buildings and monuments. He visited thirty-six states plus the District of Columbia for the purpose of identifying Swedish communities, locating landmarks, interviewing people, taking photographs, and gathering information. This material was incorporated into *Swedish-American Landmarks: Where to Go and What to See,* published in 1995 by the Swedish Council of America, in Minneapolis, Minnesota.

This popular first edition sold out. In 2003 Susan Larson, then executive director of the Swedish Council, approached us about updating and republishing the book as a joint enterprise of the Swedish Council and the Minnesota Historical Society. We agreed. While we had been developing a file of additional and lost landmarks, we knew much more research needed to be done. Granted sabbatical leaves from Taylor University in 2004, we traversed twenty-six states, from the East Coast to the Rockies. In the summer of 2003 we had also traveled through the Pacific Northwest and northern California.

This new book contains a description of the most significant landmarks, photographs, and maps. It also has historical background and anecdotes about many of these sites. Considerations regarding the book's length forced us to limit descriptions of some sites. Sites are grouped by region and state.

As we worked our way across the nation, we were amazed by the diversity of historical sites. Swedish Americans in many parts of the country clearly maintain an interest in the accomplishments of their forebears and try to preserve what has been built in the past. This is particularly true in the Midwest and Texas and to a lesser extent in the East.

We focused primarily on homes, historic towns, and churches from the early Delaware River Valley settlements and from the main Swedish immigration period, roughly the 1840s to the 1920s. When immigrants arrived, their first concern, understandably, was putting a roof over their heads. Some original immigrant

3

homes survive—for example, several log cabins in the Delaware Valley dating from the 1600s and restored nineteenth-century log homes in a number of southern, midwestern, and western states. Homes of prominent Swedish Americans have also been preserved as museums. These include Carl Sandburg's birthplace (Galesburg, Illinois) and residence (Flat Rock, North Carolina), the Charles A. Lindbergh House (Little Falls, Minnesota), the residence of the musician and composer Howard Hanson (Wahoo, Nebraska), and the homestead of John Morton (Philadelphia). Residences in unique architectural styles, built by Swedish craftsmen, include the Swan Turnblad Mansion (Minneapolis), now the American Swedish Institute, and the Hovander Homestead (Ferndale, Washington).

Historic towns dominated by Swedish immigrants include Bishop Hill, Illinois; Stanton, Iowa; Lindsborg, Marquette, and Scandia, Kansas; New Sweden, Maine; Scandia and Vasa, Minnesota; and Stromsburg, Nebraska. Within these and other towns are a number of residential areas built and owned by Swedes that are currently on or being proposed for the National Register of Historic Places.

Religion played an important role in the lives of many Swedish immigrants, and after constructing homes, they frequently turned their attention to a place of worship. A large number of their churches, particularly in rural areas, survive, but most have undergone major alterations. A notable exception is the New Sweden Lutheran Church in New Sweden, Iowa, completed in 1861. Usually a Swedish community organized not only a Lutheran church, but also Covenant and Baptist congregations and sometimes Methodist and Evangelical Free congregations. We focused mainly on churches constructed before 1900 (later on the West Coast), concentrating on those still used mainly by Swedish Americans. Other buildings are included if they played a significant historic role in the Swedish American community or if they contain unique architectural features, particularly Swedish design. Traditional Swedish architectural styles may be noted in such churches as Trinity Lutheran, Worcester, Massachusetts; Bethany Lutheran, Lindsborg, Kansas; and the former Gethsemane Lutheran, Austin, Texas. Elements of modern and traditional Swedish architecture may be seen in some of the churches designed by Swedish architect Martin Hedmark, including Trinity Baptist Church in New York City, Gloria Dei Evangelical Lutheran Church in Providence, and Immanuel Evangelical Lutheran Church in Chicago.

From the early days, Swedish immigrants were concerned with education, health, and old age. Swedes established at least sixteen schools of higher learning; only five of these colleges—North Park in Chicago and Augustana in Rock Island, Illinois; Gustavus Adolphus in St. Peter and Bethel in St. Paul, Minnesota; and Bethany in Lindsborg, Kansas—still survive. The Frank Carlson Library, Concordia, Kansas, and Ericson Memorial Public Library, Boone, Iowa, are named for Swedish Americans. Swedes were also active in founding hospitals, retirement homes, and orphanages. Swedish-oriented fraternal organizations and clubs, including the Vasa Order of America, the Independent Order of Svithiod, the International Organization of Good Templars, and the Independent Order of Vikings, also served immigrants' needs.

Businesses begun by Swedes stretch from coast to coast. For example, Swedish immigrants John Jeppson and Sven Pålson (Swen Pulson) were involved with founding the Norton Company of Worcester, Massachusetts, which became the world's largest maker of abrasives and grinding machinery. In Chicago, Charles R. Walgreen began a drugstore business that developed into a nationwide chain. Headquartered in Seattle, Nordstrom is another enterprise begun by Swedish Americans that has expanded its retail stores across the country.

Chronicling the immigrant experience with renewed interest in the Swedish contribution to American culture and life are a number of Swedish American museums. The well-established American Swedish Historical Museum, Philadelphia, and the American Swedish Institute, Minneapolis, are outstanding examples. Chicago's Swedish American Museum Center was begun modestly, but in 1987 it purchased a four-story building that multiplied its square footage significantly. Smaller museums are scattered throughout the country in such places as New Sweden, Maine; Scandia, Minnesota; Andover, Illinois; Stanton, Iowa; Swedesburg, Iowa; and Scandia, Kansas. The McPherson County Old Mill Museum and Park, Lindsborg, Kansas, includes displays about Swedes along with other ethnic groups. The Nordic Heritage Museum in Seattle focuses on all five Nordic countries. The Institute of Texan Cultures in San Antonio features more than two-dozen Texas ethnic groups, including an extensive display of Swedish contributions.

Monuments, statues, and plaques commemorate important Swedish Americans and events, officially recognizing Swedish contributions to our history. Minnesota, Texas, Nebraska, Pennsylvania, Illinois, Kansas, and South Dakota lead in this type of recognition. Church markers may commemorate the beginning of a denomination, an important conference, or a former church building. Markers also depict such specific events as the founding of New Sweden in the Delaware Valley and the deaths in 1862 of Swedish settlers near New London, Minnesota. Perhaps the most unusually located is the plaque at the summit of Pike's Peak in Colorado honoring Kansas artist Carl Lotave.

Swedish inscriptions on monuments, plaques, church and educational buildings, and gravestones have also drawn our interest. Church congregations frequently placed Swedish inscriptions over altars or pulpits, but when English replaced Swedish during the 1920s and 1930s, most original inscriptions were removed. Some are now being restored, such as in the Fish Lake Lutheran Church, in Harris, Minnesota.

We have noted art depicting historical events in Sweden or related to Swedish immigrants, as well as altar paintings by Olof Grafström and Birger Sandzén. We have also located sculpture created by Swedish or Swedish American artists, particularly Paul Granlund, Carl Milles, Claes Oldenburg, and Kent Ullberg.

We have added significant websites and updated telephone numbers for many landmarks. New appendixes list sites on the National Register of Historic Places (identified in the main text with a symbol) and sites with other significant national and state designations.

We have commented on the landmarks' physical conditions and noted structures that are endangered. We have also paid more attention to the role of women and expanded anecdotes that make the narrative more interesting.

Many additional landmarks have been added to the original list, including Faraway Ranch in Chiricahua National Monument, Arizona; Tallman Ranch, Golden Gate Canyon State Park, Colorado; Jacobson House, Norman, Oklahoma; the Stockholm Church, Shickley, Nebraska; and the town of Thorsby, Alabama. Some sites have been deleted. Others have had name changes or are being used in different ways, for example, Linnea Hall, Portland, Oregon; Palm Mansion, Round Rock, Texas; the former Trinity Swedish Evangelical Lutheran Church, Chicago; and Swede-Finn Hall, Telluride, Colorado. Restoration success stories are mentioned, for example, Fish Lake Lutheran Church, Harris, Minnesota; Salem Methodist Episcopal Church, Axtell, Nebraska; and Cordelia Lutheran Church, Moscow, Idaho. Museum expansions are noted, among them the Swedish American Museum Center, Chicago; Stanton Swedish Heritage Cultural Center, Stanton, Iowa; and Swedish American Museum, Swedesburg, Iowa. Additional research has meant changes to some interpretive material found in the first edition.

Most sites mentioned are easily accessible, although many churches, particularly in large metropolitan areas, are closed for security reasons. Rural churches should, but may not be, secured to avoid vandalization, as was the fate of Stockholm Church in Shickley, Nebraska. Others have been torn down, including Mariadahl Lutheran Church north of Manhattan, Kansas.

Balancing these forces are individuals or small groups spearheading restoration projects. The idea that certain churches and houses are worth saving is growing, though traditionally Swedish Americans have been modest in their preservation efforts and reluctant to memorialize what is so familiar to them.

Our project has always been challenging and stimulating. The best part of our work has been meeting interested people of Swedish extraction who can often recount fascinating anecdotes about the sites.

This guide is as accurate and as comprehensive as possible, in part because many local fact checkers assisted us in our work. Despite our best efforts, the information will nevertheless be incomplete. Because time passes, people change, and so do places, we advise phoning sites before visiting.

In tribute to the Swedes and Swedish Americans who have gone before us, we offer this guide as an aid to readers wishing to learn more about the Swedish immigrant story and its vital impact on the development of the United States.

Alan Winquist and Jessica Rousselow-Winquist

 This symbol indicates the building is listed on the National Register of Historic Places.

Holy Trinity (Old Swedes) Church, Wilmington

THE NORTHEAST

DELAWARE

Wilmington

 This guidebook to Swedish American landmarks fittingly begins in the city of Wilmington with **Fort Christina State Park** (302-739-4266), on Seventh Street adjacent to the Christina River, a tributary of the Delaware River. It was here on March 26, 1638, that the first Swedes landed in North America, establishing the New Sweden Colony. While nothing remains of the Swedes' original fort, the state park located on the original site is on the National Register of Historic Places. The park commemorates the expedition led by Peter Minuit and his two ships, the *Kalmar Nyckel* and the *Fogel Grip*. In 1938 a monument by Swedish sculptor Carl Milles was dedicated in the presence of President Franklin D. Roosevelt, Crown Prince Gustav Adolf, Crown Princess Louise, and Prince Bertil. It is a hexagon of black Swedish granite surmounted by a stylized wave bearing the ship *Kalmar Nyckel*. On the granite shaft are inscriptions and bas-reliefs depicting various seventeenth-century historical events pertaining to the New Sweden Colony.

Along the walk near the Milles monument are historic plaques noting that the log cabin was unknown in the New World until introduced by Swedes at Fort Christina. It "proved cheap, quickly and easily built." A nearby log cabin is identified as "the early Swedish type with rough-hewn round logs saddle-notched at the ends, chinked with sticks, twigs, and grass-mixed clay. It has one large room with a fireplace and a huge shelf above for extra sleeping and storage space." Several other early Swedish cabins stand in the Delaware Valley.

At the end of Seventh Street on the Christina River is the East Seventh Street Park, a historical site opened in 1988. It houses a partial replica of Fort Christina.

A replica of the Dutch-built *Kalmar Nyckel*, located at the **Kalmar Nyckel Shipyard**, 1124 E. Seventh Street (302-429-7447; www.kalnyc.org), was designed, built, and launched by the Kalmar Nyckel Foundation in 1997. The three-masted pinnace, painted blue and gold and featuring decorative wood carvings, measures ninety-three feet in length, with a beam of twenty-five feet and a draft of more than twelve feet.

 Holy Trinity (Old Swedes) Church, 606 Church Street (302-652-5629; www .oldswedes.org), was erected in 1698–99, making it the oldest original sanctuary in the United States that still holds regular religious services. Established in 1638, the church initially conducted services in Fort Christina. In 1667, the Lutheran community built a new church two miles to the south at Crane Hook, which was more convenient for Swedes and Finns on that side of the river. This wooden church was used for thirty years. (Its former site, west of the intersection of Pigeon Point Road with the railroad spur serving the Castlewood Industrial Park, is indicated by a stone marker on the grounds of an oil refinery.)

In 1697, three Church of Sweden missionaries—Jonas Aurén, Eric Björk, and Andreas Rudman—arrived in the colony, and on Trinity Sunday, July 4, 1699, the present church was consecrated. It remained a Swedish Lutheran congregation until 1791, when it was transferred to the Protestant Episcopal Church. Eight "Old Swedes" churches remain in the Delaware Valley—in Wilmington; Pennsville and Swedesboro, New Jersey; Philadelphia, Kingsessing, Upper Merion, and Douglasville, Pennsylvania; and North East, Maryland; they are now all Episcopalian.

The sanctuary of Holy Trinity contains historically significant features, including the original raised, canopied pulpit made of black walnut and believed to be the oldest in the United States. The herringbone bricks in the main aisle and the hinges on the main door were imported from Sweden. A large church chest for storing valuables dates from 1713; it has two keyholes requiring different keys, making it similar to modern safe-deposit boxes. Three portraits of early pastors—the first pastor, Eric Björk, the fifth, Peter Tranberg, and the sixth, Israel Acrelius—grace the front of the balcony. The church's stained-glass windows were added between 1885 and 1897. On the south side is a Tiffany window portraying the Holy Family—Mary spins, while the boy Jesus carries a carpenter's square.

Although there is a surrounding cemetery, eight graves are inside the church. In the cross-aisle is the burial site of the infant son of the last Swedish pastor of Old Swedes, who died of whooping cough in 1786. In the south porch under the steps to the balcony is the grave of Carl Christopherson Springer (1658–1738), head warden to Pastor Björk. Springer grew up in Sweden, was sent abroad to school, and, while returning home, was kidnapped and put on a boat to the New World. When the ship reached Virginia, he was sold as an indentured servant. Learning that there were Swedes in the Delaware Valley, he worked off his indenture in five years and walked 400 miles to join them. The graveyard surrounding the church, which predates the church by sixty years, was a burial ground for the early settlers of Fort Christina. Most identifiable burial markers indicate settlers of English descent.

On the opposite side of the cemetery from the church is **Hendrickson House**. The stone dwelling was built in 1690 for Andrew Hendrickson, a young Swedish farmer, and his wife, Brigitta, daughter of Mårten Mårtensson. In the late 1950s

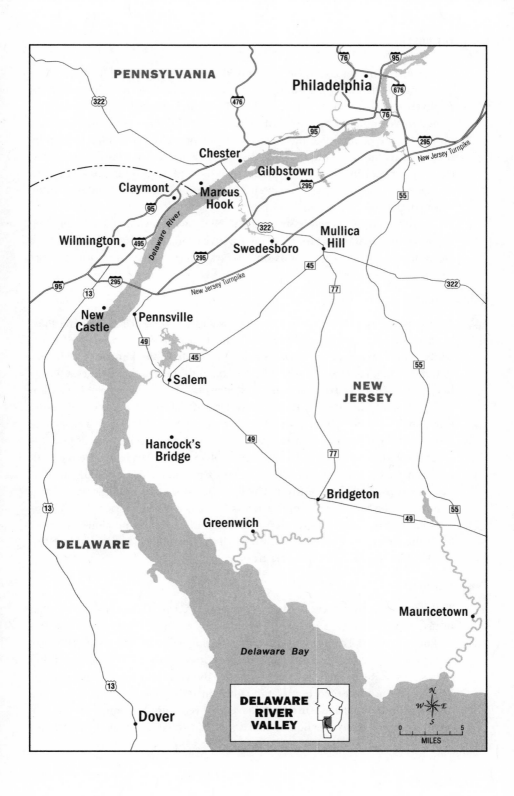

PENNSYLVANIA

Philadelphia

Chester

Claymont

Gibbstown

Marcus
Hook

Delaware River

Wilmington

Swedesboro

Mullica
Hill

New
Castle

Pennsville

New Jersey Turnpike

Salem

NEW
JERSEY

Hancock's
Bridge

Bridgeton

Greenwich

DELAWARE

Mauricetown

Delaware Bay

DELAWARE
RIVER
VALLEY

Dover

MILES
0   5

the seventeenth-century house was moved to the present site. One of the two rooms on the first floor is a gift shop. In the other can be seen the Hendrickson family Bible, Hendrickson's 1722 will, and a model of the *Kalmar Nyckel* presented to Wilmington by the Maritime Museum of Gothenburg, Sweden. Also on display are paintings of the church and the altar cloth presented in 1950 by the Swedish ambassador to the United States on behalf of the king of Sweden. At age ninety-two, King Gustav V partially embroidered the central cross. The large fireplace contains the original mantel. Although the house has been extensively restored, the walls are original.

Nearby, at 819 E. Seventh Street, is the **New Sweden Centre** (302-426-1638; www.ColonialNewSweden.org), an interpretive center for colonial history of the Delaware Valley, featuring hands-on displays of prehistoric times through the American Revolution.

Claymont

 On the property of the Robinson House, Naaman's Road at Philadelphia Pike, in the northeastern corner of the state stands a small, one-and-one-half-story, whitewashed structure locally known as the **Swedish Blockhouse**. The house, however, is not constructed with the horizontal timbering that defines a blockhouse in Sweden. Narrow slits in the stonework of the upper level have been interpreted as rifle ports, but they may have had a more prosaic ventilating function. The interior has a Swedish-style corner fireplace to which a separately roofed external beehive oven was attached. Some sources have identified this structure with New Sweden's last governor, Johan Rising. His residence was built on Timber Island, seven miles closer to Fort Christina and overlooking it from just across the Brandywine River. The blockhouse may be the oldest surviving building in the state. Nearby on Naaman's Creek is a state historic plaque claiming that in 1655 a local Native American leader deeded the land along the creek to Rising. Gustavus Hesselius and Adolf Ulrik Wertmüller, two noted Swedish artists, lived on plantations on this creek.

New Castle

The New Castle settlement began its days as Fort Casimir, erected by the Dutch in 1651 and taken by the Swedes on Trinity Sunday, 1654. They renamed it Fort Trefaldighet (Fort Trinity), but the Dutch reclaimed it the next year. The state historical marker for the fort is on Chestnut Street between Second Street and the Delaware River. English rule, first under the Duke of York and later under William Penn, succeeded that of the Dutch in 1664. New Castle is one of the most important towns in America to have survived with its colonial appearance relatively intact; many fine homes date from the eighteenth and early nineteenth centuries. The pulpit of Immanuel Church (Episcopal) was frequently occupied by visiting Swedish pastors from its beginning. The oldest part of the present church dates from 1703.

Dover

In the **Delaware Agricultural Museum**, 866 N. DuPont Highway on U.S. Highway 13 (302-734-1618), is a Swedish-style log house. Seven logs in height, the house has a low entry door, three windows, a loft, and a brick fireplace. It is decorated with seventeenth-century furnishings.

NEW JERSEY

Swedesboro

Southern New Jersey was originally part of the New Sweden colony. Several Swedish historic sites remain, particularly in and around Swedesboro, originally known as "Raccoon."

For years, the early Swedes of southern New Jersey crossed the Delaware River to attend religious services in present-day Delaware and Pennsylvania. In 1702, a log structure built on the banks of Raccoon Creek became **Trinity Episcopal (Old Swedes) Church**, the first Swedish Lutheran church in New Jersey. Today's two-story, red-brick Georgian-style structure was built between 1784 and 1786. The church, designed by the Reverend Nicholas Collin, pastor of the congregation, stands at 208 Kings Highway at Church Street, also known as County Road 551 (856-467-1227; www.colonialswedes.org). In 1838 a five-story tower topped the church. The white interior has a flag and a plaque unveiled by Prince Bertil in June 1938 in commemoration of the 300th anniversary of the Swedish settlement on the Delaware. When King Carl XVI Gustaf visited the Swedesboro church on April 8, 1976, a plaque in front of the church describing the construction of the first sanctuary was unveiled. In a small park across the street is a plaque commemorating the visit on April 4, 2003, of Sweden's Crown Princess Victoria to celebrate the 300th anniversary of the congregation.

Swedes built the **VanLear-Schorn Log Cabin** in New Sweden Park on the churchyard's north end and the C. A. Nothnagle Log House, both seventeenth-century log cabins. The VanLear-Schorn log cabin was acquired by the Gloucester County Historical Society and moved to the churchyard. It is a 12 by 15 foot cabin that dates from the early eighteenth century. Originally it sat a mile down Raccoon Creek on Swedesboro-Bridgeport Road on land purchased by Mårten Mårtensson, who arrived in New Sweden in 1654. Because of massive insect damage and weathering, roughly half of the log timbering required careful replacement.

The **C. A. Nothnagle Log House**, 406 Swedesboro Road in Gibbstown, New Jersey, is believed by some to have been built shortly after the first Swedish settlers arrived in America. A plaque on the cabin claims it dates between 1638 and 1643. Authorities suggest that a more probable date is 1680 and that Israel Helm or Benjamin Bramman was the first owner. Attached to the 16 by 22 foot cabin of dovetailed, hand-hewn logs with a corner fireplace is a house built between 1730 and 1750. Privately owned, the log house can be seen by appointment (856-423-0916).

Pennsville

At the end of Church Landing Road on the banks of the Delaware just south of the Delaware Memorial Bridge is a historic sign noting that "this is the site where Swedish-Finnish colonists who settled in Penn's Neck would depart by boat to attend church in Wilmington. The trip was hazardous." As a result, the colonists purchased land and constructed a log church, which was dedicated in March 1717. But when the Reverend Nicholas Collin visited the parish in 1770, he noted that the congregation demonstrated few distinctively Swedish characteristics. Twenty-four years later, the congregation became Episcopalian. The present small red-brick church, now known as **St. George's Episcopal Church** (856-678-7979), was built in 1808 to replace the earlier Swedish log structure. The church, which has an adjoining cemetery, is at 305 N. Broadway, immediately south of the bridge on State Highway 49, and may be visited by appointment. East of the main church door is a plaque commemorating the earliest Finns in the United States.

Monument to Swedish colonists, Pennsville

In 2004, Sweden's ambassador dedicated a new monument in River View Beach Park, about two and one-half miles south of St. George's Church, that commemorates the pioneering role of the Swedes and Finns on the eastern bank of the Delaware. The striking monument contains two bronze plaques designed by Alesa Hogate, a descendant of Anders Larsson Dalbo, an early Swedish settler in Pennsville. One plaque, entitled "The Delaware River Colonial Highway of the Swedes and Finns," portrays a church boat, while the other, "Land of the Lenape Settlement of the Swedes and Finns," shows a colonist's farmstead. Daniel Gantenbein designed the large granite sculpture.

The descriptive plaque notes that "Swedish and Finnish farmers, fisherman, and craftsman settled this area and built log cabins. They navigated the waterways in canoes, plank boats and ferries to manage commerce and attend church on the west bank. . . . They also served in the militia, were Indian interpreters and legislators."

Bridgeton

In commemoration of the 350th anniversary of the New Sweden Colony, a reproduction of a seventeenth-century farmstead of the type built by the early Swedish colonists was constructed in Bridgeton City Park on Mayor Aitken Drive near Commerce Street, crowning the efforts of the New Sweden Company that had begun in 1983. An ongoing organization of volunteers, the company was chaired through its early years by the late Thorsten Karlsson, a native of Eskilstuna who became a New Jersey businessman and was active in many Swedish American causes. Partly through his influence, Bridgeton and Eskilstuna became sister cities.

Called the **New Sweden Farmstead Museum**, the site features seven log dwellings and outbuildings. The Swedish historic preservation society Riksförbundet för Hembygdsvård was actively engaged in the project. Gunnar Zetterqvist of Dala-Floda, Dalarna, supervised construction and also designed the furnishings of the farmstead, assisted by Severin Johansson and several American laborers. King Carl XVI Gustaf and Queen Silvia dedicated the museum in 1988, presenting candleholders to the museum for display. A living history museum, the farmstead was a venue for teaching seventeenth- and eighteenth-century crafts, but the site is currently closed to visitors. Its future status is uncertain.

Mauricetown

In Mauricetown at the corner of Second and South Streets is the **Caesar Hoskins Log House**, 1232 Second Street, an early eighteenth-century dwelling built of dovetailed logs. Clapboard siding has been placed on the exterior. Privately owned and located in the former Maurice River Swedish community, this structure features an incised drawing of a schooner on an interior wall.

Swedish Granary, Greenwich

Greenwich

 Behind the Gibbon House in Greenwich is a **Swedish Granary**, considered the sole surviving example of a farm building erected by the early Swedes in the Delaware Valley. A plaque notes its construction about 1650. Built of cedar logs, the granary originally sat in Lower Hopewell Township. The structure contains a large front door for wagons as well as a smaller door. The granary was moved four miles to its present location on the grounds of the Gibbon House on Main or Greate Street. The town of Greenwich, established in 1675, has been placed on the National Register of Historic Places because of its unique colonial architecture. The restored Gibbon mansion is the headquarters of the Cumberland County Historical Society (856-455-4055).

Mullica Hill

Eric and John Mullica, sons of Swedish pioneer Eric Mullica, settled the community of Mullica Hill, which is now a mecca for collectors of antiques and handicrafts. When the Mullica family arrived in America from Sweden, they found recent immigrants from another Mullica Hill—Mullikannäki, near the present town of Pylkönmäki in central Finland.

Hancock's Bridge

Sitting on the grounds of the Hancock House (856-935-4373) in Hancock's Bridge, on the southwest side of the Salem–Hancock's Bridge Road and Front Street, is a **Swedish cabin**. The impressive brick Georgian-style Hancock House was the home of a prominent Salem County colonial family. Outside the log house a sign notes: "This single-room cabin is a rare remaining example of hand-hewn, white cedar plank construction and reflects a traditional Swedish cabin. This cabin, with its glazed windows, is more elaborate than those typically constructed in the seventeenth century. . . . The cabin's construction follows the traditional building techniques of the seventeenth century, with four-inch thick sideplanks, dove-tailed corners, a fireplace and wooden pins instead of nails. White cedar was 'mined' from the swamp by teams of men excavating the logs."

Salem

Four miles southwest of Salem on the Fort Elfsborg–Salem Road (County Highway 625) near the Delaware River are two historic markers commemorating **Fort Elfsborg**. The New Jersey state plaque notes: "Not far from here on the New Jersey side of the Delaware River in 1643, the Swedes erected an earthwork fort with three angles on order of Governor Johan Printz to control the River. It was commanded by Lieutenant Sven Skute, and was abandoned in 1651." In front of the Elsinboro Elementary School attached to a large boulder is a white stone marker erected in 1988: "This memorial is presented by the citizens of Göteborg, Sweden, to Elsinboro Township and the People of New Jersey, from the wall of the original Fort Elfsborg at Göteborg. It honors those who served 1643–1653 at Fort Elfsborg on Elsinboro Point, and left the lasting legacy of the New Sweden Colony."

Behind the Salem County Historical Society's building at 79–82 Market Street (856-935-5004; www.salemcounty.com/schs) in historic Salem is a **log cabin** built between 1840 and 1855 as a one-room home. It shows construction techniques utilized by the early Swedish and Finnish settlers in the Delaware River Valley. A couple of blocks away on Market Street (State Highway 45) next to the old railway tracks in the Salem Historic District is a small log structure, presumably a replica of an early dwelling, identified as the Johan Printz Memorial, constructed by Gunnar Zetterqvist.

East Orange

The former **Upsala College** at Springdale and Prospect in East Orange, founded in 1893 and closed in 1995, was named for the Uppsala decree establishing the Lutheran creed of the Church of Sweden 300 years earlier. The first classes for the sixteen enrolled students were held in the Bethlehem Lutheran Church in Brooklyn. Dr. Lars H. Beck, president during the college's first seventeen years, moved Upsala to the forty-five-acre campus in East Orange, sixteen miles from New York City. In the fall of 1979, a second campus (Wirths) was opened in Wantage, New Jersey. The school planned to build a campus there on 240 acres of farmland.

Many of the twentieth-century buildings on the East Orange campus were designed by Jens Fredrick Larson (1891–1982), born in Boston of Swedish-Danish parents. Larson was also responsible for designing other college and university buildings in the United States and overseas, including buildings at Dartmouth, Colby College, Wake Forest University, and the Institute for Advanced Study at Princeton University. Some Upsala College buildings were named for Swedish Americans or Swedes, including Beck Hall (honoring Upsala's first president), Bremer Hall (Swedish writer Fredrika Bremer), Froeberg North and South Residence Halls (Dr. Peter Froeberg was Upsala's second president and claimed he was the first student to register in 1893), Nelsenius Hall (the Reverend Gustav Nelsenius, first chairman of the board of trustees), and the Agnes Wahlstrom College Center (a Swedish-born donor).

Upsala was under the Augustana Lutheran Synod until the merger in 1963, when it became affiliated with the Evangelical Lutheran Church in America. In 2005 the Beck and Wahlstrom buildings were part of the East Orange Campus High School. Other parts of the former campus were slated to become a new residential area.

Kearny

First Lutheran Church, at 65 Oakwood Avenue (201-991-1623; www.firstlutheran .netfirms.com), was organized in 1890 as the Swedish Evangelical Lutheran Church of Gustavus Vasa. A frame church had been built in 1891 but was replaced in 1930 by the present brick sanctuary, designed by Swedish architect Martin Hedmark (1896–1980). Visitors enter the church through a free-standing red-brick bell tower with a parabolic arch and a pointed steeple.

The interior of the sanctuary has a pine ceiling in the shape of a ship's hull. The ceiling and beams have painted designs reminiscent of Viking art. The raised, light-colored wood pulpit, trimmed in gold paint, is surmounted by a canopy.

Budd Lake

New Jersey Vasa Home and Park (201-691-8383) is a 126-acre site purchased in 1936. Located on Wolfe Road, the park contains recreational facilities, summer cabins, and retirement homes operated by the twenty lodges of District 6, an active division of the Vasa Order of America.

PENNSYLVANIA

In the eastern part of Pennsylvania, many Swedish American sites are associated with the seventeenth-century New Sweden Colony. In the northwest region, including Chandlers Valley–Sugar Grove, sites relate to the nineteenth-century immigration story and nearby Jamestown, New York.

Philadelphia

Institutes and Museums

American Swedish Historical Museum—1900 Pattison Avenue, in Franklin Delano Roosevelt Park (215-389-1776; www.americanswedish.org). This website has links to related sites in the Delaware Valley, the United States, and Sweden.

This museum is one of the three largest museums in the United States devoted to Swedish American culture (the other two are the American Swedish Institute, Minneapolis, and the Swedish American Museum Center, Chicago). Organized in 1926 to preserve and record the accomplishments of Swedish Americans with particular emphasis on the Delaware Valley, the museum was founded and guided by Dr. Amandus Johnson. He wanted the museum to be a national repository of Swedish culture in the United States, and it contains an impressive, diverse collection.

The museum is housed in the John Morton Memorial Building, Swedish America's contribution to the sesquicentennial celebration of the Declaration of Independence. In 1926, Crown Prince Gustav Adolf laid the cornerstone, and the building opened in 1938, which was the 300th anniversary of Swedes in America. The museum's exterior design, by John Nydén, a Swedish American from Chicago, is based on the seventeenth-century Eriksberg Manor in Södermanland, Sweden.

On the first floor, the impressive grand entrance hall features three large frescoes of historic subjects painted in 1928 by Swedish artist Christian von Schneidau. The ceiling painting illustrates the arrival of Swedish settlers in the Delaware Valley aboard the *Kalmar Nyckel*. One of the two wall paintings depicts John Morton, a descendant of original Swedish settlers, signing the Declaration of Independence, and the other features Swedish army officer Axel von Fersen, who was present at the surrender of Lord Cornwallis at the battle of Yorktown in 1781.

At the right of the main entrance is a room containing several small Carl Milles sculptures, including a miniature of Johan Printz and two pioneer women. In the adjacent Nobel Room is an interactive internet experience featuring Nobel Prize recipients and wall charts identifying all the Nobel winners from 1901 to the present.

American Swedish Historical Museum, exterior and ceiling, Philadelphia

To the left of the main entrance is the George and Marion Anderson Wing, a gallery devoted to special exhibits, and the Golden Map Room, where visitors may imagine themselves in the middle of the Baltic Sea surrounded by Sweden's seventeenth-century empire. The New Sweden Room, designed originally by Hans Asplund of Stockholm in 1959, depicts the daily life of the Swedish colonists among the Lenape Indians. Dominating the room is a large tapestry entitled *Nova Suecia*, based on a cartoon by Kurt Jungstedt and woven in Aubusson, France. A family chest came from Sweden in the seventeenth century. Also on the first floor is the Stuga or Pioneer Room, a somewhat idealized view of the interior of a nineteenth-century Swedish farmhouse. Important features of this room are the Swedish corner fireplace, a floor loom, a seventeenth-century trestle table, and a floral folk art ceiling painted by Olle Nordmark. Also on the first floor are the gift shop and the Nord Memorial Library, which has several thousand volumes available to researchers by appointment.

The second-floor balcony is an exhibition gallery where items from the collection are displayed, including Swedish furniture and paintings by artists Carl Oscar Borg and Birger Sandzén. Proceeding clockwise around the balcony, one first encounters the John Ericsson Room, designed by Martin Hedmark in 1930 in an art deco style. Wall murals by Swedish artist Olle Hjortzberg show Ericsson presenting his design for the ironclad *Monitor* to Abraham Lincoln's war cabinet and the subsequent battle between the *Monitor* and the *Merrimack*.

Across the balcony is the Chicago Room, designed in 1936 with an inlaid-wood mural by the Swedish artist Ewald Dahlskog (1894–1950) using 103 different types of wood. The mural focuses on Swedish contributions to construction in the New World. On the left is a log structure in the Delaware River Valley. On the right is Holy Trinity (Old Swedes Church) in Wilmington, Delaware, and in the center is the Chicago skyline showing Andrew Lanquist, founder of the prestigious Chicago construction firm of Lanquist and Illsley, in his office.

The Jenny Lind Room contains two works by Carl Larsson (1889–1959), the watercolor *My Bedroom* and a large-scale cartoon for a tapestry called *Kräftfisket (Crayfishing)*. The museum owns a number of etchings by Swedish artist Anders Zorn (1860–1920), and usually one or two are displayed. The Fredrika Bremer Room is dedicated to the accomplishments of Swedish women, including Bremer (1801–1865), a nineteenth-century Swedish writer and advocate of women's and human rights, and author Selma Lagerlöf (1858–1940). The next gallery features glass by Orrefors and Reijmyre Glassworks. In this room is a plaque honoring Axel Halstrom, a pioneer in Florida horticulture (see Vero Beach, Florida). The museum's office contains a bronze sculpture of Emanuel Swedenborg—inventor, philosopher, and theologian—by Carl Milles.

The American Swedish Historical Museum sponsors special events, including a pea soup and *punsch* event in January, *midsommarfest* in mid-June, and Lucia Fest including a *julbord* (Christmas smörgåsbord) and *julmarknad* (Christmas market) in early December.

Historic Places

City Hall—Market and Broad Streets (215-686-1776).

City Hall occupies all of Penn Square at the intersection of Market and Broad Streets. This square was at the center of the original seventeenth-century Philadelphia city plan. A plaque at City Hall commemorating the Swedish settlements on the Delaware River lists the four Swedish governors of New Sweden and other prominent settlers.

Near the top of City Hall (below the large statue of William Penn that surmounts the building) is a sculpture of a woman holding a child, representing early Swedish settlers in Pennsylvania. The official flag of Philadelphia is in the blue and yellow of the Swedish flag in recognition of the first settlers to arrive.

Governor Printz Park—Taylor Avenue and Second Street, Essington (610-583-7221).

The seven-acre park on Tinicum Island on the western shore of the Delaware River occupies the site of New Sweden's capital from 1643 to 1654. The first European settlement in present-day Pennsylvania, it consisted of Fort New Gothenburg, a log chapel, simple settlers' houses, and Printzhof, the hewn-log home of Governor Johan Printz (1592–1663). None of these buildings survive. An imposing bronze statue of Printz by Carl Lindborg looks over the waterfront park on the Delaware. Administered by the Pennsylvania Historical and Museum Commission, the park has sixteen interpretive display panels featuring key events and descriptions of life in the New World. A gravel path leads to a children's board game embedded in a concrete sidewalk. The squares contain quotations from Governor Printz's letters and journals.

To the east of the park is a yacht club at whose gate is a large stone monument commemorating Governor Printz. At the main entrance to the clubhouse stands a small plaque, attached to a porch column that notes the location of the chapel of Fort New Gothenburg and the burial ground. The large stone beneath the plaque was the step of the chapel. It is not widely known or advertised that this was the first regularly consecrated house of worship for Lutherans in America. Its few surviving artifacts are preserved in Gloria Dei Church in Philadelphia.

A historic marker outside the Tinicum Township Memorial Building on Fourth Street (not far from the park) notes that Tinicum, the first permanent settlement in Pennsylvania, was founded in 1643 by Johan Printz.

Lower Swedish Cabin—Darby Creek, Drexel Hill, Delaware County (610-623-1650). Driving directions from Philadelphia: Go west on Baltimore Pike to Maple Avenue in Clifton Heights. Turn right over Lindberg Bridge to Dennison Avenue. Turn left, go two blocks to stop sign. Turn right onto Creek Road. Take this to its end (less than one mile).

This one-and-one-half-story log structure, owned by Upper Darby Township, was constructed in the seventeenth century. It may be the oldest log house in North America still in existence. Originally the cabin consisted of one 20 by 15 foot room with a corner fireplace and a large stone mantle. At a later date, a log addition with a corner fireplace was constructed. In the early twentieth century, the Lower Swedish Cabin's interior was plastered and wallpapered, and electricity was installed. Between 1904 and 1906, pioneer film maker Sigmund Lubin used the cabin in several of his western films. The Friends of the Swedish Cabin maintain it today.

 Morton Homestead—100 Lincoln Avenue, Darby Creek north of Governor Printz Park (610-583-7221). Driving directions: From Interstate 95, exit at State Highway 420 in Prospect Park and follow signs to Morton Homestead.

The Morton Homestead, begun by Swedish settler Mårten Mårtensson, features two seventeenth-century Swedish log houses. For many years, the property remained in the hands of the family, the most famous member being the great-grandson of Mårtensson, John Morton (1727–1777), who signed the Declaration of Independence.

One part of the Morton Homestead dates from 1654. An adjacent building was constructed in 1698. Around 1800, the two buildings were connected by stone walls and a higher roof added, thus creating a half-story above the cabins. The house contains late seventeenth-century furniture. The date 1698 is carved on the fireplace in the newer cabin. The earlier cabin was built of hewn oak logs fitted together without the use of nails. Wooden pegs hold the timbers in position.

Churches

 Gloria Dei (Old Swedes) Episcopal Church—Delaware Avenue near Christian Street (215-389-1513; www.gloriadei-oldswedes.org).
Swedish colonists built this red-brick structure of English architectural design between 1698 and 1703, making it the oldest church in Philadelphia. The steep-roofed building features a square belfry and small spire probably added in the 1730s. In the entrance vestibule a stairway leads to a balcony that extends on three sides of the sanctuary. President Franklin D. Roosevelt declared Gloria Dei a National Historic Site in 1942.

The church congregation had its origins in Fort New Gothenburg at Tinicum. A small log church with bell tower built in 1643 was destroyed by fire two years later. A larger log church and bell tower was built the following year. Many of the Swedish settlers moved north along the Delaware River to Wicaco (now South Philadelphia), where about 1677 a blockhouse just south of present Gloria Dei was converted into a church. That structure was succeeded by the present church at the end of the seventeenth century.

Gloria Dei preserves several items from the log church at Tinicum, including the baptismal font and the golden sprays on the front of the lectern. Significant are the two wooden cherubs, brought from Sweden in 1643, on the rear balcony under the organ. Below the cherubs is an open Bible whereon is written in Swedish: "The people who wander in darkness shall see a great light and over them that dwell in dark lands it shone clearly. Glory to God in the Highest."

Models of the *Kalmar Nyckel* and *Fogel Grip* are suspended from the ceiling. The models as well as the candelabra were given by Carl Milles, noted Swedish sculptor. The wood carving of the angel Gabriel over the pulpit is a replica of an earlier one.

Buried beneath the church floor are several early Swedish missionaries, including Andrew Rudman, pastor at the time of the present church's construction. The last missionary, Nicholas Collin, served the church from 1784 to 1831. He was a friend of Thomas Jefferson and Benjamin Franklin, who supplied lightning rods for the church. In June 1777, Betsy Ross was married in Gloria Dei. Jenny Lind gave a religious concert here in 1851. On the left side of the sanctuary are old Bibles, including one presented by the Swedish king and queen in 1926 and a reproduction of the 1541 Gustav Vasa Bible. A small museum in the church compound holds interesting documents associated with the early pastors. Gloria Dei Church and grounds have been beautifully restored with funds collected in the United States and Sweden.

One of the most famous persons buried in the adjacent cemetery is Swedish artist Adolf Ulrik Wertmüller (1751–1811), who arrived in America in 1794. Also in the graveyard is the statue of the Seven Johns. It is a seven-sided black-granite monolith from Sweden, surmounted by a bronze bust of John Hanson (1715–1783), the first president of the United States under the Articles of Confederation, and seven bronze, low-relief plaques by local artist and sculptor Carl Lindborg. The seven plaques memorialize Hanson, whose Swedish ancestry is now doubted by serious historians, and six famous men of Swedish descent—Johan Printz (1592–1663); Johan Rising (1617–1672), the last governor of New Sweden; John Dahlgren (1809–1870); engineer, inventor, and author John Nystrom (1824–1885); John Ericsson (1803–1889); and John Morton (1727–1777).

In 1876, a Maryland Hanson of authentic New Sweden ancestry wrote that he was patriot John Hanson's relative. This report gave the living Hanson an important kinsman; to the deceased Hanson it gave a huge population of recent immigrants from Sweden, who were as eager to adopt an early patriot as they were to make this country their own. In 1988, a short scholarly article by George E. Russell titled "John Hanson of Maryland: A Swedish Origin Disproved," gave convincing evidence that the patriot's immigrant ancestor, John Hanson (also spelled *Henson)*, was an English indentured servant who arrived in the winter of 1661–1662 and lived in Charles County, Maryland, where his numerous documented associations never included the Delaware Swedes or their descendants. Since 1988 historian and genealogist Peter Stebbins Craig has brought to light at least two additional points of evidence from the contemporary records of New Sweden refuting the 1876 Hanson claim.

St. James Church of Kingsessing—6838 Woodland Avenue (215-727-5265). This stone structure is the sixth oldest church building in Philadelphia and the oldest west of the Schuylkill River. Although constructed in 1762, the building was not dedicated until 1765. In 1844 it became an Episcopal church.

Christ Church (Old Swedes), Upper Merion, and Cemetery—
740 River Road, State Highway 23, Swedesburg, one-half mile east of
Bridgeport (610-272-6036; www.colonialswedes.org).
By 1712 Swedes had gradually migrated from the Delaware Valley and Philadelphia northwestward along the Schuylkill River to the Upper Merion Township area. They established a village known as Swedesford, today Swedesburg. The original log cabin that housed the congregation and school was built in 1753 on land donated by Gunnar Rambo, a direct descendant of Peter Rambo, a colonist who arrived in 1640. In 1760 Christ Church (Old Swedes), today covered by yellow plaster, was dedicated.

The interior of Christ Church is significant for its stained-glass windows depicting early Swedes in America. They were installed in 1938 for the 300th anniversary of the landing of the Swedes at Wilmington. Another historic memorial is the baptismal font presented to the church in 1876 by Prince Oscar (1859–1953), the second son of King Oscar I, during a visit to the United States. Also in the sanctuary is Prince Oscar's flag (the union flag of Sweden and Norway), which flew on the *Norrköping* when it was anchored in the Delaware River during the prince's visit.

The oldest grave in the adjacent cemetery is that of twenty-six-year-old Diana Rambo, who died in 1744. A plaque in the path near the main door honors the Reverend Nicholas Collin, George Washington, Benjamin Franklin, and Anthony Wayne. During the winter of 1777 when the Continental Army was encamped at nearby Valley Forge, Washington and his officers occasionally came to this church for worship services. It is an annual tradition at Christ Church to celebrate Lucia Day (December 13). After the Lucia enters the sanctuary, men costumed as Continental soldiers knock on the church door, and the congregation sings "America" in response.

Bryn Athyn Cathedral Church of the New Jerusalem (Swedenborgian)— 900 Cathedral Road at Huntingdon Pike one mile north of intersection with Pennsylvania Highway 63 in Bryn Athyn (215-947-6225; www.brynathyncathedral.org).
Bryn Athyn serves as the Episcopal seat of the Church of the New Jerusalem (Swedenborgian). Most of the population of this community is associated with the church and its educational institutions. The most outstanding building in the complex is Bryn Athyn Cathedral. Groundbreaking for the Gothic and Romanesque edifice took place in 1913, and its dedication was six years later. The original endowment was a gift of John Pitcairn, and the design and construction was supervised by his son, Raymond Pitcairn. The three parts of the site are the church (inspired by Gothic architecture of the thirteenth and fourteenth centuries), the Council Hall (twelfth-century Romanesque style), and the Choir Hall (also twelfth-century Romanesque). The church's stained-glass windows depict biblical scenes. The cathedral is on one of the highest points in Montgomery County, making it an unexpected and spectacular sight in the rolling countryside.

Other Points of Interest

Historic Bartram's Garden—Fifty-fourth Street and Lindbergh Boulevard (215-729-5281; www.bartramsgarden.org).
Historic Bartram's Garden, the oldest botanic garden in the United States, was originally part of the 1,100-acre Aronameck plantation granted under the English government to Hans Månson in 1669. Månson, who was connected with the New Sweden Colony, sold it in 1681 to his stepson, Peter Peterson Yocum. Several years later, Mouns Jones, Yocum's brother-in-law, acquired the property on which the John Bartram house is located. It was formerly believed that the inner core of the 1731 Bartram House was the Mouns Jones cabin before he moved to present Douglassville, Pennsylvania. However, recent archaeological studies cast doubt on this claim.

John Bartram (1699–1777) is remembered as the first American-born botanist. A founding member of the American Philosophical Society and a close friend of Benjamin Franklin, he was sought out by Swedish botanist Pehr Kalm during his lengthy stay in America. Seeds and sample plants from Bartram's collection were prominent among those sent by Kalm to Linnaeus in Sweden. The mountain laurel, the state flower of Pennsylvania, is named in Kalm's honor (*Kalmia latifolia*).

**Grave of Rear Admiral John A. Dahlgren—Laurel Hill Cemetery,
3822 Ridge Avenue (302-228-8200).**
A reddish granite stone marks the grave of Swedish American Rear Admiral John
A. Dahlgren (1809–1870), a famous U.S. Navy officer, scientist, scholar, teacher,
and author. Other members of the Dahlgren family are buried nearby.

Sculpture and Other Art

**John Ericsson Fountain—near the Philadelphia Museum of Art,
Twenty-sixth and Benjamin Franklin Parkway.**
This marble fountain is dedicated to John Ericsson, the scientist and inventor,
who was born in Sweden in 1803 at Långbanshyttan in the Swedish province of
Värmland and died in his adopted United States homeland in 1889. On his birthday, Filipstad, Värmland, annually celebrates John Ericsson Day with a mock battle
on Lake Daglösen reenacted by replicas of the *Merrimack* and Ericsson's *Monitor*.

Carl Milles Sculpture—Fairmount Park along the Schuylkill River.
Carl Milles created three angels blowing wind instruments atop large stone columns, approximately thirty-five feet high. Elsewhere in the park near the river
stands a statue, presented in 1974 by the Leif Ericson Society of Philadelphia, in
honor of the explorer.

**Claes Oldenburg's Sculpture—Centre Square Plaza, Fifteenth and Market
Streets, and Levy Park, University of Pennsylvania, Philadelphia.**
Claes Oldenburg's *Clothespin* (1976) stands opposite Philadelphia's City Hall. His
Split Button (1981) is in Levy Park. Oldenburg, born in Stockholm in 1929, is a
naturalized American citizen.

**Kent Ullberg Sculpture—Nineteenth Street and Benjamin Franklin Parkway
in Logan Square, in front of the Academy of Natural Sciences.**
The sculpture, a twenty-five-foot bronze, is entitled *Deinonychus* (the "terrible
claw" dinosaur). It was dedicated in 1987 to commemorate the 175th year of the
Academy of Natural Sciences in honor of Academy Women's Committee. (See
Corpus Christi, Texas, for additional Ullberg works.)

Chester

Chester is the second-oldest settlement in Pennsylvania. Called Upland by
the Swedes, the city got its new name from William Penn. In the **Old Swedes
Cemetery**, State Highway 291, across from the city's administration building, is
the grave of John Morton (1727–1777), marked with an obelisk. Inscriptions on
this and on many other old stones are almost completely illegible. Not far from

this cemetery, at Second and Penn across from the William Penn monument, was an official state historic marker (undergoing restoration in 2005) noting the location of the farmhouse of Armegott Printz, daughter of Johan Printz, New Sweden's governor from 1643 to 1653. Armegott Printz returned to Sweden in 1676 and died in 1695.

On the northwestern edge of Chester in Crozer Park stands one of the most elegant of all the memorials relating to the New Sweden Colony—a large red-granite monument by the Finnish sculptor Väinö Aaltonen, donated to the people of Pennsylvania and the city of Chester in 1938 by the government and people of Finland. With scenes in bas-relief on both faces, the monument has inscriptions in Finnish and English. It honors the many colonists who came from Finland or were Finns living in Sweden (especially in Värmland) just before remigrating to New Sweden.

Marcus Hook

First settled by Swedes, Marcus Hook is one mile from the Delaware-Pennsylvania border. A plaque outside Marcus Hook Municipal Building, at the southwest corner of W. Tenth and Green Streets, describes the contribution of the early settlers.

Douglassville

 St. Gabriel's Church and Cemetery, 1188 E. Ben Franklin Highway, Route 422 (610-385-3144), was established in 1720, making it the first Swedish Lutheran church in Berks County. The sanctuary, built in that year, was a log cabin that served as a school between 1801 and 1832, when it was destroyed by fire. The present stone church was built in 1841, some forty years after the congregation became Episcopalian. A larger Gothic-style church was constructed to the west in 1881, the same year the name St. Gabriel's was first employed. From that time until 1959, when it was restored as a chapel, the old stone church served as a parish house. It contains an impressive raised, canopied pulpit and a balcony on three sides.

 The **Mouns Jones House** (610-385-3870) on Old Philadelphia Pike is near St. Gabriel's. The two-and-one-half-story stone structure, which is also known as **Old Swede's House,** is the oldest dated building in Berks County. It was erected in 1716 by early settler Mouns Jones, who, with fourteen other Swedes in 1701, acquired 10,000 acres of land. The first structure built on the site was a small log cabin, the foundation of which remains. The present 24 by 30 foot house is constructed of squared stone with two chimneys, including one for a corner fire-place. The restored structure and grounds are maintained by the Historic Preservation Trust of Berks County. Since it is located close to the Schuylkill River, the structure was used as a ferry house. It has also been known as Lamb's Inn.

Mouns Jones House, Douglassville

Jones's name is a puzzle. It is an Anglicized version of his traditional Swed-ish name—Jönsson. His father, Jöns Nilsson (sometimes called Jonas), arrived in 1643 with Governor Printz. A descendant believes the name should be Jonas, not Jones, and historians have noted that county court records consistently spell his last name *Jones* but that his first name has variant spellings. Records of the time were kept in English and sometimes German. In the fall of each year, St. Gabriel's and the Historic Preservation Trust of Berks County hold a popular country fair in Jones's name on the church grounds and near the house.

Birdsboro

Hopewell Village National Historic Site—2 Mark Bird Lane, six miles south of Birdsboro on State Highway 345 (610-582-8773; www.nps.gov/hofu). Hopewell Village, a restored ironworks and ironworkers' residential community that includes both eighteenth- and nineteenth-century structures, is operated by the National Park Service. Hopewell Furnace was founded by Mark Bird in 1771. Interpretation at the site does not highlight its Swedish connection, but Bird's mother was a descendant of New Sweden colonists. Her father, Marcus

Huling, was a partner in nearby iron mines for forty years before the founding of Hopewell. Her maternal grandfather was Mouns Jones, mentioned above.

Bird and his parents were active in the Swedish church in Douglassville that became St. Gabriel's. His sister was the wife of James Wilson, a signer of the Declaration of Independence and the Constitution of the United States. As one of the primary suppliers of American-made cannons to the Continental Army and a founder of other early ironworks in New Jersey, Virginia, and North Carolina (where he died in poverty in 1816), Bird may rightfully be considered alongside John Morton as a significant contributor to the struggle for independence.

Harrisburg

The State Finance Building, bounded by North Street, Seventh Street (Fisher Street), North Drive, and Commonwealth Avenue (across from the Pennsylvania Capitol), has twelve bronze doors designed by Carl Milles. On the North Drive side, they depict the state's agricultural enterprises, and on the North Street side they show industries, including oil drilling, glass making, steel manufacturing, and coal mining.

Grassflat-Lanse

In central Pennsylvania, near the Kylertown exit on Interstate 80, are the small mining communities of Grassflat and Lanse. In 1883 thirty Swedish men, who had been part of a migration beginning in 1875 from Dalsland to the coal fields of McIntyre in Pennsylvania's Tioga County, moved west and south to this area. The following year, 181 more Swedes arrived. In nearby Peale, no longer extant, Swedish Evangelical Lutheran Nebo Church was organized in 1884. Gustavus Adolphus, a daughter congregation, sprang up in Lanse shortly afterward, and the congregation built a chapel in 1892. Other congregations also formed, and eventually some merged to form **Holy Trinity Lutheran Church of Lanse**, 1167 Maple Street (814-345-5204). This church on Lanse Road holds several items from the old Gustavus Adolphus Church, dismantled in 1986. Included in the collection are the 1901 altar painting by Olof Grafström of Jesus praying in the Garden of Gethsemane, the remodeled pulpit, the altar, and most of the altar rail. Several graves in the **Grassflat-Lanse Lutheran Cemetery** on State Highway 53 have Swedish inscriptions (go north from Interstate 80 on State Highway 53 for two miles and then drive east for one-half mile). In the center is the grave of Pastor P. A. Bergquist (1855–1912), who served all the Swedish congregations in the area. Several early markers give Älvsborg län, Sweden, as the birthplace of a number of early Swedish settlers in the area. Organized in 1892, the Evangelical Free Church of Lanse has Swedish roots; its present sanctuary was constructed in 1977.

Pittsburgh

University of Pittsburgh's Cathedral of Learning (Nationality Classrooms)—4200 Fifth Avenue (412-624-6000).
The University of Pittsburgh's Cathedral of Learning contains more than two dozen classrooms honoring different ethnic groups' achievements in education. Room 135 is the Swedish classroom; it has the atmosphere of a peasant cottage and murals in the style of the eighteenth-century Hälsingland painter Gustav Reuter. The Bollnäs cottage of Stockholm's Skansen inspired a hooded brick fireplace, a central feature of the room. Murals depict biblical events and personifications of virtues. Swedish sculptor Carl Milles was the university's adviser in creating the room.

Chandlers Valley–Sugar Grove

The first Swedes in northwestern Pennsylvania were connected with the colony in New Sweden, Iowa, organized in 1845 by Peter Cassel. His glowing letters about Iowa encouraged additional Swedes to emigrate in 1846, but when they arrived, they were robbed and stranded in Buffalo, New York. Two young girls with the group were offered homes by families in Warren and Sugar Grove. These girls—the first Swedish-born persons in that area—arrived in December 1846, and the centennial of their arrival is commemorated in a Chandlers Valley wayside park by a monument bearing the biblical inscription, "A little child shall lead them." Another interpretation of the events maintains that after losing their money, Germund and Catherine Johnson were obliged to place their two daughters, Louise and Josephine, in an orphanage. When they returned to retrieve their children, the girls had been "bound out" or indentured to two families in Chandlers Valley. The parents traveled to the valley to find them and decided to stay.

In 1848, other Swedes began arriving in Chandlers Valley–Sugar Grove, where the men became woodsmen and acquired farms. The settlement became known as Hessel Valley for three brothers from Hässleby, Småland. Later, Swedes worked in the area's oil fields.

The Chandlers Valley–Sugar Grove area became a center from which Swedes spread to parts of western Pennsylvania and western New York, particularly Jamestown. By 1870, Swedes were actively engaged in that city's developing furniture business. In 1930 there were about 8,000 Swedish-born inhabitants.

With the exception of the churches established in the Delaware Valley in the seventeenth century, the **Hessel Valley Lutheran Church** on Brown Hill Road in Chandlers Valley (814-489-0228) is the oldest Swedish Lutheran church in the eastern part of the United States, having been organized in 1854. It is thus the mother church of the New York conference of the former Augustana Synod. In

1856, the Reverend Jonas Swenson of Unnaryd, Småland, became pastor; a year later, his son, Carl Aaron Swensson, the future founder of Bethany College in Lindsborg, Kansas, was born in Chandlers Valley.

The original Lutheran church was built at the location of the **Hessel Valley Lutheran Cemetery**, one and one-third miles northwest from Chandlers Valley on County Route 88. After this sanctuary burned, half of the congregation wanted to move to Chandlers Valley to build a new church, but the other half decided to remain in Sugar Grove Township, where they founded the Evangelical Free Church (later the **Sugar Grove Mission Covenant Church**). Three years later, they built a small white clapboard sanctuary with a central bell tower at Jackson Run and Youngsville Road (814-489-3044). The Covenant Cemetery is adjacent to the church, and Hessel Valley Lutheran Cemetery is across Youngsville Road.

In 1883, the Chandlers Valley congregation decided to build a brick church, completed two years later. The church, situated on a high point of land, has a tall central bell tower, a steeple, Gothic-style windows, and a small apse in the back of the structure. The Ascension altar fresco was painted by Maria Kristina Petersson in 1890. Above the chancel is the inscription: *Tror Du På Guds Son?* (Do you believe in the Son of God?). A large Victorian chandelier dating from the 1870s, formerly used for kerosene lamps, hangs in the center of the sanctuary. The chair used by King Carl XVI Gustaf on his 1976 visit is at the right of the altar. Also on the right wall is a picture of the king, a Swedish flag, and a plaque noting the visit. Over the exterior door leading to the basement is a bronze plaque with a brief history of the congregation. A glass case in the basement fellowship hall displays other historical mementos.

Mount Jewett

Mount Jewett, separated from Chandlers Valley and Sugar Grove by the Allegheny National Forest, is home to the octagonal **Nebo Evangelical Lutheran Church**, which dates from 1887. The members had organized one year earlier, making it the oldest church in town. Located on W. Main Street (U.S. Route 6), the church is reportedly patterned after Ersta Kyrka in Stockholm. It has an altar painting of the Ascension by Birger Sandzén. In 1950 this congregation merged with Mount Jewett's Zion Lutheran to form **St. Matthew's Lutheran**, 13 E. Main Street (814-778-5971). In the fellowship hall of St. Matthew's is an Olof Grafström painting of the Good Shepherd, formerly located in the Zion Church. The faithful gather at the old Nebo church on several occasions throughout the year—Easter sunrise and one Sunday per month between May and August. A Swedish festival is also held at the Nebo in August, including a smörgåsbord and a worship service using the former Augustana liturgy.

Kanesholm

Lebanon Lutheran Church, three and one-half miles east of Kane off U.S. Highway 6, is the mother church for several Pennsylvania Swedish Lutheran congregations in McKean County. Lebanon Lutheran was organized in 1870, and the present sanctuary, a white frame structure with a short steeple, was constructed in 1871–1872.

Kane

Tabor Evangelical Lutheran Church, 200 Dawson Street at Greeves and Dawson (814-837-6920; www.taborlutheran.com), is an old congregation with Swedish roots. **Emmanuel Mission Church**, 100 Biddle Street (814-837-8760), was built in 1902, twenty-four years after the church was first organized.

Wilcox

Nazareth Lutheran Church on Kane Street was organized in 1875, and the present white-frame church, built in 1881, has windows and a high steeple in the popular nineteenth-century Gothic style. Eleven other Lutheran congregations in northwestern Pennsylvania founded by Swedes remain active, most worshiping in their old church buildings.

MARYLAND

North East

St. Mary Anne's Episcopal Church, 315 S. Main Street (410-287-5522; www .stmaryanne.org), was organized in 1706 as North Elk Parish of the Church of England. Its original resident pastor was Jonas Aurén from Ekshärad, Värmland, whose marriage to a local Swedish woman is the first entry in the church book. As early as 1702, Aurén was living and holding services in the North East area. This was probably the beginning of the congregation. Aurén also taught school, was a surveyor, and operated one of the very few printing presses in America before his death in 1713.

The present church building, on its original lovely waterfront site, dates from 1743. In recent years the congregation has hosted or participated in several events commemorating its early Swedish and Finnish ties. One possible explanation of the odd name (there being no saint named Mary Anne) is that the Värmland Finns who settled here and attended the church referred to it by the common Finnish church name *Marian Kirkko* (Mary's Church). Another explanation is

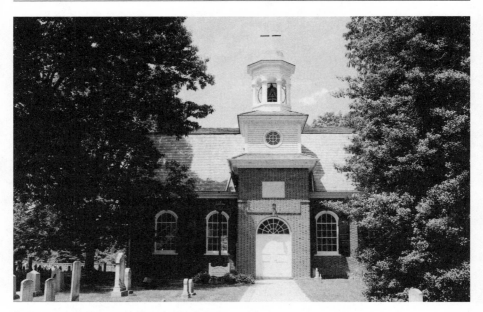

St. Mary Anne's Episcopal Church, North East

that Queen Anne of England bequeathed a large sum of money to support the Church of England in the colonies, and after the congregation received some funds, it added "Anne" to the parish name in gratitude.

Elkton

Seven miles from North East is Elkton, known as Swedestown at least until 1710. A dilapidated stone shell is located there in historic **Elk Landing** (www .elklanding.org). Until recently it was thought that this was the remains of the late seventeenth-century residence of John Hansson Steelman. Archaeological evidence now challenges this interpretation.

Steelman, an Indian trader and interpreter prominent in the history of Maryland and Pennsylvania and the son of New Sweden colonists, was the nation's wealthiest Swedish American for much of his career. Through a combination of donations and loans, Steelman advanced about one-third of the cash to finance the construction of Holy Trinity (Old Swedes) Church in present Wilmington. Pastor Eric Björk referred to Steelman as his *svärfaders svåger;* he was the brother-in-law of the pastor's father-in-law. Steelman's family and several neighbors were nominally parishioners of the Swedish Church in Delaware, but most Cecil County Swedes were active in Anglican parishes closer to their Maryland homes.

Annapolis

U.S. Naval Academy Museum—118 Maryland Avenue (410-293-2108; www.usna.edu/museum).
The U.S. Naval Academy museum recognizes Rear Admiral John A. Dahlgren's contributions to weapons development. Dahlgren's father arrived in Philadelphia from Sweden in 1806 and later served as Sweden and Norway's consul. The academy's Dahlgren Hall, a large stone structure formerly an armory and drill area, is named for the rear admiral. Today it is an activity center for the midshipmen, and a plaque notes Dahlgren's accomplishments. Outside the building are two heavy armaments—the Dahlgren rifle, a thirty-pound weapon he invented, and a 25-mm machine gun presented to the U.S. Navy by the Swedish Navy. Over the entrance immediately inside the hall hangs a portrait of Dahlgren, who had three naval ships named for him. In the Naval Academy museum's Civil War display are Dahlgren's frock coat, his pearl-hilted sword, and models of the various guns he invented.

WASHINGTON, D.C.

In Potomac Park, directly south of the Lincoln Memorial, is a monument to **John Ericsson** (1803–1889), Swedish-born builder of the *Monitor*, the first modern warship clad in iron. Unveiled in 1926 before President Calvin Coolidge and Crown Prince Gustav Adolf, the monument depicts Ericsson seated above an inscription recognizing his building of the *Monitor* and the revolution in navigation resulting from his invention of the screw propeller. On the statue, labor, adventure, and vision are represented respectively by a man, a Viking warrior, and a woman.

In the **Great Hall of the Supreme Court Building**, 1 NE First Street (202-479-3211; www.supremecourtus.gov), is a bust of Earl Warren, whose mother was born in Hälsingland and whose father was from Norway. Warren served as the fourteenth chief justice of the U.S. Supreme Court from 1953 to 1969.

In the older section of **Arlington National Cemetery** is buried William Rehnquist (1924–2005), the sixteenth chief justice of the Supreme Court from 1986 to 2005. His paternal grandfather was from Värmland, and his paternal grandmother from Östergötland; they emigrated separately to the United States in 1880 and settled in Chicago. Rehnquist was born in Milwaukee, Wisconsin. Also in that cemetery section is the grave of Earl Warren.

The **National Air and Space Museum**, Sixth Street at Independence Avenue (202-357-2700; www.nasm.si.edu), prominently displays Charles Lindbergh's *Spirit of St. Louis,* the first aircraft flown solo across the Atlantic.

At the **National Museum of American History** (202-633-1000; www.american history.si.edu) can be found Swedish American artifacts. Exhibits change regularly.

In Leutze Park in the **Washington Navy Yard** is a plaque in the northwest corner describing the early history of this important Washington, D.C., landmark. U.S. Navy Rear Admiral John Dahlgren, a Swedish American born in Philadelphia, was twice commandant of the Navy Yard (1861–1862 and 1869–1870).

At 1611 NW Sixteenth Street is the Swedenborgian **Church of the Holy City** (202-462-6734).

At the **U.S. Holocaust Memorial Museum**, 100 Raoul Wallenberg Place (202-488-0400; www.ushmem.org), the street name honors Swedish diplomat Raoul Wallenberg (1912–1947?), who is featured in a museum exhibit. Wallenberg saved the lives of thousands of Hungarian Jews during World War II. In 1981, the U.S. Congress granted him honorary citizenship (see New York City for the Wallenberg monument).

NEW YORK

New York

Most Swedes and millions of other European immigrants first set foot on American soil in New York City. Although Swedes usually continued westward, many stayed, and no other urban center except Chicago had more Swedish-born inhabitants. By 1910, the city claimed about 35,000 Swedish inhabitants, half of them living in Brooklyn. Important immigrant churches established in New York helped ease the transition from the Old Country to the New Land.

Institutes and Museums

Ellis Island National Monument and Statue of Liberty National Monument— New York Harbor (212-363-3200; www.nps.gov/stli; www.nps.gov/elis). Take the Circle Line Statue of Liberty Ferry from Battery Park in Lower Manhattan or Liberty State Park in New Jersey.

It was through Ellis Island, a 27.5-acre plot of land in New York's harbor, that more than 12.5 million immigrants (70 percent of all immigrants between 1892 and 1924) were admitted to the United States. Because more than 100 million Americans today are descended from these 12.5 million, Ellis Island and its buildings have been preserved as a fitting memorial to the largest voluntary immigration in world history.

In 1890, the federal government took over from the state of New York the processing of immigrants at Castle Garden (see Castle Clinton entry below) and moved operations to Ellis Island. It remained the central depot for immigrants until 1924, when quotas were adopted and the inspection process thus transferred overseas. Ironically, after 1924 Ellis Island became a detention and deportation center, and for a while it also served as a military hospital and Coast Guard station. Abandoned between 1954 and 1965, it then became part of the Statue of Liberty National Monument. From 1976 to 1984, guides conducted tours of the crumbling buildings, which then closed for restoration. Since 1990 this national monument has featured an outstanding museum that attracts many tourists.

Work on the main building restored its turn-of-the-century French Renaissance style and its baggage, legal, medical- and hearing-inspection, dormitory, and immigrant-aid rooms. Renovated to its 1918–1924 appearance is the second floor Registry Room, where as many as 5,000 people were processed daily. Exhibits tracing American history and displaying thousands of items brought by immigrants to the United States help visitors appreciate immigration's complexity and the immigrant's plight. Outside stands the Wall of Honor bearing the names of more than one-half million individuals and families who immigrated to the United States, many of whom passed through Ellis Island. About two-thirds of all the immigrants from Europe and Asia went west; one-third stayed in New York.

A short distance away, the Statue of Liberty, designed by Alexander-Gustave Eiffel and given to the United States by France in 1876, holds her torch 152 feet above ground, the symbol of American freedom for people around the world.

New Jersey has restored the Central Railroad of New Jersey Passenger Terminal, which is part of Liberty State Park, opposite Ellis Island.

United Nations—First Avenue between E. Forty-second and E. Fiftieth Streets (212-963-8687; www.un.org).

Swede Dag Hammarskjöld (1905–1961) served as the United Nations' second secretary-general from 1953 until his tragic death in 1961 in the Congo. His work for international peace and justice is recognized throughout the United Nations headquarters.

The Dag Hammarskjöld Library, funded by a $6.6 million Ford Foundation gift, is on Forty-second Street east of First Avenue (southwest corner of the complex). Dedicated in 1961, the library has in its main reading room a portrait of the former secretary-general.

North of the library and west of the Secretariat Building is a fountain with the sculpture *Single Form* by Barbara Hepworth. In 1964, this twenty-one foot abstract bronze standing on a granite base was erected in memory of Hammarskjöld. A portrait by Swedish artist Bo Beskow (1906–1989) hangs on the north wall of the Secretariat lobby.

The plaza on E. Forty-seventh Street between First and Second Avenues is named in honor of Hammarskjöld. An official city plaque describes the achievements of the second secretary-general of the United Nations. On the sidewalk near First Avenue is inscribed the following quotation by Hammarskjöld: "Never, 'for the sake of peace and quiet,' deny your own experience or convictions." At Second Avenue and Dag Hammarskjöld Plaza is a bust by Carina Ari, a Swedish sculptor, ballerina, and choreographer.

Outside the United Nations' Meditation Room, Hammarskjöld and Count Folke Bernadotte (1895–1948) are recognized by plaques. In a glass case near the stained-glass window by Russian painter Marc Chagall is a book inscribed in French by Chagall—"To all who served the purposes and principles of the United Nations Charter, for which Dag Hammarskjöld gave his life." Within the small Meditation Room are two gifts from Sweden—a large iron-ore slab and an abstract painting also by Beskow.

The United Nations' Economic and Social Council Chamber was designed by the Swedish architect Sven Markelius and furnished by the government of Sweden. The burgundy window curtains came from Märta Måås-Fjetterström's studio in Båstad; the marble floor was donated by Sveriges Stenindustriförbund. Markelius left the ceiling unfinished to represent the ongoing work of the council. He was one of eleven members of an international team of architects who worked on the plans for the United Nations Headquarters.

Raoul Wallenberg Monument—Forty-seventh Street and First Avenue (United Nations Plaza).
Opposite the Dag Hammarskjöld Plaza is the Wallenberg monument, entitled *Hope,* by Swedish sculptor Gustav Kraitz; it memorializes Wallenberg's efforts in saving thousands of Jews from the Nazis. The monument consists of five black-marble vertical slabs, each approximately twenty-five feet in height. One has a sphere on top. Each slab has a description of Wallenberg's heroic deeds during World War II. On the sidewalk is a bronze briefcase with the initials "R. W." The monument was dedicated in 1998, a gift of the family of Hillel Storch of Stockholm. This is one of thirty monuments honoring Wallenberg that have been raised around the world. They include a bronze bust in the New York Public Library by Lotte Stavisky and a stainless-steel-and bronze monument in Los Angeles (Beverly Boulevard and Fairfax Avenue) by Franco Assetto with an inscription that identifies Wallenberg as the "Angel of Rescue." Additional monuments are planned in other American locales, including Chicago and Redwood City, California.

Scandinavia House—58 Park Avenue between Thirty-seventh and Thirty-eighth Streets (212-879-9779; www.scandinaviahouse.org).
Identified as "the Nordic Center in America," Scandinavia House features the cultures and traditions of the five Nordic countries. It presents numerous changing

Raoul Wallenberg monument, New York City

exhibitions as well as concerts, films, and lectures. Included in the building are the 168-seat Victor Borge Hall for performances and lectures, the Heimbold Family Children's Learning Center, and the Halldór Laxness Library. The center also houses the Aq Café, operated by New York City's Restaurant Aquavit, and the American-Scandinavian Foundation, which promotes international understanding through educational and cultural exchange between the United States and the five Nordic nations. The Foundation was established in 1910 by Danish American industrialist Niels Poulsen.

Historic Places and Monuments

Castle Clinton National Monument—Battery Park (southern end of Manhattan Island).

From 1855 to 1890, Castle Clinton was the country's principal immigrant depot, with more than seven million immigrants passing through the "Gateway to the New World." Originally an untested harbor fortification during the War of 1812, in 1824 the structure was leased by New York as a place of public entertainment. Performers included Jenny Lind, whose 1850 appearance at Castle Clinton was arranged by P. T. Barnum.

In the twentieth century, when it was known as Castle Garden, it was been a city aquarium and, after 1950, a national monument. Only the lower part of the original structure remains.

Swedish Cottage Marionette Theatre—Central Park, near Seventy-ninth Street and W. Central Park (212-988-9093).

Part of the Swedish display at the 1876 Centennial Exhibition in Philadelphia was a timbered schoolhouse made in Sweden. After the exhibition closed, the City of New York purchased the building for $1,500 and moved it to Central Park. In 1947, the Parks and Recreation Department's Marionette Theatre touring company began using it for a workshop and headquarters. In 1973, a permanent theater was constructed inside the cottage, and since that time it has been a marionette theater presenting contemporary and classical shows that enchant the young and the young at heart.

New York City sites honoring John Ericsson (1803–1889), Swedish designer of the naval vessel *Monitor*.

Battery Park in lower Manhattan is the site of a John Ericsson statue by sculptor Jonathan Scott Harley (1845–1912). It was erected in 1893 and modified and dedicated August 1, 1903, a century after the Swedish inventor's birth. It depicts Ericsson holding blueprints of the *Monitor* in one hand and a model of the ship in the other. On the marble base are bronze bas-reliefs depicting scenes from the Civil War and some of Ericsson's other mechanical inventions. An official sign near the monument gives a biographical sketch of Ericsson's life and significance. It notes that at the age of eleven he built a miniature sawmill in Sweden and three years later was in charge of 600 soldiers building a canal. In 1836, three years before traveling to the United States, he invented and patented the screw

Swedish Cottage Marionette Theatre, New York City

propeller, which along with his other inventions helped to revolutionize naval technology.

Special ceremonies regularly take place around this monument, including a March 9 commemoration of the 1862 Civil War battle between the *Monitor* and the *Merrimack;* a July 29 celebration of his birthday; and a late June Midsummer festival. The John Ericsson Society, founded in 1907, furthers interest in Ericsson's accomplishments.

On the west side of lower Manhattan, just south of Canal Street, is Ericsson Place, a one-block stretch of Beech Street between Hudson and Varick Streets, where Ericsson lived and died (the building at #36 no longer exists). His remains were buried in Filipstad, Värmland.

Three sites are noteworthy in the Greenpoint section of Brooklyn, where on January 30, 1862, the *Monitor* was launched. In Monsignor McGolrick Park, which is bounded on one side by Monitor Street, stands the impressive bronze *Monitor* memorial monument. It commemorates the Battle of Hampton Roads (March 9, 1862) between the *Monitor* and the *Merrimack;* the men of the *Monitor;* and designer John Ericsson. Rising from a nine-foot-square base, the figure of a sailor strains at a hawser (a heavy rope for mooring or towing). On West Street near its intersection with Calyer Street, a historic plaque notes the spot where the *Monitor* keel was laid and, several months later, the ship was launched. A nearby intermediate school is named in Ericsson's honor (John Ericsson Intermediate School, 424 Leonard Street).

Statue of John Ericsson, New York City

Alfred Nobel Monument—near Columbus Avenue and W. Eightieth Street, west of the Museum of Natural History.

In 2003, a monument honoring Alfred Nobel, designed by Swedish sculptor Sivert Lindblom, was unveiled at Theodore Roosevelt Park. The twenty-foot-high monument features a bronze portrait of the Swedish inventor, industrialist, philanthropist, and humanist. It also lists all the American recipients of the Nobel prizes, numbering more than 270 and beginning with Theodore Roosevelt in 1906.

Long Island sites honoring aviator Charles A. Lindbergh Jr.

At Roosevelt Field in Garden City, near the spot where Lindbergh took off in 1927 for the first transatlantic solo nonstop flight from New York to Paris, is a monument honoring that feat. A thirty-foot, abstract, stainless-steel sculpture, dedicated in 1981, is at the Old Country Road entrance to the Roosevelt Field Shopping Mall. Lindbergh Park in Huntington is the site of the annual Midsummer Day festival celebrated by Long Island Swedish Americans.

Lutheran Augustana Home for Extended Care and Rehabilitation— 5434 Second Avenue, Brooklyn (718-630-6000).

Founded in 1908 at the Bethlehem Lutheran Church, Augustana Lutheran Home preceded the Swedish Home for the Aged (*Solhem*) at 20 Bristol Avenue on Staten Island by one year. In 1912 the Swedish Home purchased a residence formerly occupied by the Vanderbilts as its new site. In 1995 new facilities were added at Second Avenue.

Churches

Gustavus Adolphus Lutheran Church—155 E. Twenty-second Street, near Third Avenue (212-674-0739).

Organized in 1855, Gustavus Adolphus was one of the main Swedish immigrant churches in New York City. During its early years, the congregation was beset by several problems including a theological dispute. This resulted in the formation of Bethesda Covenant Church, which became a large immigrant church in midtown Manhattan. The Bethesda building no longer exists, but the congregation has temporarily relocated to the Vanderbilt YMCA on Forty-seventh Street between Second and Third Avenues. Gustavus Adolphus also had debt problems and was rocked by frequent pastoral changes. The "golden age" for the congregation was Reverend Mauritz Stolpe's forty-seven-year ministry, which began in 1891.

Four years before Stolpe's arrival, the cornerstone was laid for the present church sanctuary, a turn-of-the-century Romanesque stone building. It was designed by the architect responsible for the old Metropolitan Opera House, and the curved balconies are reminiscent of those found in an opera-house auditorium. A noteworthy Tiffany window graces the ceiling of the sanctuary. The congregation has preserved the old marble baptismal font with a Swedish inscription. In 1926, Crown Prince Gustav Adolf and his wife, Crown Princess Louise, attended a morning service, leaving a signed Bible and a chasuble, which is worn by the pastor on special occasions.

Trinity Baptist Church—209 E. Sixty-first Street (212-838-6844).

Organized in 1867 as the First Swedish Baptist Church of New York, the church changed its name to Trinity in 1942. The congregation worships in a sanctuary designed by Swedish architect Martin G. Hedmark and built in part by Swedish craftsmen.

Trinity has a towering straight-edged brick-front façade with a stepped gable described as late Scandinavian Art Nouveau. At the top of each side tower is a miniature Swedish bell steeple made of lead-coated copper. The steeples are different: one represents a bell tower in Västergötland, the other a tower in northern Sweden with a distinctive Russian influence. At the base of the central tower are two black-marble cornerstones imported from Sweden that were a gift from Mrs. A. K. Fernstrom of Karlshamn. The decorative ironwork on the front oak door is also of Swedish origin.

Creating "an atmosphere of rustic strength and austerity," according to one account, the narthex ceiling has a fresco painted by Olle Nordmark, a Swedish artisan. A circular dome tops the square sanctuary. Nature's colors—tan, brown, and red in the birch, oak, brick, and polished-marble appointments—predominate. Stairway railings curve like vines, and columns are entwined with sculpted grapevines. Hedmark designed Expressionist stained-glass windows, which were executed by Sten Jacobson, another Swedish craftsman. At one time the inscription "God bless you" in Swedish was visible on the rose window, at the rear of the sanctuary, which portrayed the hand of Christ.

Architect Hedmark was born in Sweden and graduated from Tekniska Högskolan (Stockholm) in 1921. He and another architect worked on Engelbrekt's Church, Stockholm, and in 1923 Hedmark designed the Boo Church on Värmdö, an island near Sweden's capital city. Hedmark then came to the United States and designed several churches on the East Coast and in Chicago and the John Ericsson Room in Philadelphia's American Swedish Historical Museum. He eventually left the United States and returned to Sweden, where he died in 1980.

The Salvation Army Central Citadel Corps—212 E. Fifty-second Street, between Second and Third Avenues (212-758-0763).

The Salvation Army Citadel Corps, organized in 1888, maintains a Swedish heritage. Known as *Tvåan*, it has had several Manhattan locations. On the present building, erected in 1940, on the west side of the front door is the inscription, *Frälsnings Armén Tillbedjen Herren i Helig skrud* (The Salvation Army Prays to the Lord in Holy Raiments).

The Church of Sweden—5 E. Forty-eighth Street, near Fifth Avenue (212-832-8443).

The only Swedish Seaman's church in the United States, the Church of Sweden was organized in 1873. In 1978, the church moved to its present facility, formerly owned by the New York Bible Society. A plaque inside the front door of the church honors Raoul Wallenberg. The facility has become a cultural and social center for visiting Swedes and Swedish Americans.

Other churches of Swedish background in Manhattan include the **Lexington United Methodist Church** at 150 E. Sixty-second Street (212-838-6915), organized in 1882, and the **Rock Church (Swedish Pentecostal)** at 153 E. Sixty-second Street (212-838-2724). The churches stand almost directly across from each other. **New Church (Swedenborgian)** is at 112 E. Thirty-fifth Street, between Park and Lexington Avenues (212-685-8967).

Bethlehem Lutheran Church—490 Pacific, corner of Third Avenue and Pacific Street, Brooklyn (718-624-0242).

Bethlehem Lutheran is the second Swedish Lutheran mother church in New York City. It has been said that some 10,000 children who later moved west with their parents were baptized in this church. The congregation organized in April 15, 1874, and the present Romanesque light-brick building with its tall tower was erected twenty years later. Over the main door in marble is the inscription, "Swedish Evangelical Lutheran Bethlehem Church."

The church sanctuary contains an outstanding raised, hand-carved wood pulpit with various Christian symbols. Above the pulpit are the words, *Predika Ordet* (Preach the Word). There are stained-glass windows throughout the sanctuary, including one in the front of the east balcony by Olaus Petri, and stenciling on the walls near the ceiling. On the altar is a copy of Bertel Thorvaldsen's sculpted Christ. The altar cloth was embroidered by King Gustav V in honor of the congregation's seventy-fifth anniversary.

Bethlehem Lutheran Church was the cradle for two of the strongest institutions of the former Metropolitan New York Synod of the Augustana Lutheran Church—Upsala College (East Orange, New Jersey) and the Augustana Lutheran Home (Brooklyn). Plaques in the rear of the church describe them.

Immanuel Swedish Methodist Episcopal Church (today Immanuel and First Spanish United Methodist Church)—424 Dean Street, between Fourth and Fifth Avenues, Brooklyn (718-453-2316).

The light-brick church and its congregation boast direct lineage from the first Swedish Methodist Church organized in the world. At one time a bronze plaque in front of the church noted that in 1845 Olof Gustaf Hedstrom (1803–1877) organized the oldest Swedish Methodist Episcopal Church in the world on the *John Wesley*, also called the *Old Bethel Ship*, anchored at a pier on the Hudson River. Hedstrom died in 1877 and is buried in Brooklyn's Green Wood Cemetery, where on a gray-granite obelisk is the inscription "Founder of Swedish Methodism." After his death, a group of Norwegians purchased the vessel and brought the *Old Bethel Ship* to Brooklyn, but it was not successfully used again as a floating chapel and was sold in 1895 as scrap. Today there is a church at 5523 Fourth

Avenue (Fourth Avenue and Fifty-sixth Street) in Brooklyn called Bethelship United Methodist Church (718-439-6541). In its sanctuary is a large painting of the *Old Bethel Ship.*

Not far from Bethlehem Lutheran and Immanuel Swedish Methodist Episcopal Church is Atlantic Avenue, once known as "Swedish Broadway." At one time, Swedish merchants ran nearly all the stores.

Salem Lutheran—450 Sixty-seventh Street, between Fourth and Fifth Avenues, Brooklyn (718-748-7770).

Located in the Bay Ridge section of Brooklyn, the Salem Lutheran congregation was established in 1904. The present cut-stone, English Gothic-style church was built between 1934 and 1945. In the sanctuary is a stained-glass window of Gustavus II Adolphus. Opposite the church in a small park is a monument to explorer Leif Eriksson, dedicated in 1939 by Crown Prince Olav of Norway. The monument is a replica of a runestone found in Tune, Norway.

Jamestown

Churches

At least seven Swedish-speaking congregations were established in Jamestown, beginning in 1852 with the first Swedish Methodist Episcopal Church. The largest sanctuary belongs to **First Lutheran Church** at 120 Chandler (716-664-4601), organized July 26, 1856. The only Swedish church in the United States designated a cathedral, it was an outgrowth of the Hessel Valley Lutheran congregation. In 1864, Dr. Carl O. Hultgren became the third pastor, beginning a thirty-one-year ministry at the church. Increased membership and the desire to conduct one service in which all the communicants could worship together led to the decision in 1892 to begin construction of a great Romanesque sanctuary. Aaron Hall, a local architect and contractor who had designed the Governor Fenton Home, supervised construction of the enormous church, which was not completed until 1901, in part because of the economic depression of the 1890s.

The cruciform church built of sandstone is 136 feet long and 64 feet wide. It boasts two towers, one 153 feet and the other 96 feet tall. Seating 1,300, the spacious sanctuary, which soars 65 feet to the ceiling, features a large raised pulpit with canopy, stenciling on the ceiling and chancel walls, and large stained-glass windows, including one in the east transept memorializing Gustavus II Adolphus. The west transept window is dedicated to Reverend Hultgren. In the rear of the sanctuary, a plaque placed by the New York Conference of the Augustana Evangelical Lutheran Church commemorates the church. The church bell bears a Swedish inscription.

First Lutheran Church, interior
and Gustavius II Adolphus
window, Jamestown

On the second floor adjacent to the church office is the Heritage Room, where pictures of former pastors and the old church remind visitors of previous eras. The altar and altar rail from the 1856 church can be seen in a small room adjacent to the main sanctuary. The parsonage stands across the street from the church and was built from the same rough stone and in the same nineteenth-century Romanesque style.

The First Swedish Methodist Episcopal Church met in a church at Foote and Chandler, one block from First Lutheran. The red-brick sanctuary was built in 1891. The building is now identified as the **New Covenant Church of Christ Christian Center**. Today, as a result of a merger, the former Swedish Methodist congregation is now **Christ First United Methodist Church**, 663 Lake View Avenue (716-664-5803). Located across the street from First Lutheran, the red-brick building of the former First Swedish Baptist Church (the congregation is now the **Hillcrest Baptist**), at 40 Hallock Street (716-483-3331), was constructed in 1907. Today the poorly maintained structure houses another congregation.

First Covenant Church, at 520 Spring Street (716-483-9825), was organized in 1878 (an 1897 building was destroyed by fire in 1950). Currently the congregation meets in an attractive 1952 Georgian colonial-style structure. The church's history exhibits are collected in its Heritage Room. A second Covenant Church, **Zion Covenant**, 520 Fairmount Avenue (716-488-9310), was originally located two blocks from First. Now outside central Jamestown, the church celebrated its centennial in 1994.

Salvation Army Church is located at the corner of S. Main and Allen Streets (716-664-4108). The church retains a *julotta* service at Christmas, and until recently it broadcast a religious program, largely in Swedish, each Sunday morning over radio station WKSN.

Museums and Other Historic Landmarks

 The Fenton Historical Center—67 Washington Street (716-664-6256).
The Italian villa-style **Governor Reuben E. Fenton Mansion** houses the collections of the Fenton Historical Society. This impressive building features exhibits on life in Jamestown and Chautauqua County. Its library has the finest genealogical records in southwestern New York. In the basement is the Jennie Vimmerstedt Swedish Heritage Room, commemorating the contributions of Vimmerstedt, an indefatigable, dedicated worker and honored citizen. The room, which is a replica of a Swedish *stuga,* was designed and executed by wood-carver Russell Chall and contains authentic Swedish items. In recognition of the 1976 visit of King Carl XVI Gustaf, this room displays a chair made specifically for the king by the Union National Furniture Company of Jamestown and a place setting from the 1976 royal luncheon held in the Jamestown Municipal Building.

The Fenton Historical Center owns a secretary made by the Lindblad Brothers Furniture Company of Jamestown, an Ahlstrom Company piano of 1875, and a bag of greetings dropped by Charles Lindbergh Jr. to Mayor Carlson as he flew over the city on August 1, 1927. In the stairway hang pictures of famous Jamestown citizens. Two Swedish Americans—Roger Tory Peterson, the noted ornithologist, and Samuel Carlson, a former Jamestown mayor—are among the group. Jamestown has had eight mayors of Swedish ancestry. The center also exhibits photographs of some of the more than forty former furniture establishments in Jamestown, many of which were headed by Swedish Americans. The tower of the Fenton Mansion affords a good view of the city, including First Lutheran Church.

Though it does not have a Swedish cemetery, Jamestown has said farewell to many of its Swedish citizens at Lakeview Cemetery on Lakeview Avenue. One of the more interesting graves at this lovely place is that of the Reverend Hultgren, the long-time pastor of First Lutheran. His grave is near the main entrance, marked by a lengthy Swedish inscription.

Historic Plaques

Samuel A. Carlson (1868–1961)—E. Third Street between Spring and Prendergast Streets, near the Municipal Building.
The plaque notes that Carlson was mayor from 1908 to 1927, 1929 to 1933, and 1933 to 1937. Robert H. Jackson, former justice of the U.S. Supreme Court and a resident of Jamestown, stated that Carlson was "a steadfast steward of municipal affairs."

New York State Armory site—S. Main and Harrison Streets.
The historic plaque placed by the Jamestown Historical Marker Committee and the Ingjald Lodge #65 Independent Order of Vikings notes that "the Fenton Guards, organized in 1875 by Swedish immigrants, was the local National Guard unit which occupied the first armory here in 1888." The Guards was founded by John P. Hollers, editor of the Jamestown Swedish newspaper *Folkets Röst*, and Conrad Hult, owner of a haberdashery.

Boyhood Home of Roger Tory Peterson (1908–1996)—16 Bowen Street.
The Jamestown Historical Marker Committee and the Roger Tory Peterson Institute placed this marker to commemorate the world famous naturalist, father of bird watching, and author of the two field guides of North American birds, which have sold more than seven million copies. Peterson's father, Charles Gustav, emigrated from Värmland and worked in a metal working company in Jamestown. As a teenager, Roger worked at the Union Furniture Factory in Jamestown

before studying drawing at the Art Students League in New York City. In 1934 Houghton-Mifflin published Peterson's first book on birds, which sold out in less than three weeks. Peterson won numerous awards, including the Linnaeus Gold Medal of the Royal Swedish Academy and the Presidential Medal of Freedom, presented by President Jimmy Carter in 1980. He and his wife, Virginia Marie, worked and traveled as a team, and a major culmination of their work was the founding of the Roger Tory Peterson Institute of Natural History, located at 311 Curtis Street (716-665-2473; www.rtpi.org).

Gustavus Adolphus Children's Home—715 Falconer Street.
The historic marker erected in 1993 notes that this institution "admitted its first twelve orphans on January 27, 1886. It was established on this site by the New York Conference of the Scandinavian Evangelical Lutheran Augustana Synod. The home became the foundation for Lutheran Social Services of Upper New York, Inc." The site today is owned by the Lutheran Social Services, and its facilities include the Lutheran Retirement Home and the Gustavus Adolphus Child and Family Center.

Fraternal Societies

The Jamestown Vasa (known as Thule Lodge) and Vikings are large and active Swedish lodges. The Vikings have their own downtown building at 318 Washington Street (716-487-9305), and both lodges operate summer facilities on or near Lake Chautauqua. The Thule Lodge supports a Swedish folk dancing group, and the Viking Lodge, divided into Ingjald Lodge (for men) and Diana Lodge (for women), is known for its Viking Male Chorus. The Norden Club, the Norden Women's Club, and the American Scandinavian Heritage Foundation also are active. During the weekend after Labor Day, a Scandinavian Folk Festival, first organized by Lutheran Social Services, is held. Jamestown Community College sponsors a Scandinavian Studies program.

CONNECTICUT

In the 1870s, Swedish immigrants arrived in Connecticut, settling in Portland, south of Hartford, and near the Connecticut River, attracted by employment opportunities at the sandstone quarries and silk mills in nearby Middletown. Other Swedes migrated to Cromwell and New Britain. Swedes also settled in Bridgeport and New Haven. Others were drawn to farming possibilities in northeast Connecticut, particularly in Woodstock Township. In Rhode Island, most Swedes settled around Providence. With the exception of Woodstock and

New Sweden, Maine, New England's Swedish population concentrated in cities and industrial areas.

Darien

The **Convent of St. Birgitta and Vikingsborg Guest House**, at Tokeneke Trail and Runkenhage Road (203-655-1068), is the only convent in the United States of the worldwide order of the Sisters of St. Birgitta (Bridget), founded by St. Birgitta of Sweden (1303–1373). Maria Elisabeth Hesselblad, born in Fåglavik, Västergötland, in 1870, became a Roman Catholic convert and joined this order because of the high regard she had for St. Birgitta. Mother Elisabeth was instrumental in breathing new life into the order, reintroducing the Sisters of St. Birgitta into Sweden for the first time since the Reformation. Just before her death in 1957, she obtained Vikingsborg, a mansion nestled at the head of a rocky cove on Long Island Sound that had belonged to a Swedish evangelist and his wife, who used it as a meeting center and a missionary rest home.

A few sisters reside here and wear the full fourteenth-century-style habit. They offer twelve rooms to guests and prepare three meals daily. The house features antique furniture, a library with books in several languages, a chapel, and sun porches overlooking the sound.

Bridgeport

 Barnum Museum—820 Main Street (203-331-1104; www.barnum-museum.org).
This heavily decorated Romanesque building in downtown Bridgeport focuses on the remarkable life of P. T. Barnum, entrepreneur, museum owner, and impresario. The Jenny Lind Room displays memorabilia focusing on the "Swedish Nightingale's" famous American performance tour in 1850–1851, which Barnum sponsored. When she arrived in New York on September 1, 1850, she was greeted by nearly 40,000 people as a result of the publicity staged by Barnum. Her opening concert took place in New York City's Castle Garden, and she gave an additional ninety-two concerts over the next nine months. In less than a year Barnum had grossed $535,000 and Lind had earned $176,000 plus $10,000 for her first concert.

New Haven

Berzelius Hall, at the corner of Temple and Trumbull Streets and Whitney Avenue, near the campus of Yale University, is a large, white granite building named for the famed Swedish chemist Jöns Jacob Berzelius (1779–1848). The structure is used by a Yale society.

New Britain

First Lutheran Church of the Reformation, 77 Franklin Square (860-224-2475; www.1stlutherannb.org), is a large, impressive early twentieth-century, twin-tower Gothic building in light Vermont granite. It represents the dream of the congregation's dynamic pastor, Sven Gustaf Ohman, who served the church from 1895 (fourteen years after its founding) to 1922. Inspired by Uppsala Cathedral in Sweden, Ohman used similar design elements at First Lutheran. When it was completed in 1906, the church had two soaring spires above the present towers, but these were removed in 1938 because of structural weaknesses. The Swedish bell bears an inscription from Psalms in Swedish.

The impressive interior (remodeled twice) is notable for its vaulted ceiling, large stained-glass windows depicting scenes from Christ's life (also small windows at the rear of the sanctuary portraying Gustavus Adolphus and Martin Luther), a large balcony on three sides, and three large paintings by Olof Grafström (1855–1933) at the front of the sanctuary. The altar painting depicts the Crucifixion. The two side paintings portraying the Resurrection and Ascension are in large niches made specifically for Grafström's works. The sanctuary also features a magnificent Casavant organ installed in 1968.

One block from First Lutheran on Franklin Square is the former sanctuary of **Bethany Covenant Church.** The light-colored brick church, built in 1920, is now owned by the Church of Jesus Christ of the Latter-Day Saints.

Nearby, at 57–61 Arch Street, is a three-story, light-colored brick building identified as **Vega Hall,** constructed in 1897. It was the former headquarters of the Vega Benefit Society. Visible under the roof line is an elaborate ship sculptured in stone.

The **Klingberg Family Centers,** 370 Linwood Street (860-224-9113), were founded by the Reverend John Eric Klingberg. Born into a poor Västmanland family, Klingberg worked in a steel mill near Chicago before earning a theology degree at the University of Chicago. Remembering his difficult childhood, Klingberg in 1903 founded an orphanage in New Britain. It remained nondenominational though closely connected with Swedish Baptists. Today it is a large residential treatment facility for emotionally troubled children. The site's oldest building was constructed in 1920.

Buried in Fairview Cemetery, whose office is at 110 Smalley Street, is Swede Nils Pearson (1850–1938), founder of the Vasa Order of America. This Swedish American fraternal organization, first established in 1896 in New Haven, currently has lodges throughout the United States, Canada, and Sweden (see Bishop Hill, Illinois). Pearson's grave is marked with a red-granite memorial stone.

Cromwell

Cromwell is famous for the extensive nurseries and greenhouses of Andrew N. Pierson (Anders Nils Persson; 1850–1925), from Håslöv, Skåne. Pierson, head of A. N. Pierson's, Inc., became known as the "Rose King of America." The town of Pierson, Florida, was named for one of his brothers, a citrus grower.

Also located in Cromwell is a large complex run by the Evangelical Covenant Church of America (860-635-2690; www.covenantretirement.org). It includes the Children's Home of Cromwell, Covenant Village of Cromwell, Pilgrim Manor (a retirement center), and the East Coast headquarters of the Covenant Church of America.

Woodstock

A charming town in an idyllic setting in northeastern Connecticut, Woodstock first attracted three Swedes in 1871 to work in the cranberry business owned by Dr. George Bowen. One of them, Carl Anderson, was so impressive that Bowen asked him to invite his friends and relatives to join him as indentured workers. Although the cranberry business did not become profitable, the Swedes prospered as local farmers. By the early 1900s, about one-fifth of the local population was Swedish. Area road names testify to the Swedish influence.

The Evangelical Covenant Church is at 24 Child Hill Road (860-928-0486), across the road from Woodstock Academy. Although there was a Congregational church in Woodstock, none of the Swedes became members. It has been said that the Swedes were obliged to sit in the church's balcony during the services because the established residents did not want the newcomers in close proximity. In response, the Swedes organized their own church—the Swedish Evangelical Mission Congregation of Woodstock. The first Swedish service was held in 1875; fifteen years later, the congregation was offered the blacksmith shop on Woodstock Hill. The cornerstone of the white clapboard church has the following inscription: "Sw. Congl. Church erected 1891 remodeled 1906." The Elmvale Cemetery contains the graves of many of the early Swedish settlers. It is located on Woodstock Paine District Road about one mile northeast of the Covenant Church.

Many Swedish American children attended the **Old Quasset School** on the east side of State Highway 169, behind the Woodstock Elementary School. It was used as a school from 1748 until 1945. It claims to be the oldest existing one-room school in the United States. The building was moved to its present site in 1954.

North Grosvenordale

The congregation of **Emanuel Lutheran Church** on Main Street was first organized in 1882, and the brick building with its tall steeple was dedicated in 1897.

This is one of the oldest Swedish church buildings still surviving in the state. Its members were mainly workers in the local cotton-weaving company.

Other Historic Connecticut Churches

Several significant congregations established by early Swedes continue to thrive in various Connecticut locals. **Salem Lutheran Church**, at 14 Salem Street, Naugatuck (203-723-0246), was organized in 1887 and the church building dedicated in 1888. An old Covenant congregation is Hillside Covenant, 100 Hillside Avenue, Naugatuck (203-729-2444). **Salem Evangelical Covenant**, 96 Baldwin Hill Road, Washington (860-868-2794), is another old Covenant congregation. Stained glass from the former sanctuary decorates the windows in its new building. **Emmanuel Lutheran Church**, 311 Capitol Avenue, Hartford (860-525-0894), was organized in 1889 and the building dedicated in 1924. **Christ Lutheran Church**, 300 Washington Street, Middletown (860-347-6068), is opposite the campus of Wesleyan University. The congregation was organized in 1891. This light-brick church was built in the Gothic style in 1958 and has a 1910 altar painting of the Crucifixion by Olof Grafström. **Zion Lutheran Church**, 183 William Street, Portland (860-342-2860; www.zionlutheranportland.org), was organized in 1874, making it the oldest Swedish Lutheran congregation in Connecticut. The first sanctuary, built in 1877, was destroyed by fire. The second church building at 13 Waverly Avenue was dedicated in 1879 and is currently owned by another congregation. In 1968, the Lutherans built a new sanctuary on William Street, opposite the Swedish cemetery, which offers a wonderful view of the Connecticut River Valley. An altar painting by artist Olof Grafström of Christ in Gethsemane (1901) hangs in the fellowship hall. **Bethlehem Lutheran Church**, 1 East High Street, East Hampton (860-643-1193), was organized in 1899 and the building constructed in 1900. This church was originally Congregational. **Emanuel Lutheran Church**, 60 Church Street, Manchester (860-643-1193; www.emanuelmanchester.org), was organized in 1881 and the church dedicated in 1923. **Ebenezer Lutheran Church**, 96 Oak, Willimantic (860-423-2193), was established in 1889 and the church building dedicated in 1894. Except for its steeple, it is almost an exact replica of the former Zion Lutheran Church in Portland, about thirty miles away.

RHODE ISLAND

Providence

 Organized in 1889, **Gloria Dei Evangelical Lutheran Church**, 15 Hayes Street (401-421-5860), is probably the most architecturally outstanding Swedish church in Rhode Island. At one time there were seven Swedish churches in the city. Two blocks from the State Capitol, the church was designed by Martin Hedmark and dedicated in 1928. Hedmark may have been influenced by Gripsholm Castle in Mariefred, Sweden, in designing the church's exterior. The combination of brick and limestone facing is used on the circular corner towers with their small windows and sheet metal caps. A weathervane on the left tower has the form of a Viking ship, symbolic of the church sailing through the ages. The highest part of the dramatic edifice contains a stepped gable.

On the doors leading into the nave from the narthex are small metal medallions of people who have greatly influenced the Swedish Lutheran Church—St. Ansgarius, St. Botvid, St. Eric, St. Birgitta, Martin Luther, and Olaus Petri. The sanctuary can best be described as Art Nouveau in detail. It is marked by an array of Christian symbols. The stained-glass windows have Swedish inscriptions honoring the contributors. The window to the right of the altar depicts the Last Supper from a perspective above the table. At the top of the window is an inscription in Swedish: "Given for you for the forgiveness of sins." The eight-sided raised pulpit with a canopy has a wood panel in gold leaf with the image of the Reverend J. E. Morton (1869–1913), a popular pastor during the first decade of the twentieth century. Morton died in Sweden and is buried in Svenljunga, where Gloria Dei and a congregation in Gävle have erected a monument in his honor.

Swedish Lutheran congregations existed in other Rhode Island towns, including East Greenwich (First Lutheran, 124 Division Street, is the oldest Swedish Lutheran congregation in the state, having been organized in 1874), Pawtucket (St. Matthew–Trinity Lutheran, 690 Newport Avenue, was organized in 1893 and its building constructed in 1896), and West Warwick (Emanuel Lutheran, 9 New London Avenue, www.emanuelww.org, was organized in 1893 and its building constructed in 1896). Covenant congregations are found in Cranston, East Greenwich, Pawtucket, and West Warwick. The Scandinavian Home in Cranston is run by a corporation.

Several Providence Swedes were instrumental in organizing the Mayflower movement to raise money for the Swedish National Sanatorium (today called the Swedish Medical Center) in Denver. The Berkander Plant in Providence, founded by George Berkander, made little mayflowers (celluloid wood anemones) that were sold to raise the money. This sale follows the Swedish custom of making and selling mayflowers in May and using the proceeds to support health care.

MASSACHUSETTS

New England's first group of Swedish immigrants arrived in Brockton, Massachusetts, in 1851. Nineteen years later, fifty-one Swedish settlers headed for the remote northeast corner of Maine to establish the New Sweden colony. Beginning in the 1870s, large numbers of Swedes settled in Worcester, Massachusetts, attracted by the Norton Company (a grinding machinery and abrasives concern founded in 1885) and various steel industries. Many early Swedes in Worcester arrived from Skåne, particularly around Höganäs. One was John Jeppson, who settled in Worcester in 1869 and by 1885 was superintendent of the Norton Emery Wheel Company. His son, George Jeppson, eventually became chairman of the board of Norton Company. By the late 1880s, there were some 5,000 Swedes living in Worcester, mainly in the Belmont Hill, Greendale, Vernon Hill, and Quinsigamond Village sections. By 1920, the Swedish-born and second-generation population made up about one-fifth of Worcester's population. Other Massachusetts cities with large Swedish populations included Boston (particularly in the Dorchester and Roxbury sections) and the nearby communities of Beverly, Lynn, Waltham, and Newton.

Worcester

Churches

Trinity Evangelical Lutheran Church—73 Lancaster Street, at Salisbury Street, opposite the Worcester Art Museum (508-753-2989; www.trinityworc.org).
The Trinity Lutheran Church congregation began on January 1, 1948, after a merger of three congregations, including the Swedish First Evangelical Lutheran Church, organized in 1881. Since the merger involved more than 2,000 communicants, a new larger sanctuary was needed. George Jeppson was appointed the chairman of the building committee, and Jens Fredrick Larson, known for his work at former Upsala College (East Orange, New Jersey), was selected as the architect. Jeppson thoroughly researched Scandinavian church architecture, and Larson's design employed both Swedish and New England architectural features. The exterior of this impressive church is faced with cream-colored brick trimmed with limestone. The curved base of the tower is of seventeenth-century Swedish design. The tower above it is New England Georgian in design.

The nave of the large sanctuary is cream-colored brick penetrated by arches in Norman style supported by limestone columns. The sanctuary is believed to contain the only decorated ceiling of its kind in the United States—128 plywood panels depicting through symbols stories from the Old and New Testaments. They were painted by Arthur Covey (1877–1960), who was influenced by the important ceiling paintings of the thirteenth-century church in Dädesjö, Småland. He also was influenced by the decorations in Swedish provincial houses. Hanging from the ceiling are eight Swedish-designed silver chandeliers of clustered lotus leaves. In the church nave are commemorative plaques and the cornerstones of the three churches that merged in 1948. Behind a glass is a golden crown worn by

Trinity Evangelical Lutheran Church, Worcester

the church's brides at their weddings. The sanctuary also features a Noack organ dedicated in 1969.

The altar and reredos are a modification of a design by Nicodemus Tessin the younger (1654–1728) for the Cathedral in Kalmar, Sweden, completed and installed in 1712. Trinity's carved oak altar contains a painting of Christ in Gethsemane by Olof Grafström. The baptismal font is a replica of one dating from about 1200 in the church of Träne, Skåne, and the stone comes from the same quarry used for the Lund Cathedral. Stained-glass windows from the former Swedish First Lutheran Church sanctuary have been incorporated into Trinity Lutheran's facilities.

The exterior of the Parish House reflects the manor-house type of Swedish architecture. The door and entrance on the Lancaster Street side were inspired by one designed by Ernst Torsten Torulf, a Swedish architect. In the Parish House is the Olander Memorial Library, honoring a pastor from the 1950s. It contains a number of rare, old Bibles. Also in the Parish House is the 360-seat Jeppson Hall.

On May 26, 1959, the octagonal Christ Chapel was dedicated. It was inspired by the work of Swedish architect Nicodemus Tessin the elder (1615–1681), who built several eight-sided churches in Sweden. The altar cross is made of ground-quartz crystal and brass by Lars Fleming of Stockholm, who was the silversmith to the Swedish royal family. The Jeppson family financed this lovely chapel.

Zion Lutheran Church—41 Whitmarsh Avenue, Greendale section of Worcester (508-853-2009).

The Zion Lutheran Church congregation has included many employees of the Norton Company (near the church are a number of large three-story houses formerly owned by Swedes). The congregation was organized in 1914 and the sanctuary dedicated in 1920.

In 1948, groundbreaking for Zion Lutheran's Faith Chapel took place, with the Swedish Archbishop Erling Eidem in attendance. The architect was Martin Hedmark of Sweden.

Historically, the most interesting feature of the chapel is the pastel fresco depicting the history of this Greendale congregation. Scenes from right to left include a potter representing John Jeppson peacefully working in front of his Skåne home near a church with a stepped gable; two trees, a willow (on the wind-twisted trunk is a Viking looking toward the potter) and an elm (with a Native American peering toward a New England valley to his left and Abraham Lincoln symbolizing integrity and love of freedom); a white New England–style church and homesteads in the valley; and an angel carrying the banner, "Peace be with you," who looks down on a worker with Nordic features employed at the Norton

Company. At the top of the fresco are the hands of God blessing the valley and its people, churches, and homes.

Epworth Methodist Church—64 Salisbury Street, across from Worcester Art Museum and Trinity Lutheran Church (508-752-2376).
Swedish immigrants organized this church in 1885 as the Thomas Street Methodist Episcopal Church. It is a large, red-brick, Gothic-style structure.

Belmont Street Baptist Church—25 Belmont Street, at Fountain Street (508-753-0312).
Organized in 1880 as First Baptist Church, this congregation originally built its sanctuary at the corner of Eastern Avenue and Mulberry Street. The present church is a large, red-brick, Romanesque edifice.

Bethlehem Covenant Church—46 Greenwood Street, at Halmstad Streets in Quinsigamond Village (508-752-1459; www.bethlehemcc.org).
The congregation of Bethlehem Covenant Church is an offshoot (organized in 1894) of the Salem Square Church, now the **Salem Covenant Church**, 215 E. Mountain Street, established in 1880 and known as the First Swedish Evangelical Congregational Church of Worcester. This church was made famous by the Reverend John A. Hultman (1861–1942), who gave concerts throughout the United States. A singing evangelist known as *Solskenssångaren* (the Sunshine Singer), Hultman was pastor of Salem Square from 1900 to 1906; he also served Bethlehem Covenant from 1917 to 1919. Bethlehem Covenant's white clapboard church was built in 1901. The congregation was the Second Swedish Congregational Church of Worcester until 1924, when it joined the Evangelical Mission Covenant Church of America and adopted the name "Bethlehem Evangelical Church."

Near the Bethlehem Church is the former Swedish Methodist Church (Quinsigamond United Methodist Church), 9 Stebbins Street (508-755-6237) and former Emanuel Lutheran (now the Quinsigamond Village Community Center) with its tall spire. It is located two blocks north of Bethlehem Covenant on Greenwood Street. The Emanuel Lutheran congregation is now at 200 Greenwood Street, Quinsigamond Village (508-756-6620), and the Salvation Army is at 884 Millbury Street. The local Roman Catholic Church, two blocks south of Bethlehem Covenant at 3 Wiser Avenue, is called St. Catherine of Sweden.

Other Points of Interest

Norton Company Administration Building—1 New Bond Street (508-795-5000).
Saint-Gobain Abrasives, of which the former Norton Company is a part, manu-

factures abrasives and produces technologically sophisticated ceramics, plastics, and chemical-processed products.

As late as 1914, about 75 percent of the workers of Norton Company were of Swedish extraction. On the fourth floor of the Administration Building is Norton Hall. On the walls is a unique family tree showing the founders and all employees who have worked for the company for twenty-five years or more. Murals depict various aspects of the company's operations, and glass cases show its numerous products.

Before World War I, Norton Company built single-family houses for its employees, which it sold for $1,500. When the first village was built on Indian Hill Road, Theodore Roosevelt was present at the dedication. Other houses were constructed on Ararat and New Bond Streets.

In 1903, the Swedish National Federation was organized. At its 1921 meeting, it was proposed that a Swedish hospital be established, and the following year the Fairlawn Hospital, now **Fairlawn Rehabilitation Hospital**, was opened.

Lutheran Home of Worcester, 26 Harvard Street (508-754-8877), was established in 1920 as the Swedish Lutheran Old People's Home. Five years later, the Jeppson Building, the first part of the existing structure, was constructed.

In **Old Swedish Cemetery**, 154 Webster Road, and **New Swedish Cemetery**, Island Drive, which is opposite 240 Webster Street, lie the early Swedes of Worcester. Upon entering Old Swedish Cemetery, visitors see a marble monument "in memory of those Swedish pioneers of Worcester who in 1885 founded this cemetery." Probably the most imposing of the monuments is the Jeppson family marker. Viking ships and part of the Twenty-third Psalm decorate the vertical stone whose border has a swirling Viking motif. Not far from the Jeppson monument is a marble seat in memory of Pehr G. Holmes (1881–1952), former mayor of Worcester and a member of Congress.

To the right, immediately upon entering the New Swedish Cemetery, is a monument erected in 1967 by the Vasa Order of America in memory of deceased members. At the southwest end is a large stone honoring former residents of the Swedish Lutheran Old People's Home.

Sculpture and Other Art

Two works by Carl Milles—*Man Riding Fish* (a fountain made of pewter) and *Head of Nereid*—have been collected by the **Worcester Art Museum** at 55 Salisbury Street (508-799-4406). On Boylston Street near Bourne Street, in front of the **Saint-Gobain Abrasives Building**, is Milles's *Eagle,* a war memorial made of black granite. In the Administration Building's executive dining room is Milles's *Sun Glitter,* a mermaid riding on a dolphin.

Orange

Originally known as the Swedish Lutheran Church, **Bethany Lutheran Church**, 62 Cheney Street (928-544-3541), was organized in 1889. The present church was built in 1896. Orange is northwest of Worcester, near Athol.

Holden

Immanuel Lutheran Church, 346 Shrewsbury Street (508-829-5516), is the largest of the Swedish congregations located in communities near Worcester. Its attractive building was built in 1948.

Shrewsbury

The **Scandinavian Athletic Club**, 435 Lake Street (508-757-3948; www.sacsoccer .com), is the last of numerous Swedish clubs in and around Worcester. In the early 1920s, a large clubhouse was erected. Today the facility focuses on soccer and is rated one of the best private sports complexes in the Worcester area.

Boston

Isabella Stewart Gardner Museum—280 The Fenway (617-566-1401; www .gardnermuseum.org).
This Venetian palace–style museum is the former home of Isabella Stewart Gardner and contains an art collection that includes a number of works by Swedish artist Anders Zorn (1860–1920). Of special interest is a portrait of Gardner that Zorn painted in Venice. A long-time friend who introduced Zorn to patrons and helped him arrange exhibits in Boston, Gardner first met Zorn at the Chicago World Columbian Exposition in 1893 when she purchased his *The Omnibus,* now also part of the museum's collection. In the Short Gallery are several etchings by Zorn.

Two churches in the Boston metropolitan area have Swedish roots. **Resurrection Lutheran Church** (formerly Emanuel Lutheran) at 94 Warren Avenue, at Kearsarge Avenue (617-421-2066), in Roxbury was organized in 1873. The large, stone, Romanesque church with a tall tower designed by architects Carl Enebuske and Hilding Hanson was constructed between 1923 and 1934. Over the front door, under a statue of Christ, is the inscription in Swedish, "Come to me all ye who are heavy laden."

Covenant Congregational Church, 455 Arborway in Forest Hills (617-524-0775; www.bostoncov.org), began on November 1, 1881, when twelve men met in a home in Cambridge and signed the organizational document making them charter members of the Scandinavian Free Church of Boston. The church later became known as the Swedish Congregational Church and Covenant Congregational. The present sanctuary was dedicated in 1936. Built in a Romanesque architectural style, the church has a modified stepped gable on the bell tower reminiscent of southern Swedish design.

Quincy

Faith Lutheran Church (formerly Salem Lutheran)—201 Granite Street (617-472-1247).

Organized in 1889, Salem Lutheran Church (originally Swedish) became Faith Lutheran in 1974. Its present structure was dedicated in 1894 and enlarged in 1909.

Brockton

First Lutheran Church—900 S. Main Street (508-586-9201).

The mother church of the former Augustana Lutheran churches of New England, First Lutheran was organized in 1867, but its roots go back to 1853, when the first service was conducted by Olof Gustaf Hedstrom (1803–1877), founder of Swedish Methodism. The present structure was dedicated in 1923 with Swedish Archbishop Nathan Söderblom in attendance.

Gethsemane Lutheran Church—906 N. Main Street (508-586-7975).

The church was organized in 1895, and the building was dedicated in 1923.

North Easton and Attleboro

Two old congregations are **Covenant Congregational**, 204 Center Street (508-238-6423), North Easton, and **First Evangelical Covenant Church** at 841 North Main (508-226-6221), Attleboro.

West Newton

Following Prince Wilhelm's visit to Boston in 1907, the Swedish National Union was founded. In 1911 it became the Swedish Charitable Society of Greater Boston, Inc., for the purpose of establishing and maintaining a home for aged and incapacitated Swedish Americans in the area and for providing charitable social assistance. In 1917 the Home for Aged Swedish People (now the **Swedish Home for the Aged**), 206 Waltham Avenue (617-527-9751), was established. In 1926 Crown Prince Gustav Adolf and his wife, Crown Princess Louise, visited the home, as did King Carl XVI Gustaf in 1976. At the right of the front door is a historic plaque placed there at the 1917 opening. In 1991 the society voted to allow any persons of Nordic heritage—not only Swedes—as residents.

Cambridge

Faith Lutheran Church—311 Broadway (617-354-0414; www.faithchurchcambridge.org). This sanctuary, formerly Augustana Lutheran, features a central tower in the Gothic style, dedicated in 1909. The congregation was organized in 1892.

Also in Cambridge is the **Church of the New Jerusalem (Swedenborg Chapel)** at 50 Quincy Street (617-864-4552). The Swedenborg School of Religion is in Newton at 1320 Centre Street (617-244-0504).

Waltham

By 1885 there was a growing number of Swedes in the Boston suburb of Waltham. Two congregations formed: the Swedish Lutheran Church, now known as **First Evangelical Lutheran**, 6 Eddy Street (781-893-6563), and the Swedish Free Mission, which became the **Covenant Congregational Church**, now at 375 Lexington Street (www.walthamcovenant.org). In 1894 the Swedish Free Mission constructed a building on Central Street, but in 1950 the congregation began holding services in the lovely Gothic-style stone building of the **Waltham Church of the New Jerusalem (Swedenborgian)**. In 1960 the church on Lexington Street was sold to the Covenant congregation. The First Evangelical Lutheran congregation worships in a twentieth-century English Gothic church designed by Hilding Hanson and built in 1927 at the corner of Eddy and Weston.

On United Nations Day, October 24, 1961, the Waltham Junior Chamber of Commerce erected a plaque of red Swedish granite on Waltham Common (east side near Elm Street) honoring Dag Hammarskjöld's life with the words, "In tribute for service and sacrifice to the cause of world peace."

Woburn

Lutheran Church of the Redeemer, 60 Forest Park Road (781-933-4600), was organized in 1893 and its building dedicated in 1897. It was originally called the Swedish Evangelical Lutheran Church.

Medford

On the campus of **Tufts University** (617-627-5000; www.tufts.adm) are two buildings named for Swedish Americans. Arthur Anderson Hall (Tufts College of Engineering) takes its name from the former chairman of the university board of trustees who was Boston's Swedish consul and had a successful career in the insurance business. The Nils Yngve Wessell Library is named for Tuft's president from 1951 to 1966. A Carl Milles bronze casting of an elephant welcomes visitors to a library courtyard fountain. Inside the library is a reduced-size copy of *Man and Pegasus* by Milles.

Malden

First Lutheran Church—62 Church (781-324-7133; www.firstlutheranmalden.org).
This congregation was organized in 1893, and in 1897 its members dedicated the present white-clapboard Gothic-style sanctuary.

Pigeon Cove

Cape Ann, northeast of Boston, was known for its quarries of granite, the stone used to build the Bunker Hill Monument in Boston and to pave the streets of several eastern cities, including New York. Swedes and Finns were attracted to the area by employment possibilities. The first Swede arrived in 1879. Most of the early Swedish quarry workers lived on Pigeon Hill Street or in the immediate vicinity. In the early 1890s, three Swedish churches were built. The former **Swedish Lutheran Church**, 20 Stockholm Avenue, is now a private residence. In 1891, Swedish Methodists built a church at 147 Granite Street. Today the building is used as a silversmith's studio. Down the block at 111 Granite Street is the former **Swedish Evangelical Church (Mission Covenant)**, built in 1894 and now a private residence. Although none of the former Swedish congregations currently exist, there are Lutheran and Covenant Churches with Swedish roots in nearby West Peabody, Beverly, and Lynn.

Rockport

In Rockport at 18 Broadway is the **Vasa Order's Spiran Lodge**, chartered in 1906. The Vasa Order still meets regularly in the hall and has Swedish festivals.

VERMONT

Vermont attracted few Swedish settlers, but several churches of Swedish heritage still exist. In Brattleboro, the entire congregation of **Trinity Lutheran Church**, 43 Western Avenue (802-254-4220; www.trinitybrattleboro.com), was originally from Dalsland. The altar rail is believed to have been designed after one found in the Tisselskog Church in Dalsland. Some other Dalsland natives settled twenty miles north of the Vermont borders in Waterville, this being Canada's first Swedish settlement. In Proctor, **St. Paul's Lutheran Church**, 6 Gibson Street (802-459-2728), was organized in 1890 by Swedes employed by the Vermont Marble Company. They built a sanctuary in 1894.

NEW HAMPSHIRE

Like Vermont, New Hampshire had only a scattering of Swedish settlers. Evidence of their settlement remains today in **Gethsemane Lutheran Church**, 65 Sagamore Street, Manchester (603-623-3451). It was organized in 1882, and the congregation erected its building in 1887. **Concordia Lutheran**, 211 North Main Street, Concord (603-224-0277; www.concordialutheranchurch.org), was an Augustana Lutheran congregation. Bedford has a Covenant congregation identified as the **Bethany Covenant Church**, One Covenant Way (603-472-5545; www.bethanycovenant.com). The building is an attractive white, New England Gothic–style with a tall steeple. At West Swanzey, near Peterborough, the Evangelical Covenant Church created a conference center and summer campground called **Pilgrim Pines** (603-352-0443). **St. Paul Lutheran Church**, organized in 1887, is located in Berlin at 101 Norway Street (603-752-1410) near White Mountain National Forest in northern New Hampshire. Scandinavians were attracted to Berlin by employment opportunities on the local railway and the timber industries. Swedes in Berlin were known for ski jumping.

MAINE
Monson

 Monson is nineteen miles northwest of Dover-Foxcroft, the largest town in central Maine. Monson-area slate quarries first drew Swedes in 1874 and 1875. They established two churches—a Swedish Mission Church (1890), which became the Lutheran church, and a Swedish Methodist church (1892). Both had ministers who conducted services in Swedish. The **Swedish Lutheran Church** at Wilkins and Hebron Streets has been a hostel for Appalachian Trail hikers but currently serves as a Christian study center. The former Swedish Methodist Church on Water Street was a small clapboard structure that burned in 1982.

Monson has a small town museum (207-997-3792). The Welsh were the first ethnic group to arrive, followed by Swedes and later Finns. While the Swedes have moved on, they left behind many tombstones with Swedish epitaphs. Persisting in the area is an interest in kick sledding, which Swedes first introduced to Maine. Sleds were once manufactured in Monson. The museum has two kick sleds on display, and the community still sponsors kick-sled races.

Caribou

Built in 1938, **Nylander Museum**, 657 Main Street (207-493-4209; www.nylander museum.org), honors Olof O. Nylander (1864–1943), the Swedish American botanist and geologist. An Ystad shoemaker's son, Nylander began work as a housepainter but became a self-taught geologist. In 1893, he discovered fossils in Chapman Plantation, Maine, and joined the U.S. Geological Survey.

Nylander contributed articles to many magazines around the United States. He collected fossils, minerals, and shells in many areas of Maine. The museum houses Nylander's extensive geological, marine life, and natural history collection.

New Sweden

New Sweden (www.visitaroostook.com; www.geocities.com/maineswedishcolony) is in the extreme northeastern Aroostook Valley, an area of vast stretches of pine- and birch-covered hills and mountains, crystal lakes, and potato growing. Swedish settlement dates from 1870, when twenty-two men, eleven women, and eighteen children from Gothenburg arrived at the urging of William Widgery Thomas Jr., a native of Portland, Maine, who had been the American consular agent in Gothenburg between 1863 and 1865 and later served as American minister to Stockholm. Thomas believed that the hardy Swedes he saw emigrating from Gothenburg for the western United States would be ideal settlers for his home state as well, so he advertised 100-acre Aroostook Valley land grants in the Swedish press after persuading the state legislature to provide the lands. Emigrants were required to pay for their own journeys, be in good health, and present letters recommending their moral character. Thomas particularly sought farmers with additional skills in carpentry and tailoring.

The first group of Swedes came from several provinces, particularly Skåne. Because they arrived late in the summer, the only good crop harvested the first year was turnips. The settlers spent their time building a central gathering hall, called the Capitolium, where they lived the first winter. (They had expected that the state would build log cabins before their arrival but found only six.) By 1873, some 22,000 acres of land had been cleared. The population grew to 600, including many new arrivals from Jämtland. This contingent decided to build their log cabins immediately north of New Sweden, naming their settlement Jemtland. To the west of New Sweden is a township called Westmanland, which was settled as early as 1879. In 1881 a few Swedish immigrants moved north from New Sweden, and fourteen years later the township of Stockholm was organized. Mainly because of the vast timber resources and the construction of a new lumber mill, Stockholm expanded industrially between 1900 and 1910.

New Sweden and the surrounding area prospered during the late nineteenth and early twentieth centuries. In the early 1960s one could still hear Swedish spoken, see Swedish food prepared, and enjoy Swedish songs and dances. In 1978 the town observed its centennial, stimulating even greater interest in its Swedish heritage. In the vicinity of New Sweden are several geographic features named

New Sweden Historical Museum, New Sweden

for the early Swedish settlers, including Fogelin Hill and Pond, Jacobson Hill, and Stockholm Mountain.

The **New Sweden Historical Museum** (207-896-3018) on Capitol Hill Road is housed in a replica of the old Capitolium, the immigrants' first home, place of worship, school, store, community hall, and the office of the commissioner of immigration. The local historical society later converted the original capitolium into a museum, but in 1971, a fire destroyed it. Three years later, thanks to a special fund collected in the United States and Sweden, the present replica was dedicated. Displays feature the area's historical collection saved from the fire, including photographs of early settlers, hand-hewn skis, the original altar rail and pews from Gustaf Adolph Lutheran Church, various farm implements, and a portrait of New Sweden's immigration commissioner, William W. Thomas Jr., in Stockholm, Sweden.

Adjacent to the museum is the former **Capitol School** (207-896-3199). Built around 1926, it is the last of the one-room schoolhouses in New Sweden. It retains its early character, with the original blackboard, teacher's desk, and student desks, and was used as a school until 1950. It is now a Scandinavian gift shop.

Two markers near the museum—a state plaque on a large boulder in front of the New Sweden Museum and a nearby granite monument inscribed, *Mina Barn I Skogen* (My children in the forest)—recognize New Sweden's heritage. Close to the museum is the restored **Lindsten Stuga**, an immigrant log cottage dating from around 1894 that was moved from Westmanland.

Nearby on Station Road is another restored Swedish homestead. Known as the **Noak Larson–George Ostlund log house** and built in the early 1870s, it is the only two-story log home in Maine that has survived. It was owned and occupied by the George Ostlund family from 1910 to 1989. Across the road is the **Lars Noak Blacksmith and Woodworking Shop** built around 1900. All the equipment is in working order. These two buildings, which are in the Larsson-Noak Historic District, are in the care of Maine's Swedish Colony, Inc. (207-896-5728), which is also responsible for Capitol School.

The **Gustaf Adolph Lutheran Congregation** was organized in 1871, and the present sanctuary on Capitol Hill Road (207-896-3068) was built in 1880. The stained glass in the balcony is in memory of the early pioneers; the church bell came from William W. Thomas Jr.

In March 1871, eight settlers organized the First Swedish Baptist Church, now the **First Baptist Church of New Sweden** (207-896-3392), making it the oldest congregation in New Sweden by several months. The first church building was erected in 1892 but destroyed by fire ten years later. The present building dates from 1902. The stained-glass windows are memorials to the Swedes of New Sweden. The **Evangelical Covenant Church** (207-896-5202) was founded in 1886 as the Free Christian Gospel Mission Church with twenty charter members. The attractive white clapboard church was dedicated in 1891, and ten years later the high steeple was given by William W. Thomas Jr. The colored windows are memorials given by Swedes of the congregation.

New Sweden Cemetery, near the New Sweden Historical Museum on Capitol Hill Road, includes the graves of the early Swedish settlers. Adjacent to the cemetery to the northwest in a grove of trees is a granite monument, bearing the inscription, "In loving memory of the first Swedish pioneers laid at rest here 1871–1875." There is also a small **Swedish cemetery** on State Highway 161 one-half mile south of the New Sweden–Woodland town line.

W. W. Thomas Memorial Park, to the east of the New Sweden Historical Museum, is named for the founder of New Sweden. Here and at other sites on the weekend nearest June 21, the annual Swedish Midsummer festivities, including an interdenominational community worship service and Swedish folk dancing and singing, take place.

New Sweden claims nearly thirty log houses built by pioneer Swedes, though none of the original State of Maine–built cabins survives. The privately owned **Timmerhuset** (the log house), a one-and-one-half-story dwelling, was built sometime between 1871 and 1873. The interior has been totally restored, and hand-hewn logs can be seen in the living room, which has a cathedral ceiling. The front of the house formerly had an exterior balcony, as do homes in northern Sweden. This characteristic has been preserved in the upstairs interior balcony.

In Woodland, south of New Sweden, are two sites maintained by the Woodland Historical Society: the **Snowman Schoolhouse Museum** (1895) on Woodland Center Road and the **Lagerstrom House Museum** on Beckstrom Road. The latter was built in 1896 by Julius Hammer for his parents. It was sold to Carl Beckstrom in 1900 and resold three years later to Carl Lagerstrom Sr. The house was donated to the Woodland Historical Society in 1996; few changes have been made to the structure since its construction.

Westmanland

Westmanland School House is a one-room, white clapboard schoolhouse built in 1925 (take Westmanland Road west three miles from the New Sweden Historical Museum; turn north on Westmanland Road and travel one mile to the schoolhouse, which is on the west side of the road). The interior walls and pressed-metal ceiling are painted white. Today it is the township hall. Almost directly east of the school is the Westmanland cemetery with old stone markers.

On the east side of Westmanland Road, less than a mile north of the schoolhouse and cemetery, is a restored privately owned log house (the logs are visible only on the interior). The cabin was probably built in 1880 by Carl August

Peterson, an early Swedish settler. Later the family of Algot Andersson (the first person born in Westmanland) lived in the house.

On the west side of Westmanland Road is a birch-tree-lined drive leading to a farmhouse. Between the house and barn, built in the 1870s, is a log house built in 1871 by settler A. G. Ohlson at the **Anders and Johanna Ohlson Farm**, 114 W. Lebanon Road. The site is privately owned.

Jemtland

The **West Jemtland Cemetery** is located on Hedman Road west of State Highway 161, and **Rista Cemetery** is east of State Highway 161 on Rista Road. On State Highway 161, about one-half mile north of Rista Road, was the Everett Larson Store, where the community Sunday school was held.

Stockholm

The **Stockholm Historical Society Museum**, 280 Main Street (207-896-5759), is in a 1901 building that housed the first store in Stockholm, which was run by Lewis and John Anderson and known as the **Anderson Brothers Store**. Among the museum displays are the Swedish flag given to the town by King Gustav V marking the 700th anniversary of Stockholm, Sweden; items from the Fogelin store and family; a Stockholm centennial quilt depicting buildings in the town; old photographs; skis and sleds; a lumbering display; and a schoolroom and old kitchen displays.

The white clapboard **First Baptist Church** (207-896-5279), south of the Stockholm Historical Museum, is the oldest church building in town, constructed in 1905. **Trinity Lutheran Church** (207-896-7960; formerly the Oscar Frederick Evangelical Lutheran Church) was organized in 1906 and constructed in 1907.

On the east side of Stockholm Road, on top of a hill overlooking Stockholm, is the cemetery containing graves of early Swedish settlers. The north end of the cemetery offers a fine view of the pine forests and the town of Stockholm in the valley. St. Theresa Catholic Church is located across the road from the cemetery.

THE EASTERN MIDWEST

ILLINOIS

Among the states, the greatest number of Swedish immigrants chose Illinois as their first destination. Chicago, Rockford, Rock Island, Moline, Galesburg, and parts of Cook, Winnebago, Rock Island, Knox, and Henry Counties developed into Swedish strongholds. But it was Carl Sandburg's Chicago—"Hog Butcher for the World,/Tool Maker, Stacker of Wheat,/Player with Railroads and the Nation's Freight Handler,/Stormy, husky, brawling,/City of the Big Shoulders"—where Swedes created the state's largest community and from which came the second-stage migration to new destinations throughout the Midwest and West.

Chicago

The first Swedes arrived in the 1840s, and by 1900 Chicago had 49,000 Swedish-born residents, whose 96,000 children quickly swelled their ranks. Only Stockholm, the capital of Sweden, boasted more Swedes and their children.

At first they settled and established churches in Swede Town, just north of the Chicago River, but the great Chicago Fire of 1871 wiped out that settlement, reducing four of the churches to ashes. The next Swedish settlement was farther north in the Lake View district around Belmont Avenue (3200 North). By the 1890s, the Swedes had moved into the area surrounding Clark and Foster Avenues (5200 North), which became known as Andersonville. There were also Swedish settlements on the south side on Twentieth and Twenty-first Streets; on Buffalo Avenue between Eighty-sixth and Eighty-eighth (known as Englewood); on the northwest side (Irving Park and Logan Square); west side (Humboldt Park); and the far south side (Grand Crossing, Pullman, Roseland, and Indiana Harbor). In nearby Evanston to the north was another Swedish community.

Swedish architects, contractors, carpenters, and engineers helped make Chicago into Sandburg's "City of the Big Shoulders." Estimates of major buildings by Swedes range from 35 percent in 1928 to 75 percent in 1948. Research funded by the Swedish American Museum Center has shown that Swedish architects helped shape Chicago and Evanston: Eric Edwin Hall (born in 1883 in Östergötland) designed Chicago Stadium, home of the Bulls and Blackhawks, built in 1929; Lars Gustaf Hallberg Sr. (born in Vänersnäs, Västergötland) designed what was formerly the Swedish Theological Seminary and later Kendall College in Evanston; John A. Nydén (born in 1878 in Småland) founded the John A. Nydén Company in 1907 and was responsible by the time of his death in 1932 for some one-third of the buildings in Evanston (he is buried at Memorial Park Cemetery in Evanston); and Arthur F. Hussander designed school buildings, including Lindblom High School.

Swedish and Swedish American builders shaped Chicago's skyline. They included Henry Ericksson (born 1862 in Småland) and Andrew Lanquist (born 1856 in Ving, Västergötland), who in 1891 erected the Monon Building, considered Chicago's first skyscraper. In 1904 Lanquist organized and became president of the Lanquist & Illsley Company, responsible for the Wrigley Building and several additional downtown buildings. Other builders included Henry Ericsson's brother John (born 1868 in Småland); John Adolph Lindstrom (born 1883 in Versås, Västergötland), who built the Baha'i House of Worship in Wilmette, Illinois, in the 1920s; Louis M. Nelson (born 1867 in Värmland); Nils Persson Severin (born 1861 in Skåne); Eric E. Skoglund (born 1878 in Närke); and Erik Peter Strandberg Sr. (born 1860 in Jämtland).

In Chicago, Swedes founded or helped establish five colleges and seminaries (North Park and Trinity remain in or near the city), two hospitals, a number of Swedish-language newspapers, and two national societies (Svithiod and Vikings) as well as many local ones. Four Swedish churches—Lutheran, Covenant, Methodist, and Baptist—had homes for the aged. Two Swedish-founded church denominations—the Evangelical Covenant Church of America (originally known as the Mission Friends) and the Baptist General Conference (formerly Swedish Baptist Church)—continue to have their headquarters in the Chicago area. Along with Minneapolis–St. Paul, Chicago retains a central position among Swedish Americans.

Institutes and Museums

Swedish American Museum Center of Chicago—5211 N. Clark Street (773-728-8111; www.samac.org).

This museum sprang from seeds planted by local residents, particularly Kurt Mathiasson, after the 1976 U.S. Bicentennial. Originally on the west side of Clark Street (one stretch of Clark Street in Andersonville is identified as Honorary Kurt Mathiasson Street), the museum moved after the Swedish American Museum Association of Chicago purchased in 1987 the four-story building on the east side of Clark. King Carl XVI Gustaf and Queen Silvia officially dedicated the center in 1988.

This museum has greatly expanded its exhibits and programs. "The Dream of American Swedish Immigration to Chicago," the museum's permanent collection on the second floor, features Swedish immigrant trunks, linens, tools, kitchen utensils, various immigrant documents and photographs, and Bibles from the late nineteenth and early twentieth centuries. Displays include a Swedish American home in Chicago in the early part of the twentieth century, with an Ostlind and Almqvist pump organ from Sweden; religious life featuring the communion silver donated in 1990 by the Swedish Mission Covenant Church of Bucklin, Missouri, and the altar (about 1895) and altar painting from the Immanuel Swedish

Swedish American Museum Center, Chicago

Evangelical Lutheran Church of Delaware, Iowa; Swedish national costumes; and photographs of various Swedish fraternal clubs and the Swedish Athletic Association of Chicago. There is a large photograph of the American Union of Swedish Singers festival concert in Orchestra Hall, Chicago, in 1933.

The second floor also contains the Bolling Immigrant Room with displays of Swedish American businesses in Chicagoland, such as Albert Ivar Appleton's Appleton Electric Company; Andrew Lanquist's Lanquist Construction Company; Pehr Samuel Peterson's Rose Hill Nursery; Charles R. Walgreen Sr.'s Walgreen Drug stores; and Pehr Bolling and others' Overland Bolling Company. The Raoul Wallenberg Room on the second floor contains a plaque presented to the Chicago Art Institute for Carl Milles's *Triton Fountain,* which commemorated the service rendered to the United States by inventor John Ericsson.

On the second-floor landing of the museum's main staircase is one of the four original muses of the Linné Monument now located on the Midway at the University of Chicago. Four models of the muses were shipped from Sweden in 1893 for the Linné monument, which was in Lincoln Park. The models were to be cast in bronze in the United States, a project stymied by lack of funds. Instead, the models themselves were used with the statue. In 1976 when the Linné statue was relocated to its present location, the four muses were simply stored. One has survived and is kept at the Center.

The museum's third floor contains an interactive exhibit for children entitled "From Vikings to Visionaries." The displays cover children's lives in a Swedish stuga in the 1870s, the emigration shipboard experience, and early agricultural life in the Midwest. Skillfully painted wall murals depict life in both Sweden and America.

Concerts, cultural events, and classes draw visitors year-round. At the Midsummer celebration during Father's Day weekend, four blocks of North Clark are closed to traffic. The center celebrates *julmarknad* with an arts and crafts festival the first weekend of December and Lucia Fest on December 13.

Nobel Hall of Science, Museum of Science and Industry—Fifty-seventh Street and Lake Shore Drive (312-684-1414; www.msichicago.org).
The Nobel Hall of Science at the Museum of Science and Industry commemorates Swedish inventor Alfred Nobel (1833–1896) and is dedicated to the American Nobel laureates in physics, chemistry, physiology, and medicine.

Historic Places

Andersonville—bounded by Peterson (north), Broadway (east), Lawrence (south), and Damen (west).
Andersonville is the only remaining Chicago district that attempts to be distinctively Swedish, though it is now ethnically mixed. In this city of neighborhoods,

Andersonville's Swedish heritage can be felt on Clark Street north of Foster Avenue. A plaque on the southwest corner of Foster and Clark identifies the location of the former Andersonville School, from which the area took its name. Several restaurants and businesses with Swedish roots or featuring a Swedish décor are located along Clark Street, but these are only an echo of the former Swedish commercial offerings, such as Gustafson's Haberdashery, Hedstrom's Shoes, and Johnson Brothers' Grocery, that once drew Chicagoans six miles north of downtown on horse-drawn streetcars. Today, Svea Restaurant and Ann Sathers recall with traditional Swedish dishes the time when Swedes were the largest ethnic group in Andersonville. Wikström's Delicatessen, The Swedish Bakery, Erickson's Delicatessen, and Erickson's Jewelry continue to flourish. Annually Andersonville celebrates Midsummer Day festivities, which thousands attend, and enjoys a Lucia Fest at the Swedish American Museum Center and nearby Ebenezer Lutheran Church.

Churches

Cristo Rey Iglesia Episcopal Church—2514 W. Thorndale at Maplewood (773-561-8189).
Among the early Swedish arrivals in Chicago was Gustaf Unonius (1810–1902), who emigrated from Sweden in 1841 and was ordained an Episcopal priest in 1845. He founded the Swedish-Norwegian St. Ansgarius parish in Chicago and became its pastor in 1849. Nine years later he returned to Sweden after conflicts with newer immigrant Scandinavian Lutherans. A church Unonius built on Indiana (today Grand) near Wells Street with financial assistance from Jenny Lind burned during the 1871 fire. A second, erected in 1872 on Chicago Avenue, was razed in 1920 after also burning. In 1929, the present church was built farther north, and in the 1940s the name was changed from St Ansgarius to St. Francis and more recently to Cristo Rey Iglesia Episcopal Church. Over the main door of this red-brick church is inscribed in stone "Jenny Lind Memorial Chapel"; the cornerstone reads, "AD 1849–1929." Nothing inside the church is of Swedish origin.

One item remaining from the mid-nineteenth century is the beautiful silver communion chalice and paten presented by the Swedish singer Jenny Lind to St. Ansgarius Church, on which is the inscription, *Gifven till den Skandinaviska Kyrkan St. Ansgarius Chicago af en Landsmaninna* A.D. *1851* (Gift to the Scandinavian Church St. Ansgarius Chicago from a Fellow-Countrywoman A.D. 1851). The chalice and paten are kept at the Episcopal Church Center, 65 E. Huron (312-751-4200).

Immanuel Evangelical Lutheran Church—1500 W. Elmdale Avenue at Greenview (773-743-1820; www.immanuellutheranchicago.org).
This is the mother church of Chicago's Swedish Lutherans. The congregation was organized in 1853 by the Reverend Tuve Nilsson Hasselquist (1816–1891), the first president (1860–1870) of the Augustana Synod. The church's first pastor was the Reverend Erland Carlsson (1822–1893), a powerful preacher and strong advocate of temperance. The present church building, dating from the early 1950s, is the fifth in the congregation's history, earlier ones having been located on Superior Street and at Sedgwick and Hobbie Streets. The modified Gothic-style church of red brick trimmed with Indiana limestone was designed by the firm of Adolph Hanson and Einar Olson. On the lawn outside the church are three 1886 bells with Swedish inscriptions from a former sanctuary.

Many of the interior appointments are attributed to Swedish architect Martin Hedmark and to Swedish American craftsmen. The church sanctuary and adjacent Lanquist Chapel have numerous historic reminders. At the rear of the sanctuary are five stained-glass windows depicting historic events at Immanuel Lutheran, including the first classes of Augustana College and Theological Seminary from 1860 to 1863; the organizing of Augustana Hospital in Chicago by Immanuel members in 1882; the establishing of seven Chicago daughter congregations; and the founding in the late 1800s of the Augustana Women's Missionary Society, with special recognition of Dr. Emmy Evald. Four wood statues on the north side of the sanctuary represent St. Birgitta; the somewhat legendary twelfth-century king of Sweden and patron saint, Erik IX; Nathan Söderblom, archbishop of Sweden; and Pope John XXIII. The chancel is said to be of Swedish style, and the ends of every pew are painted in floral designs reminiscent of Swedish folk art.

The Lanquist Memorial Chapel, to the south of the main sanctuary, is in memory of Andrew and Elsa Lanquist. Andrew Lanquist (1856–1931) was one of Chicago's major building contractors, responsible for such structures as the Wrigley Building (410 N. Michigan Avenue) and Wrigley Field (1060 W. Addison). The chapel's ceiling, embellished with frescoes depicting the heavenly host, has chandeliers from Orrefors Glassworks. The frontal on the altar was handmade by Solvig Westerberg of Sweden, who is known for her artistic embroideries. The baptistery contains a silver flagon used in the congregation's former church sanctuaries. Stained-glass windows represent scenes from the history of Immanuel Lutheran.

On the north side of the main sanctuary, on the same level as the rear balcony, is the St. Ansgar Room, named in honor of the ninth-century missionary to Sweden. A stained-glass window and a small altar commemorate the missionary. On the north wall are depicted various churches associated with St. Ansgar's ministry. In Founders Hall, also to the north of the main sanctuary, are stained-glass windows with the coat of arms of the Swedish provinces.

Ebenezer Lutheran Church—1650 W. Foster Avenue at N. Paulina (773-561-8496; www.ebenezerchurch.org).

Ebenezer Church, one of the daughter congregations of Immanuel Lutheran, is faced with rusticated limestone and topped by a tall silver spire and a shorter one. Founded in 1892, the congregation dedicated the building in 1912. The sanctuary with its high, vaulted ceiling contains two large Gothic-style, stained-glass windows. The ornate Gothic altar includes a statue of Christ patterned after Bertel Thorvaldsen's Christ in Vor Frue Church in Copenhagen, and on either side of the altar are paintings of the life of Christ. High above the exterior Foster Avenue door is carved *Svenska Ev. Lutherska Ebenezer Kyrkan* (the English inscription is on the Paulina Street side).

A second daughter congregation of Immanuel Lutheran is **Salem Lutheran**, 318 E. Seventy-fourth Street (773-783-7776). Its former sanctuary, currently St. Jerome Croatian Catholic Church, was designed in brick Romanesque style by a Swede and dedicated in 1885. It is located at 2819 S. Princeton Avenue.

Other Churches

Another older Chicago Swedish church building is the former **Trinity Swedish Evangelical Lutheran Church** at the northeast corner of Seminary and Barry (one block south of Belmont). It is a red-brick edifice with Gothic-style windows and a soaring steeple. The church has been converted to condominiums.

The mother church of the north side Chicago Covenant churches was originally identified as the North Side Church, and its roots go back to 1868. Many of its early members were associated with Immanuel Lutheran. Later it became First Covenant at 280 N. Franklin, closed in 1976 and now gone. Other early Mission Friends (Covenant) groups in the greater Chicago area merged with various congregations, and their early buildings have disappeared. An exception is the Gothic-style brick building of the former **Englewood Covenant Church**, currently the Rust Memorial United Methodist Church, at W. Fifty-ninth and Carpenter Streets, which was constructed in 1898. Over two doors on the Carpenter Street side are floral stained-glass windows with the words *Svenska Missions Kyrkan*. The former **Edgewater Covenant Church**, 1400 Bryn Mawr (at Glenwood) dates from 1909. It is now Iglesia Dei Pacto Belin.

The **Addison Street Baptist Church** at 1242 W. Addison (between N. Magnolia and N. Lakewood) was the First Swedish Baptist Church in Chicago. On the east side of the large red-brick building is a cornerstone reading "First Swedish Baptist Church AD 1911." The church is now the Wrigleyville Worship Center

(773-935-2357). The former **Edgewater Swedish Baptist Church**, at Hollywood and Glenwood, dates from 1910. There is a plaque on the Glenwood side.

The sanctuary of the former **All Saints Lutheran Church**, 5846 N. Spaulding at W. Thorndale, now the Church of Christ, Presbyterian (773-267-6290), was constructed in the 1930s. The sanctuary contains a triptych altar painting (1918) by Carl Emil Zoir (1861–1936), an internationally known Swedish painter born in Gothenburg. He studied at l'Ecole des Beaux-arts in Paris and at the Institute of Fine Arts in Boston. Another work by this artist on display in the United States is his etching entitled *Grief*, which is in the Fine Arts Collection at Luther College, Decorah, Iowa.

Schools

Lutheran School of Theology at Chicago—1100 E. Fifty-fifth Street (773-256-0700; www.lstc.edu).

When the Lutheran Church in America was created in 1962 through the merger of four Lutheran bodies, including the Augustana Lutheran Church, the Augustana Theological Seminary in Rock Island, Illinois, closed, and its facilities became part of the Augustana College campus. The Lutheran School of Theology at Chicago, built in 1967, now is one of the seminaries of the Evangelical Lutheran Church in America (ELCA), organized in 1987 by the merger of the Lutheran Church in America, the American Lutheran Church, and the Association of Evangelical Lutheran Churches. In the archives and library are paintings of the early presidents of Augustana College and Seminary. The school owns an altar cloth embroidered by King Gustav V. The seminary's Augustana Chapel recognizes the contributions of the Augustana Synod to the ELCA.

North Park University and Theological Seminary—3225 W. Foster Avenue (773-244-6200; www.northpark.edu).

As early as 1884, the Reverend Erik August Skogsbergh (1850–1939) began a school, first in his home in Minneapolis and shortly thereafter in the basement of the Minneapolis Swedish Tabernacle. At the 1891 annual meeting of the denomination, Skogsbergh and David Nyvall (1863–1946) successfully proposed that it become a training school for pastors, and on September 19, 1891, the Covenant school was born. Two years later in Chicago, thirty-one men formed a real estate group known as the Swedish University Land Association. It acquired ninety acres of land on and around Foster Avenue in North Park for the purpose of dividing it into 725 housing lots. The association also offered a donation of 8.5 acres of land to the Covenant school and contributed $25,000 for a building to become, they hoped, a focal point for a new Swedish community. The school became known as North Park College and eventually North Park University.

Today it offers liberal arts and professional undergraduate degrees and graduate programs in several professional areas, including theology. It serves about 3,000 undergraduate and graduate students on its thirty-acre campus.

To encourage better understanding between the United States and Scandinavia, North Park in 1982 launched the Center for Scandinavian Studies. The Center hosts public events, lectures, concerts, and exhibits from Scandinavia and administers exchange programs with universities in Denmark, Finland, Iceland, Norway, and Sweden. It is housed in Caroline Hall, designed by Swedish American architect John A. Nydén in 1925. Nydén also designed Philadelphia's American Swedish Historical Museum.

On Foster Avenue at N. Sawyer is a building known as **Old Main** (3225 W. Foster Avenue). Construction began in the summer of 1893; the contractor was J. A. Modine, one of the founders of the Swedish University Association. When completed, it was one of the very few structures in largely rural North Park. Old Main, a three-story brick building in the "academic" Georgian Revival style, has a lighted cupola that served as a guide in the 1920s for aviators. Over the porch under the third-floor window is inscribed, "SEMC College," meaning Swedish Evangelical Mission Covenant College, the original name of North Park. The cornerstone verse in Swedish is from Psalms 111:10: *Herrens fruktan är vishetens begynnelse* (The fear of the Lord is the beginning of wisdom). During the first eight years, until Wilson Hall was completed in 1901, the entire school was housed in Old Main. Later it was the home of North Park Academy, a secondary school that closed in 1969. Renovations completed in 1987 converted it into the college's central administrative offices.

Nyvall Hall, built in 1947, was named for the first president of North Park College and Theological Seminary. It formerly housed the Covenant Archives and Historical Library. In the stairwell are two large wood plaques with biblical verses inscribed in Swedish and carved by Axel Larson of the Covenant church of Cambridge, Massachusetts, in 1921. Nyvall Hall houses the seminary and the Isaacson Chapel. The chapel is in a simple dignified Georgian style. In the foyer are a memorial plaque and a picture of John Isaacson (1875–1939), founder of Isaacson Steel in Seattle and a generous contributor to the Covenant Church. Isaacson was born in Medelpad, Sweden.

A bronze statue of Caroline (Lina) Sandell (1832–1903), famed Swedish hymn writer, is found in front of Nyvall Hall. Created by artist Axel Wallenberg, the original statue stands in the Fröderyd Church in Småland, and the plaster cast of the statue is in the narthex of Immanuelskyrkan, Stockholm. Another bronze is at Mount Olivet Lutheran Church in Minneapolis.

Nearly all the buildings on campus are named for Swedish Americans. Wilson Hall, the second oldest building, was dedicated in 1901 and later named for a

North Park science teacher. The "Old Gym," now known as Hamming Hall, was constructed in 1915 and named for an academy alumnus who provided funds for its restoration. The "Old Gym," along with Wilson Hall, was funded by money from Alaskan gold claims. The Modine Learning Center honors Arthur B. Modine—scientist, inventor, industrialist, and philanthropist and son of Swedish University Association member J. A. Modine. Parts of the center include the Carlson Tower (named for Paul Carlson, martyred Covenant missionary who served in

Statue of Caroline (Lina) Sandell, North Park University, Chicago

the Congo until his tragic death in 1964) and Wikholm Laboratories (named for Donald Wikholm, a professor of chemistry).

Other campus buildings named for Swedish Americans include Caroline Hall (Caroline Sahlstrom was a former faculty member); Lund House (Nils Wilhelm Lund was dean of the seminary); Burgh Hall (J. Fredrik Burgh was a faculty member and the college's vice president); Ohlson House (Algoth Ohlson was a former president of the college); Sohlberg Hall (Helen Sohlberg was a dean of women); Magnuson Campus Center (named for a donor and businessman); Anderson Hall (Anna Anderson was a Covenant layperson who contributed significant funds for the construction of this women's residence); and Hanson Hall. Connected to Hanson Hall is the A. Harold and Lorraine Anderson Chapel, dedicated in October 1993 and donated by builder Harold Anderson.

In August 2001 the Paul W. and Bernice P. Brandel Library opened. Paul Brandel was an entrepreneur and Covenant layman who also gave extensive resources to Swedish Covenant Hospital. In addition to having a significant collection of books in Scandinavian languages and the valuable Jenny Lind Collection, the Brandel Library maintains the archives of North Park University, the Evangelical Covenant Church, and the Swedish American Historical Society. The denominational archives contain a collection of written records and memorabilia associated with the history of the Covenant Church. Significant memorabilia include the Skogsbergh round pulpit used in the Mission Tabernacles built by Skogsbergh in 1877 (it was located at Thirtieth and LaSalle but torn down in 1960 to make way for the Dan Ryan Expressway); hymn writer and minister Nils Frykman's rocking chair; the collapsible portable organ used by J. A. Hultman, the "Sunshine Singer," from the 1890s to 1942 on his concert tours in the United States and Sweden; a lectern made by Algoth Ohlson, former North Park president; and two large Rörstrand urns of King Oscar II and Queen Sophia.

On October 2, 2004, the Holmgren Athletic Complex was dedicated honoring Mike Holmgren, former Green Bay Packers football coach who currently coaches the Seattle Seahawks, and his wife, Kathy. The football field honors Ted Hedstrand, former North Park football and baseball coach. The Covenant Church's main bookstore is on the northwest corner of W. Foster and N. Kedzie.

Sawyer Avenue, leading north from Old Main, was North Park's most important north-south street in the 1890s and the first developed for residential use by the Swedish University Land Association. By 1897, five buildings in addition to Old Main stood on it. Large frame houses soon lined the street, housing faculty and students. C. A. Björk, the first president of the Covenant Church, built the first house—a three-story frame building at 5240 Sawyer—in 1894. Two years later, Axel Mellander, North Park Seminary dean and a professor of theology (one wing of Nyvall Hall is named in his honor), constructed a residence at 5226

N. Sawyer (the house, supposedly built in the shape of a cross, has been extensively remodeled). Swede John Hagström, early pastor, writer, and inventor, built at 5223 N. Sawyer; on his second floor lived A. F. Boring, an early local photographer. The top half of the house burned in 1909. J. A. Modine built a house at 5308 N. Sawyer, and his son-in-law, North Park professor C. J. Wilson, lived in that house and in one at 5302 N. Sawyer.

Other Points of Interest

Swedish Covenant Hospital—5146 N. California Avenue (773-878-8200; www.swedishcovenant.org).
In the 1880s, two Swedish hospitals were founded in Chicago—Augustana (1884) and Swedish Covenant (1886). The idea for Swedish Covenant began with Henry Palmblad from Gränna, Sweden. Palmblad was distressed by the appalling health conditions among the newly arrived immigrants in Chicago. At the first annual meeting of the Covenant Church in Princeton, Illinois, in 1885, Palmblad spoke strongly of the need for a health facility. The following year, a Home of Mercy was opened. A historic plaque on the California Avenue side of the hospital between Foster and Winona commemorates this event.

In 1891 and 1903, two buildings were erected. The North Wing, completed in 1918, is still extant (at Foster). The South Wing, constructed in 1928, has been modernized. The hospital continues to grow and expand its facilities.

West of Immanuel Covenant Church on Foster Avenue is the **Covenant Home of Chicago** at 2720 Foster Avenue. The Evangelical Covenant Church of America administers twelve retirement communities nationwide.

Evangelical Covenant Church of America (Administration Building)—5101 N. Francisco Avenue (773-784-3000; www.covchurch.org).
The Evangelical Covenant Church of America is rooted in the great religious revivals that swept Sweden between the 1840s and 1870s. Members of the pietistic wing of the Church of Sweden, the Mission Friends, formed the Swedish Mission Covenant in 1878 under the leadership of Paul Peter Waldenström (1838–1917). In the United States, several mission societies were formed, and in 1885, two rival synods merged into the Swedish Evangelical Mission Covenant Church in America, a name later changed to its present name. The church's administration building dates from 1947.

 Swedish Club of Chicago—1254–1258 N. LaSalle (on the southwest corner of LaSalle and Goethe).
The only significant structure with a Swedish connection in the old Swede Town section on the near North Side is the former Swedish Club, which incorporated

three buildings dating to the 1860s. They have served in more recent years as private residences.

Cafe Idrott—3206 N. Wilton.
The inscription, "The Cooperative Temperance Cafe 'Idrott,'" is still visible on this building on N. Wilton near W. Belmont. By the turn of the century, it was a well-known meeting and eating place for many of Chicago's Swedes. Immigrants gave this address to relatives in Sweden, knowing they could receive mail there until they were settled. Ironically, the building is now a bar. Another similar outpost was at 5248 N. Clark.

Near the former Cafe Idrott at 929 W. Belmont is the popular **Ann Sather Restaurant** (773-348-2378; www.annsather.org), which identifies itself as Chicago's Swedish Diner. A plaque outside the door notes that it is the last of the Swedish restaurants in the area, which until the 1940s was predominantly Scandinavian. Other Ann Sather restaurants are at 3411 N. Broadway (773-305-0024), 1448 N. Milwaukee (773-394-1812), 3416 N. Southport (773-404-4475), and 5207 N. Clark (773-271-6677).

Landmarks honoring Carolus Linnaeus (Carl von Linné).
In 1885, a large statue by sculptor Johannes Kjellberg (1836–1885) commemorating the Swedish botanist Carolus Linnaeus (1707–1778) was unveiled in the park named Humlegården in Stockholm. Eight years later, during the Columbian Exposition, the city of Chicago received a bronze copy, placed in Lincoln Park. In 1976, the statue was moved to the University of Chicago. Present at the rededication was King Carl XVI Gustaf. The large statue, on the north side of the Midway, east of Ellis Avenue and immediately south of the Harper Library (1116 E. Fifty-ninth), originally also included four allegorical pewter muses (the originals are on the Linnaeus statue in Humlegården) at the base corners, each representing a scientific discipline. One is now housed in the Swedish American Museum Center of Chicago on N. Clark.

In 1983 a bronze sculpture by Robert Berks was dedicated at the Chicago Botanic Garden, 1000 Lake Cook Road, Glencoe (847-835-8208; www.chicago-botanic .org). It depicts a young, kneeling Linnaeus collecting plants, with his notes lying on the ground. He is studying a rose about to be placed in his collection case. Surrounding the twelve-foot Linnaeus are clusters of flowers also made of bronze. Behind him is a toad about to capture an insect.

The **Carl von Linné Elementary School**, 3221 N. Sacramento Avenue, near Belmont (773-534-5262), is named for the famed Swedish scientist. In the lobby is an impressive bust by Carl J. Nilsson donated in 1937 by the Swedish Cultural Society of Chicago. The pedestal is made of Swedish marble. In Room 211

Statue of Carl von Linné, University of Chicago, Chicago

is a charming wall mural by artist Ethel Spears depicting the eighteenth-century Swedish botanist's life.

Robert Lindblom College Preparatory High School—6130 S. Wolcott Avenue (773-535-9300).

Robert Lindblom (1844–1907) emigrated from Sweden to the United States in 1864, settled in Chicago in 1877, and made a fortune as a grain dealer. He became president of the Chicago Board of Trade and served on the Chicago Board of

Education. In 1893, he was one of the principal backers of the Columbian Exposition. Several blocks west of the school is Lindblom Park, 6054 S. Damen Avenue (773-776-8788), also named in his honor.

Peterson Park—5801 N. Pulaski Road.

Per (Pehr) August Peterson (1830–1903) came to the United States via Canada in 1852 from Sweden and in 1856 began a nursery in Chicago. He was known for planting trees along Lake Shore Drive and as at one time being the largest landowner in Chicago. Peterson Park and Peterson Avenue are named for him. The Mary Gage Peterson School at 5510 N. Christiana Avenue (773-534-5070) is named in honor of Peterson's wife, who was not Swedish.

Swedish Engineers Society—503 Wrightwood (at Hampden).

The Swedish Engineers Society, founded in 1908, used this outstanding baroque mansion built in 1896 by Francis Dewes, noted brewer and collector of Old World art, as its headquarters after it purchased the building in 1920. It was designated a Chicago landmark in 1974.

Carl Sandburg Residence—4646 N. Hermitage.

Swedish American writer Carl Sandburg lived in this three-story house, now a private residence, from 1913 to 1916. The Chicago Department of Cultural Affairs with the *Chicago Tribune* erected an official marker in 1997, which begins with Sandburg's famous 1914 poem "Chicago." The inscription continues in part: "Poet, journalist and historian, Carl Sandburg was one of the most famous literary figures of the twentieth century. Born in Galesburg, Illinois, the son of Swedish immigrants, he left home in his early teens to travel, earning money digging potatoes, harvesting wheat, blacking stoves and working on railroads and steamboats. Many of the themes and images Sandburg used in his poems were the laborers he encountered. Sandburg published his first book of poetry, *In Reckless Ecstasy,* in 1904. Shortly thereafter, he moved to Milwaukee and married Lillian Steichen, sister of photographer Edward Steichen. The family moved here to 4646 N. Hermitage Avenue in 1912, and Sandburg began writing for the *Chicago Daily News.* It was here that the famous poem "Chicago" was written."

On Chicago's near north side at 135 N. Clark Street is the Carl Sandburg Village, a modern condominium complex.

Queen of All Saints Basilica—6280 N. Sauganash Avenue, between N. Lemont and N. Keene Avenues (773-736-6060).

Queen of All Saints Basilica is a large Gothic-style Roman Catholic church noted for its lovely stained-glass windows featuring Christian saints. St. Birgitta of Sweden is depicted in the second window from the narthex end of the basilica on the west side. Clearly visible is a yellow cross on a blue field.

Cemeteries

No cemeteries in Chicago are specifically Swedish, but Rosehill, 5800 Ravenswood Avenue at Rosehill Drive (773-561-5940); Graceland, 4001 N. Clark at Irving Park (773-525-1105); Mount Olive, 3800 N. Narragansett (773-286-3770); and Oak Hill, 11900 Kedzie Avenue, Blue Island (708-285-0130), contain the graves of many Swedish Americans. Johan A. Enander (1842–1910), buried in Oak Hill, was the first editor and owner of *Hemlandet,* a leading nineteenth-century U.S. Swedish Lutheran publication. His monument, imported from Sweden, is in the form of a runestone. In the southwest corner of Montrose Cemetery, 5400 N. Pulaski (773-478-5400), are the simple graves of David and Louise Nyvall. David Nyvall (1863–1946) was the first president of North Park College and Theological Seminary, and his wife, Louise (1857–1940), was E. August Skogsbergh's sister. In October 1991, a commemorative stone was placed at the grave during the centennial celebration of North Park. (See www.graveyards.com for information on Chicago cemeteries.)

Sculpture and Other Art

Besides the two sculptures of Carolus Linnaeus previously mentioned, one at the University of Chicago campus and the other at the Chicago Botanic Garden, Chicago has several other works and monuments created by or celebrating Swedes. Swedish philosopher Emanuel Swedenborg is honored by a monument on the Outer Drive (east side), just north of Fullerton Avenue. A stone obelisk quotes Franklin D. Roosevelt: "In a world in which the voice of conscience too often seems still and small, there is a need of that spiritual leadership of which Swedenborg was a particular example."

The Art Institute of Chicago, 111 S. Michigan Avenue (312-433-3600; www .artic.edu), exhibits Carl Milles's *Four Tritons Fountain* in the McKinlock Court, site of the Garden Restaurant.

In front of the Harold Washington Social Security Center at 600 W. Madison Street is the 1977 abstract sculpture *Batcolumn.* The painted steel piece featuring crisscrossing structural latticework by Swedish American sculptor Claes Oldenburg and Coosje van Bruggen is 101 feet high. Oldenburg was born in Stockholm in 1929, the son of a Swedish diplomat. The family moved to Chicago in 1936, where he attended Chicago Latin School; he graduated from Yale University in 1950 and became an American citizen in 1953. By the early 1960s he was one of the leading figures of American pop art.

Other large-scale works by Claes Oldenburg and Coosje van Bruggen on display in the United States include *Lipstick (Ascending) on Caterpillar Tracks* (1969–1974), Samuel F. B. Morse College, Yale University, New Haven, Connecticut; *Clothespin* (1976) and *Split Button* (1981; see Philadelphia); *Trowel II* (1976), Donald M. Kendall Sculpture Gardens at PepsiCo, Purchase, New York; *Crusoe Umbrella* (1979; see Des Moines, Iowa); *Flashlight* (1981), University of Nevada, Las Vegas;

Claes Oldenburg and Coosje van Bruggen's *Batcolumn*, Chicago

Hat in Three Stages of Landing (1982), Sherwood Park, Salinas, California; *Stake Hitch* (1984; see Dallas, Texas); *Knife Ship II* (1986), Museum of Contemporary Art, Los Angeles; *Knife Slicing through Wall* (1986), Margo Leavin Gallery, Los Angeles; *Toppling Ladder with Spilling Paint* (1986), Loyola Law School, Los Angeles; *Spoonbridge and Cherry* (1988; see Minneapolis); *Dropped Bowl with Scattered Slices and Peels* (1990), Metro-Dade Open Space Park, Miami; *Binoculars* (1991), 340 Main Street, Venice, California; *Free Stamp* (1991), Willard Park, Cleveland, Ohio; *Shuttlecocks* (1994; see Kansas City); *Torn Notebook* (1996), Madden Garden, University of Nebraska, Lincoln; *Typewriter Eraser* (1999), National Gallery of Art, Washington D.C.; and *Cupid's Span* (2002), Lincoln Park, San Francisco.

On the front façade of the Chicago Tribune Tower, 435 N. Michigan Avenue, to the north of its main door, a stone from the Royal Castle in Stockholm is imbedded in the wall along with stones from other internationally known buildings and structures. Across Michigan Avenue is the Wrigley Building, 410 N. Michigan, built by Lanquist and Illsley Construction Company, which was founded in 1904 with Lanquist as president.

A Raoul Wallenberg monument is being planned at State Street and Wacker Drive. The location has been designated Raoul Wallenberg Place.

Evanston

Swedish Theological Seminary—southwest corner of Orrington and Lincoln.

Evanston was the site of a Swedish Methodist seminary. The Swedish Theological Seminary began in Galesburg, Illinois, in 1870, moved to Galva, Illinois, in 1872, and then went to Evanston in 1875, where it operated until 1934. The dark reddish-brick building has a cornerstone with the year 1907. The Kendall College Library acquired the school property, but recently it was sold to a realtor. At the time of this book's publication, its future use had not been determined.

Pioneer Place and the Swedish Retirement Association (Three Crowns Park)—2320 Pioneer Road, bounded also by Colfax, McDaniel, and Grant (847-328-8700).

In 1894, the Swedish Societies Central Association was organized in Chicago for dispensing charity to needy countrymen. In 1908, the organization's name was changed to the Swedish Societies Old People's Home Association. One year later the present property was purchased and the cornerstone laid for the first building. In 1923, a larger facility was constructed and dedicated in the presence of Nathan Söderblom, the Swedish archbishop. This building still stands and is called "Pioneer Place." On the Grant Street door are commemorative plaques. In October 1975, the Robert E. Landstrom Manor building was opened.

Immanuel Lutheran Church—616 Lake at Sherman (847-864-4464).
Immanuel Lutheran was organized in 1888, and the nineteenth-century Gothic, light-brick building with its tall steeple was built ten years later. The interior has been modernized except for the old stained-glass windows. At 1101 Church (the northwest corner of Church and Oak) is the small Evangelical Covenant Church (847-864-0365) with 1910 marked on its cornerstone.

Deerfield

The Swedish Evangelical Free Mission, later renamed the Swedish Evangelical Free Church, was organized in 1884 in Boone, Iowa. Later other free church groups of Danish and Norwegian origin joined. In the early 1950s, this fellowship of independent churches became known as the Evangelical Free Church.

Trinity International University, 2077 Half Day Road (847-317-2065; www.tiu.edu), traces its roots to 1887, when the Swedish Evangelical Free Church began a ten-week Bible course in the basement of a Chicago church. This became the Bible Institute of the Swedish Evangelical Free Church of America. Between 1946 and 1949, it merged with a Norwegian Danish school to form Trinity Seminary and Bible College, located in Chicago. During the 1960s, the seminary was renamed Trinity Evangelical Divinity School, and the college became Trinity College. During that decade, they both moved to Deerfield, Illinois. In 1995, the Trinity College and Trinity Evangelical Divinity School became Trinity International University. In recent years the university has expanded to develop campuses in other locations, including one in Miami, Florida (305-770-5100), and Trinity Law School and Graduate School, 2200 N. Grand Avenue, Santa Ana, California. Though the new campus has buildings named for Swedish-descended donors, the Evangelical Free Church of America does not demonstrate so strong a tie with its Scandinavian heritage as do other groups. The denominational headquarters is in Bloomington, Minnesota.

Arlington Heights

The Baptist General Conference International Center, 2002 S. Arlington Heights Road (847-228-0200; www.bgcworld.org), is headquarters for the Baptist General Conference, formerly known as the Swedish Baptist Conference. The modern brick building, dedicated in 1981, features a stone in its lobby taken from the Village Creek, Iowa, home of Eric Sandman, a founding father of the denomination. In the reception area is a 1923 painting depicting a mid-nineteenth-century baptism in the Mississippi River at Rock Island, Illinois. The denomination's archives are at Bethel Seminary in St. Paul, Minnesota.

Geneva

Geneva hosts an annual Midsummer Festival in Good Templar Park, showcasing its Swedish heritage, still evident in gift shops and a restaurant.

Batavia

The Holmstad, 700 W. Fabyan Parkway (630-879-4100; www.covenantretirement .org), is an Evangelical Covenant Church retirement center.

Joliet

The former Salem Home for the Aged, now known as the **Nursing and Rehabilitation Center and Salem Village Retirement Homes,** 1314 Rowell Avenue (815-727-5451), was founded by Augustana Lutherans and came to Joliet from Stony Island and Ninety-fifth in Chicago.

Rockford

In 1852, about thirty immigrants from Sweden settled in Rockford. Others followed, and by 1930 about 10,000 Swedish-born residents lived there, forming about one-quarter of the town's inhabitants. The majority of Swedes were from Östergötland, Västergötland, and Småland. Among sizable North American urban areas, only Jamestown, New York, had a larger percentage of Swedes.

In the late 1800s, Rockford, like Jamestown, emerged as a center for furniture-manufacturing, in large part because of the immigrants' woodworking skills. The Chicago fire of 1871 created a demand for replacement furniture, which stimulated the industry's growth. In the mid-1870s, Swedes founded the Forest City Furniture Company. In 1876, Union Furniture Company was organized, owned, and operated entirely by Swedes. By 1885, Rockford had become the second leading furniture-producing center in the United States. In addition, Rockford Swedes contributed to making the city a leading producer of tools and dies and hardware.

Per August Peterson (1846–1927), who arrived in Rockford at age six, made a name for himself as a venture capitalist. Rising through the ranks from broom maker to one of Rockford's wealthiest men, he was known for his entrepreneurial skills and his extraordinary work ethic. He helped start a variety of businesses involved with manufacturing furniture, pianos, sewing machines, glass products, farm equipment, and hardware. These enterprises provided employment opportunities for the newly arrived Swedes. John Nelson (1830–1883), another successful entrepreneur, is credited with the invention of the automatic knitting machine capable of making a seamless sock. Levin Faust (or Fast; 1863–1936) was known for his machine and tool production.

Swedes frequently settled in **East Rockford**, particularly along Kishwaukee Street. Seventh Street, a parallel artery, included the old Swedish business district. Later, Fourteenth Avenue (Broadway) took its place. The corner of Seventh Street and Fourteenth Avenue was the heart of the Swedish business district, and the East Rockford District is now on the National Register.

Rockford Standard Furniture, 1100 Eleventh Street, is one reminder of the manufacturing era that saw furniture factories prosper on Railroad Avenue between Seventh and Eleventh Streets. The building, now owned by the Benson Stone Company, features an attractive restaurant and furniture gallery. Although the exterior has been dramatically changed, the careful restoration of the interior has preserved the beautiful wood beams and flooring. The third floor is being considered as a heritage center.

Railroad Station—Sixth Avenue and Seventh Street.
In front of the former railway station at Seventh Street is a historic plaque commemorating the 150th anniversary of the arrival by train of Rockford's first Swedish settlers. The plaque notes that "at this place Swedish immigrants arrived in Rockford with their vision of a new life in America. From here they began their future as Swedish-Americans." The old railway station is currently the office of the Seventh Street Area Development Council.

The **Stockholm Inn**, 2420 Charles Street (815-397-3534), is a well-known restaurant dating from the 1950s that continues to serve Swedish specialties.

Institutes and Museums

Erlander Home Swedish American Museum—404 S. Third Street, southeast corner of Grove and Third Streets (815-963-5559; www.swedishhistorical.org).

The Swedish Historical Society of Rockford operates the beautifully renovated Erlander Home Museum. It is located in **Haight Village Historic District**, which is on the National Register. During the late 1980s and early 1990s, the first floor of the museum was restored, and the exterior underwent renovation. The house was once the home of John Erlander (1826–1917), one of Rockford's first Swedish settlers, who was born in Småland and emigrated to America in 1854. The two-story, fourteen-room Italianate house, built in 1871, was the first brick residence for a Swedish family in Rockford. Five years later the Union Furniture Company was organized in this house, with John Erlander as president and P. A. Peterson as secretary. Erlander was also the first president of the Swedish Mutual Fire Insurance Company and was actively involved in Rockford's business and political community. His daughter Mary, who lived in the house until 1951 and studied art at Rockford College, painted the exquisite floral watercolors and family

Erlander Home Museum,
exterior and parlor, Rockford

portraits hanging throughout the house and did the wall stenciling in the parlor and her bedroom. When the house become a museum in 1952, Sweden's Prime Minister Tage Erlander, who was related to these American Erlanders, attended the dedication.

Upon entering the house, visitors encounter a bronze plaque inscribed with a poem written by Carl Sandburg honoring the Swedish pioneers who built Rockford. The first floor features nicely restored rooms offering an insight into the lifestyle of the Erlander family. Throughout the house is fine wood furniture made in Rockford. In the front parlor is a nineteenth-century decorative Swedish *kakelugn* (ceramic tile stove). The music room contains a Rockford-made dolcette with vertical strings and forty-four keys. Only two were ever produced in Rockford—the one in the Erlander Home and another now in the Smithsonian Museum. Visitors can also see the first piano made in Rockford by the Haddorff Piano Company and a psalmodikon, a one-stringed Scandinavian musical instrument. An orientation film on Swedish immigration to Rockford and the house itself may be viewed.

Rockford's Swedish Historical Society spearheads annual Midsummer Day activities on the third Saturday in June. During the Lucia Fest, the home is decorated and Swedish coffee and delicacies are served. In the nearby First Lutheran Church, a Lucia queen is crowned in a candlelight service. A *julmarknad* gives people the opportunity to purchase Swedish craft items and traditional foods.

Midway Village and Museum Center—6799 Guilford Road (815-397-9112; www.midwayvillage.com).
Several museum exhibits highlight Swedish life and achievements. One of the most unusual is devoted to Colonel Bert R. J. Hassell (1893–1974), who attempted to fly from Rockford to Stockholm in 1929 to prove that the shortest journey between those cities was along the great circle route. The plane crashed in Greenland, but the aircraft was eventually brought to the museum. Hassell, a Rockford resident and employee of Rockford Products Corporation, was born in Wisconsin to parents who had emigrated from Värmland.

The Industrial Gallery presents an interesting roundup of Swedish American business entrepreneurs. A display on the American Union of Swedish Singers includes photographs dating to 1892. The archives of the organization, which promoted Swedish choral singing and knowledge of Swedish songs, are housed here.

A Swedish farm model, patterned after the boyhood home of Carl Severin, a Rockford business superintendent, depicts his life as a boy in Kalmar län, Småland. He donated the first sixteen acres of land for the Midway Village and Museum Center.

Airplane at Midway Museum Center, Rockford

Historic Places

Lake-Peterson Home—1313 E. State Street, adjacent to Swedish American Hospital (815-963-2821).
This nineteenth-century Gothic Revival house built by lumber dealer John H. Lake in 1873 later became the home of Per August Peterson, a native of Södra Ving, Västergötland, who became a Rockford commercial leader and financial supporter of the Swedish American Hospital. Peterson was president of more than a dozen industrial firms.

Swedish American Hospital—1400 Charles Street (815-963-2821; www.swedishamerican.org).
In 1918, Swedish American Hospital opened as a fifty-five-bed facility in a building that still stands. The following year, the school of nursing was established. Today Swedish American Hospital is a major medical facility.

Faust Landmark—618–632 E. State Street, at Third Street.
This former hotel was named for Levin Faust, one of its principal investors. A penniless Swedish immigrant, Faust amassed a large fortune. Ericson, Benson Construction Company built the eleven-story building for Faust, but the stock

market crashed in 1929, and the hotel was never successful. Today Rockford's tallest building is used for low-cost housing. Faust's portrait hangs in the lobby.

Churches

First Lutheran Church—225 S. Third Street, at Oak Street (815-962-6691).
First Lutheran, a large, Gothic-style brick structure with two tall steeples, is known as the mother church of at least seven other Swedish Lutheran congregations in Rockford. First Lutheran was organized in 1854. The first church and parsonage were built in 1856, and the second in 1869. The church was rebuilt in 1883 and remodeled in 1928. The impressive walnut altar, altar rail, and pulpit were made by Rockford Central Furniture Company. In the back of the sanctuary are artifacts including a psalmodikon used by the first congregation, a velvet heart used on the pulpit of the second church, and the cornerstone box from the second church.

Zion Lutheran Church—925 Fifth Avenue (815-964-4609).
Zion Lutheran is probably the most Swedish of current Rockford Lutheran congregations. The red-brick, Gothic-style church and its steeple were completed in 1885. In the Fellowship Hall are memorabilia from former times, including the old church sign written in Swedish.

Emmanuel Lutheran—920 Third Avenue, at Sixth Street (815-963-4815).
The cornerstone of Emmanuel, a light-brick church, bears the dates 1882, when Emmanuel was organized, and 1922, the year the sanctuary was built.

Salem Lutheran Church—1629 Sixth Street, at Sixteenth Avenue (815-965-5131; www.salemrockford.org).
The Salem Lutheran congregation was organized in 1907 and its building erected in 1911. The front exterior of the reddish-brick church wall is inscribed, "Swedish Evangelical Lutheran Salem Church South Park." The church building is topped with a pair of spires.

Other Churches

At 714 Third Avenue, at Kishwaukee Street, stands a reddish-brick structure identified by its cornerstone as a former Covenant Church building—Swedish Evangelical Lutheran Mission Society of Rockford, organized in 1888. Currently the congregation of **First Evangelical Covenant Church** (815-398-4247; www .firstcovonline.com) worships in an impressive sanctuary built in 1966 at 316 Wood. The former Swedish Baptist Church was located on the northeast corner of Fifth Avenue and Eighth Street. The **Salvation Army** on the corner of Hooker and Hollister Streets near the Stockholm Inn continues to hold an annual *julotta* service in Swedish.

St. Anskar's Episcopal Church, 4801 Spring Creek Road (815-877-1226), is named for the ninth-century missionary to Scandinavia.

Schools

Five elementary schools are named for notable Rockford Swedish Americans, including inventor and manufacturer John Nelson (623 Fifteenth, 815-229-2190); mayor Henry Bloom (2912 Brendenwood Road, 815-229-2170); screw manufacturer Swan Hillman (3701 Greendale Drive, 815-229-2835); schoolteacher Maud Johnson (3805 Rural Street, 815-229-2485); and school board president Clifford P. Carlson (4015 Pepper Drive, 815-654-4955).

Other Points of Interest

Scandinavian Cemetery—1700 Rural at Prospect (815-965-6625).

Locally renowned men buried in this cemetery include P. A. Peterson, Levin Faust, John Erlander, Henry Bloom, and August Erickson. John Laurentius Haff, pastor of First Lutheran (1862–1896), rests beneath a monument that identifies him as Joel Laurentius Haff. The marker has the Swedish inscription *Saliga äro de döda som i Herren dö* (Blessed are the dead who die in the Lord).

P. A. Peterson Center for Health—1311 Parkview Avenue (815-399-8832).

When P. A. Peterson died in 1927, he bequeathed substantial funds to various charitable institutions, including a facility for the elderly.

Pecatonica

Several old Swedish Lutheran congregations still exist in towns surrounding Rockford. The oldest one meets in the red-brick First Lutheran Church of Pecatonica at E. Sixth and Taylor Streets (815-239-2390). Organized in 1857, the congregation built this church in 1881.

The Quad Cities

Swedes who settled in the Quad Cities—Moline and Rock Island, Illinois, and Bettendorf and Davenport, Iowa—helped make the area a national center for the manufacture of farm implements. John Deere & Company, a billion-dollar farm, construction, and lawn machinery and equipment business, is the most outstanding example.

Moline

Churches

First Lutheran Church—1230 Fifth Avenue, at Thirteenth Street (309-764-3517).

The congregation was organized in 1850 by the Reverend Lars P. Esbjörn, who also led the founding of the church in Andover, Illinois. Many early parishioners were unskilled laborers employed by such companies as John Deere. Young women worked as maids, laundresses, cooks, and nursemaids. In 1853, the Mississippi Conference of the Evangelical Lutheran Augustana Synod was organized in the first sanctuary of First Lutheran. Honoring this event is a plaque quoting the minutes of the meeting in both Swedish and English. Among the exhortations was the need for pastors "to awake men among us . . . who will travel among our countrymen and preach the Word of Life." The eighth resolution implored Lutherans to refrain from visiting churches where they might hear "preachers teaching strange and false doctrines."

In 1875, the church made a decision to build a large Gothic-style red-brick building featuring a high, three-tiered clock tower (visible above the Moline skyline). Some members objected and formed Gustav Adolph's Church in Moline, eventually joining the Mission Covenant Church. The former church is on the corner of Fifth Avenue and Tenth Street. Over the front door of the red-brick building is the inscription, *Missions Tabernaklet*. The Covenant congregation has relocated to 3303 Forty-first Street.

The inaugural service in First Lutheran's new church was held October 13, 1878. The sanctuary features impressive memorial stained-glass windows with Old and New Testament personages and Christian symbols made by German craftsmen. Local artist F. A. Lundahl rendered the altar painting of the Ascension. A recent $1 million renovation has returned the church to its early magnificence.

Continued use of Swedish in church services brought about tensions and congregational splits, including one producing **Trinity Evangelical Lutheran**, 1330 Thirteenth Street (309-762-3624; www.trinitylutheranmoline.org), in 1912. Despite the schism, First Lutheran was in the forefront in organizing Lutheran Hospital four years later. The hospital is now part of Trinity Medical Center, 500 John Deere Road (309-779-2200).

Bethany Baptist Church—701 Thirty-eighth Avenue, at Seventh Street and Black Hawk Road (309-764-3041).

In the lobby of Bethany Baptist Church, organized in 1876, is a plaque noting that in 1852 in Rock Island the First Swedish Baptist Church in the United States was

First Lutheran Church, exterior and sanctuary, Moline

organized under the leadership of Gustav Palmquist (1812–1867) from northern Småland. He was one of three pastors who laid the foundation of the Swedish Baptist Church in the United States; the other two were Fredrik Olaus Nilsson (1809–1891) from Halland and Anders Wiberg (1816–1887) from Hälsingland.

Bethel Methodist Church—1201 Thirteenth Street, at Twelfth Avenue.
Bethel Methodist is an offspring of the congregation in Victoria, Illinois. The present red-brick building dates from 1910 and is identified as the Moline Bethel Wesley Church (309-764-0619).

Other Landmarks

Riverside Cemetery—Sixth Avenue and Twenty-ninth Street (309-797-0790).
The graves of two early presidents of Augustana College and Theological Seminary, Tuve Nilsson Hasselquist and Olof Olsson, are located in this cemetery. From their graves near the Deere Cross is a good view of the Mississippi River.

Deere & Company World Headquarters—John Deere Road (309-765-8000; www.deere.com).
This company is the world's largest producer of farm equipment, with $7 billion annual sales and 35,500 workers in the early 1990s. Though not founded by Swedes, Deere has employed many Swedish immigrants since being established in 1837. The headquarters, designed by Eero Saarinen (1910–1961), the son of Finnish architect Eliel Saarinen (1873–1950), offers lovely surrounding grounds and a display of Deere's products. The John Deere Commons at 1400 River Drive in downtown Moline includes the John Deere Pavilion (309-765-1000; www.johndeerepavilion.com) where one may observe a variety of farm equipment produced by the company.

Rock Island

Augustana College—639 Thirty-eighth Street (800-798-8100; www.augustana.edu).
The Scandinavian Evangelical Lutheran Augustana Synod was organized in 1860 at Jefferson Prairie, Wisconsin, and Reverend Lars Paul Esbjörn became the first president of Augustana Theological Seminary, the country's oldest Swedish educational institution. The name Augustana honored the 1530 Augsburg Confession (in Latin, *Confessio Augustana*).

Organized in 1863, the college was until 1875 in Paxton, Illinois, under the leadership of Reverend T. N Hasselquist. Two of the four great pioneer leaders of nineteenth-century Swedish Lutheranism in the United States, Esbjörn and Hasselquist, were presidents of Augustana. The other two, Erland Carlsson

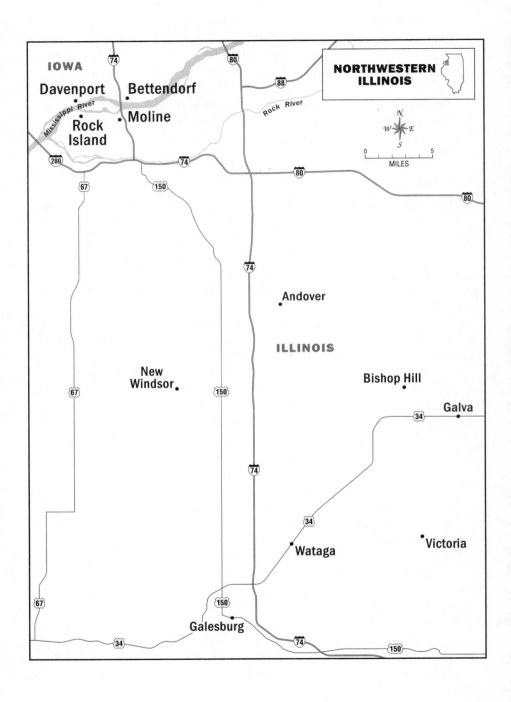

(1882–1893) and Eric Norelius (1883–1916), were Lutheran leaders who chaired Augustana's board of directors. On September 22, 1875, fifteen years after its founding, Augustana College and Theological Seminary, 639 Thirty-eighth Street, opened its doors in Rock Island. The college, which had ninety students, now enrolls about 2,000 students on its 115-acre campus.

A plaque on a stone bench behind Old Main notes that the stones are from the foundation of the first Augustana College and Theological Seminary building in Paxton. The Bell Tower on Zion Hill, a replica of a Swedish *klockstapel,* was constructed in 1936 from beams used in the first college building; the bell is also from that building.

 Old Main, on Seventh Avenue between Thirty-fifth and Thirty-eighth Streets, was originally called Memorial Hall. Begun in 1884, it was constructed of buff-colored dolomite limestone and represented the largest undertaking for any Swedish group in the United States up to that time. With the college and seminary rapidly expanding in the early 1880s, an additional, larger building was needed. The board of the college wanted a Renaissance-style building; one member expressed the wish that it include a dome for an American look. Former college president Conrad Bergendorff (1895–1997) suggested that the design may have been influenced by the Renaissance-style main building at Uppsala University in Sweden, completed in 1879.

Old Main's architects were L. G. Hallberg of Chicago, a graduate of Chalmers Polytechnic Institute in Gothenburg, and E. S. Hammatt of Davenport, Iowa. Since its completion in 1893, Old Main has been remodeled extensively. Cable Hall on the second floor honors the building's benefactor, and this room has been restored to a nineteenth-century classroom with portraits of the early college presidents, two of which were painted by Olof Grafström. On the third floor was his art studio.

Grafström (1885–1933), born in Medelpad near Sundsvall, studied at the Royal Academy of Art in Stockholm. He came to the United States in 1886 and arrived at Augustana in 1897, teaching art there until his retirement in 1926. He was responsible for at least 200 altar paintings in Lutheran churches. He also painted landscapes. Many paintings are in the school's art collection, along with works by Birger Sandzén and Carl Milles.

Denkmann Memorial Library on Seventh Avenue, dedicated in 1911, is an example of Beaux Arts style with Prairie School architectural detailing. In it is the oldest Department of Scandinavian Studies of any American college or university, having offered courses in Swedish language, literature, and culture since 1860. Also in the building is the Swenson Swedish Immigration Research Center (309-794-7204). It is a national archives and research institute providing resources for the study of Swedish immigration to North America, the communities the

Old Main, Augustana College, Rock Island

immigrants established, and the role the immigrants and their descendants have played in American society. Another major role of the research center is assisting people researching their Swedish American family history. Its holdings include a specialized library, an extensive collection of church records, and an excellent collection of Swedish American and Swedish Canadian newspapers.

The Augustana College Library has a significant number of Swedish books, including a collection donated by Sweden's King Karl XV in 1863. Many book bindings bear monograms of the Swedish monarchy.

Sorensen Hall is the former site of the Augustana Book Concern, the largest Swedish American publishing house in the United States. A stained-glass window in the stairwell leading to Ascension Chapel depicts four historic sites of collegiate Lutheran learning—Springfield (Illinois State University in Springfield was a Lutheran institution serving English and German Lutherans), Chicago, Paxton, and Rock Island.

The Carl E. Swenson Hall of Science includes the Fryxell Geological Museum, developed by Dr. Fritiof Fryxell, founder of Augustana's geology department. Swenson was an inventor who left a significant bequest to the college. Outside the building is a large boulder inscribed with the names Lindahl and Udden.

Johan Harald Josua Lindahl (1844–1912), a native of Halland, Sweden, was the first professor of natural sciences at Augustana and the organizer of the college Museum of Natural History. His student, Johan August Udden, who was from Västergötland, succeeded him. In 2003 a courtyard was named in honor of Glen E. Brolander "in recognition of forty years of service to Augustana College." Brolander is a professor emeritus of Augustana and longtime officer of the Swedish Council of America.

Ericson Field and Stadium, on the site of Ericson Hall, the former science building, is named for Iowa state senator Charles J. Ericson (1840–1910), who gave $30,000 in 1901, some of which was used for a professorship in Swedish.

Carlsson Hall is named for the Reverend Erland Carlsson. This women's residence hall dedicated in 1928 was funded largely by gifts from the Women's Missionary Society of the Augustana Lutheran Synod. Other campus buildings named for Swedish Americans include Bergendorff Hall of Fine Arts (Conrad Bergendorff was president from 1935 to 1962); Wallberg Faculty Complex (Marie Wallberg was an alumna and generous donor); Abrahamson Hall (Reverend L. G. Abrahamson was a Chicago pastor considered for the college presidency); Mauritzson Hall (Jules G. Mauritzson was a professor of Swedish and a dean); Wald Hall (Arthur E. Wald was a dean); Andreen Hall (Gustav A. Andreen was president from 1901 to 1935); Westerlin Residence Center for Women (J. M. and Elsa Westerlin were longtime school financial supporters); Erickson Residence Center for Men (Knut E. Erickson was vice president and treasurer); Jenny Lind Hall (the nineteenth-century Swedish singer); Brodahl Student Services Building (Betsey Brodahl was a faculty member and dean of women); I. M. Anderson House (I. M. Anderson was a professor of Greek); and Esbjorn House (C. L. E. Esbjorn was a professor of German).

At 3400 Tenth Avenue is the Cervin-Ryden House, which belonged to the family of local architect Olof Z. Cervin, who designed this 1914 structure. Cervin also designed many other buildings in the Quad Cities as well as the Zion Chapel in Axtell, Nebraska. E. E. Ryden was the former chair of the Augustana College Board and longtime editor of *The Lutheran Companion,* the periodical of the Augustana Synod. On the third floor of this structure, which serves as the College Center, is the Hammarskjöld Room, named for the former United Nations secretary-general.

Davenport, Iowa

Putnam Museum—1717 W. Twelfth at Division (563-322-5910; www.putnam.org).
This extensive modern museum includes exhibits in the River, Prairie, and People Section focusing on the Quad Cities' immigrants, including Swedes. A

1912 photograph taken in the Cable Room in Old Main of Augustana shows faculty members with Norwegian polar explorer Roald Amundsen. There are also copper objects, wood cabinets, immigrant trunks, and photographs of early Swedish settlers.

Andover

 Jenny Lind Chapel—Sixth and Oak Streets (309-476-8228).
The chapel is considered a shrine of Swedish Lutheranism. The Reverend Lars Paul Esbjörn (1808–1870), a Swedish state church minister, led the founding of the Andover Lutheran congregation on March 18, 1850, and the chapel, dedicated on the first Sunday of Advent in 1854, was named for Swedish soprano Jenny Lind, whose gift of $1,500 made its construction possible. The intended steeple was never built because the wood was used to make coffins for the cholera victims. The church's basement served as a hospital and immigrant home. Soon the congregation outgrew the building, which was finally restored in 1975.

The chapel's plain but dignified interior complements an annual Swedish-language vesper service held the last Sunday afternoon in September, a Founders Day service, and a candlelight service in early December. A kerosene lamp used by the early church is in the sanctuary. Originally a large opening in the floor

Jenny Lind Chapel, Andover

permitted people to hear the service from the basement, which now houses a small museum.

The adjoining cemetery contains many graves of Swedish pioneers and Civil War soldiers. A touching gravestone, memorializing the young daughter and son of Anders and Catrina Peterson, depicts a girl and boy with clasped hands and the phrase "Not dead but sleeping."

Nearby is the **Augustana Lutheran Church**, 625 Sixth Street (309-522-8127), a large, impressive brick church with a high steeple. Dedicated in 1869, it is of solid masonry construction, and its dimensions rival those of churches the immigrants left behind in Sweden. Among the main features in the sanctuary are beautiful dark-wood appointments, wall stenciling above the altar, a high ceiling, and a rear balcony.

Also near the Jenny Lind Chapel was the second Swedish Methodist congregation organized in the Midwest, in 1849, known as the Andover Methodist Church. The small, white clapboard church built in 1854 is now a private residence. Nearby is the Mix-Lobeck House, built in 1837, where the Lutheran and Methodist Churches were organized.

The work of the Reverend Esbjörn and his wife, Amalia Maria, is commemorated by a historical marker on the south side of State Highway 81 at the west end of Andover. Near the marker are the graves of cholera victims.

Near State Highway 81 on Locust Street is the **Andover Historical Museum**, formerly the Rehnstrom house (309-547-8378). The umber clapboard structure, built about 1860, was originally a boardinghouse where men who built the Augustana Lutheran Church stayed. The interior furnishings are from the late 1800s and were donated by Andover residents. Next door is a white clapboard structure constructed in 1879, which served a local business. Upstairs was the Carlson Brothers Hall and Stage, which was added in 1910.

Swedish immigrants who came to Andover often first stayed in the **A. E. "Brick" Anderson House (Brick House)** at the corner of Osco and Cambridge Roads. Built in 1854 and greatly altered over the years, the house is now a private residence. Historic markers identify all the aforementioned structures.

About six miles south of exit 24 (Kewanee, Cambridge, Andover) on Interstate 74 is the **Krisdala Baka Rest Stop**. A plaque inside the building notes that settlement in this part of Henry County began with the arrival of Swedish immigrants in the 1840s. The hilly timbered terrain reminded the Swedes of their home community of Krisdala in Småland.

New Windsor

New Windsor's inhabitants are largely of Swedish ancestry. **Calvary Lutheran Church**, 121 Meridian Street (309-667-2415), was organized in 1869 and the church building constructed in 1876. Of nineteenth-century Gothic-Revival style in vertical board-and-batten construction, the church boasts an impressively tall steeple. The altar bears the inscription, *Helig, Helig, Helig* (Holy, Holy, Holy).

New Windsor suffered a fire in 1898, but the Opera House in the east business block survived. At the northeast corner of Main and Fifth is the brick mercantile building, dated 1911.

Bishop Hill

Bishop Hill State Historic Site—(309-927-3345; www.state.il.us/hpa).
Bishop Hill Heritage Association—(309-927-3899; www.bishophill.com).
During the 1840s, the first three Swedish colonizing efforts took place in the United States since the ill-fated New Sweden on the Delaware River in the mid-1600s. They were Gustaf Unonius's New Upsala colony at Pine Lake, Wisconsin, in 1841; New Sweden, Iowa, in 1845; and Bishop Hill Colony in 1846. The last was the largest.

Eric Janson (1805–1850), leader of Bishop Hill, was born Erik Jansson in Biskopskulla, Uppland, not far from Uppsala. By the time he settled in Hälsingland in the early 1840s, Janson was convinced that all religious books except the Bible were superfluous, even harmful, and that simplicity was the only way to salvation. To him, the Swedish Church had seriously strayed from its mission. When authorities attempted to suppress what was regarded as fanaticism, Janson and others looked to America as a haven. He sent Olof Olsson, his most influential associate, to scout land in western Illinois, and in 1846 a site about 160 miles west of Chicago was selected. Some 1,200 men, women, and children sailed for the United States that year, arrived in Chicago, and walked to Bishop Hill, the English translation of Janson's birthplace, Biskopskulla. Arriving in autumn, they built dugouts where the bleachers now stand on the town's central ball field. Ninety-six died during the first winter from inadequate food and shelter. With the coming of spring, the business of organizing and building a settlement commenced, but problems—including a cholera epidemic, weariness with the communal lifestyle, and disillusionment with Janson's messianic claims—plagued the community. Many transferred loyalties to the new Swedish Methodist Church in nearby Victoria, Illinois, and Bishop Hill Colony shrank to between 600 and 800 people.

During the fifteen years Bishop Hill existed as a Jansonist communal colony, twenty large commercial buildings were erected, many in classical style, and some 15,000 acres of land were farmed. After Janson was murdered in 1850 by a disenchanted colony member, management passed to a board of trustees, though for a time Jonas Olsson (brother of Olof Olsson) ruled with a firm hand. From 1853 to 1861, economics motivated the colony rather than religious zeal. The colonists excelled in producing linen, furniture, wagons, brooms, and farm products and opened a hotel. In the 1850s Bishop Hill became a commercial center between Rock Island and Peoria, but in the early 1860s, the colony dissolved and divided the property.

The state of Illinois operates two of the original buildings—the Colony Church and the Bjorklund Hotel. The Old Settlers' Association, Bishop Hill Heritage Association, and private owners manage the others. Visitors are always impressed by the size of many of the buildings. Though no longer standing, a communal apartment with ninety-six rooms on three floors, known as "Big Brick," was 200 by 45 feet. Bishop Hill buildings generally were made of kiln-dried bricks, with the exception of the Colony Church.

These original buildings are open to the public: Colony Church (1848); Steeple Building (1854); Colony Hotel (Bjorklund Hotel, 1852–1864); Colony School (1861; open by appointment); Colony Store (1853); Blacksmith Shop (1857); Carpenter and Paint Shop (1851); Eric Krans House (1848); and Hospital (1855; open for overnight accommodations). Other early buildings not open include: Boys' Dormitory (about 1847); Apartment House (1855); Administration Building (1856); Swanson House (1862–1863); Jacobson House (1866); Krusbo House (1855); Meat Storage Building (1851); Janson House (1847); Dairy Building (1854); and Red House (1855). Other structures in Bishop Hill include the Poppy Barn (1882; open to public); Cobbler Shop (1905; open to public); Olson Barn (1856–1860); Vasa

Colony Church, Bishop Hill

National Archives (1974; open to the public); and the Bishop Hill Museum (1988; open to the public). Visitors may also view the bandstand (about 1860), the cemetery (1846), and the Dugout Site.

The **Colony Church**, a gambrel-roofed building, was erected in 1848. Because of the initial housing shortage, colonists built a combination apartment-church. The basement and first floor each had ten rooms where twenty families were lodged. The first-floor rooms have been made into a museum. On the second floor is the sanctuary where a thousand people—men on the west side, women and children on the east—worshiped. The white walls contrast sharply with the black walnut pews. The pulpit panels were painted by Olof Krans, the colony's artist, to resemble marble. The church is not Swedish in design, but the wood and wrought-iron chandeliers are copies of brass chandeliers the colonists had known in Swedish churches. The spindles in the railing in front of the pulpit were turned by the colony's women.

The **Steeple Building**, erected in 1853 and 1854, is a striking contrast to the unembellished exterior of other Bishop Hill structures. Its classical Greek Revival style, colonnaded front, pediments, and symmetrical clock tower are unique. In the tower is a clock with four faces, each of which has one hand. Installed in 1859, it was operated by two sets of weights attached to ropes in a chute that

Steeple Building, Bishop Hill

extends the entire height of the building. Parts of the building have served as a communal home, school, general store, bank, newspaper office, doctor's office, and telephone exchange.

Early visitors to the colony were first accommodated in "Big Brick," but soon a regular hotel was needed. In the 1850s, Bishop Hill became the overnight stop on the stage route between Peoria and Rock Island. The **Bjorklund Hotel** was built between 1852 and 1864, and in 2004 was being restored by the state of Illinois. It is a three-story structure with a large cupola on top. On the first floor is a dining room with adjacent bar, men's parlor, ladies' parlor, pantry, and kitchen. Eleven guest rooms are on the second floor, and a large ballroom is on the third floor, which was added in the early 1860s.

The colony's schoolhouse, completed in 1861, was the last major building erected by the Jansonists. It served as the town's educational center until 1953. The original tower contained a bell purchased by Eric Janson in 1846. Mary Sandburg, sister of author Carl Sandburg, was a teacher in the school from 1899 to 1901. Her brother visited her there several times.

The colony store, erected in 1853, was a center of daily community life. The Bishop Hill Post Office occupied the corner of the building for about one hundred years. Still used as a general store and gift shop, the building contains the original shelving and fixtures.

The **Bishop Hill Museum** contains a large number of paintings by Olof Krans. They depict the original settlers and preserve a remarkable record of the colony's early years.

One block south of the Steeple Building is the **Vasa Order of America National Archives**, 1095 Bishop Hill Street (309-927-3898). This fraternal group works to perpetuate Swedish culture and traditions in America. A library, exhibits, and records room are housed in the building. In front of the building is a plaque honoring Bertil G. Winstrom (1904–2001), longtime Grand Master of the Vasa Order. Currently the Vasa Order has around 225 lodges in the United States, Sweden, and Canada representing some 20,000 members.

In the **Bishop Hill Park** are two historic landmarks: a monument and plaque "dedicated to the memory of the hardy pioneers" and a statue honoring the Bishop Hill Company that fought during the Civil War. In the nearby **Bishop Hill Cemetery** are the graves of Eric Janson and many early colonists. Three miles northwest of Bishop Hill is a district called Red Oak where the original colonists' log house was built (it does not survive). Also there is a marker in memory of colonists who died during the first winter. A similar marker was erected on a colony farm three miles southeast of Orion in memory of seventy Bishop Hill cholera victims. An island in Rock Island, Illinois, also has graves of some Bishop Hill victims who ran a fishing station.

Events celebrating Swedish culture and heritage include a Midsummer Music Festival and Maypole Celebration in June; Old Settlers' Day (the second Saturday in September); and Agricultural Days, known as *Jordbruksdagarna* (the last full weekend in September), featuring crafts, music, and folk dancing. Also popular near Christmas are the *julmarknad,* Lucia Nights, and a *julotta* candlelight service in the Colony Church.

Galva

Although founded in 1853 by New Englanders, Galva was shaped by Bishop Hill colonists who owned seventy town lots. It was from Galva that the Bishop Hill Colony shipped and received goods by railroad, and the 150-foot-long Bishop Hill Colony warehouse, on the west side of Exchange Street south of the Burlington railroad tracks, was erected in 1855. Passengers heading for the colony could stay overnight at the **Bishop Hill Colony Boarding House**, 415 SW Third Street, now a private residence, before going on to the colony.

 Several houses in Galva have colony ties. After Janson's murder in 1850, the **Olof Johnson House**, 408 NW Fourth Street, housed a trustee who was the liaison between the colony and Galva. He was accorded the honor of naming the town after the Swedish seaport of Gävle, from which many colonists sailed. In time, the name was changed to Galva, a name easier for English-speaking people to pronounce.

The **Jonas Erickson House**, 420 NW Fourth Street, was also owned by and named for a Bishop Hill trustee. At 17 NW Fifth Street is a private residence that was formerly the **Bishop Hill Mission Church**, a Covenant church built in the 1880s near the Colony Church and moved to Galva around 1900.

Churches

Churches in Galva include the Swedish Methodist Church, now **Galva Grace United Methodist Church**, 318 N. Center Avenue (309-932-3143), which was organized in 1867 by the Reverend A. J. Anderson, then a pastor in Bishop Hill.

Messiah Lutheran Church, 317 SW Third Street (309-932-3346), organized in 1869 and built in 1873, was the town's first red-brick church. The congregation now worships in an imposing red-brick, Gothic-style sanctuary (1915) with a soaring 146-foot steeple visible as one approaches Galva. The dramatic interior is dominated by an impressive high altar of Gothic design, a gift of Alfrida Appell, daughter of Swedish immigrants Charles and Sophia Appell. The central focus of the altar is a copy of nineteenth-century Danish sculptor Bertel Thorvaldsen's statue of Christ. Two striking brass chandeliers are suspended from the ceiling. A part of the central chandelier hung in the 1873 church.

In the **Galva Cemetery** outside the town are buried many Bishop Hill trustees.

Olof Krans (1838–1916) and his family are probably the best-known Swedes buried there. The **Galva Historical Museum** is at 906 W. Division (309-932-2100).

Victoria

Many local people claim that Victoria is the birthplace of Swedish Methodism, pointing to a red-granite monument on the west end of town opposite the school on the south side of State Highway 167. However, most Methodists identify *Old Bethel Ship*, a floating chapel in New York harbor, as the first congregation, organized on a ship, not on land. Olof Gustaf Hedstrom (1803–1879) established Swedish Methodism in New York City in 1845, while Jonas Hedstrom (1813–1859) began working in Illinois in 1846.

The Victoria Swedish Methodists built their sanctuary in 1854, but it was replaced in 1909 by a red-brick Gothic-style building, still in use. They merged with an American Methodist congregation and now worship at **Victoria United Methodist Church**, 102 W. Washington Street (309-879-2511). A handmade wooden pulpit, its base in the shape of a lyre and its top a closed Bible, is the only church item commemorating the founding Swedes. A plaque on the pulpit reads, "Hand carved by Octavius Seibolt for the first Swedish Methodist church in the world."

Wataga

Faith Lutheran Church, 405 S. Sparta Street (309-335-6509), was built in 1876. The nineteenth-century Gothic Revival, white-frame church is of vertical board-and-batten construction. Organized in 1853 by the Reverend T. N. Hasselquist, the congregation built its first church in 1860, but it was struck by lightning and burned.

Galesburg

Swedes first came to Galesburg because they were dissatisfied with the Bishop Hill Colony thirty miles to the northeast. The town became a railroad center and attracted Swedish immigrants seeking employment. By 1912 more than one-third of the city was Swedish by birth or descent. The third-oldest Swedish Methodist Church in the Middle West was organized in Galesburg.

First Lutheran Church, 364 E. Water Street (309-343-3176; www.luther95 .com), is one of the oldest congregations of the former Augustana Synod and one of the earliest congregations in Galesburg. The present sanctuary was built in 1928.

The **Carl Sandburg Birthplace**, 331 E. Third Street (309-342-2361; www .sandburg.org), owned by the state of Illinois, is a workman's cottage purchased by the writer's parents several years before Carl was born in 1878 and sold more than a year later when the family outgrew the small, vertical siding–clad structure.

Carl Sandburg's birthplace, Galesburg

Sandburg's father had come to Galesburg for employment opportunities with the Chicago, Burlington, and Quincy Railroad. The family moved several times to houses on East, South and Berrien Streets.

In the years following, the house changed considerably. The unplastered interior once had newspapers pasted over the drafty cracks. The new owner, a carpenter, put clapboard on the exterior. Few Sandburg family possessions other than photographs and the family Bible (Carl was confirmed in the Swedish Elim Lutheran Church in Galesburg) remain in the house. The house had no indoor plumbing and only a single woodstove for cooking and heating, conditions typical of a working-class family a century ago.

The Lincoln Room, devoted to Sandburg's life and accomplishments, includes an autographed collection of his books and the typewriter used to write *The Prairie Years* and *Rootabaga Stories*. Behind the house is Remembrance Rock, named for Sandburg's only novel; it is here that Sandburg's ashes are buried.

Also in Galesburg is **Carl Sandburg College**, 2400 Tom L. Wilson Boulevard (309-344-2518; www.sandburg.edu.). It has a branch campus in Carthage, Illinois.

Springfield

Lindbergh Field, northwest of Springfield, was the city's first airport; it is no longer used. In April 1926, Charles A. Lindbergh Jr. assisted in selecting the field. He flew mail into Springfield on the St. Louis–Chicago route until he began preparing for his historic 1927 transatlantic flight. In August 1927, the field was named to honor this aviator who first crossed the Atlantic alone and nonstop. There is a historical marker north of State Highways 97 and 125.

Monticello

In **Allerton Park and Conference Center** (217-762-2721; www.allerton.uiuc.edu), between Champaign and Decatur just off Interstate 72, is Carl Milles's impressive sculpture *The Sun Singer,* a bronze male nude with uplifted arms mounted on a granite column. It sits on the former estate of Robert Henry Allerton (1873–1964), art collector, one-time painter, and heir to a large fortune. His estate, The Farms, was a gift to the University of Illinois in 1946. The sculpture is reached by driving one and one-half miles past the main conference center through a wooded area to a large clearing at the end of the road. Castings made from the same mold may also be found at the National Memorial Park, a private cemetery in Falls Church, Virginia, and on the waterfront near the Royal Palace in Stockholm.

Paxton

In 1863, Augustana College and Seminary moved from Chicago to Paxton as the result of a land agreement made with the Illinois Central Railroad. Dr. Tuve N. Hasselquist, college president at the time of the move, replaced the Reverend Lars Esbjörn, who had headed the school in Chicago. The school remained in Paxton until the fall of 1875, when it was relocated to Rock Island, Illinois. In 1957, a marker was dedicated on the former site of Augustana College and Seminary at Summer and Park Streets, opposite Glen Cemetery.

Augustana's move to Paxton brought an influx of Swedish immigrants. They organized the **First Lutheran Church**, 301 S. College Street (217-379-2985), in Hasselquist's home in June 1863. In 1907 the third and present church at the southeast corner of College and Orleans was built. It is a large, red-brick structure that originally had two spires. Olof Grafström's *Crucifixion* (about 1910) hangs behind the altar. In the chapel in the sanctuary's rear are two stained-glass windows depicting Hasselquist and Martin Luther. The sacristy has pictures of all the former pastors as well as an old communion set. The **Evangelical Covenant Church**, 260 S. Union Street (217-379-3554) at the northwest corner of Union and Orleans, was organized in 1878 as the result of a split from First Lutheran.

INDIANA

Porter

In the late 1840s and early 1850s, young Swedish men in Chicago were attracted to northwestern Indiana by employment opportunities, including a sawmill established by the son-in-law of Joseph Bailly, a French Canadian fur trader.

In 1858, Reverend Erland Carlsson of Chicago organized the Swedish Lutheran Church of Baillytown (Augsburg Lutheran Church) with thirty-one charter members. In 1864, this congregation erected its first sanctuary in Porter, about a mile northeast of Baillytown. The log church is now gone, as is the second church, which burned in 1933. The present handsome stone church, **Augsburg Evangelical Lutheran Church**, was completed in 1938 on the site of the second sanctuary at 100 N. Mineral Springs Road (219-926-1658). In the church's basement is a well-organized archives that includes a Hillstrom organ made in nearby Chesterton. On the front lawn is the Swedish-inscribed bell of the second church. The cemetery to the south contains many Swedish graves.

Because Swedes wanted their children to maintain their heritage, children were taught Swedish during the summer months. Across the road from the old Swedish cemetery, on the north side of Oak Hill Road, about .2 mile southeast of the intersection with U.S. Highway 12 (the intersection is three miles west of Indiana Highway 49) was a small tool shed belonging to Frederick Burstrom that in 1880 was moved near the cemetery and renamed Augsburgs Svenska Skola (Augsburg's Swedish School). Today it is known as the **Burstrom Chapel and Svenska Skola.** Residents used the building as a public school until 1885, when Porter County built a local school. After that it served until the 1920s as a Swedish-language summer school where the community also gathered for midweek prayer meetings and vesper services. A granite marker stands near the front door, and the site is particularly attractive in the fall season with the colorful maple foliage.

The old cemetery holds the graves of many early Swedes, including Jonas Asp, who initially encouraged his fellow countrymen to settle in Porter County, and Frederick Burstrom, Porter County's first trustee.

At Indiana Dunes National Lakeshore, 1100 N. Mineral Springs Road (219-926-7561; www.nps.gov/indu) is **Chellberg Farm**, the homestead of Anders and Johanna Kjellberg (anglicized to "Chellberg"), now part of the national park system. The farm is one and one-half miles south of U.S. Highway 12 near Augsburg's Swedish School. Christmas and Midsummer are celebrated at the farm in a Swedish fashion.

The Chellbergs left Sweden in 1863 and settled on this eighty-acre farm in 1874. Anders was a tailor and farmer who served the Augsburg Evangelical Lutheran Church as a deacon and lay preacher. Three generations of Chellbergs made their living from the farm, where they grew wheat, oats, corn, and rye. The farm produced milk and butter for sale, especially after 1908 when the South Shore Railroad provided faster transportation to the Chicago market.

The brick farmhouse, built in 1885, replaced a frame house that burned. The barn, constructed in 1880, has a frame held together by wooden pegs. Six other

Burstrom Chapel and Svenska Skola, Porter

Chellberg Farm, Indiana Dunes National Lakeshore, Porter

structures stand on the restored farm, on which the Solar Energy Research Institute has demonstrated renewable energy.

Chesterton

 Stockholm-born Carl Oscar Hillstrom moved his organ factory from Chicago to Chesterton in 1880. He made it the main industry in town, attracting a number of Swedish immigrants and producing thousands of organs before the factory closed in 1920. Many of the stores in the **Chesterton Commercial Historic District**, 109–130 N. Calumet Road, were owned by Swedes in the late nineteenth and early twentieth centuries.

La Porte

Bethany Lutheran, 102 G Street (219-362-3312; www.bethanylaporte.org), is northwest Indiana's oldest Swedish Lutheran congregation, having been organized in 1857 by Erland Carlsson. The first church was built in 1860, and the present one in 1883. A red-brick, Gothic-style structure with a tall central spire, the church has a sanctuary that is extensively remodeled.

Besides Bethany Lutheran, nine other Augustana Lutheran congregations were organized in Indiana before 1900: First Lutheran (1858), 204 E. Pike Street,

Attica (765-764-4364); Augsburg Evangelical Lutheran (1858), 100 N. Mineral Springs Road, Porter (219-926-1658); Augustana Lutheran, 207 N. Kelly Street, Hobart (219-942-3574); Augustana Lutheran (1873), 1133 Kilbourn Street, Elkhart (574-294-3823); Bethel Lutheran (1874), 411 N. Montgomery Street, Gary (219-938-6677); Immanuel Lutheran (1876), 6835 Union Road, Donaldson (574-936-8365); Bethlehem (1879), 2050 W. 1100 North, Chesterton (219-926-5596); and Gloria Dei Lutheran (1880), 225 E. Honey Avenue, South Bend (574-288-5266). Zion Lutheran (1887), Michigan City, is no longer a separate congregation.

West of La Porte on S. County Road 50, near 700 West and Forrester Road, is the small, simple white clapboard structure known as **Carmel Chapel.** Built in 1872, it is the oldest Swedish Lutheran sanctuary in northern Indiana. Members of the Bethany congregation of La Porte constructed it because winter weather conditions frequently made it difficult to get to worship services in town. Bethany's pastor visited the chapel on Sunday afternoons. Although regular services ended in 1918, the chapel is used for events, including an Easter sunrise service, annual church picnic, harvest festival service in October, weddings, and youth retreats. The chapel is surrounded by maple trees that make fall a good time to

Carmel Chapel, La Porte

visit. A well-kept cemetery contains the graves of early Swedish settlers. To reach the chapel from La Porte, drive west on Indiana Highway 2 for six miles, turn north on Forrester Road to County Road 50, and proceed west for a short distance; the chapel is surrounded by Garwood Orchards.

On the northeast corner of Indiana and Maple in La Porte is the small **New Church Swedenborgian**, 812 Indiana Avenue (219-362-1959), constructed in 1859. The church is known as a wedding chapel. Probably the most prominent Swedenborgian in the state of Indiana was John Chapman, better known today as Johnny Appleseed.

Donaldson

In Donaldson, nine miles west of the intersection of U.S. Highways 30 and 31, are two churches of Swedish origin—the modern **Evangelical Covenant Church**, 7810 Union Road (219-936-8354), and the older, white-clapboard **Immanuel Lutheran Church**, 6835 Union Road, northwest of town off U.S. Highway 30 (574-936-8365). South of Immanuel is a large cemetery with many Swedish graves.

Attica

Swedes from the Gränna district in western Småland settled in or near Lafayette near Attica as early as the 1840s. Many moved on to Waseca County, Minnesota, in 1857. **First Lutheran Church**, 204 E. Pike Street at S. Brady (317-764-4364), is a white clapboard church, built for a congregation organized in 1858 by the Reverend Erland Carlsson.

Indianapolis

 Oldfields-Lilly House and Garden is on the grounds of the Indianapolis Museum of Art, 4000 Michigan Road (317-923-1331; www.ima-art.org). Colonel Eli Lilly, founder of the Eli Lilly Pharmaceutical Company, claimed Swedish ancestry. His family tree can be traced back to the 1200s in the province of Södermanland. In the mid-1450s, one of his ancestors adopted the name Lillja; later generations moved to France, where the spelling was changed to Lilly, then to the Netherlands and England, before emigrating to Maryland in 1789. The restored Lilly house is the former home of Josiah K. Lilly Jr., son of Eli Lilly.

OHIO

Ohio attracted few Swedish immigrants in comparison to other midwestern states. Most of them settled in Cleveland, Akron, and Youngstown. Some found their way to Ashtabula, which had a "Swedetown." Swedes organized Lutheran and

Covenant congregations in the four cities, the largest being Bethlehem Lutheran Church in Cleveland Heights, now within metropolitan Cleveland. A bronze sculpture of a young Carl von Linné by sculptor Carl Eldh is outside the Cleveland Museum of Natural History (1 Wade Oval, University Circle).

Cleveland Heights

The **Bethlehem Lutheran Church** congregation was organized in 1885 and the first church built in 1890 at 434 Central Avenue. A second sanctuary was constructed in 1903 at 7505 Wade Park Avenue adjacent to Cleveland's "Swedetown," roughly bordered by NE Superior Avenue, E. Seventy-ninth, NE Lexington Avenue, and Fifty-fifth. Swedish Baptist, Covenant, Methodist, and Salvation Army congregations also organized in Swedetown. In 1953 Bethlehem Lutheran sold its second church to an African Methodist Episcopal congregation and one year later dedicated a large stone Gothic sanctuary at 3740 Mayfield Road (216-382-4545; www.bethluth.org). The architects of this impressive church were Adolph Hanson and Einar Olson of Chicago.

Urbana

Urbana University, 579 College Way (937-484-1301; www.urbana.edu), has a 128-acre campus in southwestern Urbana. Although founded in 1850 by followers of the Swedish philosopher, theologian, and scientist Emanuel Swedenborg (1688–1772), the school today has only an informal relationship with the Church of the New Jerusalem in the United States. The Swedenborg Memorial Library, built in 1968, contains a Swedenborgian book room; the small Harvey chapel, named for the Reverend Dorothea W. Harvey, the first woman ordained by the Swedenborgian Church in 1975, has portraits of Swedenborg. At 330 S. Main Street is the Romanesque-style **Urbana Swedenborgian Church**, with the year 1880 on its cornerstone. Constructed of limestone, it has been used as a wedding chapel.

Gambier

At **Kenyon College** (740-427-5000; www.kenyon.edu), the Victorian-style building that houses the Department of Anthropology and Sociology, 101 Ward Street, is named in honor of former Swedish prime minister Olof Palme. Small plaques identify Palme (1927–1986) as a distinguished 1948 graduate, and one has the following Palme quotation: "The road to democratic change requires knowledge, effort, and beyond all, patience."

In 2003 an ensemble of Carl Milles's sculptures was installed on the attractive campus near Rosse Hall, which houses the Music Department. It is a series of angels poised on columns and playing various musical instruments.

MICHIGAN

Swedes arrived in 1853 and 1854 at the Lower Peninsula settlement of Lisbon, now known as Kent City, north of Grand Rapids. Industrial opportunities in the Detroit area drew others to that part of the state. Additional early Swedes settled near the logging centers of Saginaw and Bay City, at Alpena, and along the western shore from Muskegon to Manistee. In rural Osceola County, Tustin was founded in 1871 by about eighty Swedish families, whose men were laborers on the Grand Rapids and Indiana Railroad. The families originally called Tustin "New Bleking" after Blekinge in their homeland. Because nearby Cadillac was a lumbering town after the Civil War, it became the funnel for most Swedish immigrants who came to settle and work in northern Michigan after 1865.

Beginning in the 1860s, a larger concentration of Swedes settled in Michigan's Upper Peninsula. After the iron mines were depleted, Swedes stayed on and turned to other sources of employment—lumbering, farming, and railroad construction. Ishpeming, in the heart of an iron-ore region, became a leading center for Swedes. Other communities included Escanaba, Iron Mountain, Norway, St. Ignace, Skandia, and Skanee. The Upper Peninsula also attracted settlers from Finland, some of whom were Swede Finns. In Hancock, on the Keweenaw Peninsula, is Suomi College, now called Finlandia University.

Bloomfield Hills

The architecture and art of the magnificent campus of the **Cranbrook Academy of Art**, 39221 N. Woodward (248-645-3323; www.cranbrook.edu), near Detroit was greatly influenced by two men, Eliel Saarinen and Carl Milles. From 1931 to 1951, Milles was the resident sculptor at Cranbrook, and Cranbrook owns the largest collection of Milles's sculpture outside Sweden. Outdoor sculptures include *Fountain of Jonah and the Whale, Orpheus Fountain, Triton Pool, Europa and the Bull,* and *Siren with Fishes.* A number of Milles's works are also in the Cranbrook Academy of Art Museum. A fountain, *Sunday Morning in Deep Waters,* is on the University of Michigan campus at Ann Arbor, on the main quadrangle near the Burton Memorial Tower.

Finnish architect Eliel Saarinen (1873–1950) was first asked to draw plans for the Cranbrook Educational Community in 1924 by its founder, financier George C. Booth. In the following years, Saarinen served as chief architectural adviser, president of Cranbrook Academy, and a department head. It was Saarinen who persuaded his good friend Carl Milles to join him at Cranbrook, which became recognized for its cutting-edge art, architecture, and design.

Sawyer

Early in the twentieth century, the Swedish Baptist churches in the Chicago area formed the Illinois Sunday School Union. Concerned that city children, particularly of poor families, should spend some summer vacation days in rural surroundings, the Union began purchasing farmland in southwestern Michigan's Sawyer. **Bethany Beach** is now a large summer religious conference center as well as a community of permanent year-round residents. At its heart is the Tabernacle, built in 1924. Ecumenical services have been held at Bethany Beach since 1906, the year the first tabernacle was constructed.

Harbert

 Carl Sandburg's family began spending part of their summers along the southeastern shore of Lake Michigan in Harbert in the late 1920s. The **Carl Sandburg House** on Birchwood Court (still a private residence) later became the family's year-round home. Here Sandburg wrote the volume of poetry *The People, Yes* and completed the Pulitzer Prize–winning biography *Abraham Lincoln: The War Years*.

Grand Rapids

The Swedish Covenant congregation, organized in 1880, built its first sanctuary at Broadway and First Streets three years later and its second red-brick church in 1895. The interior woodwork reflects the skilled craftsmanship of the Swedes engaged in the city's furniture business. In 1961 the building was sold to another congregation. The 1895 cornerstone is in the foyer of the present modern **First Evangelical Covenant Church**, 1933 NW Tremont Boulevard (616-453-6346).

The **Bethlehem Lutheran** (616-456-1741; www.blc-grmi.org) congregation was organized in 1873, and the present large light-brick sanctuary at 330 NE Crescent was built in 1932, in what is now the Heritage Hill Historic District.

Kent City

The congregation of the **Mamrelund Lutheran Church**, 406 NW Lutheran Church Road (616-887-8873), between Sparta and Kent City, is important historically as the first Swedish church in Michigan. The congregation was organized in 1866, and six years later, the present site was selected for a church building. At the turn of the century, the church was enlarged, but it was torn down for the new sanctuary, completed in 1979. The colored windows in the present sanctuary are from the old church.

Big Rapids

Immanuel Lutheran Church, 325 Linden Avenue (231-796-8273; www
.immanuelbr.com), is the result of merged Swedish and Danish congregations.
The first Swedish Lutheran sanctuary, which no longer exists, was located on
the northeastern side of town's Swede Hill. A plaque erected in a small park on
Baldwin Street, two blocks east of N. State Street, commemorates the Swede Hill
settlement. Swedes came to the high bluffs above the Muskegon River as early as
the 1870s and 1880s. They found work on the Grand Rapids and Indiana Railroad
and in lumber camps, sawmills, and factories.

Tustin-LeRoy

Three miles south of the Wexford-Osceola County line on U.S. Highway 131 is
a rest stop with a State of Michigan marker reading: "Unto a New Land. Swedish immigrants, anxious to escape famine and an unsympathetic government,
flowed into the Midwest frontier of America from the 1870s to 1890s searching for land and work. Railroads and lumbering industries offered attractive
opportunities to these immigrants. The Grand Rapids & Indiana Railroad sent
the Rev. J. P. Tustin to Sweden to recruit laborers for construction of its line.
As an inducement, the railroad donated 80 acres to the Swedish colony of New
Blekinge (Tustin). Swedes swarmed to this vicinity, building the railroad, logging
the forest and laboring in the sawmills. As the forest became depleted, many
moved on but others became permanent settlers whose descendants still reside
here. Children of these settlers have in this century gone across the country to
make their contributions to America."

In nearby Tustin, at 18499 Twenty Mile Road, is the white-frame **Augustana
Lutheran Church** (231-829-3837). In 1872 the Reverend Josiah Tustin, rector of
St. Mark's Episcopal Church of Grand Rapids, organized an Episcopal congre-
gation known as St. Johannes' Church of New Bleaking (later changed to New
Bleking and ultimately to Tustin). Few Swedes, however, showed much interest
in the Episcopal Church, and in 1874 a group broke away to form the Swedish
Evangelical Lutheran Church of Tustin. St. Johannes' Church closed in 1938.

Also in Tustin near the church is Hoaglund Hardware, housed in the former
bank building at 107 E. Church Street. In a former potato warehouse across from
the post office on Howard Street is the local museum. Many early Swedish settlers grew potatoes in the summer and logged in the winter. A Swedish Baptist
Church in town is currently identified as the **First Baptist Church**, 301 E. Church
Street (231-829-3894). The former Covenant church is now a private house, its
congregation having merged with the local Presbyterian church.

Outside Tustin are several cemeteries with numerous Swedish graves, including Burdell Township Cemetery, one mile west of Tustin on Twenty Mile or Marion Road just west of U.S. Highway 131; Sherman Township Cemetery, four miles northeast of Tustin on Twenty-one Mile or Ina Road; and Maple Hill Cemetery, two and one-half miles south of Tustin on Mackinaw Trail or old U.S. Highway 131.

Zion Lutheran Church of Le Roy, 202 S. Albert Street (231-829-3537), was constructed in 1902 approximately five miles south of town. Originally the congregation was known as the Swedish Evangelical Lutheran Emanuel Church. The small Covenant church originally used by a Swedish Baptist congregation was

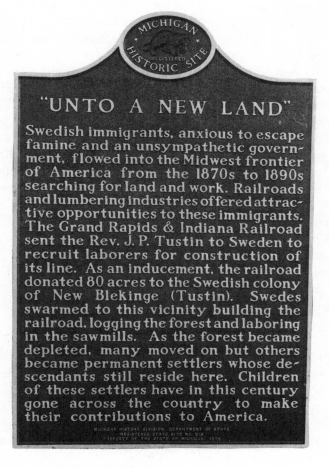

Swedish immigration marker, Tustin–LeRoy

built in the late 1870s or early 1880s. In 1890 the Covenant congregation was organized in Le Roy. The present **Evangelical Covenant Church** is located at 201 E. Cherry Street (231-768-5011). Southwest of town is the Dewings Cemetery where Swedes are buried.

Cadillac

The original sanctuary of **Zion Lutheran Church**, organized in 1874, stands on the corner of Shelby and Nelson (now owned by another religious group). It was moved here in 1909 from the corner of Nelson and Simons, when a new red-brick building with a tall steeple replaced it (also now owned by another congregation). Zion's present sanctuary at 350 Pearl Street (231-775-9821; www.zion-cadillac.org) dates to 1973. In a small chapel are altar objects from the former sanctuary.

Other churches with Swedish links in this community include Swedish Christian Mission Church, organized in 1880; the next year the congregation constructed a church building that was not replaced until 1913, when the red-brick Covenant church was built. The present **First Covenant** is at 315 E. Pine Street (616-775-3191).

One block west on Pine Street is the Free Methodist Church, whose predominantly Swedish congregation was organized in 1870. The Swedish Baptist Church was organized in 1883 and later renamed **Temple Hill Baptist Church**. The old church, constructed in 1888, is one block north of the old Zion Lutheran Church on N. Simons Street. The present Baptist congregation built a new sanctuary at 1601 W. Division (231-775-4942; www.thbc.org).

The Gotha Society, operating as a mutual aid and fraternal society, constructed a building at 422 N. Mitchell Street that it used for about forty years. The building is now owned by the American Legion.

About four miles south of Cadillac is Clam Lake Township's Lutheran cemetery, the graveyard for the former Swedish Lutheran church at Hobart, which disbanded in the early twentieth century.

Gilbert

Trinity Lutheran Church, 2780 N. Forty-first Road, south of Manton, was constructed in the late nineteenth century and continues to have a Swedish connection. Gilbert was a sawmill town on the Grand Rapids and Indiana Railroad.

Jennings

Jennings, northeast of Cadillac, was a lumbering community that attracted Swedish immigrants from 1882 until the early 1920s, when the timber reserves petered out and people moved away. St. John's Lutheran, the community church which was similar in appearance to Gilbert's Trinity Lutheran, was moved to a new site south of Lake City, but it was eventually demolished. The old Lutheran cemetery at Jennings is maintained.

Ludington

Emanuel Lutheran Church, 501 E. Danaher (231-843-3686), was organized in 1874 by Swedish and Norwegian immigrants. The present sanctuary was built near the turn of the century.

Manistee

 Completed in 1870, the white-frame **Our Savior's Historical Museum Church**, 304 Walnut (231-723-0077), is the oldest extant Danish church in the United States and Manistee's oldest house of worship. A number of Swedes helped build the church, then called Our Saviour's Evangelical Lutheran Church, and attended services there. Across the street is the red-brick former Evangelical Covenant Church, 349 Third Avenue, with its cornerstone reading "Swedish Ev. Mission Church 1882 Ad 1913." The present Covenant church is **Faith Covenant** located at 475 Eighth Street (231-723-7173).

In 1970 three congregations, including the Swedish Messiah Lutheran, merged to form **Good Shepherd Lutheran Church** (231-723-7161; www.goodshepherd manistee.org). Worship is conducted in the former Messiah Lutheran Church, a brick structure at 521 Cypress with Gothic-style windows and a central steeple.

The **Manistee County Historical Museum**, 425 River Street (231-723-5531), has a large collection of local artifacts and memorabilia.

St. Ignace

In St. Ignace, gateway to the Upper Peninsula, stands the **Zion Lutheran Church** at 950 Huron Street (906-643-7870), which was organized by Swedes. The sanctuary was built in 1957. The building provides a view of the Straits of Mackinac and Mackinac Island to the east.

Moran

The small, white-frame **Trinity (Brevort) Lutheran Church**, 3820 W. Highway 2 (906-643-7870), whose congregation was organized by Swedes, is near a scenic beach on the north shore of Lake Michigan not far from the Mackinac Bridge. Its Olof Grafström altar painting, *The Good Shepherd,* dates to 1912.

Escanaba

The sanctuary of **Bethany Lutheran Church**, 202 S. Eleventh (906-786-6642), is perhaps the most impressive of northern Michigan's Swedish churches. Built in 1912, the large brick church (the congregation's third building) features two tall spires. Stained-glass windows depict Christ and the children with the pine-covered hilly landscape near Skandia in the Upper Peninsula. Three windows, now in the Fellowship Hall but formerly at the rear of the sanctuary, each portray Swedish leaders—King Gustavus Adolphus (1594–1632); Dr. Tuve Hasselquist, the Swedish Lutheran leader in America; and the Reverend Carl Olander, pastor of the Zion Lutheran Church of Marinette, Wisconsin, who presided at the 1879 organizational meeting of Bethany Lutheran.

Norway

Bethany Lutheran Church, 815 Iron Street (906-563-8472), began in 1880, and the sanctuary still in use dates from the late 1880s. The whitewashed frame building was first located in the hills above Norway, but it was moved to town in the early 1890s. The bell tower and chancel were additions. Above the Iron Street door is a stained-glass window inscribed, "Swedish Lutheran Church." Nearby is the white-frame **Evangelical Covenant Church**, 1200 O'Dill Road (906-563-9480), whose congregation was organized in 1883.

Au Train

 Two miles south of Au Train and State Highway 28, in the Hiawatha National Forest, stands the **Paulson House**, 6915 Forest Lake Road (906-892-8892). Swedish pioneer and homesteader Charles Paulson built the two-story log house in the early 1880s on the shores of Au Train Lake, constructing first a single story and adding a second-floor dormer later. Built of hand-hewn cedar logs, some thirty-four feet long, cut at the site and dove-tailed at the corners, the home was one of the first farmhouses in Alger County. The Paulson family lived in it for more than fifty years. The cabin houses a museum of pioneer furnishings and implements.

Skandia

The light-red brick **Emanuel Lutheran Church**, at 9812 U.S. Highway 41 (906-942-7245), sits surrounded by woods. An old structure with transparent Gothic-style windows, the church has a sanctuary featuring a small 1913 altar painting of Christ by Olof Grafström.

Ishpeming

Bethany Lutheran Church (906-486-4351) was organized in 1870, making it the oldest original Swedish Lutheran church in the Upper Peninsula. Today the congregation worships in a facility located at 715 Mather and dating from 1962. On a separate tower hangs the 1912 bell with a Swedish inscription.

Also in Ishpeming is the **National Ski Hall of Fame and Museum**, located on U.S. Highway 41 and Second (906-485-6323). This modern facility traces the history of skiing and emphasizes the importance of Norway and Sweden in developing the sport. Outstanding skiers are also featured.

Skanee

Skanee is in an isolated area to the east of the Keweenaw Peninsula in the far northern Upper Peninsula. Lumbering and dairy farming attracted Swedes to the area. **Zion Lutheran Church**, Upper Skanee Road (906-353-6541), was organized in the late 1880s and is Baraga County's oldest congregation. The white-frame sanctuary was constructed in 1892, making it the county's oldest existing house of worship. The impressive large altar painting is by Olof Grafström and is dated 1900. Two miles to the west is a cemetery with Swedish graves.

WISCONSIN

The first identifiable Swedes in Wisconsin were Carl Friman (1781–1862) and his family (descendants changed the spelling to "Freeman") from Västergötland. They settled in 1838 in Racine County near Genoa City and what is today New Munster. By 1900, nearly 49,000 Swedes lived in Wisconsin.

One immigrant, Gustaf Unonius, a young graduate from Uppsala University, arrived in Milwaukee in 1841 with his wife and two friends. He established a colony named New Upsala at Pine Lake, some thirty miles west of Milwaukee, creating the first organized nineteenth-century Swedish settlement in the United States. (New Sweden, Iowa, holds the distinction of being the nineteenth century's first permanent Swedish settlement.) Although some Swedes responded to his positive letters, the colony was unsuccessful. Following his training at an Episcopal seminary at Nashotah a few miles southwest of Pine Lake, Unonius was ordained and served as a minister to three Wisconsin congregations. In 1849 Unonius moved to Chicago, where he served St. Ansgarius Church until his return to Sweden in 1858.

Northwest Wisconsin attracted a significant number of Swedish immigrants, and a sizable percentage of people in Burnett, Polk, Douglas, Pierce, Pepin, and Barron Counties are of Swedish ancestry.

Milwaukee

As early as the 1840s, Milwaukee drew Swedish immigrants. By the early 1900s, Swedish Americans had numbers great enough to support three Swedish-language churches and a lodge of the Independent Order of Vikings. At the southwest corner of Scott and S. Tenth Streets stands the original building of the Swedish Congregational Church (later Mission Friends-Covenant). Olaf Rehnquist, grandfather of former Supreme Court Chief Justice William Rehnquist, helped found the congregation.

Swedish artist Thorsten Lindberg's large wall murals celebrating Milwaukee history, painted between 1942 and 1944, may be seen in the **Milwaukee Theatre**, 500 W. Kilbourn Avenue (414-908-6000). Lindberg, who was born in 1878 in Stockholm, was a Works Progress Administration (WPA) artist during the 1930s and 1940s. His work may also be seen in the Milwaukee Courthouse and Milwaukee City Park.

At the Milwaukee City Hall, E. Wells and N. Water Streets, Swedish American author Carl Sandburg served in 1910 as private secretary for Emil Siedel, Milwaukee's Social-Democratic mayor. John Olaf Norquist, Milwaukee's mayor from 1988 to 2003, is of Swedish descent.

Genoa City

In the community park under a freestanding log structure, the Swedish-American Historical Society of Wisconsin placed a plaque recognizing Carl Friman as the first identifiable Swedish immigrant to Wisconsin. Friman, who settled on eighty acres he purchased near Genoa City, emigrated in 1838. The Friman farm site is nearby. Freeman Street in Genoa City is named in honor of Adolph Freeman, Carl's son, who anglicized the family name.

Pine Lake

In 1948, the Wisconsin Swedish Pioneer Centennial Commission commemorated the founding of New Upsala by Gustaf Unonius (1810–1902) by erecting a marker at the junction of State Highway 83 and County Highway K. Two years after **Nashotah House**, 2777 Mission Road (262-646-6500; www.nashotah.edu), an Episcopal seminary, was founded in 1842, thirty-three-year-old Unonius became a student and, subsequently, the seminary's first graduate. On the library's second floor is a picture of Unonius, and in its collection are some of his papers. The seminary has preserved two wood buildings dating from the 1840s that would have been familiar to Unonius—Blue House, originally the dormitory, and Red Chapel, still used for religious services. Near these buildings in 1991 the Swedish-American Historical Society of Wisconsin erected a monument noting the 150th anniversary of Unonius's immigration to the United States and recognizing Unonius as Nashotah House's first graduate.

St. Anskar Episcopal Church (262-367-2430), whose 1968 sanctuary stands west of Hartland on Hill Road, north of the intersection of Highways 16 and 83, combines two former congregations, including Holy Innocents. In the northwest corner of Holy Innocents Cemetery on Highway C west of Pine Lake is an early grave belonging to K. N. Peterson (or Bengt Pettersson; 1797–1845), who arrived in Pine Lake in 1842. St. John's Lutheran Cemetery in Stone Bank, a small crossroads community on Highway K north of Pine Lake, also contains graves of Swedes. Five or six miles north of Stone Bank on Roosevelt Road is St. Olaf's Lutheran Church, which was organized and served by Gustaf Unonius.

North of Holy Innocents Cemetery off Route C on Oakland Road near the south end of Pine Lake is a restored log cabin built in 1849 by John O. Rudberg for his new Danish bride. Rudberg later added wings and a clapboard exterior to the original structure. It became a large frame house that eventually was converted to a hotel. When the house was being torn down in 1951, the cabin was rediscovered. Believed to be the only log cabin that has survived near Pine Lake from the early New Upsala settlement, it was moved and restored as a private residence.

Clinton

In the Jefferson Prairie settlement south of Clinton near the Wisconsin-Illinois line, the Scandinavian Evangelical Lutheran Augustana Synod was organized in June 1860. In the cemetery near the Jefferson Prairie Lutheran Church, established in 1844 by Norwegians, is a plaque commemorating the synod's founding. In 1894 the synod replaced "Scandinavian" with "Swedish" in its name. Included in the list of ministers who gathered here in 1860 were L.P. Esbjörn, T. Hasselquist, Erik Norelius, and Erland Carlson. The cemetery is five miles south of Clinton on Wisconsin Highway 140. Nearby is a marker titled "Jefferson Prairie Settlement," which notes that Ole Knutson Nattestad was the first Norwegian settler in the state, coming to Clinton Township in 1836 from Numedal, Norway. His brother, Ansten, organized a settlement to the west in Rock Prairie or Luther Valley. The plaque reads: "They are regarded jointly as the first Norwegian settlement in Wisconsin and the fourth in the United States."

Albion

In 1843, two years after New Upsala was founded at Pine Lake, Thure L. Kumlien (1819–1888) from Västergötland led a group of colonists to the Lake Koshkonong area. From 1865 to 1870, Kumlien taught natural history at Albion Academy. The school no longer exists, but **Kumlien Hall**, its main building built in 1853, is now a local museum. On the two-story, light-colored brick building is a marker outlining the academy's history that refers to Kumlien as a "world famous naturalist." Kumlien and his family are buried in the town cemetery.

Although Kumlien's settlement was not permanent, members of the party remained, including Carl Edvard Abraham Reuterskiöld (1796–1847) from Västmanland. He arrived in 1843 with his wife and seven children, and they are buried in the Busseyville Cemetery in Jefferson County, northwest of Lake Koshkonong on State Highway 106, about five miles east of Albion. A curious stone inscribed "Abraham—Royal family of Sweden," marks the grave site, but Reuterskiöld was not royalty.

Madison

On the grounds of the State Capitol (608-266-0382), 2 E. Main Street, is a statue commemorating Hans Christian Heg, who was born in Norway in 1820 and died in the Civil War at the battle of Chickamauga in 1863. Heg was colonel of the Fifteenth Wisconsin Volunteers, or Scandinavian Regiment, during the war. Swedes including surgeon A. F. Lindsfelt, Lieutenant Colonel Kiler K. Jones, and Captain Charles Gustafson were among the regiment's 900 men, one-third of whom were killed on the field or died of wounds.

La Crosse

Several works by sculptor Paul Granlund can be found in La Crosse. One of his most delightful and interesting bronzes, *The Dancing Francis*, dedicated in 1989, stands on the campus of Viterbo University between Ninth and Tenth across from Mary of the Angels Chapel. The bronze St. Francis has one foot on a curved crescent moon and balances the orb of the earth above his head. Carved on the orb is the figure of Christ on the Cross.

A second work, *Damascus Illumination*, was installed in 1966 outside St. Paul's Lutheran Church, 420 S. West Avenue. This dramatic bronze shows Christ with arms outstretched in invitation, positioned on the brick wall of the church building several feet above Paul, depicted with bowed head, his hands and feet extended toward Christ.

Reflections III is located in front of the main branch of the La Crosse Public Library on Eighth and Main. This bronze is a seated female nude posed on a bronze pedestal gazing into a reflecting pool. Inside the library near the main desk is a small Granlund piece entitled *Ascendance*.

Eau Claire

Three Paul Granlund sculptures are located here, two on the campus of the University of Wisconsin–Eau Claire. *Resurrection* is in front of the Ecumenical Religious Center, 110 Garfield Avenue, in a garden of "rest and contemplation" provided by the members of University Lutheran Church and the Roman Catholic Newman Parish "to commemorate the signing of the Joint Declaration on the Doctrine of Justification by the Roman Catholic Church and the Lutheran World Federation." *Resurrection* is a bronze human figure breaking free from an enclosure.

The second work, a casting of *Sprites*, is found on the lawn between Scofield Hall and Zorn Arena. This bronze depicts three fifteen-foot nudes arranged on a cement cylinder on a round brick plaza. (The original *Sprites* is in the courtyard of Hennepin County Medical Center, 900 S. Eighth Street, Minneapolis.)

Family Circle is outside the main entrance to Luther Hospital, 1221 Whipple Street. This bronze sculpture is of a mother, father, and child.

Paul Granlund's *The Dancing Francis*, La Crosse

Stockholm and Lund

In 1851, Eric Peterson (1822–1887) of Karlskoga, Värmland, sighted the wide Mississippi River with its towering bluffs south of Red Wing, Minnesota (the part of the river known as Lake Pepin). Two years later, his brother arrived with a group of settlers and founded the community of Stockholm. A small museum in town on County Road J contains memorabilia of this community's heritage.

In June 1856, the first Swedish Lutheran congregation was organized in the area, but eleven years later the congregation split. Two churches were built: one in Stockholm and the other in the country six miles inland. Around the turn of the twentieth century, the country congregation constructed a large, stately red-brick church with a soaring steeple, calling it the **Sabylund Lutheran Church**, 11137 W. County Road J (715-448-4044). The church is attractively sited on a rise at the end of a tree-lined drive. The striking sanctuary has a Gothic-style white altar with a statue of Christ. The chancel wall is painted with white clouds on a blue background, and the wall on either side of the altar has a cross and chalice motif on a red background. Other walls are stenciled with various designs. One cemetery is adjacent to the site, and another one is halfway between Stockholm and the church on County Road J.

A number of Lutherans in the nearby Lund area became Mission Friends, and a church was organized in 1874. The present Gothic-style, white-frame **Lund Mission Covenant Church**, W. 10899 County Road CC (715-445-3580), dating from 1904, is the second sanctuary of the congregation. A separate bell tower sits in front of the extensively altered church. From the adjacent cemetery, looking out over the farm fields, one can see the spire of Sabylund Lutheran. Three miles west, on Moravian Road off Highway J, is the white-clapboard Moravian church, an offshoot of the Covenant congregation; a cemetery nearby has many Swedish graves.

Hager City

Svea Lutheran Church was organized in 1875 near Red Wing, Minnesota, and two years later the sanctuary was built. The white-frame church with a tall, attractive steeple is located three miles east of Hager City off Route 63 on 770 Street or Church Road (715-792-2883).

Dresser

Bethesda Lutheran Church, 1947-110th Avenue (715-755-2562; www.bethesda lutheran.ws), on Sand Lake is a daughter congregation of Chisago Lake Lutheran Church in Center City, Minnesota. Bethesda Lutheran's Swedish heritage seems more apparent than that of other churches in northwestern Wisconsin. Over

Sabylund Lutheran Church, Lund

the main door of this red-brick church is the inscription, *Sv. Ev. Luth. Bethesda Församl's Kyrka Byggd. Ad 1888 Församlingen Stiftades 21 April Ad 1872* (Swedish Evangelical Lutheran Bethesda Parish Church built A.D. 1888. The parish was founded April 21, 1872). Set in a lovely location on the south shore of Sand Lake, the church stands immediately north of the Swedish cemetery, also established in 1872.

Balsam Lake

 Polk County Museum (715-483-3979; www.co.polk.wi.us/museum), a well-organized museum, is housed at 300 Main Street in the former Polk County Courthouse, built in 1899. Exhibits feature the area's ethnic and religious heritage. Several Swedish congregations have contributed to the collection. The Polk County Historical Society has been active in placing historic plaques throughout the county, and a number of the historic sites are of interest to Swedish Americans. The museum offers a complete directory.

Frederic

Grace Lutheran, 11810 County Road Z (715-327-8384), originally known as the Swedish Evangelical Lutheran Church of West Sweden, was founded in 1873. In 1931 electricity was installed in the 1884 sanctuary. Most gas lamps were replaced, but the congregation retains two old ornate chandeliers. A cemetery is nearby. The small community of West Sweden at one time had a creamery, dance hall, blacksmith shop, school, large merchandise store, and church. Only the last structure has survived.

Trade Lake

Zion Lutheran Church, 11840 County Road Z, Frederic (715-327-8384), is the oldest Swedish Lutheran congregation in northwest Wisconsin, having been organized in 1870. Zion's present red-brick church with its tall steeple and Gothic-style window was completed in 1914. In the adjacent cemetery, Swedish names predominate. The church is located at what local people call "Four Corners." At one time there were three Swedish churches—Lutheran, Baptist, Methodist (now in Atlas)—at this crossroads.

Additional old Swedish congregations in Burnett County include Bethany Lutheran, one-half block north of Main Street, Siren (715-349-5280), which has a contemporary building; Siren Covenant, 7686 Lofty Pines Drive, Siren (715-349-5601); Trinity Lutheran, 10394 State Road 70, Siren (715-689-2271), a small white-frame church; and Bethany Lutheran, three and one-half miles south of Grantsburg (715-463-5746). Although the congregation has disbanded, the old Mission Church in Trade Lake is maintained. The Trade Lake Mission congregation

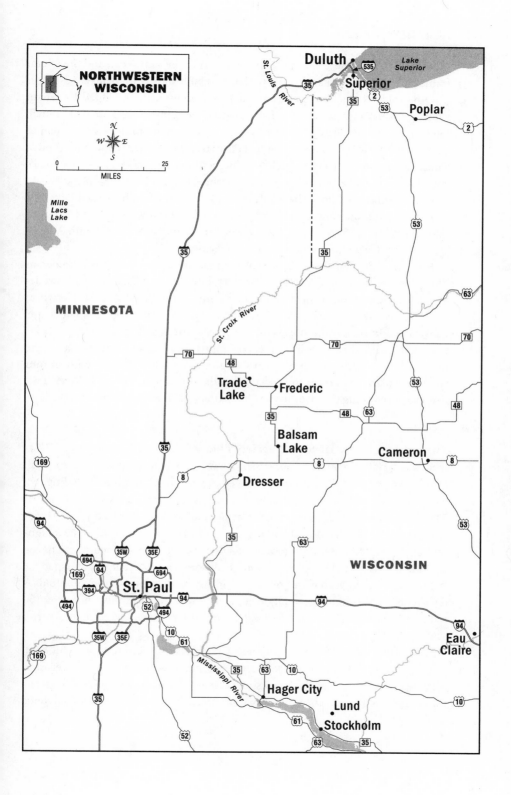

was organized in 1886. Property was purchased in the same year, and the white-frame church made of hand-hewn timber was built shortly thereafter.

Other old Swedish congregations in Polk County include United Covenant Church, 348 NW Fifth Street, Clear Lake (715-263-2665); Immanuel Lutheran Church, four miles south on State Highway 63, Clayton (715-948-2494); Fristad Lutheran Church, 501 State Highway 35, Centuria (715-646-2357); Atlas United Methodist Church, 2110-295th Avenue, Luck (mailing address Grantsburg; 715-463-2624); and Faith Lutheran Church, 305 E. First Avenue, Balsam Lake (715-485-3986). In nearby Washburn County, the lovely Salem Lutheran Church in Shell Lake was demolished, but the congregation saved the stained-glass windows and incorporated them into its new church at the corner of Second Street and Eighth Avenue (715-468-7718; www.salemlutheraninshelllake.org).

Southwest of Trade Lake, in an isolated part of western Wisconsin known as "The Barrens," is the Old Settlers' Cemetery. On the grounds, a group of Swedes began a congregation in 1878 and built a church completed in 1881, known as the Sterling Swedish Lutheran Church. The church is gone, but a small chapel constructed in 1984 is the site's sentinel. To visit the cemetery from Trade Lake, take County Road 48 west five miles to County Road 87 and turn south. At the north end of Cushing, turn west on Evergreen Avenue. Follow Evergreen four and one-half miles west through several bends and turns to the Trade River. Take the bridge spanning the river to the Old Settlers' Cemetery, which is on the left.

Cameron

The **Barron County Historical Society's Pioneer Village Museum**, 1870 Thirteen and a Half Avenue (715-458-2080; www.barroncountymuseum.com), is an impressive open-air site with more than twenty historic buildings, including two structures of Swedish origin. It is two miles east of Barron on County Road W. The 14 by 24 foot Hedin Log House was built about 1890 by Swede A. P. Hedin (1865–1941). Hedin lived in the log house with his wife, five sons, three daughters, and a grandmother until 1909, when they moved to larger quarters. The log cabin had only a kitchen–dining room, bedroom, and loft that slept six people. Before 1967, the log cabin was on a farm in the nearby township of Stanfold. A few items in the cabin originally belonged to the Hedin family, including the religious songbooks in the kitchen hutch, the butter churn, and a large cast-iron scalding pot.

The white-frame Ebenezer Lutheran Church, where weddings are still held, was built in 1908 between the towns of Poskin and Almena. The congregation was organized in 1908 as the Swedish Evangelical Lutheran Ebenezer Congregation of Poskin. In 1972, the sanctuary was moved to the museum. Original items in the church include two pews, a hymn board, communion service pieces, and two velveteen collection pouches on long poles.

Ogema

One mile outside Ogema is the one-room **Lars and Charlotta Ek Log Home**, built in the late nineteenth century when the Eks moved to Wisconsin from Bällefors, Skaraborg. Ek bought the land in 1881. Because of remodeling, the house had been masked until it was rediscovered in the 1970s. It is now cared for by the Ogema Historical Society.

The Gothic-style frame **First Lutheran Church**, 4950 W. State Road 86 (715-767-5155), was built in 1900, and the Olof Grafström altar painting is dated 1905. On the west side of Ogema is the town cemetery where many stones bear Swedish names.

Spirit

Around 1878, a Swede named Charles Hilmar Olson, who worked on a boat that brought immigrants to Michigan's Upper Peninsula, heard about the giant white-pine stands on the Spirit River in north-central Wisconsin. More interested in logging than sailing, Olson brought his family and friends, including Albin Johnson, to the area. The one-and-one-half-story **Albin Johnson Log House**, known as "Our Yesterday House," was built in 1885 in one of the last-settled regions of Wisconsin. The Johnsons lived in the structure only briefly. In 1972 it was moved to the Roy Meier farm and converted into a local museum. To see the log house, drive east on State Highway 86 for three and one-half miles and then south on County Road Y for four miles. The farm is on the east side of the road, near the German Lutheran Church.

Superior

Numerous Swedes settled in this most northwesterly section of Wisconsin. Many came to Superior, a city with several churches of Swedish background, including Pilgrim Lutheran, 820 Belknap Street (715-392-4731); Zion Lutheran, 2022 E. Second Street (715-398-3663); and First Evangelical Covenant, 3311 Hammond Avenue (715-392-4051). Superior and its sister city, Duluth ("The Twin Ports"), drew immigrants to the shipping trade.

The **Richard I. Bong World War II Heritage Center**, 305 Harbor View Parkway at the intersection of U.S. Highways 53 and 2 (715-392-7151; www.bongheritage center.org), honors Richard I. Bong (1920–1945) and other World War II veterans. Bong was a Swedish American fighter pilot in World War II who was credited with shooting down forty Japanese aircraft. His father was born in Dalarna and

Richard was brought to Wisconsin when he was six years old. The pilot was killed on August 6, 1945, during a training exercise in California. The museum building is shaped like an aircraft hanger, and a Lockheed P-38 fighter plane is now the museum centerpiece. Superior's airport is named for this World War II hero.

Poplar

In Poplar, about twenty miles east of Superior, is a state marker honoring Major Richard I. Bong, called "America's Ace of Aces." This marker is on the north side of U.S. Highway 2 in a rest area at the west end of town. The local school is also named in his honor. Bong is buried in the Poplar Cemetery on Cemetery Road off U.S. Highway 2.

Door Peninsula

Nordic immigrants, especially Norwegians and Icelanders (on Washington Island), settled the Door Peninsula, which juts into Lake Michigan. Towns such as Ellison Bay, Sister Bay, and Ephraim have a distinctly Scandinavian atmosphere and feature Nordic restaurants and gift shops. Because of its scenic beauty, Door Peninsula attracts many tourists. A recently developed vacation resort known as Little Sweden features homes built of pine logs, 8984 Highway 42, Fish Creek (920-868-9950; www.little-sweden.com).

THE WESTERN MIDWEST

IOWA

Iowa is significant in the story of Swedish immigration because it was the site of the United States' first permanent nineteenth-century Swedish settlement. "New Sweden" in southeastern Jefferson County was established in 1845 by Peter (Per) Cassel (1790–1857), a well-to-do farmer, who brought along seventeen Swedes from Kisa Parish, Östergötland. A year later, a second party heading for New Sweden lost its way and eventually settled along the Des Moines River, north of Des Moines, at Swede Point, later renamed Madrid. Boone, Hamilton, and Webster Counties in central Iowa, with towns including Boone, Boxholm, Stratford, Dayton, Harcourt, Gowrie, and Fort Dodge, attracted large numbers of Swedish settlers.

Across the southern tier of Iowa's counties are other pockets of Swedish settlement, including Burlington, Swedesburg, and Munterville, and towns in Montgomery and Page Counties. In addition to the congregations specifically mentioned in the following pages, several old Swedish Lutheran congregations in southeastern Iowa carry on, though the early buildings no longer survive: Messiah Lutheran of Burlington (1859), First Lutheran of Chariton (1869), First Lutheran of Ottumwa (1871), First Lutheran of Centerville (1881), and First Lutheran of Keokuk (1883). The most important Swedish settlement in the southwest part of the state is Stanton, founded by the Reverend Bengt Magnus Halland (1837–1902) from the province of Halland. The First Swedish Baptist congregation, now known as the Center Baptist Church, was founded in 1853 near Lansing in northeast Iowa. Swedes were also attracted to Kiron in Crawford County.

Lockridge

While New Sweden was never incorporated and never claimed more than a few hundred residents, the community's historic significance in the history of Swedish immigration is far reaching. The gravel road known as the "Swedish Highway" historically unified the churches and farmsteads, running west from County Road 40 through the New Sweden Historic District, which is about three miles northwest of Lockridge.

On the south side of the Swedish Highway is **New Sweden Chapel**, New Sweden's most significant existing structure. The 50 by 30 foot white-frame church is basically unchanged since its construction in 1860 (the Lutheran congregation

New Sweden Chapel, exterior and sanctuary, Lockridge

was organized in 1848). It has a two-tiered steeple with a spire, and the lower part of it contains a bell manufactured in St. Louis. Inside, the sanctuary is elegantly simple. The wood pulpit, altar and rail, hymn board, plaster walls, wainscoting, wood floor, and dark, walnut ceiling are original, as are two early light fixtures, each containing four kerosene lamps now supplied with electricity. A large altar painting by Olof Grafström, completed in 1919, depicts Christ at prayer with his right arm extended toward the darkened heavens where an angel appears. The chapel replaced a smaller log church, built in 1851 with the assistance of Jenny Lind. In 1948, on the 100th anniversary of the congregation, about 3,000 people gathered at the church with Prince Bertil and the Archbishop of Sweden in attendance. The building is recognized as a historic shrine of the former Augustana Lutheran Synod. Many settlers who died of cholera or diphtheria in the early years are buried in the cemetery south and east of the chapel.

In 1944 the New Sweden congregation merged with the **First Augustana Lutheran Church of Lockridge**, 301 W. Main Street (319-696-3191), which now owns the New Sweden Chapel and Cemetery. Several summer services are held annually in the chapel. First Augustana features stepped gables and a striking embossed-tin ceiling.

In 1850 a theological dispute resulted in the organizing of the Swedish Methodist Church, the first in Iowa, by the Reverend Jonas Hedstrom, brother of Olof Gustaf Hedstrom, founder of Swedish Methodism in the United States. Jonas conducted an aggressive and successful campaign for members in New Sweden. The white clapboard **Methodist Church**, which replaced a log church built in 1871, stands one mile west of New Sweden Chapel on the Swedish Highway. Additions have been made to the structure, but the original pressed-metal ceiling remains in the sanctuary. In the cemetery east of the church are buried early pioneers, including Cassel and Danielson family members, many of whom converted to Methodism. A bronze tablet in the churchyard identifies "many of the first band of people of Swedish birth who settled west of the Mississippi River in 1845." There is also a plaque honoring the Reverend Peter Cassel and others who organized the church in 1850, the third Swedish Methodist Church in the United States.

The Swedish Baptist Cemetery, one-quarter mile east of New Sweden Chapel on the Swedish Highway, shared its location with the New Sweden Baptist Church, no longer extant. A plaque states that in 1854 this was the first house of worship in America organized by Swedish Baptists. However, the Swedish Baptist congregation in Rock Island, Illinois, asserts that it was founded in 1852. Gustaf and Inga Schillerstrom are two of the pioneers buried in this small cemetery, which commands a lovely view of the New Sweden Chapel.

Swedesburg

Eleven miles east of Lockridge and nine miles north on U.S. Highway 218 is Swedesburg, a tiny unincorporated community of barely one hundred people that includes five historic landmarks listed on the National Register of Historic Places. These include the **Swedesburg Historic Commercial District** (four buildings); the **Charles E. Hult House**; the **John Hultquist House**; **Swedesburg Evangelical Lutheran Church**; and the **Red Ball Garage**. Approaching the town, one is greeted by a large "Welcome to Swedesburg" sign featuring the Swedish flag, a large straw *julbok* (Christmas goat), and a *majstång* (maypole).

Swedes came to the area, then called Freeport, after Pastor Hakan Olson of the New Sweden Lutheran congregation visited in the 1860s. Although the land was swampy, Olson believed that Swedish settlers had the knowledge to drain and convert it into productive farmland, so he encouraged people from New Sweden and Biggsville, Illinois, to establish a colony. (They had originally come from three Swedish provinces, Blekinge, Östergötland, and Småland.) The first Swedish settlers, the S. P. Swenson family, arrived in 1864; by 1866 a congregation had organized as the Swedish Evangelical Lutheran Congregation of Freeport, Iowa, today called **Swedesburg Lutheran Church** (319-254-2216). The red-brick church, built in 1927, is the third sanctuary on the site. A large cemetery is adjacent.

In recent years the Swedish Heritage Society has purchased four buildings, including the former local co-op, the Bergh Tinsmith Shop and home, the Brown

Swedish American Museum, Swedesburg

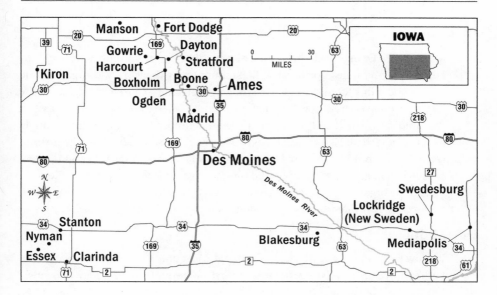

Shoe Company, and the S. L. White Grocery Store. With a Dala Horse prominently placed over the front door, the society opened the **Swedish American
Museum** (319-254-2317). Visitors may watch a video discussing early Swedish settlers in southeast Iowa, tour a reconstructed country store, and view a replica of a
nineteenth-century huckster wagon that local merchants used to take goods to
surrounding farms and trade for farm products. The upstairs two-room apartment of Charles Bergh, local tinsmith and emigrant from Sweden, has been
reconstructed. In an additional building is a Swedish *stuga*, painted in traditional
red and white colors.

The museum has received Iowa's Best Preservation Award. The Swedish Heri-
tage Society organizes several annual festivities, including Midsummer and Lucia
Fest. The venue for some of these activities is the Parish Hall, formerly a Female
Academy established by the Reverend Olson.

Mediapolis

Swedish immigrants near the southeastern Iowa community of Amityville founded
Immanuel Lutheran Church in 1868, and in 1872 they constructed the congregation's first building. As time passed, the Swedish population grew and shifted
from the country into Mediapolis. By 1892 so many members had moved from
Amityville that they built a new church in Mediapolis at 606 Orchard (319-394-
3600) in 1954. Eventually, the church in Amityville was closed, but its cemetery
is well maintained.

Blakesburg

Munterville Evangelical Lutheran Church, 23981 Eighty-seventh Street, on U.S. Highway 34 six miles northeast of Blakesburg (515-938-2870), was organized in 1856 by about fifty Swedes. In 1865 the congregation built a church and marked off a cemetery on five acres. At the turn of the century, when the congregation erected the building where it still worships, it used the lumber from the original church to construct Parish Hall (since moved). The congregation later added the memorial belfry from stones gathered from members' farms and hung the original 1866 church bell in it. Immediately behind the church are the family graves of the congregation's organizer, the Reverend Hokanson (1811–1893), who served from 1848 to 1856. This crowded cemetery contains many stones bearing Swedish names.

Des Moines

In November 1869 Pastor Hakan Olson, president of the Iowa Conference of the Lutheran Augustana Synod, organized First Lutheran Church, today known as **Capitol Hill Lutheran** (515-244-8913). The first small building, built in 1871 at E. First and Grand Avenue, was replaced by a red-brick structure completed in 1887 at 511 Des Moines Street and still used today. Capitol Hill Lutheran with its tall Gothic-style spire is on a rise several blocks from the Iowa State Capitol, and was built about the same time. Stone rejected for Capitol construction may have been used for the church's foundation walls. Many Swedes immigrating to Des Moines built houses near the church. The church sanctuary was remodeled in 1927, but few early furnishings were retained.

The Reverend A. P. Westerberg, a pastor in the early twentieth century, presented to the Iowa Conference of the Augustana Synod in the winter of 1909 a plan for creating the Iowa Lutheran Hospital. Construction began in 1913, and other facilities were added. In 1993 Iowa Lutheran Hospital, 700 E. University Avenue (515-263-5612), Iowa Methodist Medical Center, and Blank Children's Hospital merged to form **Iowa Health System**, the largest hospital in Iowa (www.ihsdesmoines.org).

Two works by Swedish American sculptors stand in Des Moines. Carl Milles's bronze sculpture *Pegasus and Bellerophon,* completed in 1949, complements a lovely reflecting pool in the central courtyard of the Des Moines Art Center, 4700 Grand Avenue (515-277-4405). Another *Pegasus* can be found in a park in Malmö, Sweden. *Crusoe Umbrella* (1979), a sculpture by Claes Oldenburg, is at Nolen Plaza between Locust and Walnut Streets, about a dozen blocks west of the Iowa State Capitol.

Madrid

The fascinating story of how Swedes arrived in central Iowa involves Anna Larsdotter Dalander (1792–1854), a widow who in 1846 led a party of forty-two immigrants who planned to join New Sweden in response to Peter Cassel's glowing reports. They followed the wrong river—the Des Moines rather than the Skunk—and arrived instead in Boone County. Dalander platted Swede Point, later renamed Madrid.

The **Carl and Ulrika Dalander Cassel House**, 415 W. Second Street, is believed to be the first frame residence here. Carl Cassel (1820–1902), son of New Sweden pioneer leader Peter Cassel, constructed the house in 1862. In 1848 Carl had married Anna Dalander's daughter, Ulrika, in what was probably the first Swedish marriage in Iowa. He was active in politics and a charter member of St. John's Lutheran Church in Madrid.

The Cassel House is made of native black walnut (now covered by vinyl siding). It combines elements of Greek Revival and Swedish vernacular architecture. According to National Register documentation, its Swedish architectural features include "broadside orientation, projecting eaves, and a medium pitched gable roof." The same report also noted that "Cassel reverted to the architectural traditions of his native land" when several years later he built a one-story addition to the west end of the house.

Carl and Ulrika Dalander Cassel House, Madrid

Inside the house is a central hall with doors at either end, a typical arrange-ment of rooms in early homes. Woodwork and flooring are original. Carl Cassel lived in this house, a private residence, for forty years until his death in 1902.

Cassel, Ulrika, and her mother are buried in the Dalander Cemetery, whose entrance is marked by a granite monument. To reach the cemetery, take North Street (State Highway 210) west three-fourths of a mile to County Road Qm. Go north toward Swede Point Park. After passing the park, the road becomes gravel. Go about one-half mile farther until you see a small board sign on the west side indicating the cemetery.

The Greek Revival brick sanctuary of **St. John's Lutheran Church** at 414 W. First Street dates from 1924, but the congregation was organized by the Reverend Magnus Fredrik Hokanson in 1859, as noted on the cornerstone. Inside the sanctu-ary is an altar painting (1899) of the Crucifixion by Olof Grafström. This painting and the church's two large stained-glass windows hung in the former church.

The Iowa Lutheran Home, planned in 1904 and dedicated four years later, was destroyed by fire in 1948. A new building was completed in 1950, and additions have been made. Now known as the **Madrid Home**, 613 W. North Street (515-795-3007), the interdenominational center serves the elderly in a facility still having some Swedish tone.

Originally called Swede Point, the town was renamed Madrid in 1882. The only location in the area still retaining the name Swede Point is Swede Point Park, above the Des Moines River a short distance from the Dalander Cemetery.

The **Madrid Historical Museum** attracts visitors at 109 W. Second Street (515-795-2287; www.madridiowa.com/history.html). Within a block, near the library, are a doll museum and a replica of a coal mine, a remembrance of the industry that brought many to the region.

Boone

Boone hosts landmarks for two residents, Swedish descendant Mamie Doud Eisenhower (1896–1979), born in Boone and wife of the thirty-third president of the United States, and Charles John Alfred Ericson (1840–1910), a Swede who became a successful Boone businessman and Iowa state senator. At the **Mamie Doud Eisenhower Birthplace**, 709 Carroll (515-432-1896; www.mamiesbirthplace .com), visitors can tour Mamie Eisenhower's paternal grandparents' home. She was baptized in 1896 in the Evangelical Free Church (not extant). Her maternal grandparents, Carl and Marie Carlson, were both born in Sweden. Carl was the head miller at Boone's Reed Flour Mill, and his brother Joel was vice president of a Boone bank and active in the Evangelical Free Church. Mamie Eisenhower lived just nine months in the house before moving to Cedar Rapids and then to Denver.

The **Charles J. A. Ericson Memorial Public Library**, 703 Greene Street at Seventh (515-432-3727), was built by Ericson in 1901. Born in Vimmerby, Småland, he was president of the City Bank of Boone, which he helped found in 1872, a six-term state senator, and a benefactor of Augustana College in Rock Island, Illinois.

Boone is the home of the mother congregation of the Swedish **Evangelical Free Church**, founded in 1884. Though the building dates only to 1971, the 1900 cornerstone of the old church rests in the lobby at 1407 Kate Shelley Drive (515-432-7690). **The Evangelical Free Church Home** (515-432-1393), begun in 1912 as *Frikyrkans Ålderdoms Hem* (The Free Church's Home for Old People), at 112 W. Fourth, is a newer building, but its original cornerstone, inscribed in Swedish, is in a back stairwell.

The Lutheran congregation in Boone, **Augustana Lutheran Church** at 309 S. Greene (515-432-5910), was founded in 1877. Housed in a modern building, the congregation now displays its Olof Grafström altar painting of Christ as the Good Shepherd in the Fellowship Hall.

Ogden

The mother Lutheran congregation in the Boone area is **Swede Valley Lutheran Church**, organized in 1868 (515-275-2164), located five miles south of Ogden on U.S. Highway 169. The white-frame, Gothic-style church and steeple, the congregation's second church, consecrated in 1882, is picturesquely sited on a wooded knoll with a well-maintained adjacent cemetery. The church features a large altar painting depicting Christ in Gethsemane by an unidentified artist. An impressive pipe organ was dedicated in 1921. The beautiful curved white altar rail, altar, pulpit, baptismal font, and wainscoting are original. Old pews are in the balcony. Outside the main entrance is a memorial to the Reverend A. W. Edwins (1871–1942), founder of the Augustana Lutheran Mission to China, whose stone reads, "Buried at Sea."

In 1996 the Swede Valley congregation merged with **Immanuel Lutheran Church**, 119 SW Second Street, Ogden (515-275-2164), a daughter church organized in 1914. The former Mission Covenant Church in Ogden at 120 SE Third Street, built in 1882 and rebuilt in 1914, is now a private residence.

Boxholm

Boxholm is named for the Swedish village in Östergötland, birthplace of its first postmaster, John B. Anderson. Visitors are greeted by a large sign announcing "The Home of the Swedes," a reference to the high-school teams.

Twenty-one men and women organized **Trinity Lutheran Church** in 1886, and in 1888 the congregation built a church in the country. In 1911 the sanctuary was moved to its present location at 502 Second Street (515-846-6277). Services were conducted in Swedish until 1924.

Swedish Methodists built the **Boxholm United Methodist Church**, 303 Third Street (515-846-6350), in 1886 three-quarters of a mile southeast of town but moved it to town at the turn of the century. Swedish and German groups eventually merged, forming the present congregation.

Early Swedish settlers are buried in Lawn Cemetery near Boxholm.

Stratford

Stratford is on the eastern edge of the largest (in area) Swedish settlement in Iowa, including the towns of Dayton, Harcourt, Lanyon, Boxholm, and Pilot Mound.

John Linn, born in Småland in 1826, immigrated at age twenty-three to Swede Point, now Madrid, Iowa. He and his wife continued up the Des Moines River to a location southwest of Stratford called Swede Bend, the third-oldest Swedish settlement in Iowa. Soon other Swedes arrived, coming along the bottomland of the Des Moines River with teams of oxen.

The 24 by 26 foot **John Linn House**, built in the 1850s, is made of trough-grooved logs. A staircase leads from the four-room first floor to the second floor, with its low sloping ceiling. The Linn House was moved in 1983 to Bellville Road two blocks north of State Highway 175 and Tennyson Avenue. (The unused house is presently in danger of being vandalized.)

After Linn converted to Methodism, he preached and organized churches, including the **South Marion Methodist Church**, founded in 1854, which is the second Swedish Methodist congregation in Iowa. In 1861 the first sanctuary was built in Swede Bend. This building was later sold to the Mission Church (the Mission Covenant had its beginnings in 1868 in Swede Bend). Eventually the building was moved to Twin Lakes Bible Camp in Manson, Iowa. At the first sanctuary's original site, a marker identifies the spot as the birthplace of the Evangelical Covenant Church of America, organized by Carl August Björk. To reach the marker, go west from Stratford on State Highway 175 for three miles. Turn south on a gravel road identified as S. River Road for one and one-half miles to County Road 21 (gravel road), also identified as 390 Street. The marker is just east of this intersection on County Road 21.

In 1877, Methodists dedicated the **South Marion Methodist** sanctuary, 1392-390th Street (515-838-2325), three and one-half miles east of the former one. The white-clapboard structure with a high steeple was saved from a 1936 windstorm, though altered. In the South Marion Cemetery is John Linn's grave. To reach the cemetery, go east on County Road 21 for two miles to its intersection with Fenton Avenue, also identified as Hamilton County R27. Turn north for half a mile; the old section of the cemetery is on the west side.

In 1859, with forty charter members, Pastor Magnus Fredrik Hokanson organized the **Stratford Lutheran Church**. In 1893 a white-clapboard church was completed at 824 Teneyck Avenue. The church has a tall, picturesque, Gothic-style steeple (515-838-2251). The sanctuary features a pressed-tin ceiling and an altar painting of Christ in Gethsemane by Norwegian American artist Arnold Klagstad (1898–1954). A Baptist congregation was also organized in 1856 in Swede Bend, but in 1979 the congregation relocated to the town of Stratford and the former building was torn down.

Downtown Stratford features the former **State Bank of Stratford**, founded by Swedish Americans, at 801 Shakespeare. The building, designed by architects Boyd and Herbert Moore, was constructed in 1917. It currently houses a publishing company and apartments. Many architectural details have been preserved, including the original wrought-iron spiral staircase, woodwork, tile floor, and vault.

Across Shakespeare Street is Stratford's small **Swedish Immigrant Museum**. It is housed in the old co-op gas station built in the 1920s.

Dayton

On Main Street is the former **Opera House**, a two-story, light-color brick structure. The bottom floor has been badly damaged by poor renovations, but the top floor retains interesting architectural detail, especially the Romanesque arches over the windows. The word "Opera" is still visible on the front pediment. **Emanuel Lutheran**, 208 NW Second Avenue (515-547-2405), was organized in 1868. The northwest corner of the town cemetery on State Highway 175 contains the oldest graves, many with Swedish names.

Harcourt

Settlers organized and built the Mission Covenant Church in 1888. Today the white-clapboard building is identified as the **United Evangelical Covenant Church** on E. Second and Wood Streets (515-354-5214). Three years later, Lutherans organized **Faith Lutheran**, at 113 N. Ash Street (515-354-5224), and constructed its white-frame building. The altar painting of Jesus the Good Shepherd (1912) is by Olof Grafström.

Gowrie

Zion Evangelical Lutheran, 1003 Church Street (515-352-3645), was organized in 1871. The congregation now meets in a large dark-brick, Gothic-style structure built in 1931.

Twin Lakes Christian Center, Manson

Fort Dodge

Swedes helped settle Fort Dodge, and a section of the city was known as Swede-town. Leif Ericson Park honors this well-known Scandinavian.

Manson

The Twin Lakes Bible Camp in Manson, now known as **Twin Lakes Christian Center**, 2524 W. Twin Lakes Road (712-297-7714), preserves in its compound the first Mission (Friends) Covenant Church in the United States. Organized on July 4, 1868, at Swede Bend, the congregation was led by Carl August Svenson Björk (1837–1916), a native of Lommaryd, Småland. Greatly influenced by the *läsare* (readers or pietist) movement, Björk left Sweden in 1864 to join his brother in Swede Bend. When the local Lutheran church split, Björk persuaded a group meeting in the home of Peter Englund to form the first Mission Covenant congregation. Built by Methodists in 1861 and sold to Björk and his group in 1874, the structure served the Swede Bend Covenant congregation until it was relocated to Manson in 1976.

Kiron

In west central Iowa's Crawford County, the first Swedish settlers arrived in 1867 and a year later organized the Swedish Baptist Church. In 1875 the present **Bethel Lutheran** congregation was organized with twenty-five members. In 1995 a

Swedish bell tower was dedicated on the grounds of the Bethel Lutheran Church, replacing one destroyed when lightning struck the former Bethel Church in 1961. It is a smaller version of the bell tower at the University of Uppsala in Sweden. Next to the structure is a granite marker with an inscription in Swedish and English noting that "this Swedish bell tower is dedicated to all Swedish immigrants who founded this community and brought with them the faith of their fathers."

Stanton

Stanton, sixty miles southeast of Omaha, Nebraska, retains the atmosphere of a Swedish settlement. Some business district signs are written in Swedish, buildings have Swedish décor, and the water tower is shaped and painted like a Swedish coffee pot (*see photo, page 2*). A southwest Iowa landmark, the coffee pot was created in the 1970s at a time when millions of American television viewers watched actress Virginia Christine, known as Mrs. Olson, endorse Folger's coffee with a comforting, respect-inspiring Swedish accent. Christine, whose real name was Virginia Rickett Kraft Feld, was born in Stanton and lived at 307 Hilltop. In 2000, a second water tower, this time in the form of a coffee cup and saucer, was completed on Highland and Hilltop. The tower holds 150,000 gallons, enough to make 2.4 million cups of coffee!

Stanton, known as the Halland Settlement, was established by Pastor Bengt Magnus Halland (born Johansson; 1837–1902), who arrived in Illinois in 1856 and was ordained eight years later. Early in 1869, he became convinced of the suitability of southwest Iowa for colonization. A land agent for the Burlington Railroad, Halland advertised for "non-drinking" and "God-fearing Swedes." Immigrants from Sweden, as well as from Andover, Illinois, flocked to the area and bought land at six to eleven dollars per acre. In 1870, Halland organized three Lutheran congregations: Fremont in Nyman on May 19, Mamrelund in Stanton on May 25, and Bethesda in Clarinda on December 26. Later Halland established Bethlehem Lutheran in Red Oak (1872), St. John's Lutheran in Essex (1876), and Tabor Lutheran in Wallin (1894), as well as the Iowa Lutheran Children's Home (1881). Nothing remains of the latter institution except a barn and marker one-half mile south of Stanton on County Road M63. From 1881 to 1938, the home sheltered more than four hundred children. According to the plaque, the children's home was "one of the first providers of social services for the Lutheran Church in the state and is the root of the continuing ministry of Lutheran Social Service of Iowa."

Mamrelund Lutheran Church—410 Eastern Avenue (712-829-2422).

This large, impressive stone building stands at the center of the "Little White City," a nickname reflecting the fact that many houses in Stanton are painted white. The congregation began with a small sanctuary in 1870, and thirteen years later, the "First Big White Church" was erected. In 1938 the building was struck by lightning; only the bell and four church record books were saved from the fire. The new, white Indiana-stone edifice, dedicated in 1941, is crowned with a towering spire visible from the town's outskirts. Its sanctuary features symbolic stained-glass windows, lovely woodwork on the ceiling, balcony, and pews, and a Gothic-style altar. In a room near the sanctuary is an altar with the scripture from Psalms 29:2: *Tillbedjen Herren i helig prydnad* (Worship the Lord in the beauty of holiness). The same inscription was over the main altar in the church that burned in 1938. Nearby is a picture of Halland, who, along with other early Swedes, is buried in Stanton cemetery, which is near the water tower, at the end of Frankfurt. His house, privately owned, stands at 717 Thorn Street near the cemetery.

Stanton Swedish Heritage and Cultural Center—410 Hilltop (712-829-2840; www.stantoniowa.com).

When Stanton's school closed in 1992, the Swedish Heritage Society bought the building for a museum. Near the door leading into the museum is a chain-saw sculpture of two emigrants, Karl Oskar and Kristina Nilsson, a replica of the bronze statue in Lindstrom, Minnesota.

A visit to this museum begins with a short video. The Halland Room on the first floor tells the history of the Halland settlement prior to World War I. Exhibits include a model of the Albert Lantz farmhouse south of Stanton, built around 1890, and a circa-1900 loom owned by Olof Malmberg, who emigrated from Sweden. A library features yearly scrapbooks documenting the town's history and a center for local genealogical studies. Another room continues the history of Stanton after World War I and serves as a social room. Across the hall is a room named for Alf Martin Kirkeberg (1902–1995), who was the son of Norwegian immigrants who began Future Farmers of America in southeastern Iowa. He was also instrumental in helping farmers develop contour farming techniques to prevent soil erosion.

At the top of the staircase is a rare 1890 wooden windmill from the farm of J. P. Larson and a sleigh. Also on the second floor is a banking exhibit featuring furnishings from the Essex bank, owned and operated by the Liljedahl family from 1901 to 1995.

Also on the museum grounds is a one-room country school from neighboring Page County. As a result of an Iowa legislative initiative to preserve country schools, the building was moved to Stanton in 1971. The school contains some furnishings original to the building, including the recitation bench.

In fostering its role as the cultural center of the community, the museum sponsors *Svenska Skolan* in June, during which the Swedish language and culture are

Swedish Heritage Center, Stanton

taught to children. Other activities include a community sing at the end of April, a Midsummer festival, a lutfisk supper the week before Thanksgiving, and Lucia Fest.

Tabor Lutheran Church—1711 Q Avenue (712-829-2324).
Seven miles northeast of Stanton is Tabor Lutheran Church, a white-frame structure with an 1898 cornerstone. The 1908 altar painting is by Olof Grafström. To reach

the church, drive north on County Road M63 to gravel road H34. Go east on H34 to Q Avenue. A sign here directs visitors to the church.

Nyman

The congregation of **Fremont Lutheran Church**, 1147 Ironwood Avenue (712-379-3407), was the first of three organized by the Reverend Bengt Magnus Halland in 1870. The first sanctuary, which also served as a parsonage, was built the following year. The site was approximately one-half mile north of the present church, and a cemetery, with remnants remaining, was established nearby. The old church later became part of a farmhouse and is north of the present parsonage. Between 1875 and 1880, the congregation erected a new sanctuary. On January 1, 1902, the building burned to the ground, but before the year was over, the new white-frame, Gothic-style sanctuary had been completed. Its 1902 altar painting is by Olof Grafström.

Essex

The **Faith Evangelical Covenant** (712-379-3382) congregation worships in a clapboard structure at 212 Alice Street, built in 1926. It was the sanctuary of the Fremont Evangelical Covenant Church (originally Svenska Lutherska Missionsföreningen, chartered in 1876) until the two congregations were consolidated in 1991.

Clarinda

Bethesda Lutheran Church, 2479-140th Street (712-586-4589), built in 1877, remains the oldest Swedish church sanctuary in southwestern Iowa. Remodeled in 1928, the white-frame structure is topped by a central steeple.

Lansing

In the extreme northeastern corner of Iowa is **Village Creek Center Baptist Church**, established in 1853. The congregation claims to be the second-oldest Swedish Baptist Church in America and the oldest continuing existing congregation in the Baptist General Conference. This church is ten miles northwest of Lansing. To reach it, take Great River Road, also identified as County Road X52, west out of Lansing for three miles. At County Road X42 (Lansing-Harpers) a church sign directs the visitor to turn north for six miles.

In 1849 Eric Sandman was sent from Sweden to Iowa to help immigrants, and four years later believers met in his home to organize the Village Creek Swedish Baptist Church. Also in his home were held discussions resulting in the founding of the Swedish Baptist Conference in 1879. Remnants of his house can be seen three-tenths of a mile west of the present church building.

The small congregation purchased a log cabin in 1857. At the 1864 annual meeting at Village Creek, the Iowa and Illinois churches formed the Illinois-Iowa Conference. In 1867 the second church was constructed, and the current structure was erected in 1911 at a cost of $7,000.

The present church is a white-clapboard Gothic-style structure with a short tower. The sanctuary features the folding pews from the second church and some original wall stenciling. Two large, floral-designed, stained-glass windows were given by the Ladies Aid Society. The cornerstone reads, "1st Swedish Baptist Church 1853–1911." Behind the church is the cemetery, which includes the graves of Henry and Gunhild Wingblade; he was a president of Bethel College (now University), St. Paul, Minnesota.

Near the church on County Road X42 is the former Seventh Day Adventist Church formed by a group that left the Baptist Church. The cemetery contains many Swedish graves.

MISSOURI

Relatively few Swedes were drawn to Missouri, principally because the state was already well populated when the Swedish immigration was in full swing. By 1930 more than one-third of Missouri's Swedes were living in Kansas City. Bucklin, in north-central Missouri, became a Swedish rural settlement. Other Swedes clustered in St. Louis and in southwest Missouri, particularly near Verona in Lawrence County. This settlement drew enough Swedes to organize a Swedish Methodist Church. Swedish Baptists formed churches in several Missouri communities, including Swedeborg in Pulaski County.

St. Louis

Two Carl Milles fountains grace public spaces in St. Louis. In Aloe Plaza is *Meeting of the Waters,* also known as *Wedding of the Rivers,* Milles's first monumental fountain designed for an American city. (Aloe Plaza is opposite Union Station on the north side of Market Street between Eighteenth and Twentieth Streets.) The Mississippi River is symbolized by a twelve-foot male figure riding a dolphin escorted by four tritons. He is meeting his bride, the Missouri River, attended by four sea nymphs. The plaza and fountain were dedicated in 1940. In Laumeier Sculpture Park, 12580 Rott Road (314-821-1209), is Milles's sculpture *Folke Filbyter,* an equestrian statue that is a replica of one standing in the central square in Linköping, Östergötland.

The oldest greenhouse west of the Allegheny Mountains is the **Linnean House** in the **Missouri Botanical Garden**, 4344 Shaw Boulevard (314-577-9400; 800-642-8862; www.mobot.org). Honoring Swedish botanist Carolus Linnaeus (Carl

Linnean House, Missouri Botanical Garden, St. Louis

von Linné; 1707–1778), the Linnean House was completed in 1882, the work of Henry Shaw, the garden's founder. Because he could see the Linnean House from his home, he made it the most ornate of the garden's three greenhouses. Three busts grace the main entrance; the central one is Linnaeus, flanked by two nineteenth-century American botanists, Thomas Nuttall and Asa Gray.

Shaw originally built the Linnean House as an orangery, but it has had several different uses. After a 1977 restoration, funded in part by the Swedish Council of St. Louis, the house is now the dramatic setting for the garden's camellia collections. Sculptor Paul Granlund is represented with his sculpture *Zerogee*. The Missouri Botanical Garden's library (314-577-5155) has a collection of rare books containing nearly every edition and translation of Linnaeus's writings, as well as works by his students and colleagues. The botanical garden also features the Milles Sculpture Garden, which includes *Two Girls Dancing* (1917), *Sun Glitter* (1918), *Orpheus Fountain Figures* (1936), and *Angel Musicians* (1949–1950).

Aviator and Swedish American Charles A. Lindbergh Jr. (1902–1974), who piloted the first nonstop transatlantic flight from New York to Paris, is honored at the Jefferson Memorial in Forest Park. A bust of Lindbergh dated 1939 is inscribed, "In flying, I tasted a wine of the gods." Lindbergh contributed items from his flight to the Missouri Historical Society (314-746-4599) in appreciation for the support from St. Louis citizens who helped organize the construction and flights of the *Spirit of St. Louis*. A main artery west of the city is named Lindbergh Boulevard.

Other St. Louis Swedish landmarks include the former **Swedish National Society Building** at 1157 Kings Highway Boulevard and the **Gethsemane Lutheran Church**, which was founded in 1894 by Swedish nail makers. The church's sanctuary, built in 1961, stands at 3600 Hampton Avenue (314-352-8050).

Kansas City, Missouri, and Kansas City, Kansas

Kansas City, Missouri, has the distinction of owning Carl Milles's last work, *St. Martin of Tours*, which is in the William Volker Memorial Fountain outside the Nelson-Atkins Museum of Art, 4525 Oak Street (816-751-1278; www.nelson-atkins .org). The fountain was completed eight months before Milles died in Stockholm in 1955. It portrays St. Martin of Tours sharing his cloak with a beggar. Also on the grounds of the Nelson-Atkins Museum is Claes Oldenburg's *Shuttlecocks*, installed in 1994.

Founded in 1906 by Swedish Lutherans, **Trinity Lutheran Hospital** at Thirty-first and Wyandotte was originally called Swedish Hospital. In 1915 it was moved to its current location, the highest point in Kansas City. The hospital merged with the Salem Lutheran Home for the Aged, also begun by Swedish Lutherans. A marker on Wyandotte honors the area's Scandinavian pioneers.

Three Lutheran churches are notable. **First Lutheran Church**, 6400 State Line Road in Mission Hills (913-362-4150), is the mother Swedish Lutheran congregation in Kansas City. This is its fourth location after moving from 416 W. Fifteenth Street to 1238 Pennsylvania Street to Thirtieth and Benton. The present impressive church building includes a memorial chapel containing an altar painting by Olof Grafström.

A daughter congregation, **Immanuel Lutheran**, 1700 Westport Road (816-931-8483; www.immanuelkc.org), was organized in 1899. Its original members worked mainly for the railroads and meat-packing companies. In former times, Swedes assembled their wagons on Westport Road before moving on to points west. The red-brick building still in use dates from the 1920s. Another daughter congregation of First Lutheran is **Messiah Lutheran**, founded in 1894. Its building at Grandview Boulevard and Twelfth Street was built in 1914.

Other buildings of interest to Swedish Americans include the Kansas City Power and Light Building, the U.S. Federal Courts Building, and the City Hall, at 701 N. Seventh. These three are among many built by a company owned by Godfrey G. Swenson (1876–1946), a successful city building contractor born in Vimmerby, Småland.

Bucklin

This community's history is intertwined with Olof Olsson (1841–1900), who left Värmland for central Kansas in 1869 with approximately 250 parishioners, friends, and other fellow believers. When the second group of Olsson's party arrived in Chicago, N. S. Ornsdorf, a Swede who had already settled in Bucklin, persuaded 103 of them to come to Missouri to make some money before starting out for central Kansas. They decided to stay permanently and purchased land north and south of Bucklin.

In 1870 settlers organized a Swedish Lutheran congregation. Of the thirty-three charter members, all but three were from Värmland. By 1875 the congregation peaked at 195 members. In that year, a Swedish farmer donated an acre of land nine miles north of Bucklin, where a church was built. In 1880 discontent in the church caused a split and the founding of a Swedish Covenant Church, known as Mission Covenant Church, about three miles south of the Lutheran church (now also called North Swede Church).

The little white-frame Lutheran church north of Bucklin has not been altered significantly since it was built. It has its original walnut altar rail and flooring. A cemetery association maintains the church as well as the adjacent cemetery, and some gravestones have Swedish inscriptions. By 1927 Lutheran services were discontinued. Mission Covenant Church, also called South Swede Church, is a small white-clapboard building with a short steeple. Its congregation also eventually dwindled, and the last services were held in the early 1950s. Once a year the churches are open for special services.

In the vicinity of Bucklin, visitors may see old farmhouses built by the early Swedish settlers.

Swedeborg

Largely settled by Swedes in the last three decades of the nineteenth century, Swedeborg, originally called Woodend, grew up with the railroad interests. The 1890 log school south of town, the school that replaced it in 1891, and early church buildings have given way to twentieth-century facilities. Two cemeteries, St. John's (Swede) Cemetery, on Pulaski County Road BB about one mile off State Road 133 west and north of Swedeborg, and the Bethlehem Cemetery, about three and one-half miles south of Swedeborg, hold many gravestones with Swedish names.

OKLAHOMA

Norman

 Oscar Brousse Jacobson House—609 Chautauqua Avenue (405-366-1667; www.jacobsonhouse.com).
This house was constructed in 1916–1917 by artist Oscar Brousse Jacobson and his wife, Jeanne. It sits on the northwest corner of the campus of the University of

Oklahoma and serves as the Jacobson Native Art Center, operated by the Jacobson Foundation.

Jacobson (1882–1966), born in Västervik, emigrated to the United States with his family at a young age and lived on a farm outside of Lindsborg, Kansas. He studied art under Birger Sandzén at Bethany College and went on to earn a Master of Fine Arts at Yale University. In 1915 he became the director of the Art Department at the University of Oklahoma. For the next two decades he brought in numerous artists who enhanced the school's reputation. Early on, Jacobson recognized Native American art as fine art, and he encouraged Native American artists to come to the University of Oklahoma and study formally. A group known as "the Kiowa Five" gained national and international fame. He also was influential in encouraging Native American artists in New Mexico.

Jacobson was an instrumental figure in the founding of the Oklahoma City Arts Center, and the old library at the University of Oklahoma is identified as Jacobson Hall in his honor. As a young man he traveled in the American West and became enamored of its landscapes, which can be seen in his paintings found at the Oklahoma City Art Museum, the University of Oklahoma Museum of Art, the Mabee-Gerrer Museum of Art, and the St. Gregory Abbey and College, Shawnee, Oklahoma.

KANSAS

In 1855, John A. Johnson from Horn Parish in southern Östergötland moved to Kansas. Making his home on the eastern shore of Big Blue River twenty miles north of Manhattan, he became the first Swede to settle in the state. Eight years later, he organized the Mariadahl church, the oldest Swedish Lutheran congregation west of the Missouri River.

During the 1850s and 1860s, other Swedish settlements were established at Axtell in northeast Kansas, and at Clay Center, Lawrence, Enterprise, and the Scandia area in Republic County in north-central Kansas. But the largest was in the Smoky Hill River Valley of central Kansas, centering around Lindsborg. The first Swede probably arrived in the valley in 1864, and two years later seventeen additional Swedes homesteaded. In 1868, two independently organized Swedish groups in Illinois initiated efforts to promote immigration to the Smoky Hill River Valley, the Swedish Agricultural Company of McPherson County in Chicago and the Galesburg Colonization Company in Galesburg. Affiliated with the Chicago organization, Pastor Olof Olsson (1841–1900) of Sunnemo, Värmland, brought a group of more than one hundred Lutheran men, women, and children in 1869. The Galesburg Company bought more than 38,000 acres of land and settled more than 200 families in the valley during 1869. Among this number were settlers led by Pastor A. W. Dahlsten (1839–1919).

Lindsborg was the last of the Swedish religious settlements in the United States. In 1879 the twenty-one-year-old Reverend Carl Aaron Swensson (1857–1904) arrived in Lindsborg as pastor of Bethany Lutheran Church. He founded Bethany College in 1881. Although the majority of people in the Lindsborg area have ancestors in Värmland, other provinces are represented, as demonstrated by the names of neighboring communities such as Falun and Smolan. The region known locally as the Smoky Hill River Valley includes an area bordered on the north by Salina, on the east by Roxbury, on the south by McPherson, and on the west by Marquette.

Lindsborg

Of the more than 3,000 inhabitants of Lindsborg, about two-thirds claim Swedish ancestry. The town prides itself on being "Little Sweden, U.S.A." Adopting the Dala horse as its symbol, Lindsborg uses it on lampposts and city vehicles. Throughout the town are more than thirty "Wild Dalas," fiberglass horses. Each is decorated by a Lindsborg artist. Many residents display Dala horses on their porches, and some businesses advertise in Swedish. In Main Street's Bank of America are Dalecarlian-style paintings by Lindsborg artists, including Rita Sharpe and her husband, the late Robert Walker. Paintings by Birger Sandzén, Maleta Forsberg, Lester Raymer, and others, bronze sculpture by Frank Reese, and wood sculpture by Anton Pearson may also be seen. The Lindsborg Community Library (Bibliotek) at 111 S. Main includes a heritage room with Scandinavian-motif furnishings and books in both Swedish and English.

Downtown has a Scandinavian air about it, and shops feature Swedish gifts, food, books, and maps, including several stores on N. Main: Anderson Butik, Clogs & Such, Courtyard Bakery & Kafe, Hemslöjd, Irene's Teas, Swedish Crafts, Swedish Crown Restaurant and Vasa Club, and Swedish Pastries and Emporium.

The historic J. D. Sundstrom Building, constructed in 1879 on Main at Lincoln Street, has a mural entitled *Our Founders in Architectural Heaven,* executed by artist Eldon Swensson in 2001, depicting early buildings of Lindsborg and celebrating early Swedish families. A detailed description of Lindsborg artists is on an adjacent plaque.

Among the town's distinctly Swedish traditional events are a Lucia Fest; Midsummer Festival; and its own tribute to Swedish pioneers, the biennial *Svensk Hyllningsfest* (Swedish Homage Festival), held in conjunction with the Bethany College homecoming. Celebrated mid-October in odd numbered years, *Svensk Hyllningsfest* has since 1941 paid tribute to the Swedes who came so far to settle this town in the Kansas heartland. On the third Saturday of June, *Midsommardag*

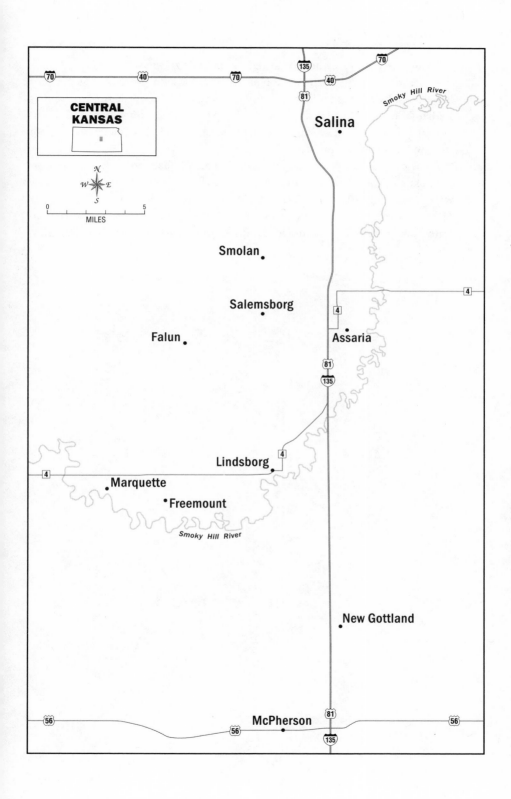

(Midsummer) activities include a traditional Swedish *majstång* (maypole) raising in front of the Swedish pavilion at Old Mill Museum Heritage Square. This is followed by Swedish folk music and dancing and a Swedish smörgåsbord at Bethany College. The next day a Swedish vesper service is conducted. Both Bethany Lutheran and Evangelical Covenant Churches still hold a *julotta* service, but they no longer are conducted in Swedish.

Lindsborg is famous for its art studios, which house more than thirty resident artists. The Chamber of Commerce, 104 E. Lincoln Street (888-227-2227; www.lindsborg.org), offers a complete list. In addition to Bethany College faculty member Birger Sandzén (1871–1954), many other gifted artists have worked in Lindsborg, attracted by the supportive community. Included are Olof Grafström

"Wild Dala," Lindsborg

(1855–1933), Carl G. Lotave (1872–1924), and Margaret Sandzén Greenough (1909–1993). Others who have taught at Bethany are Lester W. Raymer, Annie Lee Ross, Charles B. Rogers, John Basher, Rosemary Laughlin, Carl W. Peterson, and Raymond Kathmeyer. The Red Barn, at 212 S. Main (785-227-2217; www .redbarnstudio.org), is the studio of the late Lester Raymer, known for his fabrics, carvings, metalsmithing, and painting.

Oscar Brousse Jacobson (see Oklahoma) studied art at Bethany College. Gustav Nathanael Malm (1869–1928) assisted with many town and gown projects, including the Bethany Oratorio Society. Malm's daughter, Alba Malm Almquist, is noted for oil and watercolor landscapes. Other artists include Signe Larson (religious paintings), Oscar Gunnarson (landscapes), Maleta Forsberg, and Robert Walker (Swedish Dalarna peasant motifs). Lindsborg's reputation is enhanced by the oldest continuously performed Handel's *Messiah* in the United States (since 1882) during Easter week and Bach's *St. Matthew's Passion* (since 1925), both performed in Bethany College's Presser Hall.

Museums

McPherson County Old Mill Museum and Park—120 Mill Street
(785-277-3595; www.oldmillmuseum.org).

The history-rich McPherson County Old Mill Museum and Park comprises two parts: an open-air museum and the old mill, museum, and log cabin. The structures in the open-air museum grouped around Heritage Square include the **Swedish Pavilion**, the first classroom building of Bethany College, a former Lindsborg railway station, the first McPherson County above-ground structure, the workshop of the Erickson brothers, an old school, and storefronts. (The Swedish Pavilion and Old Mill are on the National Register of Historic Places.)

Designed by Ferdinand Boberg (1860–1946) and built in Sweden, the Pavilion is a reproduction of a Swedish manor house, containing a large main room and two wings. Workers reassembled it in St. Louis for the 1904 Louisiana Purchase Exposition. Afterward, William W. Thomas Jr., the American minister to Sweden and Norway, purchased and donated it to Bethany College, where it originally served as an art exhibition hall and museum. In 1969 it was moved and renovated. It was rededicated in 1976 by King Carl XVI Gustaf. Inside are historic exhibits.

Bethany College's first classroom building (Academy Building), built in 1879, now houses a library, including many Swedish Bibles and other books written in Swedish, and numerous items from the college's history.

The Union Pacific Depot, built in 1880, served as a stopping place on the line between Salina on the north and McPherson on the south. In 1975 the station was moved to the park. Nearby is a Santa Fe engine, built in 1900, one of only about four dozen steam engines of its kind on display in the United States.

Swedish Pavilion, McPherson County Old Mill Museum and Park, Lindsborg

The first above-ground building in McPherson County was erected in 1869 in Sweadal, a former community near Lindsborg, from lumber hauled from Leavenworth, Kansas. It served the local residents as the post office under the supervision of Major L. N. Holmberg, postmaster. In 1870 citizens met in this building to form McPherson County and hold the first county election. In 1872 the county seat was moved to Lindsborg.

The Erickson brothers' workshop belonged to John and Charles Erickson, pioneer developers of automatic telephone systems. Their father, Anders Erickson, who had emigrated from Värmland in 1869, was a mechanic, blacksmith, and fine metal and wood craftsman. Finding his sons also similarly gifted, he set up this cabin as a shop for them next to his own. Here the brothers worked on a variety of projects, including a horseless carriage and a player piano. It was in this small building that they invented the first workable dial telephone in 1895. John Erickson was credited with 115 patents, and Charles had 35.

The West Kentuck School, used from 1903 to 1952, belonged to the school district, organized in 1874. The first class met in a sod house, and it was not until six years later that the first frame building was constructed. A livery stable and a farm implements display are part of a recreated example of pioneer storefronts.

The Smoky Valley Roller Mill, constructed in 1898, is the second mill built for the community on the Smoky Hill River, and its nineteenth-century machinery is in excellent condition. Thousands of artifacts pertaining to natural and pioneer history, Native Americans, and Swedish heritage fill the rustic Old Mill Museum, including woodcarvings by artist Anton Pearson, cement sculpture by Oscar Gunnarson, and a chiffonier by early farmer Andrew Rosander. A painting of the Swedes landing in Germany during the Thirty Years' War is the work of Olof Grafström. Johan August Udden's Native American collection and the Bethany College natural history collection are also on display. A Swedish *stuga,* Swedish folk costumes, and a corner fireplace bespeak other Scandinavian contributions.

A cottonwood-log cabin, built by August Olson about 1870, was erected over a dugout and later became part of a six-room house. Originally southwest of Lindsborg, the cabin was moved to its current site. Interior furnishings are from pioneer days.

Birger Sandzén Memorial Gallery—adjacent to the Bethany College campus, 401 N. First Street (785-227-2220; www.sandzen.org).
This gallery houses the works of Birger Sandzén (1871–1954), Lindsborg artist and Bethany College professor. Sandzén was born in Västergötland, the son of a pastor. He attended Lund University and studied for two years with noted Swedish artist Anders Zorn before going to Paris. Sandzén joined the faculty at Bethany in 1894, and for almost six decades he gave voice lessons, sang tenor solos at *Messiah* performances, and taught French, German, architecture, and sculpture. He lived at 421 N. Second Street, where he also had a studio. The property is now a Bethany guest house. His studio can be seen behind the main house. In 1940 Sandzén received the Knight of the Royal Order of the North Star from King Gustav V.

Sandzén's love for the natural wonders of western Kansas and the mountains of Colorado is apparent in his oil landscapes and watercolors. Although this is the largest Sandzén collection, his works may also be found in churches and national and international museums, including the Nelson-Atkins Museum of Art in Kansas City, Art Institute of Chicago, Corcoran Gallery in Washington, D.C., Minneapolis Institute of Arts, Denver Art Museum, American Swedish Institute in Minneapolis, and American Swedish Historical Museum in Philadelphia. Bethany College also has many of his works.

In the gallery's outer courtyard is Carl Milles's *Little Triton,* the sculptor's only major public work in Kansas. Sandzén and Milles were personal friends; the latter presented the Lindsborg artist with the *Little Triton* as a gift. The museum also owns a number of smaller Milles works, including plaster models and bronze reductions for several of his public works. Additionally, there is a gallery exhibiting the work of Margaret Sandzén Greenough, Sandzén's daughter.

The **Lindsborg Post Office**, constructed in the mid-1930s and listed on the National Register, displays Sandzén's wall painting entitled *Smoky Hill Valley* (1938) in its lobby. Post offices at Bellville and Halstead, Kansas, also have Sandzén murals.

Historic Houses

Hoglund Dugout—from downtown take S. Main (becoming State Road 4) west about two miles; turn north on Twelfth Avenue, a gravel road, toward Coronado Peak, about seven-tenths of a mile.

The original Swedish settlement in Lindsborg was at the south side of Coronado Heights. At first settlers built dugouts into creek or river banks with buffalo hides or blankets covering the doorways. More permanent dugouts were constructed in the sides of hills or on flat ground and lined with stone chiseled by hand. In western and central Sweden there are similar cellarlike structures called *jordkulor.* The 8 by 12 by 6 foot Hoglund Dugout is made of sandstone with a sandstone bench, keystone-arch doorway facing east, and steep sandstone steps. Probably roofed with saplings and slough grass, it is one of few that have survived and is owned by the Smoky Valley Historical Association. Gustaf and Maria Hoglund emigrated from Värmland and arrived in Smoky Hill River Valley in 1864. After two years, they constructed a two-story sandstone house over the dugout, which became the cellar. Remnants of the house's foundation are visible on the south side of the dugout.

Rostad House (South Forty)—go three-quarters of a mile east of Elmwood Cemetery, and then two-fifths of a mile north on a gravel road. It is visible on the road's west side. On the way, between Elmwood and Rose Hill Cemeteries, is the first log cabin built in McPherson County. It is part of a larger private residence.

C. R. Carlson House—northwest corner of Washington and Lincoln.
C. R. Carlson, one of the founders in 1876 of the Evangelical Swedish Mission Church, forerunner of the Evangelical Covenant Church across the street, owned this brick house, now a funeral home. Carlson, who owned thousands of acres in the area, was a member of Bethany Lutheran. The house is noted for its hand-carved woodwork and spiral staircase.

Fridhem (Peaceful Home)—west side of S. Main Street on the south side of the Union Pacific Railroad track.
Built in 1879, this early parsonage was home to the Reverend Carl Aaron Swensson and his family. It is a private residence recently moved to this location.

Daniel J. Johnson House—226 W. Lincoln.
This large Italianate-style brick house was built in 1887. Daniel D. Johnson was an active member of the Covenant Church and the co-proprietor of the first department store in Lindsborg.

Churches

Bethany Lutheran Church—320 N. Main (785-227-2167; www.bethanylutheranlindsborg.com).

Bethany Lutheran, one of the most outstanding Swedish-landmark churches in the United States, resembles the cathedral in Karlstad, Sweden. Bethany's congregation is the third-oldest Lutheran church in the area, founded in 1869 by the

Bethany Lutheran Church, sanctuary, Lindsborg

Reverend Olof Olsson. (Freemount Lutheran and Salemsborg Lutheran preceded Bethany by two months.) Olsson was later McPherson County's first superintendent of schools, a state legislator, and professor of theology and president of Augustana Seminary in Rock Island, Illinois.

The congregation's first services were held in the homes of settlers and in the Community House (or *Bolagshuset*) of the Swedish Agriculture Company at the base of the butte known as Coronado Heights. In 1869 the congregation erected its first sanctuary northwest of present-day Lindsborg and south of Smoky Hill Cemetery, south of Coronado Heights. The 24 by 30 foot building made of stone and sod served the congregation until 1874. In 1993 a commemorative marker was erected on the site of the first sod church, visible to the east just north of the Hoglund dugout.

After a lengthy debate, parishioners built a new church of brown sandstone quarried near Coronado Heights. Above the front door are the words of Revelation 3:11 and John 1:29, along with the construction dates inscribed in Swedish. In 1880 the 125-foot spire was added with an additional Swedish inscription high on the steeple. In 1904 the church was significantly altered by the addition of the transepts. The exterior was plastered with stucco and painted white. Several stained-glass windows and three chancel paintings were installed. Local artist G. N. Malm was responsible for the central altar painting depicting the event in Bethany, where Mary is shown anointing Christ's feet. Birger Sandzén executed the two side works, the raising of Lazarus and the Ascension. The round stained-glass window above the altar depicts the home of Mary and Martha in Bethany.

Both bells in the tower have Swedish inscriptions, and the larger one, dated 1881, bears a brief early history of the congregation. In the church library are old gas lamps made from the original sanctuary oil lamps. A portrait of Olsson, a gift from Värmland honoring the congregation's centennial, is in the south transept along with the old communion vessels and original numbers used on the hymn board. The last pews in each transept are original, as is the original pressed-tin ceiling. Local craftsman Malcolm Esping in 1964 made the mosaic inlay of the church seal in the cement walk leading to the front door. The church's art reflects the strong artistic tradition in Lindsborg. It was in the church sacristy that Bethany College was founded on October 15, 1881. The first performance of Handel's *Messiah* was presented in 1882.

Evangelical Covenant Church—102 S. Washington at Lincoln (785-227-2447).

A group of immigrants from Östergötland settled on land later called Rose Hill northeast of present-day Lindsborg. In 1874 they organized and built the first Covenant Church in Kansas. When a theological dispute arose in the Bethany

Lutheran congregation that same year, C. R. Carlson, a friend of Olof Olsson, left with fifteen others and joined the Rose Hill group, forming the Evangelical Swedish Mission Church. In March 1876, the Rose Hill Church was dedicated, but in August a tornado destroyed it. After this disaster, the congregation rebuilt in town, completing in 1878 an unusual brick church with an onion dome. In 1905 a north wing and bell tower were added. Disaster struck again when the building began crumbling in the early 1920s because the local brick had not been fired correctly. In 1926 the congregation built the present Gothic-style red-brick church.

Other Churches

Churches with Swedish links in Lindsborg include Messiah Lutheran Church, First Baptist Church, and the former Swedish Methodist Church. **Messiah Lutheran**, 402 N. First (785-227-3972), was organized in 1908 as an English-speaking congregation. In 1911 it built a red-brick sanctuary, still standing adjacent to the Bethany College campus. G. N. Malm was commissioned to do the altar paintings. According to its cornerstone, **First Baptist Church**, 110 N. Washington Street (785-227-3826), was organized in 1880 as the Swedish Baptist Church, and its brick sanctuary was built in 1918. This building has now been sold, and the congregation worships in a new sanctuary. The former Swedish Methodist church at 202 S. Second Street is now a private residence. The present church, identified as **Trinity United Methodist**, is located at 224 S. Main (785-227-3326). This red-brick, Greek Revival–style building has a façade with four white Doric columns topped by a pediment. There are two entranceways, one on either side of the colonnade. The interior contains two large Birger Sandzén paintings depicting the Ascension and Christ in Gethsemane. Above the choir there is a painting by G. N. Malm of Christ blessing the children. The side aisles contain memorial stained-glass windows with various Christian symbols. Memorabilia from the first church are displayed in the narthex. **St. Bridget of Sweden Catholic Church**, 206 W. Swenson (785-227-3588), built in 1985, contains Nordic architectural elements and is dedicated to Sweden's patron saint. There is also a monument honoring St. Lucy (Santa Lucia).

Schools

Bethany College—421 N. First (785-227-3311; www.bethanylb.edu).
Reverend Carl Aaron Swensson founded Bethany College in 1881. The first year there were ten students and two teachers, Swensson and Johan August Udden. Originally an academy, the school in 1886 became a four-year college. On campus is a statue of Swensson with an inscription noting that he was born in Sugar Grove, Pennsylvania, in 1857 and that he was Bethany's president until his death

in 1904. The statue, unveiled in 1909, depicts Swensson wearing his academic robe with the Royal Order of the North Star.

The first college classroom building, a 16 by 24 foot, two-room frame structure, had been constructed in the late 1870s and purchased by Swensson in 1882 for $500. Originally located where the present Lindsborg elementary school now stands, it was moved to the campus. When Presser Hall was erected, the building was moved. In 1969 the Smoky Valley Historical Society relocated it to McPherson County Old Mill Museum and Park.

Old Main was demolished in 1968, but the college built Old Main Court with two capitals from the former structure and the cornerstone reading "Bethania 1886." Near the athletic field is the historic 1882 bell from the first college building. Presser Hall is a 1,900-seat auditorium where the annual *Messiah* oratorio and other concerts are performed. The Bethany Oratorio Society, organized by the Reverend and Mrs. Swensson in 1881, is now a three-hundred-voice chorus and a large orchestra. Pihlblad Memorial Union honors Dr. Ernest F. Pihlblad and his wife, Marie, the sister of Victor Sjöström, a motion-picture director. Dr. Pihlblad (1873–1943) was president of Bethany College from 1904 to 1941. In the lobby is a ceramic mural in memory of the Reverend Carl E. Lund-Quist, who was raised in the Freemount Lutheran Church near Lindsborg. He became the second executive director of the Lutheran World Federation (1952–1960). Other buildings on campus honor other Swedish Americans or Swedish American cultural ties: the Wallerstedt Social Science Center and the Wallerstedt Library–Information Center (Alvar G. Wallerstedt was a businessman and financier from Lindsborg), Kalmar Residence Hall, Nelson Science Building, Anna Marm Residence Hall (Marm was a professor of mathematics), Alma Swensson Residence Hall (Alma Swensson was founder Swensson's wife), Hahn Physical Education Building (Ray D. Hahn was a coach), and Anderson Athletic Field and Anderson Memorial Tennis Courts (E. T. Anderson was an Emporia, Kansas, cattleman, banker, and businessman). In the Wallerstedt Library is Lindquist Hall, named for former president Emory Lindquist. The Swensson Chapel is in the Burnett Center for Religion and Performing Arts.

Today this coeducational institution, which is affiliated with the Evangelical Lutheran Church in America, has about 630 full-time students and 54 full-time faculty members.

Other Points of Interest

Bethany Home—321 N. Chestnut (785-227-2846).

Bethany Home for senior citizens features paintings by local artists. In the dining room is a Signe Larson painting depicting a Swedish country scene with people in folk dress. Metal liturgical objects made by Malcolm Esping are in the chapel.

Swedish Timber Cottage (Den Svenska Timmerstugan)—125 N. Second.
The Swedish Timber Cottage, a pine log house built in Dalarna of Swedish timber, constructed by hand, and roofed with red concrete tiles from Västergötland,
was brought to Lindsborg and reconstructed after every element had been numbered and the house dismantled. Home to the Anderson Scandinavian Tours
(785-227-3210), the cottage has Swedish wood paneling.

Bed and Breakfasts

The nineteen-room **Swedish Country Inn**, at 112 W. Lincoln (785-227-2985 or
800-231-0266), creates the ambiance of a rural Swedish inn. The rooms and lobby
in this early-twentieth-century building are decorated in the Swedish-modern
style. It was originally built by C. A. Lundstrom to house grain and feeds. In
1930 it became the New Carlton Hotel. Then it was acquired by Bethany College
for off-campus housing and in 1956 sold to Mr. and Mrs. Quintin Applequist,
who named it the Scandinavian Bed and Breakfast. It is furnished with imported
Swedish furniture.

The **Rosberg House**, at 101 E. State Street (888-215-5234 or 785-227-4185;
www.1885rosberghouse.com), is a three-story Queen Anne house furnished in
the style of the Victorian era. The **Seasons of the Fox Bed and Breakfast**, at the
corner of Second and Swensson Streets (800-756-3596; www.seasonsofthefox
.com), is a three-story house designed in 1905 by G. N. Malm, who emigrated from
Sweden in 1889. Malm's daughter Alba, a local artist, lived there. At 130 N. Second
Street is the **Smoky Valley Bed and Breakfast** (800-532-4407), the former home of
Dr. William Holverda, founder of *Svensk Hyllningsfest* (Swedish Homage Festival).

In 1887 the three-story **Brunswick Hotel** was opened on the corner of Main
and Grant, at 202 S. Main. It contained a lobby, large dining room, second-floor
parlor, and thirty-three guest rooms. At various times it served as a restaurant
and a women's dormitory for Bethany College.

Cemeteries

Smoky Hill Cemetery—three miles northwest of Lindsborg, south of Coronado
Heights. From W. Swensson Street, go north on Burma Road (Thirteenth Avenue) two miles, turn left on Coronado Heights Road, and go west one mile. The
cemetery is on the north side of the road, immediately before the entrance to
Coronado Heights Park.

Near the southeast corner of the cemetery is a monument to Olof Olsson's
mother (Olsson himself is buried in Riverside Cemetery, Moline, Illinois.) Dr.
Emory Lindquist (1908–1992), author and former president of Bethany College,
also rests in the Smoky Hill Cemetery. The graves of other early Swedish setters,
some with Swedish inscriptions, can also be found in the cemetery.

An impressive view of Lindsborg and the Smoky Hill River Valley can be seen from Coronado Heights. At the summit is a stone fortress built in the 1930s by Work Projects Administration workers. It is believed that the Spanish explorer Francisco de Coronado reached this point in his 1540–1542 explorations.

Elmwood Cemetery—seven-tenths of a mile east of Bethany College campus on E. Swensson (becomes McPherson County Road 1967). A twenty-foot obelisk marks the graves of Carl Aaron Swensson (1857–1904) and family members. Artists Birger Sandzén, Gustav Nathanael Malm, Lester Raymer, and Margaret Sandzén Greenough are buried here, as is Bethany College president Dr. Peter Ristuben.

Rose Hill Cemetery—drive north from Lindsborg on Burma Road (Thirteenth Avenue); two miles north of the McPherson–Saline County line, turn east for two miles to Fairchild Road, and then turn south for one-half mile. Dotted with stones bearing Swedish inscriptions, this cemetery has a granite marker commemorating the Rose Hill Mission Covenant Church, established in 1874.

Freemount

In 1868, the Galesburg Company, formed in the Swedish Lutheran Church in Galesburg, Illinois, received from the Kansas Pacific Railroad twenty-two sections of land in southern Saline and McPherson Counties. In 1869 the Galesburg group organized a congregation. Although this community to the southwest of Lindsborg is named for explorer and soldier John C. Frémont, the congregation elected to spell its name "Freemount."

Freemount Lutheran Church is located at 2511 Eighth Avenue or McPherson County Road 1065 (785-227-3154). The first church, made of brown sandstone hauled from nearby hills, was erected in 1870. It is the oldest public building in McPherson County and currently used as a museum. Artifacts from the second sanctuary, including the gold cross from the spire, pews, and a hymn board, are in this building. The congregation occasionally meets in this historic church.

When the church immediately proved too small, a larger structure was built in 1881. Its interior copied the First Lutheran Church in Moline, Illinois. A bolt of lightning struck the high steeple on June 7, 1926, and the church burned to the ground. A third Gothic-style church made of red brick was completed the following year. In its basement is a large Swedish-inscribed stone weighing more than one ton that had been above the front door of the 1881 church. During the 1926 fire, the stone fell to the ground and miraculously remained intact. Translated, the stone's inscription reads, "Watch your step in God's house. God, we foresee Thy goodness upon Thy temple." The main sanctuary of the present church has an altar painting by Sandzén entitled *Come Unto Me*, depicting Christ with outstretched arms. Stained-glass windows portray biblical events. Graves at

Freemount Lutheran Church, Fremount

the north end of the adjacent cemetery have stones bearing Swedish inscriptions. The home south of the church was formerly the parsonage, built in the 1880s.

Marquette

Although founded by a non-Swede from Marquette, Michigan, Marquette was settled mostly by Swedes who arrived upon the encouragement of the Galesburg Land Company. Many originated from Småland and Dalarna. The town developed near the mill built on the nearby Smoky Hill River. In front of the Riverview Estates, a senior citizens home, is the old mill stone monument.

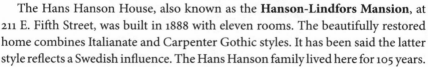

The Hans Hanson House, also known as the **Hanson-Lindfors Mansion**, at 211 E. Fifth Street, was built in 1888 with eleven rooms. The beautifully restored home combines Italianate and Carpenter Gothic styles. It has been said the latter style reflects a Swedish influence. The Hans Hanson family lived here for 105 years.

Hanson, an important leader in the development of broom corn, came to the area in 1869 and built a log cabin. Two years later he attached a one-room cabin. Here fifteen men met in 1847 and signed the original charter of Marquette. Now both Hanson's house and the 1871 cabin are on the National Register of Historic Places. Hanson was not only an early leader in civic development, but he also helped organize the Elim Lutheran Church.

In 1886 and 1887, the town built what is known as the **Opera House Block**, which included six stores with the opera house upstairs. A tornado severely damaged the opera house in 1905, and only one-third of it was rebuilt. Part of the original cornice can be seen above Olson's Furniture Store, 106 N. Washington. Inside the former Marquette Farmers State Bank, 205 N. Washington, now the Washington Street Emporium, is an interesting teller's cage. Also on the block is City Sundries, Fountain, and Gifts, which was a turn-of-the-century drugstore; the large wooden fountain still exists. Across the street from the Opera House Block is Marquette Lumber and Hardware, built in 1901. The building has an elaborate cornice and pilasters with Corinthian capitals. A colorful wall mural depicts Marquette's heritage.

Other sights in the town include the library, 121 N. Washington, built in 1887 as a bank. The Marquette Museum is being developed on the corner of Third and Washington Streets. At Fifth and Lincoln is **Elim Lutheran Church**, 403 N. Lincoln Street (785-546-2244), erected in 1906. The sanctuary's stained-glass windows memorialize those who died in the 1905 tornado. Paintings by G. N. Malm hang in the sanctuary and in a small chapel. On Sixth Street, west of town, is the Lutheran Cemetery, where a number of stones bear Swedish inscriptions.

Falun

The first Swedish settler in the vicinity of Falun arrived in 1868. Others followed, including a group from the Bishop Hill Colony and another from Galva, Illinois, led by Major Eric Forsse (1819–1889). Forsse became postmaster, justice of the peace, and member of the Kansas legislature. He named the town Falun in 1871 for the city in Dalarna where he had served in the infantry. In 1875 and 1876, organizers initiated the Falun Christian Association and built a frame building in what is now Falun Cemetery. Lutherans organized a church in 1887, purchased the association's building, and moved it to town, where it still stands at 312 E. Third Street (785-668-2551). Sandzén provided the altar painting. A flagpole and marker in the cemetery commemorate the church's original site.

Salemsborg

Salemsborg is home to the second-oldest Swedish Lutheran congregation in the Smoky Valley. **Salemsborg Lutheran Church**, 3831 W. Salemsborg Road, Smolan (785-668-2522), was organized on June 16, 1869. The church built that year was a dugout with rock walls. Today's Gothic-style brick church with two towers, constructed in 1926, is the congregation's fourth sanctuary. Over the door of the north tower is carved in stone, *Salemsborgs Sv. Ev. Lutherska Kyrka.* Over the south door is the same inscription in English. Above the north door is a stained-glass window with the words, *Vår Gud är oss en väldig borg.* The English translation,

"A mighty fortress is our God," appears on the window over the south door. On the south corner of the building is a plaque reading, "1869 The Sod Church; 1874 The Frame Church; 1893 The Spire Church; 1926 The Two Tower Church." In the south vestibule's stained-glass window is the inscription, "In memory of the charter members of the Salemsborg Lutheran church by the congregation." Four stained-glass panels depicting the parable of the sower are found in the pastor's study, which formerly was the sanctuary's overflow room. Carl Lotave was the artist of the Transfiguration altar scene that was saved from a 1925 fire. The side chancel landscape paintings are by G. N. Malm.

Some of the older stones in the adjacent cemetery have Swedish inscriptions. A monument in the shape of a pulpit with a Bible has the inscription: "In memory of the Pioneers who built the sod church on this place in the year of Our Lord 1869. Erected by the children of Salemsborg 1935."

Smolan

Two and one-half miles north of the Salemsborg Church is the small community of Smolan, the birthplace of John Carlin, a former Kansas governor of Swedish ancestry. Two cemeteries, **Smolan Lutheran Cemetery**, one-half mile north of the town on Burma Road, and **Smolan Mission Covenant Church Cemetery**, two miles south on Burma Road and one-quarter mile east, contain graves of the nineteenth-century settlers. Covenant has graves dating to the 1870s.

Assaria

Founded in 1875, **Assaria Lutheran Church** (785-667-2031) was an outgrowth of Salemsborg Lutheran. The red-brick Gothic-style sanctuary on First Street was begun in 1913 next door to the 1877 church and finished two years later. (The old sanctuary was subsequently razed.) On the altar is the Swedish inscription, *Helig, Helig, Helig* (Holy, Holy, Holy). Immigrants from the Swedish province of Blekinge settled on farms and raised crops outside Assaria.

New Gottland

Early Swedish settlers who referred to the area as *nytt gott land* (new good land) gave the town its name. The first permanent settlers arrived in 1871, and a year later the Reverend Olof Olsson organized the **New Gottland Lutheran Church**, 1822 Seventeenth Avenue, McPherson (620-654-3421). The present sanctuary was erected in 1910. Signe Larson was responsible for the altar painting.

McPherson

Swedish Lutherans and German Mennonites helped settle McPherson. Lindsborg silversmith Malcolm Esping created a life-size statue of Christ and other metal liturgical objects for **Trinity Lutheran Church**, 119 N. Elm (620-241-0424). Swedish Americans also organized Countryside Covenant at 940 E. Northview Road (620-241-4499). **Central Christian College**, 1240 S. Main (620-241-2584), formerly was known as Walden College; it had briefly been a Covenant school. Central Christian College's Science Hall, with a cornerstone date of 1904, was Walden's main building.

The imposing **McPherson County Courthouse**, at Maple and Kansas Streets, opened its doors in 1894. Swedish immigrant A. G. Linn, at the request of the county commission, supervised brick and stone work on the building. Linn also helped construct the Heceta Head Lighthouse on the Oregon coast near Florence. Exhibits at the McPherson City Museum, 1130 Euclid (620-241-8464), feature some Swedish objects, including Swedish immigrant Anna Larkin's wood carvings.

Salina

Swedes helped settle this city north of Lindsborg, establishing businesses and organizing Immanuel Lutheran, 255 S. Seventh Street (785-825-4250), and First Covenant Churches. Both churches have sanctuaries of recent origin.

Wakeeney

In the western Kansas plains, seven miles south of the Interstate 70 Ogallah exit on State Highway 147, is the small limestone **Emanuel Lutheran Church** (785-743-6629), with its short crenellated steeple. (Lightning claimed the original wood steeple.) Situated on a small hill surrounded by cedar trees, the church has an attractive interior featuring an altar painting of Christ in Gethsemane painted by Sandzén in the 1930s. The original wooden pews, pine floor, and a pressed-metal ceiling remain.

Page City, Sharon Springs, and Weskan

Swedes settled in Page City, Sharon Springs, and Weskan. The sanctuaries of Bethesda Lutheran Church, Page City, and Sharon Lutheran, 503 S. Gardner (785-852-4201), were recently constructed. The frame Bethany Lutheran in Weskan has the dates 1888, when the congregation was organized, and 1954, when the country sanctuary was moved into town from Stockholm. The congregation retained the old wooden pews.

Concordia

Frank Carlson, a former congressman, governor, and U.S. senator, was born in 1893 to Swedish immigrants who farmed in nearby Scandia. Concordia Public Library, at the corner of Seventh Street and Broadway, bears his name.

North of Concordia, the **Saron Cemetery**, where many early Swedish settlers are buried, holds the cornerstone of the Swedish Evangelical Lutheran Saron
Church, built in 1888 but no longer extant. The cemetery is about three miles
north of the Republican River and one mile east of U.S. Highway 81.

Scandia

In 1868 the Scandinavian Agricultural Society of Chicago initiated the New
Scandinavia colony, which became the settlement of Scandia. Because settlers
feared Indian attacks, they built Colony House, a stronghold recreated for the
1961 Kansas Centennial. The replica stands on the south side of U.S. Highway 36,
one-half mile west of Cloud Street. Thure Wohlfort (1835–1916), an early member
of the society and one of the twelve founders of New Scandinavia, arrived in 1869
and began homesteading one mile south of Scandia, where the large stone house
he shared with his wife, Louise Erickson, still stands. Known as the **Wohlfort
Home,** the house was the center of a large livestock enterprise that made Wohlfort
a man of influence in the area. Louise was the daughter of Andrew Erickson, one
of the first settlers. The **Scandia Library and Museum** on Main Street (785-335-
2271) displays items of local historical interest.

Courtland

In 1873 Swedes organized the Swedish Evangelical Lutheran Church of Ada, today
Ada Lutheran Church, 444 Valley Road (785-374-4267). Five years later, with the
arrival of a group from Bucklin, Missouri, the congregation built first a parsonage and then a sandstone sanctuary. Each family donated and delivered a certain
amount of building material. The church was dedicated in 1884 and the tower
added four years later. The sanctuary has an attractive chancel featuring a 1910
altar painting by Sandzén surrounded by wood panels with floral designs. Under
the altar painting are the words, *Se Guds Lamm!* (Behold the Lamb of God!). In
the basement is a glass cabinet with historic memorabilia.

Brantford

Organized in 1874, the white stucco **Zion Lutheran Church** stands in the countryside three miles east and eight miles north of Clyde (785-732-1665). Built of
untrimmed limestone quarried and hauled by ox cart from hills three miles away,
the structure took nearly four years to build. The church dedicated the building
in 1900 and in 1916 hung a half-ton bell bearing a Swedish inscription in the
belfry.

The Brantford Evangelical Covenant Church, 287 Eighth Road, Clyde
(785-446-3346), was organized in 1882. Its present sanctuary was dedicated in
1948.

Clay Center

Seven miles north and one mile west of Clay Center is the **First Lutheran Church** ("Swedesburg"; 785-926-3423), whose congregation was organized in 1871. Its former striking building was destroyed by a tornado in 1973, and the congregation then purchased a former Roman Catholic Church sanctuary south of the old church. A monument to the congregation's 100th birthday rests on the front lawn, and nearby is the congregation's old bell inscribed in Swedish. A Swedish cemetery, largely undamaged by the tornado, is west of the church.

The **Evangelical Covenant Church**, organized in 1890, was originally next to the cemetery, which is north of the city. The church and parsonage were built in 1892 and moved to town. The church is currently located at 1330 Fifteenth Street (785-632-5653).

Enterprise

Several hundred Swedes settled just east of Enterprise. Lars Jäderborg, who arrived in 1858, obtained considerable acreage and in 1873 built a large stone house. By 1890 more than fifty stone farmhouses dotted the area, mostly on eighty-acre homesteads. Some stone houses and barns still stand. Swedes became known for their skillful stone masonry, and their work was in demand regionally. They were responsible for constructing Stony Point School (1872) and the Pleasant Hill School (1878), but these two structures are no longer extant. Bethlehem Lutheran Church, built in 1877, has been torn down, but a monument is located in the church cemetery on 2100 Avenue (the continuation of Fifth Avenue) two miles east of the Enterprise town line. The stone Mission Covenant Church constructed in 1881 still exists but is not in use. It is adjacent to the Covenant cemetery. To reach this site, take 2100 Avenue east to Oat Road and turn south.

Manhattan

The **First Lutheran Church of Manhattan**, 930 Poyntz (785-537-8532), was officially organized in 1879. The congregation built a church in 1930 and erected a striking modern sanctuary in the 1960s. It contains the altar from the former Mariadahl Lutheran Church, and the impressive altar cross is made from walnut obtained from Mariadahl. Outside is the Mariadahl Memorial Bell Tower with the church's old bell. Mariadahl's large Olof Grafström altar painting (1895) hangs in a stairwell.

The **Riley County Historical Museum**, 2309 Claflin Road (785-565-6490; www.co.riley.ks.us/museum), displays memorabilia belonging to early regional Swedish settlers, as well as the altar rail from the Mariadahl Church.

Olsburg

The first Swede to settle in Kansas came to the area northwest of Olsburg along the Big Blue River in 1855. John A. Johnson (d. 1893) was joined by family members, including his mother, Maria, for whom the settlement of Mariadahl (Maria's Valley) was later named. The thriving hamlet boasted a stone schoolhouse, a blacksmith shop, a grange store, and the nearby Mariadahl Children's Home. Two stone churches, a Swedish Methodist church built in 1878 and Mariadahl Lutheran built between 1866 and 1871, graced the town. Mariadahl Lutheran, the oldest Swedish Lutheran house of worship west of the Missouri River, was made of native limestone and topped with a central steeple. The razing of this church in 1961 to make way for water impounded by the Tuttle Creek Dam evoked consternation.

Parts of the Mariadahl Lutheran Church were saved (see Riley County Historical Museum and First Lutheran Church, Manhattan), and the entire Swedish cemetery was relocated to nearby Olsburg. At Mariadahl Cemetery are monuments to the accomplishments of this community and church and artifacts from the original cemetery. A four-foot bas-relief depicts the historic church, and before it on the ground is the church's cornerstone, originally on the steeple. At the main gate are two pillars from the old cemetery, begun in 1863, and at the east end is a monument to the Children's Home.

A gravel road leads to the Mariadahl community site. Visible on a nearby hill are the Mariadahl Lutheran Church steeple, moved to higher ground after the church was razed; near the reservoir are old stone barns and the former Ekblad farm.

Across the road from the Mariadahl cemetery is the Lutheran cemetery, where most names on markers are Swedish. **Olsburg Lutheran Church** (785-468-3500), a red-brick building, has a cornerstone indicating that it was organized in 1881 and its most recent sanctuary erected in 1939. Olof Grafström produced the altar painting.

Randolph

In 1886 Swedish immigrants settled Cleburne, near Randolph and on the opposite side of the Tuttle Creek Reservoir from Olsburg. To the north the Bellegarde Cemetery, where many early Swedes are buried, offers a lovely view.

Leonardville

Walburg Lutheran Church, 12410 Union Road (785-293-2860), is four miles northeast of Leonardville. The church was rebuilt after a 1918 fire destroyed the wooden steeple and roof. Olof Grafström made the altar painting (1918). Nearby is an old stone bridge built by early Swedes. In Leonardville is the former Swedish Baptist church, a stone structure built in the early 1890s, now abandoned.

Axtell

Founded by Swedes, the white-frame **Evangelical Mission Covenant Church**, 1491 Twenty-seventh Road (785-736-2860), was built in 1910; the congregation had been organized in the early 1880s. Over the church front door is the inscription, *Svenska Evangeliska Zion Missions Kyrka.*

Lawrence

At the **Elizabeth M. Watkins Community Museum**, 1047 Massachusetts at Eleventh Street (785-841-4109), is a model of a large windmill, a landmark in Lawrence from 1863 to 1905. It was built by John H. Wilder of Massachusetts and Andrew (Anders) Palm (formerly Palmquist) of Killeröd, Skåne. Palm moved to Lawrence in 1862 and became associated with Wilder, possibly as a blacksmith, in his carriage and plow business. Palm fashioned the windmill after those of Skåne. He had returned to Sweden to learn how to construct it and brought back to the United States machinery to propel it. Built of native timber, the octagonal windmill powered a mill as well as Palm and Wilder's machine shop, where they made wagons and plows from 1864 to 1885. Though long gone, the windmill appears from time to time as the city's symbol. Also in the museum's collection is the wooden key that locked the windmill's shaft.

Another museum in the city, the **Helen Foresman Spencer Museum of Art** on the University of Kansas campus, 1301 Mississippi (785-864-4710; www.spencerart.ku.edu), has in its collection etchings by Anders Zorn and lithographs and woodcuts by Birger Sandzén.

In Lawrence, Swedes built or owned vernacular-style stone houses. A number were "mill houses" built by and for Swedish workmen who constructed and operated the windmill that stood at Ninth and Emery Road. Built in the 1860s, possibly as a hotel for the Swedish workers who constructed the windmill, was the private house at 800 Louisiana. Other stone houses under private ownership include those at 905 Michigan and 1008 Ohio. The stone house at 900 Pennsylvania is now a tavern.

Osage City

Second-stage immigrants, most from Sweden via Illinois, settled this town twenty-five miles south of Topeka beginning in 1869. The next year, twenty-two charter members formed the Swedish Evangelical Lutheran Church, now **Grace Lutheran**, 200 Holliday (785-528-4785). The present sanctuary constructed of brick was built in 1912.

Savonburg

Friends Home Lutheran Church, 3797 Arizona Road, three miles west of Savon-burg (620-754-3314), was organized in 1872 by Swedes mainly from Blekinge. Four-fifths were from the parish of Jämshög.

Their first church building was constructed in 1879. In 1898 a new white-frame church with a central steeple and Gothic-style windows designed by Olof Z. Cervin of Rock Island, Illinois, was completed. The altar painting is by Olof Grafström. The steeple's bell is one of the largest in Kansas. The adjacent parson-age was built in 1907.

The first building of Friends Home Lutheran was sold to the **Evangelical Covenant Church** in 1898 and moved one-quarter mile east of the Lutheran church to 405 W. Main Street (620-754-3711).

NEBRASKA

Swedes generally settled in five main locations in Nebraska—around Omaha, the northeast corner (Oakland, Wakefield, and Wausa), Saunders County (Wahoo, Swedeburg, and Malmo), the Stromsburg area (Polk County), and south-central (Kearney, Phelps, and Harlan Counties). Some Swedes settled in Fillmore County in southeast Nebraska, in Gothenburg along the Platte River, and around Chappell in western Nebraska. Nebraska governor Victor E. Anderson was of Swedish back-ground, as was twentieth-century composer, conductor, and educator Howard Hanson of Wahoo.

Omaha

The beginnings of the **Alegent Health Immanuel Medical Center**, 6901 N. Seventy-second Street (402-572-2121), and the adjoining **Immanuel-Fontenelle Home** (402-572-2595) date from 1887, when the Immanuel Deaconess Institute was founded by Pastor Erick Albert Fogelstrom. He was interested in organiz-ing not only a hospital but also institutions for the care of the elderly, orphans, and invalids. In 1894, a Deaconess Home was founded. With support from the Nebraska Conference of the Augustana Synod, construction was begun in 1901 on a children's home, and a school of nursing was also established.

Today the modern medical center is affiliated with the Nebraska Synod of the Evangelical Lutheran Church in America, and Swedish American support is still strong. The comfortable and well-equipped Immanuel-Fontenelle Home displays Fogelstrom memorabilia.

Another minister, the Reverend Sven Gustaf Larson, first Lutheran home mis-sionary to Nebraska, in 1868 organized the Immanuel Lutheran Church, the first

Swedish Lutheran congregation in Nebraska. Subsequently Larson established the Oakland church in 1869 and the Swedeburg, Malmo, Mead, and Lincoln congregations the following year. In 1936 Immanuel Lutheran merged with Zion Lutheran, forming the **Augustana Lutheran Church**, now at 3647 Lafayette Avenue (402-551-4728). Its Gothic-style building was constructed in 1951.

Kent Ullberg Sculpture–Sixteenth and Dodge.

One of Ullberg's largest sculptures, *Spirit of Nebraska Wilderness,* was commissioned by the First National Bank of Omaha and installed in 2002. It occupies one-fourth of a city block on the bank's property, creating a significant public green space in the center of the city.

Ullberg has created a visual story using his trademark media: polished granite, water, stainless steel, and bronze. Fifty-eight bronze Canadian geese are seen on the ground near the large black-granite fountain, taking off from the pool, flying through the air, circling the intersection, and ending up in the bank atrium. The geese appear to have been frightened by an eight-foot charging bronze buffalo approaching the fountain. Each goose has an eight-foot wingspan, is larger than life size, and weighs 200 pounds. As the geese leave the water, they are held aloft by a group of bronze trees, a traffic signal, light poles, the corner of a building, and eighteen-foot granite columns. The flight ends with several geese

Kent Ullberg's *Spirit of Nebraska Wilderness,* Omaha

suspended within a beautiful glass atrium, First National's Winter Garden. The geese dramatically transition from bronze to stainless steel to signify the evolution from the open range to a high-tech modern landscape. Ullberg describes his work on an interpretive plaque at the site.

Oakland

By 1930, about two-thirds of the foreign born in Burt County were of Swedish origin. Signs proudly proclaim it the "Swedish Capital of Nebraska." (Confusingly, Stromburg calls itself "the Swede Capital of Nebraska.") Since the 1980s, Oakland has identified with its Swedish heritage by using the Dala horse motif throughout the community. From Oakland, Swedish settlers fanned out to other areas of northeast Nebraska as well as parts of the Far West, especially Idaho.

The **First Lutheran** congregation, organized in 1869, is the second-oldest Swedish Lutheran church in Nebraska. A church built in 1878 burned in 1892. The present large Gothic-style brick edifice with a tall spire was constructed the following year at 201 N. Davis (402-685-5764) and was recently stuccoed.

About the same time the Lutheran church was organized, a Swedish Baptist congregation was also established. On the cornerstone of the **First Baptist Church**, 202 N. Fried Avenue, are the dates 1869 and 1918, the second date indicating when the present brick sanctuary was built. The **Salem Evangelical Covenant Church**, 290 County Road 1 (402-685-6111), is a white-clapboard building, whose congregation was organized in 1877. In 1989 the **Swedish Heritage Center** opened a museum and gift shop in the former Swedish Covenant Church Building at 301 N. Chard Avenue (402-685-6161). This congregation was organized in 1885 and its sanctuary constructed in 1912. When the congregation merged with Salem Covenant (see below) in 1985, the white-clapboard building was scheduled for demolition. Some of the stained glass had actually been removed when the Swedish Heritage Committee acquired the building for one dollar. Museum exhibits are now throughout the sanctuary, which has its old pews, stage, and lovely large stained-glass windows.

In 1983 the community reintroduced the dormant tradition of the Swedish festival. The festival features musical performances, folk dancing, a smörgåsbord, and an antique show on the first weekend of June during odd-numbered years.

In the country southwest of Oakland is **Salem Evangelical Covenant Church**, 290 County Road I (402-685-6111). From Oakland, take State Road 32 west for five miles, turn south onto County Road I, a blacktopped road, and travel two miles to the church. The congregation was founded in 1877 as the Swedish Evangelical Lutheran Mission Church. When the Covenant Church became an organized denomination, this congregation joined it. The present, much-altered, white-frame structure contains several smaller stained-glass windows from the former

Covenant Church in Oakland. The cemetery is located one-quarter mile west of the church on a high point in a grove of trees. There are many graves with Swedish inscriptions, including that of the Reverend O. Magnus Nyman. There is a dramatic view of the surrounding Nebraska farm fields stretching to the horizon.

West of Oakland, Stanton County was settled by Europeans, Swedes among them, as noted by a historical marker on U.S. Highway 275 several miles west of Pilger.

Wakefield

The **Salem Lutheran Church**, 411 Winter Street at E. Fifth (402-287-2681), is a white-clapboard structure with a tall dark-wood steeple erected in 1905. The exterior resembles the Tabor Lutheran Church in Wausa.

Wausa

The town's name is an anglicized form of *Vasa*. The **Tabor Lutheran Church** congregation was organized in 1885 and built its first church in 1886 and its most recent one in 1903, at 300 E. Norris Street (402-586-2533).

Wahoo

In front of the Saunders County Courthouse is a historical marker noting that Swedish settlers in Wahoo established Luther Junior College and that one of the town's native sons was composer and conductor Howard Hanson, who was of Swedish extraction.

Luther Academy opened November 10, 1883, the 400th anniversary of the birth of Martin Luther. In 1925 it became a junior college. Following the 1962 merger of several Lutheran bodies (including the Augustana Lutheran Synod, which operated Luther College), Midland College in nearby Fremont merged with Luther, creating Midland Lutheran College, 900 N. Clarkson (800-642-8382; www.mlc.edu). Luther's facilities were sold to another educational institution, but today the campus stands vacant. Among the decaying structures are a stone monument, part of the first building destroyed by fire in 1917, and an old stone gate.

The **Howard Hanson House**, 1163 Linden, is the birthplace of Dr. Howard Hanson (1896–1981), the foremost American composer of Swedish parentage. Many of his works emphasize his Swedish ancestry, such as his Third Symphony, written in honor of the 300th anniversary of the Swedish settlement on the Delaware. From 1924 to 1964, he directed the Eastman School of Music at the University of Rochester, New York. As a guest conductor, he worked with orchestras in Europe and the United States. In 1944 Hanson was awarded the Pulitzer Prize for his Fourth Symphony.

Howard Hanson House, Wahoo

The white-frame Victorian house where he was born and raised was probably built in the 1880s. Restored and opened by the county in 1967, it features exhibits emphasizing the contributions of four other Wahoo residents as well. The piano where Hanson first took lessons and where he composed his first music at the age of seven remains in the house.

Bethlehem Lutheran Church, 504 W. Eighth at Sycamore Street (402-442-3160), is a frame church topped by a tall steeple. Over its front door is inscribed, "Sw. Ev. Lutheran Bethlehem Church October 7, 1906."

Mead

Founded in 1870, the **Alma Lutheran Church** erected its white-clapboard building at 219 W. Fifth (402-624-2015) in 1886.

Malmo

The **Edensburg Lutheran** congregation dates from 1870. The church was originally in the country, but when Malmo was founded in 1886, a new church was constructed in town in 1890. Edensburg Lutheran is presently at 247 Rutland Avenue (402-642-5842). The former white-frame Covenant Church, now a private residence, has the date 1905 on its cornerstone.

Swedeburg

Located about six miles south of Wahoo, Swedeburg at one time was a lively Swedish settlement. **Grace Lutheran Church**, 739 County Road 16 (402-642-5842), organized in 1870, was known as the Swedish Evangelical Lutheran Swedeburg Congregation. Its present white-frame, Gothic-style church was completed in 1916. Olof Grafström painted Christ in Gethsemane for the altar painting. The original Swedish Mission Church, which was organized in 1876, was about two miles southwest of town at the Fridhem Cemetery. In town, the **Swedeburg Covenant Church**, 1702 Ash Street (402-443-5443), has a cornerstone inscribed, *Sw. Ev. Luth. Miss. Kyrkan 'Fridhem' 1909.*

Stromsburg

Called the "Swede Capital of Nebraska," Stromsburg prides itself on its history. In March 1872, twenty-eight Swedes arrived from Illinois, and their sod houses and dugouts were soon ready. The community persevered despite devastating grasshopper infestation, disease, and a horrible prairie fire in 1878. The Swedish royal insignia over the front door of the modern Stromsburg Bank is one of many reminders of Stromsburg's deep Swedish roots. Other evidence includes early twentieth-century mercantile buildings around the town square: the Carlson and Olson Building, the Victor Anderson Building, and the Old Opera House. In the town square, Lewis Headstrom, a Gästrikland native who died in Stromsburg in 1892, is honored with a plaque. Headstrom found no public service job too small or too large. He served as mayor, postmaster, and town and school board member. Headstrom also constructed the first residential and commercial buildings in Stromsburg.

In July 1873, northwest of town, settlers founded the Swede Home Church, now identified as **Calvary Lutheran Church of Swede Home**, NW Route 2, one mile south and one-half mile west of the junction of State Highways 92 and 39 (402-764-5981). It is the mother congregation of Lutheran churches in the city, and some of its former members were leaders in establishing churches and institutions in Oregon (see Colton; Legacy Emanuel Hospital and Health Center, Portland). The congregation built its present red-brick sanctuary with two silver steeples in 1914, replacing the original constructed in 1881–1883. In the cemetery across the road from the church are the graves of Johan and Kajsa Hult, victims of the 1878 prairie fire. Surviving members of the family became successful in lumbering in the Pacific Northwest.

Another Stromsburg landmark is the **Salem Lutheran Church**, 610 Commercial (402-764-2711), a daughter congregation of the Swede Home church. It owns a Signe Larson altar painting. Both Salem Lutheran and a Covenant congregation in Stromsburg worship in modern sanctuaries.

In Buckley Park, created with a donation from Swedish Americans John B. and Christine Buckley, is a gazebo made from the steeple of the former Covenant Church, built in 1900. The Midwest Covenant Home, 615 E. Ninth Street (402-764-2711), is on the north side of Ninth Street in town. Many early Swedish pioneers are buried in the Stromsburg cemetery, which is on Ninth Street, about one mile east of Main Street.

Buckley Park gazebo, Stromsburg

The white-clapboard Swede Plain Methodist Church, whose congregation was established in 1876 and whose building was constructed in the 1880s, was moved to Covenant Cedars Bible Camp (402-753-3241), twelve miles west of Stromsburg and three miles north of Hordville. The Methodist congregation has disbanded.

Waverly

 Peter Peterson, who emigrated from Småland, first settled in Waverly in 1879. Between 1893 and 1900, eight structures went up on his farmstead. On the privately held **Peter Peterson Farmstead** are a Queen Anne–style house and a barn, which has two octagonal cupolas and a steep gambrel roof with flared eaves. The National Register protects the private owners by not releasing the farmstead's location.

Lincoln

The first sanctuary of **First Lutheran Church**, built by Swedes in 1870, stood on the site of the present State Capitol. The congregation's 1965 sanctuary is located in east Lincoln at 1551 S. Seventieth (402-488-0919; www.flclincoln.org).

Shickley

 In the early 1870s Swedish immigrants began settling in Fillmore County between the present towns of Shickley and Ong. About two and one-half miles west of Shickley on Route 74, a Nebraska state historic marker identifies the **Stockholm Lutheran Church** and **Swedish Cemetery**. The marker reads, in part: "As the settlement grew these pioneers considered the need for a church, organized a congregation in 1875 and purchased six acres of land, although meetings were held in a school house and member's homes until 1881, when the first church was built. . . . By 1900 the old church was too small. . . . The present church, a thirty-six by sixty foot frame structure with Gothic-Revival detailing, was constructed in that year at a cost of $3549. The congregation continued to use the Swedish language occasionally for worship until 1937." The church and the Swedish cemetery are located one mile south and one-half mile west of this marker.

The congregation has dwindled, but the church is being lovingly preserved. The interior walls and ceiling of the sanctuary are covered by white embossed tin. There is a particularly attractive carved balcony balustrade. The altar, altar rail, and pulpit, white with gold trim, are original to the building, but the old pews were stolen by vandals. The sanctuary is graced by a large Olof Grafström altar painting of Christ in Gethsemane. The building's exterior is white clapboard with a central bell tower and red-shingled steeple, visible for miles across the flat Nebraska farmland. The cemetery is well maintained with impressive gravestones, some with Swedish inscriptions.

Stockholm Lutheran Church, exterior and sanctuary, Shickley

In contrast to the well-preserved Shickley church, the nearby town of Ong is in a serious state of deterioration. Its red-brick, Gothic-style Lutheran church is now abandoned, as is the local school formerly used by Swedish Americans.

Kearney

 Built in 1886, the **Hanson-Downing House (also known as Kearney Women's Club)**, 723 W. Twenty-second Street, is an ornamented frame cottage with a front recessed curved porch, gable roof, and dormer windows. Carved floral and sun decorative motifs adorn the entire house. Charles E. Hanson, who immigrated to Chicago in 1869 and came to Phelps County in 1878, opened a farm implement business in Kearney in 1882 and built the house four years later.

Keene

The congregation of the **Evangelical Free Church** was organized in 1880. Its white-frame church, constructed in 1921, was renovated in 1953.

Axtell

An inspiring institution of mercy for the mentally and physically handicapped, Bethphage Mission of the Great Plains, now known as **Mosaic at Bethphage Village** and a member of Lutheran Services in America, is located on N. Second Street (308-743-2401; www.mosaicinfo.org). It was founded in 1913 by the Reverend K. G. William Dahl (1883–1917) from Skåne. While at Augustana Theological Seminary in Rock Island, Illinois, Dahl was asked to translate from German a book on the epilepsy colony at Bielefeld, Germany. Moved by its story, he decided to build a similar institute in this country. After working for the Immanuel Deaconess Home in Omaha, Dahl accepted a call to come to the Axtell church. In 1914 forty acres of land were bought for the Bethphage Mission site. The first cottage for "guests" was dedicated Midsummer Eve 1914. Tabor Cottage, a home for women, was opened in 1916; today it serves as a museum. Although Dahl died in 1917, reportedly having overworked himself in developing the mission, additional buildings were constructed, notably Sarepta (Sisters' Home) in 1917, Emmaus Cottage for Men in 1919, Bethel Home for Children in 1929, Zion Chapel in 1930, and Kidron (for women and children with tuberculosis) in 1938.

The architect was Olof Z. Cervin of Rock Island. Of Swedish heritage, Cervin designed the buildings in a stepped-gable style with red-tile roofs, reminiscent of the architecture found in Skåne and Denmark. **Zion Chapel** is his masterpiece. Cervin described it as Klintian in style, after P. V. J. Klint of the famous Grundtvig Cathedral, built in the 1920s in Copenhagen. Zion is made of buff-colored brick enhanced by beautiful stained-glass windows. The altar window depicts Jesus surrounded by physically handicapped individuals. The chapel's interior is known for its dramatic cloister effect, and wide aisles facilitate attendance by people who are confined to beds and wheelchairs. Dr. Emmy Evald, daughter of the Reverend Erland Carlsson, spearheaded the building of the chapel by enlisting support of the Augustana Lutheran Synod's Women's Missionary Society, which she headed. In the chapel's tower is a mechanical clock donated in 1931 by a Swedish American from Smolan, Kansas.

Zion Chapel, Bethphage Village, Axtell

Trinity Lutheran Church, 104 E. Fifth Street (308-743-2196), has a brown-stucco exterior with white trim and stained-glass windows depicting Christian symbols. Reverend Dahl was the congregation's pastor for many years.

On State Road 6/34 is a Nebraska state historic marker describing the early Swedish homesteaders in the area. The marker notes that "the tempo of settlement increased with the coming of the Burlington and Missouri Railroad in 1883. . . . In the early 1900s Axtell was known as 'windmill town' because of its many windmills." Axtell's Gary Anderson won Olympic medals in rifle marksmanship in 1964 and 1968.

In the distance on the flat Nebraska landscape is the tall steeple of **Bethany Evangelical Lutheran Church**, 905 Twenty-fifth Road (308-743-2597), Kearney County's first church. The white-frame church with Gothic-style windows was built in 1885, the second church of the congregation, established ten years earlier. The altar painting, *He Dwelt Among Us,* was painted in 1900 by Olof Grafström. In the adjacent cemetery in the southwest corner is a historic marker describing the original church, a 20 by 46 foot sod structure. Inside St. Paul Lutheran Church located in the Pioneer Village Museum in Minden, 138 E. Highway 6 (800-445-4447, 308-832-2750; www.pioneervillage.org), is a model of Bethany's sod church.

West of Axtell on the county line is the former **Salem Methodist Episcopal Church**, built in 1898, a Carpenter Gothic Revival–style structure. The white-clapboard building has a tall steeple, recently restored, and the interior features the original embossed-tin walls and ceiling.

In 1878, Swedish Lutheran pioneers built a sod church, but by 1882 theological disputes within the congregation prompted the Swedish Methodists to send the Reverend Carl Charnquist to organize the dissenters. In 1883 the Methodists built a parsonage, and in 1884 they erected a small church that served the congregation until the 1898 building was constructed. Near the church is a small cemetery begun in 1882.

The Fletcher Christian Academy formerly occupied the church and moved to the site a small schoolhouse from Carter, about forty miles southwest. The academy has been closed, and the church is now under the care of the Salem Church Preservation Society. The Salem church, parsonage, and schoolhouse are on the National Register of Historic Places.

Funk

Fridhem Lutheran Church, 401 Lake (308-263-2465), the second-oldest Swedish Lutheran congregation in Phelps County, still meets in a building constructed in 1890. This structure replaced its sod predecessor, which had cost $130. First built adjacent to Fridhem Cemetery, the building was moved in 1910 to its present location. A Grafström altar painting is dated 1909.

Holdrege

Many Phelps County Swedes came from Småland. "Early settlers," reads a Nebraska state historic marker near the Phelps County Courthouse, "lured by government homestead lands and cheap railroad lands, were mainly of Swedish descent. Excellence in education, religion, and agriculture was their goal." One of the oldest buildings in Holdrege is the bank and opera building, at the northwest corner of West and Fourth, built in 1889 and much in need of restoration.

The **Nebraska Prairie Museum of the Phelps County Historical Society** (308-995-5015; www.nebraskaprairie.org), on U.S. Highway 183 one mile north of Holdrege, tells the story of communities including Funk, Loomis, Bertrand, and Atlanta. Swedish artifacts dominate the collection housed in a 65,000-square-foot building. On the museum grounds is the former Immanuel Memorial Lutheran Church, which has been moved from Ragan in Harlan County, an area known as Scandinavia Township that predates Holdrege. Founded in 1879, Immanuel was the first religious group organized in Harlan County. Its original building was superseded by this sanctuary built in 1903. Most of the congregation lived in Phelps County, and they raised the money to finance the move, to restore the church, and to establish a perpetual endowment for its upkeep. The church cemetery stands next to the church's original site in Ragan.

Also located on the museum grounds is the Snowball School, originally constructed eleven miles north of Holdrege and three miles west. The school was built in 1888 and opened in 1890 to serve a student body primarily of Swedish background. The last class was in 1954, and in 1990 the school building was moved to the museum grounds. Recently the 1906 Sam Anderson House was moved onto the property; its original location was ten miles north of Holdrege. A large Midsummer festival is held at the museum annually.

Near the museum is North Park, which contains a bronze sculpture by George W. Lundeen entitled *Promise of the Prairie*. It depicts a Nordic-looking family and is dedicated to the people of Holdrege.

Bethel Lutheran, 704 W. Avenue (308-995-5361; www.bethel-lutheran-church .com), Phelps County's oldest Lutheran congregation (established in 1877), first built a sod church, commemorated in Bethel's cemetery three miles east of Holdrege. Its sanctuary in town is of recent construction and has a Grafström altar painting.

Eight miles northwest of Holdrege near Loomis is the **Moses Hill Covenant Church** and cemetery. Organized in 1877 as the Swedish Lutheran Mission Church of Wannerburg, it is the oldest Covenant church in Phelps County. The congregation built its white-clapboard church in 1904.

North of Moses Hill is a historic marker commemorating the Christian Children's Home, founded in 1888 by the Evangelical Free Church of America. That denomination's Christian Home, two miles west of Holdrege on the south side of State Highway 23, is a residence for the elderly.

Gothenburg

Olof Bergstrom, a Baptist preacher from Delsbo in Hälsingland, had a dream for building a Swedish community near his homestead in the Platte River Valley on land acquired from the Union Pacific Railroad. He returned to Sweden to recruit people to start a new town. Some Swedes did come back with him, but they did not find the town he had promised, and many decided to move on. Although Bergstrom is generally considered to be the founder of Gothenburg, another Swede, E. G. West, may also be given credit as the town's founder. West had emigrated from Sweden in 1866 and settled in Chicago as general foreman of construction in Chicago's Lincoln Park. In 1883 he arrived in Gothenburg with a stock of lumber and coal to set up a construction company.

Bergstrom, born in northern Sweden in 1841, was involved in a number of enterprises, including being a preacher, land speculator, promoter of temperance, and dabbler in various businesses. At times in his life he amassed wealth, only to lose it in risky schemes. He died in 1910 in Tennessee, penniless and alone.

Churches and Cemeteries

Gothenburg's first church, a Swedish Baptist congregation, was organized in 1883. The congregation built their sanctuary in 1886 under the direction of E. G. West. Today they meet in a remodeled sanctuary on Avenue B and Tenth Street.

Two miles north of Gothenburg on State Highway 47 and then two miles west on County Road 769 is an unusual cemetery consisting of three artistic grave markers wrought in iron by Benjamin Palm, a loving grandfather marking his three grandchildren's graves. Palm was the first blacksmith in Gothenburg. In the early 1880s Peter and Anna Berg along with her parents arrived in Gothenburg from Hälsingland, Sweden. Between 1885 and 1889 their three children died in rapid succession. They may have been victims of an epidemic or caught in a prairie fire. Their distinctive crosses include scrollwork, hearts, and stars, each bearing a Swedish name inscription and their birth and death dates. The Bergs had four more children after these first three died. The cemetery is identified by an official Nebraska Historical Marker.

Two additional historic cemeteries may be noted. On Twenty-seventh Street east of downtown is the Gothenburg town cemetery, which has a number of Swedish graves. Four miles west on U.S. Highway 30 to the county line and then six miles north a visitor can see the Lindberg Cemetery.

Ten miles northeast of Brady, a small community thirteen miles to the west of Gothenburg, is the **Svea Dal Covenant Church and Cemetery**. The early settlers

Swedish Crosses Cemetery, Gothenburg

in Wild Horse Valley were predominantly Swedish. As early as 1893, a building committee was formed to make plans for a sanctuary, but due to frequent droughts and sickness, the church was not completed until 1912. In the nearby cemetery, the visitor can observe a number of gravestones dating back to the 1890s, including those of numerous children who succumbed to diseases.

Historic Homes

 Ernest A. Calling (Carlson), after emigrating from Sweden in 1889, made a name for himself in ranching, business, local government, and land development. About 1907 he built at 1514 Lake Avenue a small-scale Queen Anne–style residence known as the **Ernest A. Calling House.** Another historic home in Gothenburg with a Swedish connection can be found at 1315 Lake Avenue. This house was built in 1909 by Gus Dahlquist in the Scandinavian neoclassical style. Dahlquist owned a clothing store in town. The house features a classical front porch, stained-glass windows, and a symmetrical façade. At 1602 Lake Avenue, an English Tudor–style home was built in 1927 by local contractor Andrew Nordin.

Just off Interstate 80 at Exit 211 is the **Sod House Museum,** 1617 Avenue A (308-537-2076). Merle and Linda Block have re-created a two-room sod house with period furnishings, which gives the visitor an understanding of pioneer life in the late nineteenth century in western Nebraska.

SOUTH DAKOTA

In the late 1860s, Swedish homesteaders began arriving in Clay and Union Counties, not far from Vermillion in southeast South Dakota. Minnehaha County, near Sioux Falls, mainly attracted Swedes from Småland and southern Halland. Immigrants from Närke settled farther west in McCook County, where the Salem Lutheran Church was organized. In northeast South Dakota's Grant County were founded the towns of Stockholm in 1884 and Strandburg in 1888. Swedes moved from Chisago County, Minnesota, to Marshall and Brown Counties in northeast South Dakota, where they tended to settle singly rather than in groups as in other parts of the state. The first sod structures were soon replaced by log and wood-frame homes.

Vermillion

On Forest Avenue and Lewis Street is the **Forest Avenue Historic District**, a residential area of turn-of-the-century homes. A number are identified with local Swedish builders. Swedish immigrant Eric Matson's work is evident in the mansion built for the president of the University of South Dakota on E. Main Street.

At the **University of South Dakota** in Vermillion, 414 E. Clark, is the **Carl A. Norgren Hall** in the W. H. Over Museum (605-677-5257; www.usd.edu/museums .cfm). Norgren, son of Dalesburg settlers, had a number of interests, including natural history, but was best known as a designer, inventor, manufacturer, and owner of the C. A. Norgren Company in Denver.

Beresford (Dalesburg Community)

Although few remnants remain, the Dalesburg Community, southwest of Beresford, was one of the oldest and largest Swedish settlements in the Dakotas. Swedes chose the name because many of them were from Dalarna. The community included almost one hundred square miles in Clay County in the state's southeast corner; its focal point, Dalesburg Village, was north of Vermillion on University Road. Though the name Dalesburg was first given to the Lutheran and Baptist churches founded in 1871, the village took shape around the general store and post office, which Swede Andrew Lyckholm, from Leksand, Dalarna, operated on his farm in the 1890s. The name Dalesburg was originally Dahlsborg.

Daniel Peter Brown, born in Stockholm in 1827, was the most widely known Swedish settler in the area. Somewhat of a mystery man, he was the son of a minister of the Swedish state church and was educated for the ministry. When something degraded his standing, he immigrated to America and took the name Brown. He enlisted in the Civil War and participated in the siege of Vicksburg in July 1863. Six years later, he filed a homestead application in Vermillion, Clay

Marker, Dalesburg School and Village, Beresford

County. A dugout on his claim in Riverside Township served as the first home until he built a log cabin, still standing, in the early 1870s.

To get to this 12 by 17 foot one-room cabin, turn west from State Highway 19 onto 302nd Street, go two and one-half miles, turn north on Colfax, a gravel road, for one mile, then turn west on 301 Street, another gravel road. The cabin, said to be patterned after those in Dalarna, is of grooved-log construction from hardwood logs found along the bluffs of the Vermillion River running through Brown's claim. The cabin is in a bad state of disrepair. A ladder stairway had previously led to a loft, which no longer exists. The original roof was thatched.

Brown's cabin served many important functions. Here he taught school, held Lutheran services, baptized infants, performed marriages, conducted funerals, and befriended Native Americans. He also served as the government agent for settlers seeking advice on selecting a claim. Early Swedish pioneers came to this log cabin to seek counsel on a variety of subjects. In 1882 Brown sold his farm to a Norwegian and then moved on to Nebraska near the South Dakota border. On a trip to Yankton, he mysteriously disappeared. The Brown log cabin stands as a memorial to a man who aided hundreds of early Swedish pioneers.

Ten Swedish congregations were organized in or near the Dalesburg Community in Clay, Union, and Lincoln Counties between 1869 and the early 1900s. All but two (the Free Church Ansgar Meeting House and the Ahlsborg Lutheran Church) continue to exist. The first Swedish Lutheran congregation in Dakota Territory was organized at Ahlsborg, in Union County, east of Clay County, in January 1870.

The first church one sees traveling north on State Highway 19 out of Vermillion is **Dalesburg Lutheran**, 30595 University Road, Vermillion (605-253-2602; www.dalesburglutheran.org). The congregation was organized in 1871 in a sod house. The first church was built in 1874 with lumber hauled from the Big Sioux River. The present modest white-frame church with Gothic-style windows was constructed in 1897 by Swedish immigrant Eric Matson from Alunda Parish, Uppland. In 1920 the single tower was removed, and the present two towers were added. In 1978 the Ahlsborg Lutheran Church merged with Dalesburg Lutheran. This church's sister congregation is the Svärdsjö Parish in Dalarna, Sweden, and many of the first Swedes came from this parish beginning in the late 1860s. Dalesburg Lutheran, Dalesburg Baptist, and Komstad Covenant Churches host an annual Swedish Midsummer festival.

Directly across State Highway 19 from the church is a polished granite marker identifying the location of Hub City, with a detailed description of its history, people, and structures. At the top of the plaque is an etched layout of the town as it existed in the 1930s. The monument is on the site of the former Hub City garage, which operated from 1925 to 1971. Hub City was not founded until 1925, when Bill Inberg, a grandson of Swedish immigrants, opened the garage. It was given this name because the site was equidistant from the surrounding towns.

Swedish Baptists were the first group to organize in the area, forming the **Big Springs Baptist Church**, 30705-480th Avenue, five miles south of Alcester on State Highway 11, and one mile east on 307th Street at the intersection with 480th (605-547-2816), in 1869 in Union County. This congregation was the first Swedish Baptist church in Dakota Territory. A small wood-frame church begun in 1874 was not completed until the early 1880s, the delay resulting in part from a severe locust plague that discouraged many settlers, who then left the area. When the congregation experienced a spiritual revival in 1893, the old sanctuary was too small, and a new one was built across the road. The old sanctuary was relocated and used as the township hall between 1944 and 1993. In the mid-1990s, it was moved back to its original site and restored.

The old church is an informal museum with old photographs and a pre-1900 pump organ; various functions are held there. The center part of the congregation's current sanctuary across the road was built in 1893 with additions in 1920,

1965, and 2001. The congregation maintains an annual *julotta* service on Christmas morning. Adjacent to the church is the town cemetery.

In the town of Alcester is **Alcester Baptist Church**, 409 Iowa Street (605-934-2575). The white-clapboard church with a bell tower and stained-glass windows was built in 1902.

In 1871, the Swede Baptist Church of Bloomingdale was founded in the Dalesburg settlement. The present white-frame sanctuary of **Dalesburg Baptist Church** (605-253-2622) was constructed in 1919 northeast of the Dalesburg Lutheran Church and seventeen miles directly west of the Big Springs Baptist Church. To reach the church, go north from the Dalesburg Lutheran Church on State Highway 19 for one mile, turn east on a gravel road, and go one mile. There is a sign at the intersection indicating the direction to the church. The area churches hold a joint annual Midsummer festival.

Driving north on State Highway 19, one can see an impressive polished granite monument on the west side of the road. It describes the history of the Dalesburg village and the former Dalesburg school. Four and one-half miles north of the marker is the **Komstad Covenant Church and Cemetery**, 29987 University Road. The white-clapboard edifice with a central tower and Gothic-style windows was erected in 1905. Two large stained-glass windows were installed in 1924. The north window is in memory of Carolina and Gustavus Norgren, who are buried in the cemetery.

Gustavus Norgren, a local farmer, was from Dalarna, and his wife, Carolina, from Östergötland. Their son, Carl August Norgren, born in 1890 in South Dakota, became a well-known engineer, inventor, and manufacturer in Denver. Just north of the church, at the Southeast South Dakota Experiment Farm, is a state historic plaque in memory of Gustavus Norgren.

Alsen

The village of Alsen, in western Union County, was named by Olof Erickson, the area's first blacksmith, for his birthplace, Alsen Parish, Jämtland. In 1871 Erickson took out a land claim and settled on what is today the **Olof Erickson (Solomon Anderson) Farm**. He erected a house that same year, a white-clapboard structure that still stands behind the imposing main house.

Solomon Anderson, also a Swede from Jämtland, came to Alsen in 1875 from Omaha, married Erickson's daughter, and purchased the farm in 1878. The site near Beresford, one-half mile west of Interstate 29 and one-half mile north of State Highway 46, is remarkable for the twenty-one outbuildings still standing. The main house is a large, clapboard, neoclassical-style structure with Georgian characteristics, built in 1901. Of five creameries in the area, Anderson's was the most successful.

Brandon

The **Swedona Evangelical Covenant** congregation was organized in rural Brandon in 1877 by Swedish immigrants from Lockport and Joliet, Illinois. It was originally known as the Swedish Evangelical Lutheran Church of Swedona and became the Swedish Evangelical Mission Church of Swedona in 1878. The first sanctuary, a sod church, was constructed two years later. A stone marker notes the spot where the sod church stood. In 1881 the congregation built a frame church. The present white-frame Gothic building, 25843-479th Avenue (605-582-3261), dates from 1913. The sanctuary features an altar painting by Norwegian American artist Arnold Klagstad of Christ in a blessing gesture in front of a snow-capped mountain landscape. Across the road is the Swedona Cemetery, where there are several interesting gravestones, including that of Israel Granström, an early pioneer who perished in a blizzard. A number of church members came from Västerbotten, including Axel Alexius Anderson, whose gravestone has the province's coat of arms. To reach the church, go north on State Highway 11 from Interstate 90 about two and one-half miles to Minnehaha County Road 130 and turn west. Travel three miles to a county road and turn south. The church is about one-half mile south of County Road 130.

During the 1976 bicentennial of the United States, the Sioux Falls Bicentennial Commission published *Our Heritage,* a complete list of historic sites and a detailed map of the county. Of the 105 historic homesteads identified and marked with special plaques, at least ten were of Swedish origin.

Valley Springs

The **Beaver Valley Lutheran Church**, 26214-484th Avenue (605-582-3504), two and one-half miles east of Brandon, was organized in 1873. The present large brick church building dates from 1922. Birger Sandzén, the well-known Lindsborg, Kansas, artist, executed the large altar painting showing Christ flanked by two angels in the heavens while his followers watch from below. A large cemetery is adjacent to the church.

On the north side of County Road 138 near the state line is a marker honoring the memory of the state's second poet laureate, Adeline Jenney. She was a long-time Valley Springs resident who wrote a poem, "They Were Able," to honor the New England and Scandinavian immigrants into this valley from 1868 to 1873.

Crooks

Although the first church organized in Minnehaha County was the Nidaros Norwegian Lutheran Church in 1868, Swedish congregations were soon established.

The early pioneers of the late 1860s and early 1870s experienced a series of hardships, including drought, grasshoppers, hail and winter storms, and prairie fires. Despite these threats, twenty-five settlers, mainly from Halland, met in 1878 to organize the Swedish Evangelical Lutheran Church of Benton, now called the **Benton Lutheran Church** (605-543-5384), two miles west of Crooks. The church built its first sanctuary in 1885, but lightning destroyed it in 1913. The 1,325-pound bell, purchased in 1894 by the Ladies Sewing Society, fell from the steeple during the fire and cracked. In 1914 the Luther League restored and remounted the bell behind the present church sanctuary. That same year a new church bell was installed in the steeple. It is the custom to toll the bell at 10 A.M. the day after the death of a member of the congregation. Swedish pioneers are buried in the cemetery. The first burial was Peter Byg, a Dane, who died in 1880 trying to save his family and home from a prairie fire.

The white-clapboard church with its central steeple and Gothic-style windows was designed by a Sioux Falls architect. The striking interior features a lovely Gothic-style altar painted white with gold trim and inscribed, *Jag har bedt för dig* (I have prayed for thee), from Luke 22:32. Olof Grafström created the altar painting of Christ in Gethsemane. A cabinet in the back of the sanctuary holds historic memorabilia.

Mitchell

At the original site of the New Home Lutheran Church, seven miles south and two miles west of Mitchell, the bell of the old church remains, as does the cemetery. In 1883 a group of Swedish homesteaders organized the Swedish Evangelical Lutheran Nyhem Church and two years later constructed a small frame sanctuary. When the congregation in 1958 erected a new church in nearby Mitchell at 1023 S. Minnesota Street (605-996-8763), the old church building was sold. It was later lost to fire.

Lake Norden

Lake Norden in Hamlin County is a predominantly Finnish community, though many residents are of Swedish background. The Lutheran cemetery contains gravestones with Finnish and Swedish-Finnish names and a marker where the Lake Norden Suomi Synod Evangelical Lutheran Church stood from 1903 to 1944.

Charles Larson, with a business partner, bought some of the first lots in Lake Norden. Larson and his son served as mayors. The **Lake Norden Baptist Church** (605-785-3180) was established by five Swedish families in 1888, and the church building was constructed in 1909. The small white-frame **Evangelical Covenant Church**, 809 Dakota Street (605-785-3829), organized as the Scandinavian Christian Mission Congregation, was founded by Swedes and Norwegians. The building dates from 1901 and was originally located two miles east and one-half mile to the south.

Strandburg

 The beautiful red-brick **Tabor Lutheran Church** (605-676-2414) was built after the congregation's original 1892 frame structure was struck by lightning in 1905 and burned to the ground. The congregation constructed this second sanctuary between 1905 and 1910. Designed by the Reverend Erick Schöld, it is late Victorian Gothic. A tall Gothic-style steeple towers over the sanctuary with its dark shingling and white-wooden trim. Since 1910 the church's interior has remained much the same. The raised pulpit with its intricate canopy suspended from the ceiling is of natural hardwood. On either side of the Gothic-style altar are stained-glass windows with Swedish inscriptions. The congregation's well-maintained cemetery lies to the east.

Another Grant County church with Swedish roots is the **Evangelical Covenant Church**, 110 Georgia Avenue, Labolt (605-623-4242), erected in 1900.

New Effington

The rural **Walla Lutheran Church** (605-637-6409) was organized in 1894 as the Swedish Evangelical Lutheran Walla Church. The congregation built its sanctuary, where it still worships, in 1902. The church is located two miles northeast of Walla. Early pastor K. G. William Dahl, who later founded Bethphage Mission in Axtell, Nebraska, served the church from 1907 to 1909.

Rosholt

Congregants organized the rural **St. Joseph Lutheran Church** (605-537-4505) five miles southeast of town in 1894 and built its sanctuary in 1902. St. Joseph shared a pastor with the Walla Lutheran Church. Dahl was also a pastor at this church early in his career (1907–1909) and wrote a book based on his experiences in Rosholt and New Effington. Swedish was spoken in the services and Sunday school at St. Joseph until 1925.

White Rock

The **Augustana Lutheran Church** in White Rock (605-537-4505), in the extreme northeastern corner of the state, was founded in 1887. In recent years the same pastor has served the Walla, St. Joseph, and Augustana congregations.

Claremont

 In 1881 Swedish settlers, many of them from Chisago County, Minnesota, came to South Dakota to homestead land near Claremont. In 1884 they met in a home

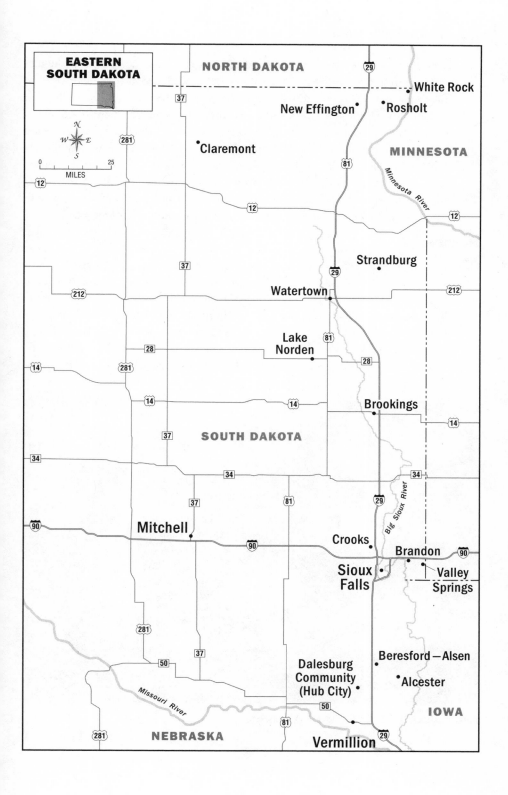

EASTERN
SOUTH DAKOTA

MILES
0   25

N
W   E
S

NORTH DAKOTA

White Rock

New Effington   Rosholt

Claremont

MINNESOTA

Minnesota River

Strandburg

Watertown

Lake
Norden

Brookings

SOUTH DAKOTA

Big Sioux River

Mitchell

Crooks
Brandon
Sioux
Falls   Valley
Springs

Beresford—Alsen

Dalesburg
Community
(Hub City)   Alcester

Missouri River

IOWA

NEBRASKA   Vermillion

for the first service of what they named the Swedish Evangelical Lutheran Augustana Church, now called the **Augustana Lutheran Church** (605-294-5340). In 1899 they built a church under the supervision of William Carlson, a Swede from Center City, Minnesota. Church sources say that Carlson did a handstand on top of the tower the day the building was completed. Dedicated in 1900, it is a large wood-frame church with both Gothic-Revival and Classical-Revival features. It has twelve long, Gothic-arched, stained-glass windows. Hand-carved furnishings, including an elevated pulpit covered by a suspended hood, are features of the interior sanctuary. The church is located eight miles west and one-quarter mile south of Langford or four and one-half miles south of Claremont.

Hermosa

Far to the west, in Custer State Park on Highway 16A, is the Peter Norbeck Visitor Center (605-255-4515). The large log structure with open front porch was built in 1927. Peter Norbeck (1870–1937), a well driller, was South Dakota's first native-born governor and a U.S. senator. He was born to a Swedish father and a Norwegian mother in a dugout in Clay County in southeastern South Dakota. Having an intense interest in the Black Hills, Norbeck was instrumental in setting aside 127,000 acres as Custer State Park. Inside the Visitor Center is a Norbeck display.

Peter Norbeck Center, Custer State Park, Hermosa

Twelve miles away is a plaque at the Norbeck Overlook on Iron Mountain Road describing this former statesman's achievement. Norbeck was responsible for designing bridges on Iron Mountain Road, which takes visitors to the nearby Mount Rushmore National Memorial.

NORTH DAKOTA

Since Swedish pioneers tended to settle singly rather than in groups in North Dakota, their influence was diluted, and relatively few of their landmarks have been preserved. Norwegians were more numerous, and Swedes frequently intermingled with them.

Grafton

The Swedish-born population was fairly evenly distributed throughout the region though many moved into the Red River Valley. On U.S. Highway 81, three and one-half miles north of Grafton and a little over five miles west on Walsh County Road 9, is a marker for the Sweden Post Office, which was established in 1879 and served the community until 1882, when the railroad reached Grafton. Less than one mile west of the marker, take a gravel road south for one half mile to where the former **North Trinity Lutheran Church** and cemetery is located. The congregation, mainly of Swedish background, was established in 1879; in 1885 it divided into the North and South Trinity churches (the latter sanctuary with its Norwegian congregation is about six miles to the south). The white-clapboard Gothic-style North Trinity Church was constructed in 1893. The congregation ceased to exist in 1953, but the sanctuary is well maintained by a local group, and a yearly service is held there.

After the congregation disbanded, members continued to support maintenance of the building. One member who lived in San Francisco sent her annual contribution with a note that in her thoughts she still listened to the bell every Christmas Eve. In the mid-1970s, Ken Johnson, a farmer whose family had rung the bell for five generations, brought his mobile phone to the church, and while the bell tolled he dialed her California number. This tradition has continued, and now a number of people gather annually with their cell phones, calling former members and friends to broadcast the lovely tolling of the old bell.

Greater Fargo Area

By the early 1960s some twenty-eight Augustana Lutheran Synod congregations were scattered throughout North Dakota. The oldest one, **Maple-Sheyenne**, 8711 N. Fortieth Avenue, Harwood (701-282-4024), was founded in 1878. To reach this church north of Fargo, from Interstate 29 exit at Harwood, go west and south on

Cass County Road 17 for three and one-half miles, and turn west on Cass County Road 20 for one and one-half miles. The sanctuary, which contains an Olof Grafström painting dated 1915, is modernized, but the original pressed-metal ceiling and walls have been retained. A well-tended cemetery is adjacent to the church.

Former North Trinity Lutheran Church, Grafton

Also near Fargo is the **Herby Lutheran Church**, 16205 SE Twenty-seventh Street, Argusville (701-484-5239). From Interstate 29, exit at Argusville, go west on Cass County Road 4 for five miles, south on Cass County Road 11 for two miles, and then west for two additional miles. The congregation was founded in 1891.

Other former Augustana Lutheran churches in North Dakota include Elim Lutheran, 321 N. Ninth Street, Fargo (701-232-2574), built in 1905 and rebuilt in 1939; Augustana, 520 University Avenue, Grand Forks (701-775-3187); Gustavus Adolphus, 207 SE First Street, Gwinner (701-678-2552); Grace, 206 Pleasant Avenue, Sheyenne (701-996-2361); Immanuel, 1403 SE Ninth Avenue, Jamestown (701-252-1211); First, 800 N. Seventh Street, Bismarck (701-223-4340); Sunne, 7701 Highway 36, six miles east of Wilton (701-734-6485; www.sunnelutheran. org); and Augustana, 321 W. University Avenue, Minot (701-838-9563).

Covenant congregations include Teien Covenant, 1270-160th Avenue, Drayton (218-455-5868); Knollbrook Covenant, 3030 N. Broadway, Fargo (701-235-4622); and Hope Evangelical Covenant, 1601 S. Seventeenth Avenue, Grand Forks (701-772-1884).

Souris

Two miles south of the Canadian border and eight miles northeast of Souris is the former Swedish **Zion Lutheran Church and Cemetery.** The fieldstone and white-clapboard church with clear Gothic-style windows was built in 1903 (the date 1903 and initials S. L. C. can be seen above the main door). Area farmers donated one cent per bushel of wheat to pay for the church's masonry work. Although the sanctuary no longer serves a congregation, it is well maintained. It contains some of the original furnishings, including the altar and altar rail, pump organ, pews, and a pot-bellied stove. Historic photographs hang on the walls. The sanctuary features a unique stenciled ceiling in cross motif. To reach this isolated church from Souris, travel east on Botineau County Road 6 for two miles, then north on a gravel road identified as NE Third Avenue for four miles, to NE 106th Street, another gravel road. Proceed on this road more than one mile to another gravel road; go north one and one-third miles to Zion Church. On NE 106th Street, travelers pass Bethesda Cemetery on the south side with a stone cairn containing a plaque honoring Norwegian pioneers who established this congregation in 1902.

Minot

Scandinavian Heritage Park—1020 S. Broadway, on the west side of U.S. Highway 83 (701-852-9161; www.realnd.com/scandiheritageindex.htm).
Although the park emphasizes Norwegian culture, it includes contributions from the other four Nordic countries. Tourists can see a very large Dala horse,

Former Zion Lutheran Church, Souris

dedicated by the Swedish Heritage Association-NW in 2000; a full-size replica of the Gol Stave Church (the original church was built in the mid-1200s, moved to Bygdøy Park, Oslo, in 1882, and reconstructed in 1884; the cornerstone was laid by King Oscar II in that year); the over 220-year-old Norwegian Sigdal house; a Norwegian *stabbur* (storehouse); statues of Norwegian skiers Sondre Norheim, identified as the "father of modern skiing," and Caspar Oimoen; a Finnish sauna; a Danish windmill built in Powers Lake, North Dakota, in 1928; and a statue of Icelandic explorer Leif Eriksson.

MINNESOTA

In 1850, Swedish novelist Fredrika Bremer visited Minnesota Territory and exclaimed, "What a glorious new Scandinavia might not Minnesota become! Here the Swede would find his clear, romantic lakes, the plains of Skåne, rich in grain, and the valleys of Norrland." Within sixty years, Swedes had become one of the largest ethnic groups in Minnesota.

Jacob Fahlström (c. 1795–1859) is the first known Swede to have settled in Minnesota. As a boy, he went to Canada, somehow separated from his party, and was adopted by the Ojibwe Indians. He later chose an Ojibwe wife. By about 1813, Fahlström arrived in the area that became the Twin Cities of St. Paul and Minneapolis, where he served as a Methodist missionary and as guide for fur trade companies. In the 1850s, Fahlström settled on a farm near Afton in Washington County.

In the fall of 1850, three Swedes—Oscar Roos, Carl Fernström, and August Sandahl—came to Washington County and built a log cabin near Hay Lake, south of present-day Scandia. During the following decades, thousands of Swedish settlers, motivated largely by economic reasons, traveled up the St. Croix River, disembarked in Washington County, and then stayed in the county or headed into Minnesota's or Wisconsin's interior. A marker, titled "Swedes in Minnesota," at the Minnesota Information Center on Interstate 94 at the St. Croix River, describes these immigrants' early experiences.

Because most modern travelers begin their exploration of Minnesota from the metropolitan Twin Cities area, Minneapolis and St. Paul open this chapter. Travelers arriving at the Minneapolis–St. Paul International Airport will see a replica of the *Spirit of St. Louis* hanging from the ceiling in honor of one of Minnesota's most famous native sons, Charles Lindbergh Jr. The terminal also bears his name.

Second only to Chicago, the Twin Cities constitute the most important Swedish American center in the United States. Swedish influence continues to be greater in Minneapolis, where the number of foreign-born Swedes once was three times more than in St. Paul.

Twin Cities

In the Twin Cities, Swedes founded three hospitals, two academies, and two colleges. Early Swedish population centers included the Cedar-Riverside area of Minneapolis, Swede Hollow (*Svenska Dalen*) near Payne Avenue in St. Paul,

South Minneapolis, and Northeast Minneapolis, including Camden. Since 1933, people have gathered on Swedish Day or Swedes' Day *(Svenskarnas Dag)* in late June in Minneapolis's Minnehaha Park. The nation's largest Lutheran congregation, Mount Olivet, and one of the most historically significant Covenant congregations, First Covenant, are in Minneapolis.

Minneapolis is also the home of the American Swedish Institute, a private, nonprofit organization that preserves the Swedish heritage brought to the United States by Swedish immigrants and promotes cultural bonds between the countries. More than seventy-five years old, the institute boasts a membership that includes six thousand households from fifty states and other countries.

Minneapolis

Institutes and Museums

 American Swedish Institute—2600 Park Avenue at E. Twenty-sixth Street (612-871-4907; www.americanswedishinst.org).
This imposing Indiana-limestone mansion built in the French Chateau style was the home of Swan J. Turnblad (1860–1933), a Swedish newspaper owner born in Småland. In 1887 he began managing the *Svenska Amerikanska Posten,* a struggling Swedish-language weekly in Minneapolis. By the turn of the century, he had turned the paper's sagging fortunes around. It claimed to be the largest Swedish newspaper in the United States.

In 1903 Turnblad and his wife, Christina, acquired property on exclusive Park Avenue and began the construction of this thirty-three-room mansion known as Turnblad's Castle. Designed by Minneapolis architects Christopher A. Boehme and Victor Cordella, it took about four years to build. With its exterior turrets and interior first-floor mahogany ornamentation, the edifice was one of the most grandiose mansions in the Twin Cities. Visitors will especially note the exterior decoration, outstanding interior woodwork, uniquely conceived ceilings, and stained-glass window on the stairway landing. Many rooms contain *kakelugnar* (large ceramic tile stoves), each of distinctive design: seven were made by Uppsala-Ekeby Ab of Uppsala, two by Rörstrand Porcelain Company of Stockholm, and two are of unknown Swedish origin. However, because Turnblad was fascinated by the latest technology, central heating was also installed.

After his wife died in 1929, Turnblad surprised the Minneapolis community by announcing he would establish the American Institute of Swedish Arts, Literature and Science (changed to the American Swedish Institute in 1949), endowed with his mansion and other properties. Today the institute promotes the Swedish cultural heritage by presenting lectures, concerts, exhibits, and educational and travel opportunities.

American Swedish Institute, Minneapolis

The mansion's major rooms house the institute's permanent exhibits. Richly decorated and paneled in African mahogany, the two-story grand hall includes a spectacularly carved fireplace featuring two male figures by sculptor Albin Polasek. On the second-story level is a Viking figure added later. At the foot of the grand staircase are two carved winged lions or griffins, believed to incorporate the Swedish lion and the American eagle. The light-colored salon in Rococo Revival style is used for special exhibits. A museum shop, also on the first floor, is housed in the former den.

The dining room walls and ceiling made of bleached Honduran mahogany are intricately carved with flowers and fruit, a motif echoed in the green marble fireplace. The wall panels and furniture were designed and carved by Ulrich Steiner, a Swiss craftsman. His work is also seen in the music room, where he carved fifty-two winged cherubs. Above the fireplace mantel is a carved scene from a Nordic legend showing a troll-like figure luring a young woman into an enchanted world. The original wool carpet was designed in Sweden and woven in Austria. Turnblad family porcelain is displayed in this room.

The light, airy breakfast room presents a stark contrast to the dark, heavy feeling of the dining room. It is decorated and furnished in the style of an eighteenth-century manor house. The white, gold-trimmed, *kakelugn* is the focal point. The room also contains furniture from the era of Gustav III, who reigned from 1771 to 1792, and a painting by Gustavus Hesselius (1682–1755), one of several by Swedish and Swedish American artists. The music room, which features mahogany decorative carvings, is still used for performances and recitals.

Visitors ascend to the second floor by way of the grand stairs. Above the landing is the Visby Window, a copy of a painting by Swedish artist Carl Gustaf Hellqvist (1851–1890) entitled *Valdemar Atterdag Levying Contributions on Visby,* which hangs in the National Museum in Stockholm. The stained-glass window, made in Sweden and installed about 1908, depicts the conquering Danish king seizing tributes from the citizens of Visby on the island of Gotland.

The Turnblad family bedrooms on the second floor are now used as special exhibit areas. In the Värmland Room are numerous items sent in 1952 as a token of friendship between the people of Värmland and the United States. Exhibits of Swedish glass as well as wood carvings by Emil Janel may be seen on this level. The library housing Turnblad's collection of books is also on this floor.

The centerpiece of the third floor is the ballroom with its proscenium stage. This floor contains an extensive exhibit featuring Swedish life in the Twin Cities, focusing on the development of the various Swedish centers. Cedar Avenue, also known as Snoose (snuff) Boulevard, was a center of Swedish American theater between 1885 and 1915. The exhibit also includes a selection of items taken by the emigrants on their journey from Sweden to America.

In the lower level of the mansion, visitors may browse the extensive *bokhandel* (bookstore) focusing on Sweden and Swedish American life. There is also a *kaffestuga* (coffee shop) and an auditorium, which features a mural in *Dalmålning* style by Bengt Engman (1925–1987) depicting Swedish immigration to America and particularly to Minnesota.

The complex also includes a carriage house that served as a garage for the first cars in the Twin Cities and was equipped with an automobile turntable. Connecting the mansion with the carriage house is a passage containing the stained-glass window from the former *Svenska Amerikanska Posten* office.

Outside in the children's garden is a statue of Selma Lagerlöf, the Swedish author who won the Nobel Prize for literature in 1909. An extensive addition to the museum is planned.

The Swedish Council of America—2600 Park Avenue at E. Twenty-sixth Street (800-981-4722; www.swedishcouncil.org).

Housed in an annex of the Turnblad mansion is the office of the Swedish Council of America, which unites more than three hundred Swedish American affiliate organizations in the United States, Canada, and Sweden. The council works to strengthen the cultural relationship between North America and Sweden and to preserve the Swedish American heritage, providing modest grants and other awards that recognize distinguished contributors to cultural exchange between Sweden and the United States.

Historic Places

Cedar-Riverside Area

Cedar Avenue was known as Snoose Boulevard. Its rows of tenement buildings were inhabited by Scandinavian immigrants who spoke Swedish, Norwegian, and Danish in the stores and other businesses in the area. Seven Corners, at Cedar and Washington Avenues, was the district's hub. Here the famous Swedish American Hjalmar Peterson, known as the "peasant comedian" Olle i Skratthult (Olle in Laughterville), entertained his countrymen. Dania Hall, at 427 Cedar Avenue near Riverside, hosted cultural events and Scandinavian performers. Built in 1886, the large red-brick edifice was destroyed by a fire in 2000.

Milwaukee Avenue between Franklin Avenue and Twenty-fourth Street— private residences, pedestrians only.

In the Seward neighborhood's **Milwaukee Avenue Historic District** are two-story houses, dating from the 1880s, which were once inhabited by so many Swedish and other Nordic working-class residents that the area was known as "Copenhagen Avenue." Many early immigrants worked in the flour mills and nearby Milwaukee Railroad yards. An unusual feature of the houses in the four-block district is the lovely lattice work on the front porches.

Hennepin County Medical Center's Medical Specialty Center (former Swedish Hospital)—900–914 S. Eighth Street at Ninth Avenue (612-875-3000; www.hcmc.org).

Swedes from several denominations cooperated in founding Swedish Hospital in 1898. In 1970 it combined with St. Barnabas Hospital to create Metropolitan Medical Center, using part of the facilities and land of the Swedish Hospital. In 1992 it closed and the building was sold to Hennepin County Medical Center for a medical specialty clinic. *Sprites,* a symbol of health and healing, is a sculpture created by Paul Granlund for the Metropolitan Medical Center in 1970. It is located in the courtyard of Hennepin County Medical Center.

The name Swedish Hospital can be seen on the Eighth Street façade of the older of the two buildings. Between the main entrance's two double doors on Eighth Street one can see the old cornerstone, partially blocked, that reads "Swedish Hospital 1901."

Swedish Hospital Nurses Home, 2215 Park Avenue, established in 1899, was built on the east side of the medical complex facing the former Central Free Church. At the top of the building can be seen the nurses-home inscription.

Floyd B. Olson House—1914 W. Forty-ninth Street (between Morgan and S. Logan Avenues).

This unpretentious house was the residence of Floyd B. Olson, governor of Minnesota from 1931 to 1936, whose father was Norwegian and mother was Swedish. A popular governor supported by the farm and labor movements during the Great Depression, he was reelected by many of the same people who voted for Franklin D. Roosevelt in 1932. Olson died in office after having been nominated to run for the U.S. Senate.

Churches

Augustana Lutheran Church—704 S. Eleventh Avenue, two blocks south of the Metrodome (612-332-8595; www.augustanampls.org).

In December 1857, the Reverend Peter Carlson preached the first Swedish Lutheran sermon in Minneapolis. Nine years later Carlson joined with eleven Swedes and Norwegians to organize the Evangelical Lutheran Augustana Church of Minneapolis. In 1867 the new congregation, now numbering twenty-nine communicants, joined the fledgling Augustana Synod and bought a lot on the corner of Washington Avenue and S. Thirteenth Avenue, just west of the Scandinavian neighborhood around Seven Corners. A year later the new church building was sufficiently finished to house the first service.

The enormous increase in Swedish immigrants in Minneapolis soon forced the congregation to look for new and larger space. By 1882 the members finished the present sand-colored church building on the corner of S. Eleventh Avenue and E. Seventh Street. On June 24, 1883, it was dedicated by the Reverend Erland Carlsson, who, with pastors Lars Paul Esbjörn and Tuve Nilsson Hasselquist, is considered a father of Swedish Lutheranism in North America.

Between 1874 and 1910, seven daughter congregations spun off from the mother Augustana congregation: Bethlehem (1847) at 2200 N. Fremont Avenue; Emanuel Lutheran (1884) at 697 NE Thirteenth Avenue (612-789-1319); St. Paul Lutheran (1887) at 2742 S. Fifteenth Avenue (612-724-3862); Ebenezer (1892) at 2720 E. Twenty-second Street; Zion (1893) at 128 W. Thirty-third Street (612-824-1017);

Messiah (1908) at 2504 S. Columbus Avenue (612-871-8831); and Grace University (1910) at 324 SE Harvard Street (612-331-8125).

Two schools founded by the church no longer exist: Emanuel Academy (1887–1894) and Minnesota College (1904–1930). The college enrolled more than 800 students in its building at Harvard and Delaware Streets in 1923, but heavy debts forced it to close.

Central Free Church—707 S. Tenth Avenue.

The cornerstone of this red-brick building, on the same block directly west of Augustana Evangelical Lutheran, identifies it as *Svenska Missions Templet 1895* (Swedish Mission Temple). Another congregation worships here now. The headquarters of the Evangelical Free Church of America is in Bloomington, Minnesota, 901 E. Seventy-eighth Street (952-854-1300; www.efca.org).

First Covenant Church—810 S. Seventh Street (612-332-8093; www.1stcov.org).

Carved on the Seventh Street façade of the large red-brick building is the inscription, *Svenska Missions Tabernaklet 1886* (Swedish Mission Tabernacle 1886). In December 1874, the congregation was officially organized with thirty-one charter members. After the dynamic Reverend E. August Skogsbergh, sometimes called "the Swedish Dwight L. Moody," assumed his post here in 1884, a larger church building was needed. A lot was purchased at Seventh Street and Chicago Avenue, the foundation was laid in 1886, and the following year, a building seating 2,500 was completed. Svenska Tabernaklet was one of the liveliest places in Minneapolis, considering Skogsbergh's forceful preaching and A. L. Skoog's powerful singing. Skoog was called "the Swedish Ira Sankey" in reference to Moody's organ-playing revival singer. For a time, it was the largest Covenant church in the United States.

The main sanctuary has been altered. The large impressive auditorium has a number of lovely stained-glass windows. Downstairs is an archival room where, among the items displayed, are the organ used by Skoog and the silk hat worn by Skogsbergh when he received the Order of Vasa from the Swedish king. In the small Skogsbergh-Skoog Chapel near the main sanctuary is a copy of Skogsbergh's round pulpit. The original one is at the Covenant Archives at North Park University in Chicago, which began at First Covenant. The reception room in the church office has a Swedish folk décor.

In Minneapolis's Lakewood Cemetery, at 3600 Hennepin Avenue, is a reddish granite marker on the Reverend Skogsbergh's grave, which lies in lot 194, section 4, grave 4½, shaded by oaks at the base of a small hill. To the Värmland native, his church inscribed: "In memory of Erik August Skogsbergh (1850–1939). A faithful pastor, a zealous evangelist, and a courageous leader who fulfilled his ministry."

Mount Olivet Lutheran Church—5025 S. Knox Avenue (612-926-7651; www .mtolivet.org). The largest Lutheran congregation (currently more than 13,000) in the United States worships in a spacious, light-colored stone, Gothic-style church designed by architect Hugo Hansen. The main sanctuary features a beamed ceiling and spectacular stained-glass windows depicting biblical figures.

The church honored the Reverend Reuben K. Youngdahl by naming its chapel for this dynamic pastor who served the church from 1938 to 1968. In the hallway on the lower level of the administration building is a statue of Caroline (Lina) Sandell (1832–1903), who composed hymns, including the favorite *Tryggare kan ingen vara* (Children of the Heavenly Father). Sculpted by Axel Wallenberg of Stockholm, it is similar to one on the campus of North Park University in Chicago.

A second Olivet campus is in Victoria, Minnesota, on Rolling Acres Road between State Highways 5 and 7 (952-443-5072).

Grace Evangelical Lutheran Church—324 Harvard Street SE (612-331-8125). This Gothic-style brick edifice was completed in 1917 to serve University of Minnesota students. The congregation is currently identified as the Grace University Lutheran Church.

Bethlehem Baptist Church (First Swedish Baptist)—720 S. Thirteenth Avenue (612-338-7653). This congregation was organized in 1871 with twenty-two charter members, and in the 1880s First Swedish Baptist bought a building at Thirteenth Avenue and Eighth Street. Through the years Bethlehem has helped start new churches in the Twin Cities area, including Elim Baptist Church at 685 SE Thirteenth Avenue (612-789-3591), which is significant in the history of Bethel University as the site of the first class sessions in 1905. Recently Bethlehem Baptist has established a North Extension site in Roseville.

Schools

University of Minnesota, Curtis L. Carlson School of Management— 321 S. Nineteenth Avenue (800-922-3622; www.csom.umn.edu). In 1986 the University of Minnesota named its school of management in honor of Curtis L. Carlson (1914–1999), founder and chairman of Carlson Companies, in recognition of a personal gift of $25 million to the university, the largest single gift ever made to a public university. Carlson was the son of Swedish immigrants; his father, Charles, had a grocery store in South Minneapolis. Curtis Carlson graduated from the University of Minnesota in 1937, majoring in economics, and founded the Gold Bond Stamp Company. In 1953 he sold it to Super Valu, a large wholesale grocery chain. Nine years later he purchased the Radisson Hotel in downtown Minneapolis and turned it into an international brand with more than 375 properties. In 1973 Carlson's global corporation became Carlson Companies, Inc., which encompasses more than one hundred companies with operations in more than 140 countries. Carlson also was a board chairman of the Swedish Council of America.

Minnehaha Academy—South Campus, 4200 W. River Parkway (612-721-3359); North Campus, 3100 W. River Parkway (612-729-8321); Bloomington Campus, 10150 S. Xerxes Avenue (952-806-0060; www.minnehaha.pvt.k12.mn.us).

Minnehaha Academy is a private coeducational school founded in 1913 under the auspices of the Evangelical Covenant Church of America. This school is an outgrowth of one founded in 1884 for children of Swedish immigrants. The academy currently enrolls about 1,200 students.

Fredrika Bremer School—1214 N. Lowry Avenue.

This former Minneapolis public school dating to 1886 honors the nineteenth-century Swedish author and social reformer. Since the 1970s the building has been an apartment complex.

Other Points of Interest

Good Templar Center—2926 Cedar Avenue (612-721-7606).

The Good Templar Center is owned by the International Order of Good Templars (IOGT), an international temperance society that began in Sweden in 1879. Built in 1983, it is a museum and archives for chapters that have been dissolved. Attached is Enigheten Hall, meeting site of the Enigheten Chapter of IOGT.

Sculpture and Other Art

Gunnar Wennerberg Statue—Minnehaha Park, Minnehaha Parkway and Minnehaha Avenue.

This statue of Gunnar Wennerberg (1817–1901), a Swedish poet, composer, educator, and statesman, is a copy of a statue by Carl Eldh that stands outside the Uppsala University library in Uppsala, Sweden. The statue portrays the famous Swede holding his student cap, and inscribed on the monument is a poem by Wennerberg. The annual *Svenskarnas Dag* (Swedish or Swedes' Day) celebrations are held near the statue.

Spoon Bridge and Cherry Fountain (1988)—**Minneapolis Sculpture Garden, 726 Vineland Place.**
This monumental sculpture by Claes Oldenburg and Coosje van Bruggen is the most visible work in the Minneapolis Sculpture Garden, a joint project of the Minneapolis Park and Recreation Board and the Walker Art Center. It has become a Minneapolis icon.

Birth of Freedom—**Westminster Presbyterian Church, Nicollet Mall at Twelfth Street.**
This bronze sculpture in front of the church is by Minnesota sculptor Paul Granlund.

Lumberman—**Webber Park, 4310 Webber Parkway.**
Minnesota sculptor Rodger Brodin (1940–1995) used his grandfather Peter (1874–1954), a Swedish immigrant from Torsby, Värmland, as the model for this bronze sculpture honoring lumbermen. As early as the 1860s, the nearby banks of the Mississippi River were the location of a number of sawmills, and Peter Brodin worked in one of them near Webber Park.

Many works of Rodger Brodin, a U.S. Marine in the Vietnam War, portray military subjects. These include *Monument to the Living*, a statue of a soldier, dedicated in 1982 on the Minnesota State Capitol Grounds near the Veterans Service Building. *The Batavia Protector,* a bronze sculpture depicting a police officer holding a young boy's hand, stands at the front entrance of the Batavia Police Department's headquarters in Batavia, Illinois, 100 N. Island Avenue. Brodin also made a model (not selected) for a statue honoring women at the Vietnam War Memorial in Washington, D.C. A model portraying a single female nurse cradling her helmet can be seen at the Brodin Studio at 130 N. Sibley Avenue, Litchfield, Minnesota.

St. Paul

Historic Places

Minnesota State Capitol and grounds—75 Reverend Dr. Martin Luther King Junior Boulevard (651-296-2881).
Minnesota has had two Swedish-born governors, Adolph Olson Eberhart and John Lind, and ten others of Swedish ancestry. Immediately in front of the Capitol is a statue of governor John Albert Johnson (1861–1909), born near St. Peter to Swedish parents. (A similar one is located on the front lawn of the Nicollet County Courthouse in St. Peter. At the monument's base are smaller statues representing miners, farmers, and traders.) On King Boulevard, just southwest of the Capitol, is a statue honoring Floyd B. Olson, governor from 1931 to 1936.

Other monuments celebrate feats of daring. West of the Capitol in a park across King Boulevard is a monument commemorating Leif Eriksson and his discovery of North America in 1000 A.D. On the mall south of the Capitol, Paul Granlund's 1985 statue depicts aviator Charles A. Lindbergh Jr. as a young boy and as a mature navigator. Casts of this sculpture are at Lindbergh Field in San Diego, California, and Le Bourget Field in Paris. Additional Granlund works in St. Paul are his garden memorial to Vietnam veterans on the grounds of the Minnesota governor's residence, 1006 Summit Avenue, and the crucified Christ in the worship space at the Luther Seminary's Chapel of the Cross, 2481 Como Avenue.

Inside the Capitol, which a publication describes as "grand in design, splendid in detail, and great in its telling of Minnesota history," are painted portraits of all the governors of Minnesota. On the first floor opposite the Governor's Reception Room is a plaque in memory of Floyd B. Olson.

South of the Capitol, across Interstate 94, is the History Center of the Minnesota Historical Society (651-296-6126; www.mnhs.org). At 345 W. Kellogg Boulevard, the Center offers a research library and a large museum and draws visitors with its restaurant and gift shops.

Churches

First Lutheran Church—463 N. Maria Avenue (651-776-7210; www.flcstpaul.org).
First Lutheran Church, the first Swedish Lutheran congregation in Minnesota, was organized in 1854 by Reverend Erland Carlsson of Immanuel Lutheran in Chicago. Originally the congregation was made up of Swedes and Norwegians, but in 1870 the groups separated, and the Swedish congregation became known as the First Swedish Evangelical Lutheran Church. The present brick structure, built in 1917, is the congregation's third building. A unique marble baptismal font supported by four columns has the Swedish inscription, *Den der tror och blivit döpt, han skall varda salig* (Whosoever believes and is baptized, he shall be blessed). In the entrance of the adjacent Norelius Hall is a plaque in memory of Swedish Lutheran leader Erik Norelius (1833–1916). In the lobby are glass cases containing a number of historical items associated with the congregation.

To the west of Norelius Hall can be seen part of Swede Hollow (*Svenska Dalen),* where many Swedes first settled before they moved on to other places. The old houses are gone; the area is now a city park. Nearby Payne Avenue was a major commercial center for St. Paul's Swedish residents, who began to arrive in St. Paul in 1852, two years after Fredrika Bremer made her visit. By 1930 almost 18,000 people born in Sweden or of Swedish ancestry lived in Ramsey County.

Schools

Bethel University and Seminary—3900 and 3949 Bethel Drive, Arden Hills (651-638-6400; www.bethel.edu).
In 1871, Dr. John Alexis Edgren from Värmland founded a Swedish Baptist theological seminary in the Morgan Park section of Chicago. During its early years, the seminary moved to several locations, including St. Paul (1884–1886); Stromsburg, Nebraska (1886–1888); and back to Morgan Park in 1888. The seminary, connected with the Baptist Union Theological Seminary of Chicago, united in 1892 with the Divinity School of the University of Chicago as the Swedish Department. In October 1905, Bethel Academy was founded in Minneapolis with twenty-nine regular students, the first class sessions being held in Elim Baptist Church.

In 1913 the Swedish Baptist Conference (now the Baptist General Conference) made the decision to bring the academy and seminary together in St. Paul under the name of Bethel Academy and Seminary. The first campus was at 1480 N. Snelling Avenue (Snelling Avenue and Arlington Street). Bethel College became a four-year college in 1947 after years as a junior college, and the seminary remained at that location until 1972, when it was relocated to a 231-acre campus in suburban Arden Hills. (The former Snelling Avenue campus is now the Hubert H. Humphrey Job Corps Center.) Enrollment in 2003 at the university was about 3,300 students in undergraduate, graduate, and adult and professional studies programs; seminary enrollment was about 1,100. The university and the seminary are owned by the Baptist General Conference of America, headquartered in Arlington Heights, Illinois.

The Bethel General Conference History Center housed in the seminary contains written historical materials related to various churches of this denomination. The archives owns Fredrik Olaus Nilsson's (1809–1881) desk and trunk and a number of portraits of early leaders. In 1854 Nilsson co-founded a Baptist congregation in Burlington, Iowa, but a year later, when that church disbanded, most of its members moved to Minnesota. In the summer of 1855, the group reached the eastern shore of Lake Waconia in Carver County, west of Minneapolis. A handful of people, including Nilsson, organized the Scandia Baptist Church and in 1857 built a small log church, which may have been the first house of worship in Carver County. In 1910 a porch and small steeple were added. In 1973 the building was moved to the Bethel University and Seminary campus, where it is preserved as a symbol of the faith of the early Swedish Baptists in Minnesota. Near the front door is a marker noting: "Scandia Baptist Church The oldest extant Baptist General Conference church building. Erected in 1857 near Lake Waconia Minnesota."

Former Scandia Baptist Church, Bethel University and Seminary, Arden Hills

In 1987 the interior was refurbished to a late nineteenth-century style. In the small vestibule is a plaque in memory of F. O. Nilsson that notes the other nine charter members of the Scandia Baptist Church. Inside, visitors can see the handmade pews and the old organ. On the exterior left side of the church, the log construction and dovetailing (the logs have been covered with clapboard) is visible. The building is used for weddings and by seminary students practicing preaching. Visitors may ask for the key at the seminary administration office across the drive.

Among the original communicants of the Scandia Baptist Church was Andrew (Anders) Peterson, who became a famous horticulturist in Carver County. From 1850 until his death in 1898, Peterson kept extensive diaries totaling twelve volumes and wrote numerous letters to Sweden. These manuscripts were a source for Vilhelm Moberg's novels, *The Emigrants, Unto a Good Land, The Settlers,* and *Last Letter Home,* and two movies based on Moberg's work. Moberg used Peterson as a model for Karl Oskar. The Minnesota Historical Society (651-296-6126) in St. Paul has Peterson's original diaries. Microfilm copies are in the University of Minnesota Immigration History Research Center, 222 S. Twenty-first Avenue, Minneapolis.

The modern Bethel University and Seminary campus has a number of buildings named for Swedish Americans, including the impressive Lundquist Community Life Center and Benson Great Hall (Carl Lundquist was president of Bethel from 1954 to 1982; Donald E. Benson, a businessman, was a generous donor to the university); Hagstrom Student Services Center (G. Arvid Hagstrom was president of Bethel from 1914 to 1941); Edgren Residence (John Alexis Edgren was founder of Bethel and its dean, 1871–1887); Bodien Residence (Mrs. Olaf Bodien was the leader of the Bethel Institute's *Kvinnoförbund* or Women's Society); Nelson Residence (Reuben Nelson was executive secretary of the Minnesota Baptists, and his wife, Effie, was dean of women); Lundquist Library in the seminary complex; and Wingblade Residence (Henry Wingblade was a Baptist pastor and president of Bethel College from 1963 to 1972). In the lobby of the Community Life Center is a 13 by 16 foot, acrylic-on-canvas wall hanging by Dale R. Johnson commemorating the 125th anniversary of Bethel College and Seminary. It is entitled *Proclaiming God's Faithfulness To All Generations (1871–1996)* and includes key Baptist events and persons.

Other Points of Interest

Jacob Fahlstrom Historic Plaque—Kellogg Boulevard and Robert Street, north end of Robert Street Bridge.

The Jacob Fahlstrom historic plaque, mounted on a seven-foot, dark-stone monument in a corner park next to a Ramsey County building, honors the first Swedish settler in Minnesota. It was unveiled in 1948 by Prince Bertil of Sweden. Fahlstrom once owned eighty acres in what is now downtown St. Paul, but he is said to have given up his claim because the land was too hilly.

Virginia Street Swedenborgian Church—170 Virginia Street (651-224-4553; www.virginiastreetchurch.org).

The church, built in 1866 (the congregation was formed in 1860), was designed by Cass Gilbert, architect of the Minnesota State Capitol and the United States Supreme Court Building, Washington, D.C.

Sculpture and Other Art

Vision of Peace by Carl Milles—St. Paul City Hall and Ramsey County Courthouse, 15 W. Kellogg Boulevard, between Wabasha and St. Peter.

A towering thirty-six-foot-high sculpture, *Vision of Peace* depicts an Indian god of peace, who holds in one hand a peace pipe and extends the other hand in a gesture of friendship. The powerful sculpture is made of cream-colored Mexican onyx and is reportedly the largest carved figure made of that variety of quartz in the world.

East-Central Minnesota

After the first Swedes arrived in Washington County, they made their first sizable settlement in what is now the Chisago Lakes area (Chisago City, Lindstrom, and Center City) of Chisago County. Chisago County and neighboring Isanti County have one of the highest percentages of Swedish American inhabitants of any comparable area in the United States. In the early 1900s, at least three-quarters of Chisago County's population was of Swedish descent. The first Chisago County leader in 1851 was Peter (Per) Andersson (or Joris Pelle Anderson). During the next two years, other families settled near Center City to form the nucleus of the Chisago Lake Lutheran Church, the county's oldest Swedish congregation.

The towns of Chisago City, Center City, and Lindstrom remain Swedish strongholds. Lindstrom was named for Daniel Lindstrom, a half-brother of Per Andersson. Northwest of Taylors Falls, the oldest town in the county, is Almelund, named for John Almquist, another very early settler. Other communities in the county, North Branch, Harris, Rush Point, and Rush City, also have a high percentage of Swedish Americans.

Chisago County's landscape of lakes, rivers, and forests is similar to parts of Sweden, which made it an attractive place for the early Swedish settlers. Their letters home about the good farming also drew more Swedes to the area. Vilhelm Moberg's novels, based on the fictitious Karl Oskar and Kristina Nilsson from Småland, continue to make Chisago County a popular tourist attraction for Swedes.

Isanti County has been called the "Dalarna of America" because of the large number of settlers from that central Swedish province. The first Swedish settlers who came in 1857 were mainly Swedish Baptists who settled south of the town of Cambridge.

In 1864 a Lutheran congregation was organized in Cambridge by people who had moved from Chisago County and Wisconsin. Two years later about one hundred families from Rättvik, Orsa, and other villages in the Lake Siljan region of Dalarna arrived to establish communities at Dalbo, Walbo, and Athens.

Kanabec County, established in 1858, is directly north of Isanti County. In 1871 Swedes from Dalarna settled around Brunswick in the southern part of the county, having been attracted by the hardwood and pine logging. Mora, the county seat, is named for Mora, Dalarna, its sister city. Both are known for annual cross-country ski races.

Afton

Jacob Fahlstrom settled on South Indian Trail Road in southern Washington County's Afton, named for a poem by Robert Burns. **Memorial Lutheran Church,**

15730 Afton Boulevard (651-436-1138), replaced the older church in 1992. Stained-glass windows from the former sanctuary are found in the Fellowship Hall, and old photographs and Bibles are in the library. The cemetery around the sanctuary contains many Swedish graves from the original Swedish members.

Stillwater

Many Swedes settled in Stillwater on the St. Croix River, once the logging capital of Minnesota. Large Victorian homes built on the bluffs still watch over the business district bustling with tourists. Several were built or owned by Swedes, including the Andrew Olson House, 107 E. Laurel, the John G. Nelson House (the Stillwater Residence), at 220 W. Olive, and the Frank Berry House (the Comfort House), at 102 School Street.

Swedish immigrants founded and built **Trinity Lutheran Church** at Oak and Fourth in 1871 but sold it in 1882 to another congregation. Lutherans erected the present sanctuary in 1883 at 115 N. Fourth Street (651-439-7400); the entrance on Fourth was created after renovation in 1983.

At the north end of Stillwater is the **Washington County Historical Society Museum**, 602 N. Main Street (651-439-5956; www.wchsmn.org), which displays artifacts from the early settler and lumbering eras. Three miles north of Stillwater on State Highway 95 along the St. Croix River is the Boom Site, which has a good view of the lovely St. Croix Valley, now designated the St. Croix National Scenic Riverway.

Marine on St. Croix

 Marine on St. Croix Historic District (www.marine.govoffice.com) was the home to many arriving Swedes. A steep dirt road behind the Marine General Store leads to the landing site on the St. Croix River where many disembarked. A scene from the film based on Vilhelm Moberg's *The Emigrants* was shot at this site. Actors Liv Ullmann and Max von Sydow starred in the Svensk Filmindustri production.

Christ Lutheran Church, 150 Fifth Street (651-433-3222), organized by Swedes in 1872, is a daughter church of the Elim Lutheran congregation in Scandia. The church building, constructed between 1872 and 1875 of rough lumber planed by hand, was originally located north of the present site. On the chancel wall above the 1890 altar painting of the Ascension by a German artist is Matthew 28:20 ("And, lo, I am with you always, even unto the end of the world"), inscribed in Swedish.

In **Township Hall**, or **the Stone House Museum**, at Fifth Street between Oak and Pine Streets, is a building considered one of the best examples of early Swedish stonework in Minnesota. Constructed in 1872, the structure has sandstone walls made of hand-tooled ashlars with uniform height, depth, and course. Gustaf

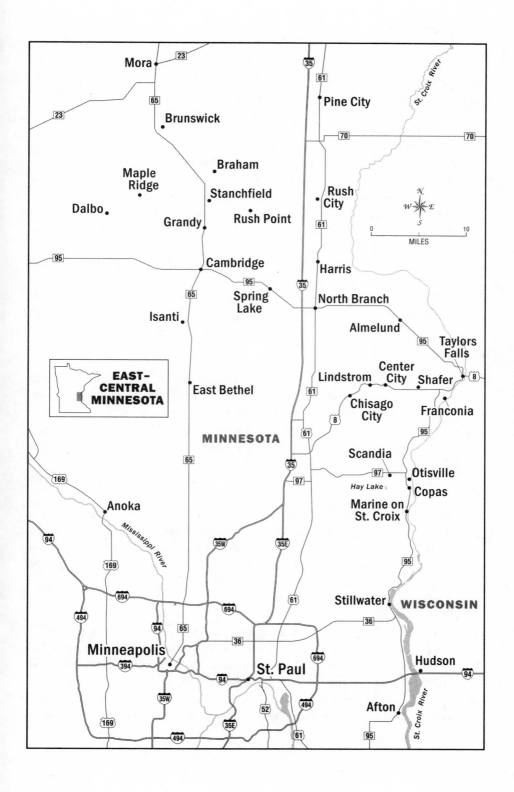

Mora

23

65

Brunswick

23

Maple
Ridge

Dalbo

Grandy

Braham

Stanchfield

Rush Point

Cambridge

65

95

Spring
Lake

95

Isanti

East Bethel

65

MINNESOTA

65

35

61

61

97

Anoka

169

94

169

694

Minneapolis

494

35W

494

169

35W

394

94

65

36

494

35E

St. Paul

94

52

61

35

61

61

Pine City

70

70

Rush
City

61

Harris

North Branch

Almelund

95

Taylors
Falls

8

Lindstrom

Center
City

Shafer

Chisago
City

8

Franconia

95

Scandia

97

Otisville

Copas

Hay Lake

Marine on
St. Croix

St. Croix River

N
W E
S

0   10
MILES

EAST-
CENTRAL
MINNESOTA

95

Stillwater

WISCONSIN

36

694

Hudson

94

Afton

95

St. Croix River

Mississippi River

Carlson, a Swedish immigrant stonemason from Småland, built it of locally quarried sandstone. Originally the three rooms served as the township offices and jail. After 1896, the building was used for a variety of purposes, including a church activity center. In 1963 it was converted into a museum with a wide assortment of memorabilia.

Marine on St. Croix Historic District includes nearly fifty significant structures and sites, a number of which are homes built by Swedish immigrants. Many Swedes were employed by local lumber companies, though some developed their own businesses as harness makers, boat builders, stonemasons, cabinet makers, wagon makers, saloon keepers, and blacksmiths. Generally the Swedish immigrants built their homes on top of the bluff and behind the homes of the New Englanders, who had arrived first and built closer to the river.

The most important historic commercial structure in town is the two-and-one-half-story **Marine General Store** at the corner of Maple and Judd Streets. The business played an important role in attracting Swedes because an early owner advertised widely that he would grant them liberal credit if they settled there. Marine Village Hall, south of the General Store, was built in 1888.

Copas

In the small community of Copas on State Highway 95, more than one mile south of State Highway 97 near Scandia, is the former general store and the old schoolhouse. Across State Highway 95 just south of the general store is the former Ames House, which was a hotel where many of the early Swedish settlers stayed. It is now a private residence. Copas is roughly halfway between Stillwater and Taylors Falls.

Otisville

Although no signs lead travelers to Otisville, it lies immediately north of Copas off County Road 53. Loghouse Landing, today a public landing on the St. Croix River, is a site where early Swedish immigrants disembarked. A log house stands near this location. To reach Loghouse Landing, from County Road 53 take N. 205th Street, a gravel road, to the St. Croix River.

Scandia

The small community of Scandia, founded in 1855, can boast having the oldest existing Swedish Lutheran Church building (1850) for the third-oldest Swedish congregation in Minnesota, the oldest Swedish Lutheran parsonage (1868) in the state, and a monument honoring the first Swedish pioneers to the region.

One of the loveliest Swedish American historic sites in Minnesota that has been developed is the complex of six pioneer structures called **Gammelgården,** or

Gammelgården (The Old Farm), Scandia

The Old Farm, 20880 Olinda Trail (651-433-5053; www.scandiamn.com/gammel garden). The two most important structures historically are the old church (*gammelkyrkan*) and the parsonage (*präst hus*). In addition, there are an authentic Swedish red *stuga*, the immigrant house, barn (*ladugård*), corn crib, and windmill. In the 1970s and 1980s, the structures were repaired and restored. The parsonage and barn have always remained in their present locations while the *stuga*, the immigrant house, and old church have been moved to the site. A Visitor's Center (*Välkommen Hus*) contains displays, an orientation room, and the Scandia Butik.

In 1867 the Elim Lutheran congregation purchased forty acres of the Ola Hansson farm and the following year built the parsonage. In 1884 another parsonage was constructed, and the old one was sold to a local family. The parsonage belonged to that family until 1970, when the house and six acres were purchased by the church. Two years earlier, five acres of the farm immediately north of Gammelgården had been bought to be converted into the Barton Johnson Memorial Park. Johnson died in Vietnam in 1968.

Elim Lutheran Church was founded in 1854 by the Reverend Erland Carlsson of Chicago at nearby Hay Lake. Two years later, the congregation erected *gammelkyrkan*, their first church, made of hand-hewn logs. When the congregation soon outgrew the building, a second church was erected on the present cemetery site, north of Gammelgården. The first church was then converted into a school and remained one until 1899, when a new brick school was constructed. The old church was sold to a school board member, who moved it to his farm, where it became a hay barn. In 1980 it was relocated to Gammelgården and rededicated in 1982 with many dignitaries, including Sweden's Prince Bertil and Princess Lillian, in attendance. Inside the church the visitor can see one original pew (the others are reproductions) and the original folding key made so that it could fit into a person's pocket. The candelabra are from the fourth church that burned in 1907.

The *präst hus* was considered a large house (five rooms downstairs and two upstairs) when it was built in 1868. The rooms are fully furnished, many of the pieces having belonged to the Nelson family. There are a number of significant items from the late nineteenth and early twentieth centuries.

Originally the *stuga* was located on the Gottlieb Magney estate near the St. Croix River. Magney was the architect who designed the Foshay Tower in Minneapolis, and he had used the *stuga* as a guest house. Built in 1930 and moved to Gammelgården in the late 1970s, the structure is divided into two rooms, one with built-in cabinets and a Swedish corner fireplace and the other with two built-in beds.

An annual event at Gammelgården on the third Saturday of August is a fiddling contest *(spelmansstämma)* featuring Swedish music. Midsummer Day is celebrated on the fourth Saturday in June with dancing and music. Lucia Fest, on the second Sunday in December, includes a prayer service in the old church. A lutfisk dinner is held in late November.

The present Elim Lutheran Church, 20071 Olinda Trail (651-433-2723; www .scandia.com/elim), a red-brick, Gothic-style building, is the Scandia congregation's sixth sanctuary. The fifth was gutted by fire in 1930, but the altar, pulpit, pews, and some furnishings were saved, as were the exterior walls. The sanctuary is noted for its dark, wood-beamed ceiling, Gothic-style altar with a copy of nineteenth-century Danish sculptor Bertel Thorvaldsen's famous statue of Christ, chancel rail, pews, and balcony. Over the main entrance, an inscription reads, "Swedish Lutheran Elim Church Scandia."

Across the street in the cemetery are the graves of pastors and early Swedish immigrants, some dating back to 1860. The Methodist Church no longer exists, but its cemetery is located south of Elim Lutheran.

Hay Lake

About one and one-half miles south of Gammelgården near Hay Lake is a twenty-two-foot obelisk honoring the first Swedish settlers in Minnesota. The monument commemorates the arrival of Oscar Roos, Carl Fernström, and August Sandahl from Västergötland in October 1850. They walked about four miles west from Marine on St Croix and built a cabin by the shore of Hay Lake.

In 1855 settlers organized a school district. A one-story brick Victorian **Hay Lake School** was constructed in the 1890s for a single teacher who taught eight grades. It was used as a school until the early 1960s. In the early 1970s ownership passed to the Washington County Historical Society, which displays school memorabilia here. The chandelier was rescued by one of the last teachers, who found it under the schoolhouse. The **Johannes Erickson Log House**, also owned by the historical society, was built in 1868. The 20 by 28 foot house of hewn oak logs with a shingled gambrel (hip) roof is now covered by red-painted vertical wood siding and is fully furnished with nineteenth-century items, but the cupboard is probably the only piece original to the dwelling. The Johannes Erickson family emigrated from Dalsland to Scandia in 1866.

Franconia

Franconia Historic District is on the flat land of the St. Croix River bottom, three miles south of Taylors Falls. During its most prosperous years in the 1870s, it was in the center of a timber area with extensive river traffic. The historic district, bounded by Cornelian, Summer, and Henry Streets, includes ten frame residences, seven of which were built between the 1850s and the 1880s. At least four of the houses—the Eric Ostrom, Jonas Lindall, Hans Hanson, and Olof Swanlund homes—are closely associated with early Swedish settlers. A stone monument honors its pioneers.

Taylors Falls

Located on the scenic St. Croix River, Taylors Falls was a tiny village of six houses when the first Swedish settlers disembarked from a riverboat in the 1850s. Oscar Roos, who arrived from Sweden with two friends in 1850 and became a prominent banker, real estate investor, and government official, made Taylors Falls his home.

The **Munch-Roos House**, 360 Bench Street (Main Street), was built in 1854 by the Munch brothers who emigrated from Prussia. This Greek Revival house became the home of the Roos family who lived in it until 1965. It is a private residence.

The **Hamilton House**, dating to 1866, is across the road at 431 Bench Street. Samuel Hamilton, a Swedish immigrant, worked as a Minnesota immigrant agent and helped many early Swedes find temporary housing after their arrival. This house is a private residence.

First Evangelical Lutheran Church, 561 Chestnut Street (651-465-5265), was organized in 1860. The present Gothic-style brick structure with its high steeple, built in 1903, has beautiful natural interior woodwork.

On the Minnesota side of the bridge that crosses the St. Croix River, the flags of the United States, Minnesota, and Sweden are displayed. Åseda, Sweden, is the sister city of Taylors Falls.

Almelund

Amador Heritage Center at County Road 12 and State Highway 95 (651-583-2883) is a local museum housed in the community's former school building, constructed in 1910. It contains items from Almelund's first Lutheran church and the former Almquist General Store. Next to the old schoolhouse is a restored Swedish log cabin.

The **Immanuel Lutheran** congregation was organized in 1887 mainly by people from Småland and its original building constructed the same year. In 1926, the congregation erected the large, handsome, Gothic-style brick building at 37515 Park Trail (651-583-2340).

Center City

Center City, along with Lindstrom and Chisago City, was a hub of Swedish immigrant activity in Chisago County. "The Swedish Circle in Minnesota," an enjoyable printed self-guided tour of Swedish American landmarks in Chisago County, is available at restaurants, motels, museums, and Chamber of Commerce offices.

Chisago Lake Lutheran Church (651-257-6300), a buff-colored brick building dating to the 1880s, may be the largest and finest rural church in Minnesota. It has been compared with the church in Madesjö Parish, Småland, a province in which many congregants have roots. This church has a lovely setting close to North Center Lake; a good viewing point is on U.S. Highway 8 near the Swedish Village Mall.

On May 12, 1854, the Reverend Erland Carlsson of Chicago organized the congregation of one hundred members, holding the first meeting in a haymow. Its site is marked by a monument in the Chisago Lake Cemetery, east of the church. That summer, Carlsson had a "meeting house" built for worship and a public school. Erik Norelius, then a twenty-year-old theological student, preached and taught there. He and his brother, Anders (Andrew), had left Sweden with the Peter Andersson group.

The first resident pastor arrived in the spring of 1855, and the following year a small frame church was begun on the location of the present church. In 1858 the church was the site for the organization of the Minnesota Conference of the Augustana Lutheran Church, an event marked by a large obelisk near the front of the sanctuary. Between 1868 and 1873, the membership of the congregation doubled from 400 to 800. By 1897, it increased to 1,495 adults and 816 children, the highest membership in the church's history. A larger sanctuary was completed in

Chisago Lake Lutheran Church,
tapestry detail and exterior view,
Center City

1882, but a bolt of lightning struck the steeple and ignited a fire that gutted the church. The present edifice, completed in 1889, is identical in size to the former church. This building is Romanesque style with round arched stained-glass windows. A soaring steeple, with clocks on each side above the belfry, is capped by a gold cross.

The sanctuary features a large raised, wood-canopied pulpit. The words *Helig, Helig, Helig* (Holy, Holy, Holy) appear on the altar under the statue of Christ. To commemorate the congregation's 150th anniversary in 2004, the sanctuary was beautifully repainted by Eric Carlisle. He enhanced the church's architectural characteristics, including the forty-foot-high ornate ceiling, curved altar alcove, and eight columns twenty-eight feet in height. The light-colored sanctuary now has gilded capitals on the Corinthian columns and stencils of twisting grape vines and intricate geometric patterns on the ceiling's borders.

In the sanctuary's narthex is a bronze casting of Reverend Erik Norelius by Paul Granlund and a display case of old Swedish-language books and church publications. Outside is a flagpole with a plaque in memory of the Swedes who organized the church, some of whom are buried in the cemetery to the east. Across the road and up on the hill is the parsonage.

In the Heritage Room in the parish building is a tapestry by Marjorie Pohlmann depicting the history of the Chisago Lake Lutheran congregation. The tapestry's history-telling threads record the agrarian roots in the immigrants' homeland, the sailing ships that brought them to the United States, the Civil War, the lightning that struck the church building in 1882 and the fire that resulted, the transformation from horse and buggy (or horse and sled) to automobiles and vans, and the metamorphosis from an agriculture-based economy to an industrial and urban one.

As a footnote, the wedding scene at the end of the film *Grumpy Old Men*, starring Jack Lemmon, Walter Matthau, and Ann-Margret, was filmed at this church.

 Immediately south of the church on the east side of Summit Avenue is the **Summit Avenue Historic District**, a residential area overlooking North Center Lake. The lots were laid out in 1888 and the fine old residences constructed between 1882 and 1910. (The Chisago County Courthouse on Main Street is also on the National Register.)

Many of the frame houses were constructed by William Carlson, owner of the local lumberyard and the town's carpenter and builder. (Carlson also created much of the woodwork in the Chisago Lake Lutheran Church.) The houses feature classical detailing, gable ornamentation, extensive use of windows, and front porches. The owners were Swedish merchants, tradesmen, politicians, retired farmers, and professionals, reflecting the growing prosperity of the area.

The oldest houses are those nearest the church. A plaque near the Swedish Village Mall commemorates the founding of Center City. It reads: "On a nearby hillside Erik Ulrik Norberg spent the winter of 1850 before guiding a group of country-men to Chisago Lake to establish Center City—the oldest permanent Swedish colony in Minnesota—a settlement immortalized by the Swedish author Vilhelm Moberg." Hassela, Sweden, is the sister city of Center City.

Shafer

The nearby community of Shafer, whose sister city is Nöbbele, Sweden, features two historic houses associated with Swedish settlers. Jacob Petterson, who arrived in 1853 from Dädesjö, Småland, was an entrepreneur and owner of Jacob Peterson General Mercantile. His house at 30405 Ridgewood Avenue is a private residence.

Around 1869, Lars J. Thorsander, from Östra Torsås parish in Småland, built his red-brick home (currently the Country Bed and Breakfast) and various farm buildings, including a large barn, at 17038-320th Street. To see it, go north on County Road 21 from U.S. Highway 8 for nearly two miles and then take Ranch Trail, a gravel road, for nearly one mile to 320th Street.

Lindstrom

 Lindstrom (www.lindstrom.mn.org) has managed to preserve several homes and churches built about a century ago. At 13045 Lake Boulevard is the two-story, red-brick **Gustaf Anderson House**, built in the Italianate style about 1879. Gustaf Anderson emigrated from Sweden in 1864 and settled in Minnesota, though later he prospected for gold in Montana. When he returned to farm in Chisago County, he constructed this house for his retirement; it is now the headquarters of the Chisago County Historical Society (651-257-5310).

 The two-and-one-half-story frame **C. A. Victor House**, 30495 Park Street, was erected about 1905. Swedish-born Charles A. Victor settled in Lindstrom in the 1880s and became one of its earliest merchants, operating the C. A. Victor General Mercantile Store behind this residence. Involved in milling and politics, he founded the *Medborgaren* (The Citizen), one of several local Swedish news-papers, in 1898.

After the arrival of the railroad, Lindstrom became a resort area. **Fridhem** (Home of Peace), also known as the **Frank A. Larson House**, on Newell Avenue on the north side of South Lindstrom Lake, is a frame structure built about 1898 for use as a summer home. It features a large porch supported by columns and a roof broken by a central gabled dormer. Larson, a Chicago publisher and owner of the *Svenska Amerikanaren Tribunen,* purchased the house in 1911, and the fam-ily spent most of their summers there until 1932. It is still a private residence.

The white, frame **Trinity Lutheran Church**, 13025 Newell Avenue (651-257-5129), was erected in 1902 for a congregation that was an offshoot of the Chisago Lakes Lutheran Church. On the southeast corner of Lake Boulevard and Elm Street is the former Swedish Methodist Church, constructed in 1892 and now a Masonic Lodge. Also on Lake Boulevard is St. Bridget of Sweden Roman Catholic Church.

Lindstrom's Swedish heritage is apparent in a plaque by the flagpole in Fairview Cemetery honoring the founder of the town, Hälsingland native Daniel Lindstrom, and other Swedish immigrants. On the west end of town on Lake Boulevard is a statue of Karl Oskar and Kristina Nilsson, based on an original work by Swedish sculptor Axel Olsson in Karlshamn, Blekinge, Sweden. The figures are characters from Vilhelm Moberg's immigration novels that dramatize the dream of the new world and the grief of losing the old. Karl Oskar looks toward the new land and Kristina takes a last look back at Sweden. In July Lindstrom celebrates Karl Oskar Days. Below the monument to Karl Oskar and Kristina is a plaque in memory of Theodore A. Norelius (1908–1993), founder of the Chisago County Historical Society, author, storyteller, and Moberg's host in 1948. Nearby is a boulder from Duvemåla, Sweden, with an inscription entitled *The Emigrant Stone* by Swedish immigrant historian Ulf Beijbom. Lindstrom's water tower is decorated like a Swedish coffee pot. Its sister city in Sweden is Tingsryd.

In Kichi-Saga Park, on Glader Boulevard, is **Nya Duvemåla** (New Dove's Home), which supposedly resembles the home described in Moberg's novels. It was dedicated in 1996 on the occasion of a Swedish royal visit. A plaque on a boulder describes Småland with a quotation from Moberg's *The Emigrants:* "And all the stones wherever he looked; broken stones, stones in piles, stone fences, stone above ground, stone in the ground, stone, stone, stone."

Nearby is the small **Glader Cemetery**, named for Anders Peter Nilsson Glader who came from Furuby, Kronobergs län, in 1853. A sign notes that this cemetery, dated 1855–1919, was the area's first burial ground for settlers. Moberg was especially impressed by this cemetery. To reach it, drive south from U.S. Highway 8 on County Road 25 to Glader Boulevard, then east a short distance.

Chisago City

Several landmarks in Chisago City are connected with Moberg's birthplace (and Chisago City's sister city), Algutsboda. A park named in his honor also includes a statue, dedicated in 1996 with King Carl XVI Gustaf and Queen Silvia in attendance, that portrays the Swedish author thoughtfully looking out into the countryside, hands in his pockets, tie loosened, with a bicycle resting against his leg. The plaque notes that Moberg (1898–1973) was "one of the foremost Swedish authors of the twentieth century. His most famous characters, Karl Oskar and

Kristina Nilsson, were representative of the over 1.2 million Swedish emigrants that landed on our shores between 1846 and 1930. During the summer of 1948 he stayed in Chisago City and explored this area by bicycle. That research helped shape his most famous work—the epic tetralogy 'The Emigrants,' 'Unto a Good Land,' 'The Settlers,' and 'The Last Letter Home.' In Sweden, thanks to Moberg's literary works, this land of Kichi-Saga—the Chisago Lakes Area—is probably the best-known area of the United States." Moberg stayed in a hotel at 29225 Old Towne Road, at the northeast corner of Old Towne Road and Lake Avenue, now a private residence.

Another landmark is **Zion Lutheran Church**, 28005 Old Towne Road (651-257-2713). Its congregation was organized in 1874, and the present church, clad in white metal siding, dates from 1908, succeeding the first sanctuary that was destroyed by fire. The building has a tall central steeple and Gothic-style windows. The **Margaret S. Parmly Residence**, 28210 Old Towne Road (651-257-0575), replaced the Bethesda Old People's Home, established by Swedish

Statue of Vilhelm Moberg, Chisago City

Lutherans in 1904, the first such home built by Swedes in Minnesota. In front of the residence is a small bronze statue entitled *Child of Peace,* erected in 2003 in tribute to "Aunt Johanna Franklund (1837–1930) by the families of Erik V. and Mary Safström-Franklund and Emil Safström. She made it possible for Erik 11 and Mary 14 to come to Bismarck, ND from Ställdalen, Sweden in 1890." It shows a young girl releasing a bird and holding a branch of flowers.

North Branch

This community and its surrounding area have a number of Century Farms, farms under the same family ownership for a century. Those with Swedish connections include the Magnison Century Farm, 9383-375th Street, Olson Century Farm, 39853 Forest Boulevard, and Sedeberg Century Farm, 51136-392th Street. For more details, consult the brochure "The Swedish Circle in Minnesota" (see Center City, Minnesota).

Rush City

First Evangelical Lutheran congregation was organized in 1876, and the Gothic-style brick church, 1000 S. Jay Avenue (320-358-4076), was built in 1909. It replaced a wood structure dating to 1877. The brick structure is now a private residence, and the congregation worships in a striking new sanctuary at S. Jay Avenue and County Road 7, dedicated in 2004.

 The large, two-story, Queen Anne–style **J. C. Carlson House** on S. Bremer Avenue between W. Fourth and W. Seventh Streets, constructed in 1899, is probably the most impressive residence in town. J. C. Carlson, a leading entrepreneur, arrived in 1882 and thirteen years later was president of the State Bank of Rush City.

Rush Point

Calvary Lutheran Church, organized in 1870, is the third-oldest Swedish Lutheran congregation in Chisago County. The present church at 600 Rush Point Drive, Stanchfield (320-358-4829), was built in 1913. It is made of light-colored brick, similar in color to that of Chisago Lake Lutheran Church, and has Gothic-style windows. Nearby is the small Baptist church and cemetery containing Swedish graves.

East Bethel and Ham Lake

 The Swedish Evangelical Lutheran Church of Ham Lake in Anoka County was organized in 1872 (the name later changed to **Our Saviour's Evangelical Lutheran Church**). The modern facility, completed in 2004, is at 19001 NE Jackson Street west of State Highway 65 (763-434-6117; www.oursaviourslc.org). Services continue to be held on Monday evenings, June through Labor Day, at the old Gothic-style, white-frame church on Swedish Drive dating from 1872. A unique architectural feature of the old church is its central pulpit. Above the altar is a portrait of Christ with the crown of thorns and the inscription, *Se Guds Lamm* (Behold the Lamb of God). To reach the church and its cemetery, drive one and one-half miles east on County Road 22 (Viking Boulevard) from State Highway 65, then south on County Road 68 for two miles, and then west on Swedish Drive (a gravel road) for one-third of a mile.

Spring Lake

The congregation of **Spring Lake Lutheran Church**, just off State Highway 95 at 8440 NE Erickson Road, North Branch (651-674-4606; www.sllchurch.org), was organized in 1874 and the present brick church built in 1942. The sanctuary

Bell Tower, Spring Lake Lutheran Church, Spring Lake

features a dark wood ceiling. In front of the church is Danielson Memorial Swedish Bell Tower, a replica of the bell tower at the Vextorps Church in Värnamo, Jönköpings län. It was dedicated to the donor's parents, Stava and Johan Danielson, whose ancestors worshipped at the Vextorps Church, and to this community's other Swedish pioneers. Across the road in a wooded area with rolling terrain is the lovely Spring Lake Cemetery. Nearby is a centennial monument in the shape of a runestone and a light-colored, carved stone statue of a couple holding their small son, entitled *Swedish Immigrants*.

Harris

Fish Lake Lutheran Church and cemetery, 43353 Cedarcrest Trail (651-674-4252; www.fishlakelutheran.org), was organized in 1867. From Interstate 35 go four miles west on State Highway 95 and then take Isanti County Road 21 north for three miles (County Road 21 becomes Chisago County Road 8).

Fish Lake is the second-oldest Swedish Lutheran congregation in Chisago County. The first church was built between 1874 and 1879, but lightning struck the tall steeple and the structure burned to the ground in 1886. The congregation immediately built a new sanctuary from 1886 to 1889. This white-frame edifice with a central steeple and Gothic-style windows still serves the congregation. The church is situated among tall maple trees, a beautiful sight in autumn.

In 1998 the church's sanctuary was completely renovated by artist Eric Carlisle to reflect the artistry of the nineteenth-century building. Fragments of the original decorative paintings survived to guide Carlisle in fashioning wall stencils. The result is a spectacular sanctuary in the Swedish tradition, featuring colorful floral stenciling. The lower walls simulate marble. In the altar alcove is a fresco painting by John Blomquist, dated 1906 and portraying Christ in Gethsemane with an angel. An intricate fresco surmounted by a crown frames the painting. On either side are painted potted palms. High above the altar in stenciling is the Swedish inscription from John 11:25, *Jag är uppståndelsen och livet* (I am the resurrection and the life). On the wall behind the impressive carved-wood pulpit with gilded Christian symbols is Revelations 22:17: *Anden och bruden säga: "Kom." Och dem som hör det, han säga: "Kom." Och dem som törstar, han komme; ja den som vill, han tage livets vatten för intet.* (The Spirit and the bride say, "Come." And let the one who hears say, "Come." And let the one who is thirsty come; let the one who wishes take the water of life without cost.) The stained-glass windows, old pews, and chandelier have also been restored. The sanctuary contains a rare tracker organ installed in 1905.

Outside the church is a granite centennial memorial stone. In the adjacent cemetery several pastors are buried. Gravestones of the Reverend P. A. Pihlgren (1836–1920) and N. J. Brink (1846–1887) note that the men were originally from

Fish Lake Lutheran Church, sanctuary, Harris

Sweden. The cemetery in the rear of the church has a number of old graves, including a ground marker to Peter and Kajsa Lof, the community's "first white settlers."

Isanti

One mile east of State Highway 65 on County Road 43 north of Isanti and a little over four miles south of Cambridge is the **North Isanti Baptist Church**, 2248 NE 313th Avenue (763-689-3576), which was the site of Tamarack Church, the first Swedish Baptist congregation in Isanti County. The founders were from Hälsingland. Outside the present building, which is the third sanctuary, is a stone monument with this inscription: "Impelled by devotion to God and a desire to worship together in their new land, fourteen Swedish pioneers met at the Olof Eastlund home June 17, 1860, to organize what became known as the 'Baptistförsamlingen i Cambridge' (Baptist Church in Cambridge). . . . The congregation's first church building, 'Tamarackyrkan,' was dedicated at the predawn 'Julotta' service on Christmas morning 1870. The Tamarack church was a well-known landmark in Isanti County until it was torn down about 1910."

The present church has an attractive Heritage Room that includes stained-glass windows, pulpit and pulpit chairs, and a communion table from the 1910 sanctuary. In the church's entrance area is a display case of early photographs and old books, some written in Swedish.

South of the church is the North Isanti Baptist Cemetery, which includes some of the oldest graves in Isanti County. In the southwest corner are buried several early ministers, including Olof Bodien (1837–1912) and his wife, Margareeta (1861–1928). Reverend Bodien was pastor of First Swedish Baptist (now Bethlehem Baptist) Church in Minneapolis who helped to establish Swedish Hospital. His gravestone contains a lengthy Swedish inscription. Reverend Olof Engberg and his wife, Sarah, are buried nearby. The gravestone notes that Engberg was a leader in early Baptist work and promoter of education in Sweden and pastor and preacher in Isanti County for twenty-four years.

South Isanti Baptist Church, 3367 NE County Road 5 (763-444-5860), six and one-half miles southeast of Cambridge, is another old Isanti County congregation housed in a white-clapboard, Gothic-style church. In the town of Isanti is the Elim Baptist Church, 114 N. Dahlin Avenue (763-444-9221).

The large, round **Linden Barn** is a unique historical landmark. Olof Linden, who arrived from Sweden in 1874, constructed the barn forty years later of ten-inch concrete blocks with four-inch tile facing the inside. The barn is 2.6 miles east of State Highway 65 near the south side of County Road 19 and is visible only from the nearby gravel road.

At the intersection of State Highway 65 and County Road 56, nine miles north of East Bethel and a short distance south of Isanti, is the **Erickson Farmstead**, first developed by Otto Erickson, who with his family came to Isanti County in 1868 from Hudiksvall, Hälsingland. His son, Edward Erickson, replaced the original farm buildings with the present ones when his farming operations prospered. The farm features a large, three-story, yellow-and-white-painted frame farmhouse, constructed in 1915, and a number of outbuildings painted red, built between 1915 and 1930. The farmstead, now privately owned, is associated with Isanti County's important potato-growing industry.

Cambridge

Cambridge, some forty-five miles north of downtown Minneapolis, was once at the southern end of great pine forests. During the 1850s the town site served as a stopping-off place for loggers on their way north. With the influx of Swedish immigrants in the 1860s and 1870s, the town gradually developed into a major service center and became the county seat of Isanti County.

The **Edblad Pioneer Cabin and West Riverside Museum School—West Riverside Historical Grounds.** Go west on State Highway 95 and then north on County Road 14 for one-half mile. Operated by the Isanti County Historical Society (763-689-4229), the Pioneer Cabin is a replica of the Edblad Cabin in which the Cambridge Lutheran Church was organized in 1864. Isak and Christina Edblad and their children came to Wisconsin from Jämtland in 1856, but in 1859 a conflict with Native Americans brought them to Isanti County. They built a two-room log cabin (a lean-to was later added) on a high bank close to the Rum River. Many alterations made to the cabin through the years made restoration difficult, but another practically identical cabin was discovered in Spring Lake. It had been built in the 1860s by the Carl H. Youngquist family, which had immigrated in 1854. This cabin was purchased and moved to this location. The visible house is mainly the Youngquist cabin, though the lean-to was completed in 1981 of logs salvaged from other old buildings. The cabin has two floors and numerous settler items, many donated by the Edblad family. The Edblads opened their home for church services from 1859 to 1868 when the first Cambridge Lutheran Church was built.

By 1880 twenty-one Swedish families who had cleared land and built log cabins on the west side of the Rum River near Cambridge were eager for a school district. School was first held in a wooden structure west of the present building. In 1898, approval of a special state bond issue allowed construction of this brick structure. In the early 1970s, when the West Riverside School ceased operations because of consolidations, the property was leased to the Isanti County Historical Society, which, along with the West Riverside Restoration Committee, has restored the building to its 1900 appearance. A plaque notes that more than 550 students attended this school, which now houses the historical society's collection.

An important purpose of the rural schools was to help the Swedish immigrants learn English and prepare them to take the examination to become American citizens. Thus, a number of people over twenty-one years of age attended school. In addition, for four to six weeks during the summer, "Swede Schools" were held here, where the Swedish language and religion were taught. Rural schools were also community centers for social and cultural events.

Historic Places

D. Olof Anderson Residence (today the Carlson-Lillemoen Funeral Home)—southwest corner of Ashland and Third Avenue.

This large white-clapboard house with many gables was the home of D. Olof Anderson, a founding father of the Cambridge business community. Anderson came from Rättvik, Dalarna, in 1867. By age twenty-three he had enough capital to enter into a partnership for general merchandising with Hans J. Gouldberg, a fellow Swede from Dalarna.

Churches

Cambridge Lutheran Church and Cemetery—621 Old North Main (763-689-1211; www.cambridgelutheran.org).

The congregation of Cambridge Lutheran Church was organized in the log cabin of the Isak Edblad family, which had become a place for Sunday meetings. In 1868

Cambridge Lutheran Church, window, Cambridge

a 40 by 26 foot frame church was completed, and between 1880 and 1884 the present large edifice was completed. While most churches of the time had two-tiered towers, a distinctive third tier was added to the Cambridge spire, making it unusual among American Lutheran churches. In 1892 brick was added to the church's exterior surface. Through the years the impressive church building was altered several times, yet it has retained a unified composition. In the main sanctuary, the nave is original, but the chancel is a later addition. The stained-glass windows are from the 1950s except for two over the rear doors that date to the 1930s.

Inside the east entrance of the church's narthex is a granite marker with a brief history of the church and a Swedish inscription. A lovely 8 by 12 foot leaded stained-glass window, installed in 1979, traces the history of Christianity from medieval Sweden to twentieth-century Minnesota. Scenes portray the introduction of Christianity in Sweden by St. Ansgar about 830 A.D., Swedish immigrants coming to America and arriving at Taylors Falls on the St. Croix River, and the pioneer settlement on the Rum River in Isanti County. In one corner, a pioneer couple walks from their cabin, similar to the Edblad cabin near Cambridge, to the original Lutheran church, which is marked by the Centennial Monument in the adjacent cemetery. In the bottom center is the present Cambridge Lutheran Church, surrounded by today's community.

The church also has an impressive collection of items from the congregation's history. Because the congregation was made up largely of immigrants from

Rättvik in Dalarna, Sweden, the church figures prominently in Swedish immigration studies.

The cemetery is located west of the church. The Centennial Monument was dedicated in 1964 to commemorate the area's Swedish Lutheran immigrants and the original church building that existed there from 1867 to 1880. There is a monument to Peter Andersson, who helped establish the Chisago Lake Lutheran Church in Center City. The inscription notes incorrectly that he and his family, along with three other families, "founded the first permanent Swedish Lutheran settlement in Minnesota, at Chisago Lake" (the first was actually Scandia in Washington County). In the cemetery are the graves of Isak Edblad, his wife, and his daughter; Oscar Viotti, who served in the early years as the "Swede School" teacher and assistant pastor of the Cambridge congregation; and several former pastors.

First Baptist Church—304 S. Main Street (763-689-1173).
This Swedish congregation was organized in 1883 and the present church constructed in 1930.

Other Points of Interest

Commissioned by the city in 1990 as a tribute to its sister city, Rättvik, a large Dala horse once stood in the Cambridge City Park one block south of State Highway 95 along the Rum River. It is brought out on special occasions. A Midsummer festival is held in Cambridge.

Grandy

Union Church on State Highway 65 was built in the 1880s as a Swedish Adventist church. It was first located southeast of town. When the church was moved into Grandy in 1905, it was a union church for all faiths, but it later served residents as a community center.

Stanchfield

Stanchfield Baptist Church (320-396-3391; www.stanchfieldbaptist.com), a red-brick building built in 1966, is a continuation of the Swedish Baptist congregation organized in 1866. People from Orsa, Dalarna, settled this town.

Braham

Rice Lake Cemetery, west of Braham on the east side of State Highway 65 near County Road 4, is particularly lovely in late June or early July when the peonies are in bloom. The cemetery has a monument noting the site of the church in which the Rice Lake Swedish Lutheran congregation worshipped from 1879 until

1932, when the congregation merged with Braham Evangelical Lutheran, 905 W. Central Drive (320-396-2755). Dr. Amandus Johnson, noted Swedish American scholar, was confirmed in the Rice Lake Church.

 The **Oscar Olson House**, 309 Beechwood, was constructed in 1914 by Fred Soderberg, a local pharmacist. The large clapboard residence is an example of Colonial Revival design. Oscar Olson, a prominent banker and leader of Braham, lived in the house for more than fifty years.

Maple Ridge

 The **South Maple Ridge Covenant Church**, a simple Gothic Revival frame building constructed in 1897, has an unadorned interior with its original woodwork and benches. The building, no longer used, is maintained by the Maple Ridge Cemetery Association. A cemetery is immediately to the north. To reach the site, from State Highway 65 drive west on Isanti County Road 3 for six miles, then south on County Road 1 for one-half mile. The Swedish Mission Church of South Maple Ridge, organized in 1884, is south of the intersection of County Roads 1 and 3.

Dalbo

Built in 1910, the former **Dalbo Grange Hall's** frame building has been the home of the Dalbo Swedish Unitarian Society and the Dalbo Church of Jesus Christ of Latter-Day Saints. Most recently it has served as the Dalbo Township hall. The structure is known for its good acoustics. To reach this building, drive north out of Dalbo on State Highway 47 for three miles to Isanti County Road 16, west on this road for two miles, and south on Jaspar Street, a gravel road, for one and one-half miles. The white-clapboard building is on the west side.

Salem Lutheran Church, 4638 NW 381st Avenue (763-689-1687), with its central steeple, was completed in 1901 (the congregation was organized in 1874). Many charter members came from Venjan, Dalarna. Testimony to that heritage is found in every stained-glass window: each displays a Bible verse or some other religious quotation in Swedish. This church is less than a mile from the center of Dalbo on Isanti County Road 3 near State Highway 47.

Brunswick

The **Immanuel Lutheran Church** of Brunswick, 2088 State Highway 70, Mora, was founded in 1885. The present congregation worships in an attractive red-brick, Gothic-style church built in 1920 at the west end of town. A cemetery is near the church.

Mora

Annually since 1973, on the second Sunday of February, Mora has hosted the Vasaloppet cross-country ski race patterned after the race in Mora, Dalarna. The thirty-six-mile (fifty-eight-kilometer) race is the second longest in the United States, beginning just north of Warman on State Highway 65 and ending in downtown Mora. The metal *Ole* statue in Mora Vasaloppet Park at the corner of State Highway 65 and E. Forest Avenue represents a race participant. In a park overlooking Lake Mora is the thirty-nine-foot tower, whose bell tolls to greet skiers who have completed the Vasaloppet. Nearby is the *Kranskulla* statue (girl with a wreath), past which the contestants ski.

The Vasaloppet headquarters is in the former railroad depot on Union Street in downtown Mora (www.vasaloppet.org). Across the street is a twenty-foot-high Mora *klocka* built in 1994 by the local Dala Heritage Society with support

Mora *klocka*, Mora

from the community and dedicated the following year as a symbol of its sister city, Mora, Sweden. North of Mora off Highway 65 is the Vasaloppet Nordic Ski Center.

The **Kanabec County Courthouse** at 18 N. Vine Street, completed in 1894, is a significant brick Romanesque building. Indicative of the Swedish influence in Mora is the twenty-two-foot-high, three-thousand-pound replica of a *Dalahäst* (Dala horse) west of State Highway 65 at the fairgrounds on Union Street. The **Kanabec History Center**, at 805 W. Forest Avenue (320-679-1665), features a large Dala horse near the front door. A log cabin is located on its premises.

Northeast Minnesota

Hinckley

Opened in the 1894 railroad depot of the St. Paul and Duluth Railroad, the **Hinckley Fire Museum**, 106 Old Highway 61 (320-384-7338), is dedicated to those who lost their lives in a tragic afternoon fire of September 1, 1894. The fire, one of the worst in American history, destroyed six villages, including Hinckley, and killed 418 people, 258 in Hinckley alone. A significant share of the victims were Swedish and Norwegian settlers. The fiery cyclone swept over central Pine County and devastated about 400 square miles of countryside. Probably the best eyewitness account, published in 1894 under the title *Eld-Cyklonen, eller, Hinckley-branden,* was originally written in Swedish by Gudmund Emanuel Åkermark, translated by William Johnson of Hinckley, and published in 1976 by the Pine County Historical Society.

In the women's waiting room is a large diorama showing the conflagration. The former freight room, now an auditorium, features an audiovisual presentation. A model of the old town, partially burned items, and various lumbering tools are displayed, as are accounts of the fire, many written by Swedish pioneers, and immigrant letters.

East of Interstate 35 is a large granite monument, fifty feet in height, dedicated in 1900 to the memory of the men, women, and children who perished in the fire. In the adjoining cemetery are a number of stones with Swedish names, some marking graves of victims of the fire.

Kerrick

 The **Louis Hultgren House**, on State Highway 23 southwest of the business district, was built in the mid-1890s. Hultgren was born in Sweden in 1863 and immigrated to the United States twenty-five years later. When Kerrick was a logging town on the recently constructed Eastern Minnesota Railroad line, Hultgren discovered fine molding sand south of town while working for the railroad. In 1892 he bought the land, began extracting the molding sand, and started a Pine County industry that supplied foundries as far away as central Canada. The house is now a private residence.

Aitkin

 Bethlehem Lutheran Church, 36696-320th Street, off County Highway 12 (218-927-3935), is the oldest Lutheran congregation in Aitkin County. Organized in 1891, the church was formed by Swedes from Klövsjö in Jämtland. The white, Gothic-style wood church with its central steeple was built in 1897; much of the lumber was hand hewn. There is also a nearby cemetery.

Duluth

Duluth and the mining area of the Mesabi Range to the northwest were settled by large numbers of Scandinavians, particularly Finns and Swedes who began arriving in the 1850s and 1860s. Among them was Swedish immigrant Carl Eric Wickman (1887–1954), the founder of Greyhound Corporation. The nearby city of Superior, Wisconsin, also attracted Swedes who, with the completion of the Northern Pacific Railroad in the mid-1880s, came to northern Minnesota to work as lumbermen.

The greatest concentration of Swedes in Duluth was in the West End along W. Third Street, marked by older houses and tall trees. Swedish congregations include Bethany Lutheran Church at 2308 W. Third Street (218-722-5108). It was organized in 1889, and the present sanctuary was constructed in 1903. First Covenant Church, 2101 W. Second Street (218-722-5451), at W. Twenty-first Avenue and Second Street, and Temple Baptist, 2202 W. Third Street, now Lincoln Park Community Church (218-722-4141), were also early churches. Temple Baptist, organized in 1884, is a red-brick classical building with a domed auditorium. The cornerstone reads, "First Swedish Baptist Church AD 1910."

South of Duluth on Midway Road is the little white-frame Augustana Lutheran Church and Cemetery (218-628-1306). The cornerstone notes that the "Sv. Ev. Luth. Midway Church" was organized in 1874 and built in 1917. There were also a number of Swedish settlers in the town of Cloquet, southwest of Duluth, but none of the old church buildings survive. The First Swedish Lutheran Church of Duluth (now Gloria Dei Lutheran Church), 219 N. Sixth Avenue East (218-722-3381), was organized in 1870 by the Reverend P. A. Cederstam, who was serving as a traveling missionary for the Augustana Lutheran Minnesota Conference.

In downtown Duluth, in a park overlooking Lake Superior on London Road, stands a statue of Leif Eriksson. The statue was erected in 1956 by the Norwegian American League of Duluth and by popular subscription.

Hibbing

Andrew G. Anderson, nicknamed "Bus Andy," was a Swedish immigrant born in 1882 who settled in this northern Minnesota community on the Mesabi Iron Range. Along with two other men, he founded a transportation service between Hibbing and Alice in 1914. The business grew, and in 1916 the Mesabi Transportation Company, the forerunner of the Greyhound Corporation, was founded. Another early Hibbing resident, Swedish American Carl Eric Wickman, is recognized as Greyhound's founder, but he later moved to Chicago. Unlike Wickman, Anderson stayed in Hibbing until his death in the mid-1960s. The **Andrew G. Anderson House**, erected in 1920, is a large two-story brick residence combining Georgian Revival and Spanish architecture, at 1001 E. Howard Street. It remains a private residence.

The **Greyhound Bus Origin Center**, at Twenty-third and E. Fifth Avenue, tells the bus line's history. Call the Hibbing Chamber of Commerce (218-262-3895) for information.

Southeast Minnesota

Vasa

In 1853 a group of immigrants led by twenty-one-year-old Hans Mattson founded a community, originally called the Mattson Settlement, in Goodhue County southeast of the present Twin Cities. Mattson became a prominent immigrant promoter of Swedes to Minnesota and founder of three Swedish-language weekly newspapers. The community was later renamed Vasa in honor of King Gustav Vasa. Like Mattson, many early settlers came from northern Skåne. By 1854 at least ten Swedish families were living in the Vasa community, and by 1880 almost 4,300 foreign-born Swedes lived in the county.

Vasa Historic District, southwest of Red Wing and ten miles east of Cannon Falls, is listed on the National Register of Historic Places as "the most intact, unchanged of the original Swedish colonies of Minnesota" and "one of the most representative of an immigrant people from which Minnesota derives so much of its national cultural image." Nineteen buildings date from the nineteenth century.

Near the community's second church, which was erected in 1862 and is today the Vasa Museum, is a marker entitled "Vasa: Mattson's Settlement," erected in 1988 by the Minnesota Historical Society. The marker reads in part: "Founded in 1853 and called 'Mattson's Settlement' after its first resident, Hans Mattson, the community was renamed Vasa in 1856 in honor of Swedish King Gustav Vasa. Once called 'the most Swedish colony in America,' the town prospered as an agricultural community until its two general stores, creamery, and post office were closed in the 1950s. . . . Two men played major roles in Vasa's development. Mattson was one of the earliest promoters of Swedish immigration to the United States. He organized and led a company of Swedish volunteers in the Civil War and later became Minnesota's first commissioner of immigration in 1867 and its secretary of state in 1869. He later served as U.S. Consul General to India and in 1888 was named national chairman of the celebration marking the 250th anniversary of Swedish settlement in America. Reverend Erik Norelius, who settled in Vasa in 1855, established about a dozen Lutheran congregations in southeastern Minnesota. A major force in establishing the Minnesota Conference of the Lutheran Church—the Augustana Synod—he also started the state's first Swedish newspaper and one of its first colleges, Gustavus Adolphus. . . . Minnesota's first private children's home and first private high school were both established in Vasa by Pastor Norelius, who was later knighted for his efforts by Sweden's King Oscar [Oscar II]."

The red-brick **Vasa Evangelical Lutheran Church**, with a tall wood spire and Gothic-style windows, was built in 1869 and dedicated the following year. Situated on a high knoll, it is the focal point of the settlement and is the congregation's third sanctuary. Along the stone wall in front of the church are iron rings for fastening horses' reins. To the right of the church are a monument and the graves of Norelius (1833–1916) and his wife, Inga Charlotte (1838–1924). In the adjacent cemetery are the graves of Olof M. Turnblad (1811–1889) and Ingegerd Turnblad (1816–1888), parents of Swan J. Turnblad, the Swedish-born newspaper publisher whose home now houses the American Swedish Institute in Minneapolis.

The Vasa sanctuary features a unique pulpit inspired by one of Reverend Norelius's visions: a closed Bible under an open one, the inside of the latter facing the pastor and the outside toward the congregation. Also noteworthy in the large sanctuary is a beautiful patterned tin ceiling and a white, carved-wood altar rail fully encircling the altar. The church's stained-glass windows date from 1954.

The Vasa congregation was organized in 1855, with Norelius as its first pastor. A small log church that also served as a school was built in 1856. The second church, a frame structure, was erected in 1862, but the congregation quickly outgrew it. In 1865 the building was moved to its present location, where it was first used as a schoolhouse and now serves as the **Vasa Museum** (612-258-4327). Both the old church and the adjacent caretaker's house, while basically Greek Revival in character, contain distinctly Swedish stylistic overtones. The museum features a large collection of memorabilia, including some items brought from Sweden and others made in the early days of the settlement. Built around 1877, the caretaker's house was first used as a boardinghouse, named the Vasa House, and later as a girls' dormitory for the Vasa school.

Vasa Evangelical Lutheran Church pulpit, Vasa

Other landmarks in Vasa include the town hall, also built about 1877, which has interior benches from the old church made by local Swedish craftsmen. The W. F. Peterson Farmstead, one-half mile south on County Road 7, is the site of the first Vasa Lutheran Church, no longer standing. It also has one of two special cabins found only in Vasa, reputedly examples of Swedish vernacular rural architecture. The Lutheran parsonage was built in 1869 of the same locally fired red brick as the Vasa Lutheran Church. The large white-clapboard house across the road from the church was built by Reverend Norelius in the 1870s; it is a private residence. The former creamery also survives in town, though it is no longer used and is deteriorating. A short distance east of Vasa on State Highway 19 is the Methodist cemetery established in 1883 and the site of the former Methodist church.

The Vasa Lutheran Home, originally known as the Vasa Children's Home, was one of the first private institutions of its kind in Minnesota. It was begun by

Norelius in 1865, when four orphan children were brought to Vasa. The original building, constructed in 1899, is now a private residence located north of the church on a gravel road immediately west of the cemetery. The Vasa Children's Home was relocated in 1926 at the junction of U.S. Highway 61 and State Highway 19, between Vasa and Red Wing, across from the farm of A. P. Anderson, inventor of the cereals known as puffed wheat and puffed rice. The present facility is the fourth building. Under the direction of the Lutheran Social Service of Minnesota, it houses children with developmental disabilities.

In the valley known as Jemtland, south of Vasa on County Road 7, some of the settlers built their homes in 1857. In a small cemetery known as Gravbacken is a large polished-granite marker honoring those laid to rest between 1859 and 1881; their names are listed. More than thirty graves in the cemetery are identified by unique white-painted crosses made from pipes. The cemetery is overgrown with tall grass. To reach Gravbacken, drive one and one-half miles south on County Road 7 from the Vasa Lutheran Church, take a sharp right at 315th Avenue, and drive one mile to White Rock Trail. Turn left and travel about one-half mile. Gravbacken is on a knoll behind a field to the right. A white flagpole in the cemetery is visible from White Rock Trail.

A historic marker at the site of Reverend Norelius's first home in America is on White Rock Trail, one-half mile north of the junction with County Road 1 or about one and one-half miles south of Gravbacken. The marker, dedicated in 1952, is difficult to spot because it is a flat stone on the ground.

Spring Garden Lutheran Church, 10239 County 1 Boulevard (507-263-5532; www.spring-garden.org), and its adjacent cemetery are four miles west of County Road 1 and White Rock Trail. Swedes first settled here in 1855. During the first two years, Reverend Norelius regularly came from Vasa to hold services. The Swedish Evangelical Lutheran Church of Spring Garden was officially formed in 1858. Over the door of the white-frame church with a central steeple is the inscription, "Sw. Ev. Luth. Kyrkan Spring Garden 1876," the date the church was built.

Welch

 Among the congregations established by Norelius is Welch Lutheran Church, now **Cross of Christ Lutheran**, 1512 Highway 61 Boulevard (651-388-3464), organized in 1873. Located at County Road 7, the church has in its sanctuary a replica of the pulpit made by Norelius for the Vasa Lutheran Church. Other congregations organized by Norelius include Cannon River Lutheran Church (1857); St. Ansgar Lutheran Church in Cannon Falls (1869); Zion Lutheran Church in Goodhue (1869), whose present congregation is the result of a merger; and First Lutheran Church in Red Wing (1855).

Red Wing

The **First Lutheran Church** congregation, organized in 1855, constructed an impressive Gothic-style building with a high steeple in 1895 at 615 W. Fifth Street (651-388-9311; www.firstlutheranrw.org). The buff-limestone structure located in the historic mall district was built on the same site as the second church. In the 1950 remodeling, a chapel was dedicated to Norelius's memory.

The congregation of **First Covenant Church of Red Wing**, 2302 Hay Creek Trail (651-388-2385), organized in 1874, now worships in a church built in 1978 at Twin Bluff Road and Pioneer. Its former church building, constructed in 1874 and 1875 at the corner of Sixth Street and West Avenue, is owned by another congregation.

Millville

 The simple former **Swedish Evangelical Lutheran Church** was built in 1874 of fieldstone with Gothic-style, clear-glass windows. It is near the corner of Bridge (County Road 2) and Oakwood Streets. The building was deeded by the Minnesota Synod of the Lutheran Church in America to the village of Millville and is maintained by the Millville Historical Association. Behind the structure is a small cemetery with Swedish graves.

Houston

The **Swede Bottom Cemetery** in Houston is important in the history of Swedish Baptists because it contains the grave of early leader F. O. Nilsson (1809–1881). The first Swedish Baptist congregation in Minnesota was organized in Houston in 1853, but the old sanctuary no longer exists.

South-Central and Southwest Minnesota

Finding difficulty expanding the settlement in Goodhue County, Swedes who had come to Minnesota from Indiana in the summer of 1857 moved on to south-central Minnesota in search of land. They called their settlement Vista in memory of their native Småland community. As early as 1854, other Swedes began to arrive in Nicollet County, some eighty miles southwest of Minneapolis, by covered wagons and riverboats from Illinois and Wisconsin. They settled in the farming areas south, north, and west of St. Peter, nestled on the winding Minnesota River. Additionally, to the east, in the 1870s Swedes were attracted to the "Big Woods" country of what is today Rice County.

New Richland

 Vista Lutheran Church, 15035-275th Avenue (507-465-3539), was organized as early as 1858 by Dr. Erik Norelius. The attractive red-brick, Gothic-style building northeast of New Richland (six miles north on State Highway 13 and one mile east on County Road 20) was constructed in 1908. The sanctuary is unusual because of the Swedish inscriptions stenciled on the walls. One-quarter mile west of Vista are two cemeteries, Lutheran and Covenant. Just west of them is **Vista Evangelical Covenant Church**, 14679-275th Avenue (507-465-8365), organized in 1876. Members constructed the present sanctuary in 1964.

Mankato

 Political leader Adolph O. Eberhart, born in Värmland in 1870, immigrated to Minnesota in 1882. The two-and-one-half-story Georgian Revival **Adolph Olson Eberhart House**, at 228 E. Pleasant Street, built around 1903, is distinctive in its irregular roofline featuring attic dormers and Palladian windows and in its open-entrance porch. Eberhart, a student at Gustavus Adolphus College in St. Peter before coming to Mankato in 1895 to study law, was a state senator (1901–1906), lieutenant governor (1906–1909), and governor (1909–1915).

St. Peter

A Swedish Lutheran congregation was established here in 1857. The present sanctuary of **First Lutheran Church** was built in 1965 at 1114 W. Traverse Road at Sunrise Drive (507-934-3060). One of the earliest Swedes to settle in the St. Peter area was Gustaf Johnson of southern Östergötland. His son, John A. Johnson, was governor of Minnesota from 1905 to 1909.

Schools

Gustavus Adolphus College—800 W. College Avenue (507-933-8000; www.gustavus.edu).
Swedish Lutherans in Minnesota began a school in Red Wing in 1862. The following year, it moved to East Union in Carver County with the name St. Ansgar's Academy. In October 1876, the school opened in St. Peter under its present name. This liberal arts institution has grown to more than 2,500 students and a faculty of 180. Situated on a hill on the west side of St. Peter, the lovely campus has a number of buildings and markers underscoring its Swedish heritage.

Near the center of campus is a bust of Gustavus Adolphus (1594–1632), the Swedish king and defender of Lutheranism. It was unveiled in 1932, on the 300th anniversary of his death at the Battle of Lützen.

Nearby is **Old Main**. This stone building dating from 1876 is the oldest structure on campus. Near the front is the millstone used in the mill at East Union, Carver County, from 1865 to 1875 to support St. Ansgar's Academy.

The modern Folke Bernadotte Memorial Library opened in 1972; it has a picture and plaque about Count Folke Bernadotte (1895–1948), noted Swedish diplomat, near the information desk. On the third floor of the library are the archives of the college and the Minnesota Synod of Augustana's successor, formerly the Lutheran Church in America (LCA).

Old Main, Gustavus Adolphus College, St. Peter

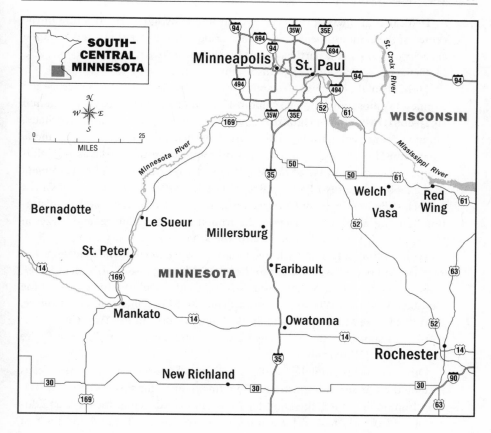

The Nobel Hall of Science was dedicated in 1963 in honor of Alfred Nobel by Dr. Glenn T. Seaborg, then chairman of the U.S. Atomic Energy Commission and the 1951 co-winner of the Nobel Prize in chemistry. Seaborg's Swedish parents immigrated to Ishpeming, Michigan, and then to California. Also present at the 1963 dedication were twenty-seven other Nobel Prize winners. In the lobby is a Foucault pendulum and four panels about Alfred Nobel's life and significance. Each fall the college hosts the Nobel Conference, attended by many world-famous scholars.

In the lobby of the Jussi Björling Recital Hall is a bust of the renowned Swedish operatic tenor, a photograph of Björling (1911–1960), and a poem by Swedish poet Bo Setterlind (1923–1991). The Björling Recital Hall is part of the Schaefer Fine Arts Complex, which includes the Anderson Theatre named in honor of Evan Anderson, professor of speech, and his wife, Evelyn, associate professor of speech and director of the theater.

Dedicated in 1962, Christ Chapel is an impressive modern structure in the center of the campus; the chapel has a soaring spire 187 feet high and a seating capacity of 1,200. In the narthex are plaques honoring two college presidents, P. A. Mattson (1904–1911) and O. J. Johnson (1913–1943).

Throughout the campus are sculptures by Paul Granlund, artist-in-residence and Minnesota's most outstanding sculptor. The son of a Lutheran pastor, Granlund (1925–2003) cast some 650 bronze sculptures for public spaces in the United States. Granlund's international commissions are in Sweden, England, France, Italy, India, Japan, and Hong Kong. Thirty of his works appear on the Gustavus Adolphus campus, including *Masks of the Muses* outside the Anderson Theatre, *Sonata* in the lobby of the Jussi Björling Recital Hall, *Luna Moth Matrix* east of Christ Chapel, *Palindrome* west of Christ Chapel, *Apogee* near the Carlson Administration Building, a bust of Linnaeus at the arboretum, and sculptures and friezes in Christ Chapel. The artist's studio was in the Schaefer Fine Arts Center.

Within Minnesota, other selected Granlund works include the following: *The Mothers,* in Louise Park adjacent to the W. W. Mayo House, North Main Street, Le Sueur; *Lofting* at the Miller-Dwan Medical Center, Duluth; *Adolescence* at the Constance Bultman Wilson Center, Faribault; and *Celebration,* St. Olaf College, Northfield. (See Minneapolis and St. Paul for his works in the Twin Cities.) His works also appear at the Five Flags Plaza in Dubuque, Iowa, and in Eau Claire and La Crosse, Wisconsin.

Other Gustavus Adolphus College buildings honoring Swedish Americans include the Carlson Administration Building, named for Edgar Carlson, president from 1944 to 1968; the Lund Ice Arena and Lund Center for Physical Education and Health, named for Minnesota grocer Russell T. Lund and his first and second wives; Norelius Hall, a student residence hall named for the college's founder, Erik Norelius; Rundstrom Hall, named for Inez Rundstrom, the first woman graduate of Augustana College, Rock Island, Illinois, and a professor of mathematics at Gustavus Adolphus for forty-eight years; Edwin J. Vickner Hall, named for the linguist and Scandinavian scholar; Mathias Wahlstrom Hall, named for the college's fifth president, 1881–1904; Johnson Student Union, built as a gymnasium in 1921 and dedicated to the college's seventh president, Oscar J. Johnson, in 1987; Hillstrom Museum of Art, named for the Reverend Richard L. Hillstrom, collector of fine art; and the arboretum's Melva Lind Interpretive Center, named for a former dean of students.

The Linnaeus Arboretum was created under the leadership of biology professor Charles Mason in honor of the Swedish immigrants who founded Gustavus Adolphus in 1862. It is named for Swedish botanist Carl von Linné, who is responsible for the binomial biological nomenclature used today. In the arboretum is an example of Swedish folk architecture: the pioneer home of the Carl J.

Borgeson log cabin, Gustavus Adolphus College, St. Peter

and Clara C. Borgeson family, who came from Sweden and settled in Minnesota. Made with twenty-five-foot white-oak logs held in place by dovetail notching, the cabin has a single room with a narrow staircase leading to a sleeping loft, a plan typical of the Swedish *stuga*. It was built in the 1860s or 1870s in Norseland, Nicollet County.

The college annually sponsors the Raoul Wallenberg Lecture, and Gustavus Adolphus was the first American school of higher education to confer a degree on Wallenberg in absentia. Scandinavian studies are a formal program of academic study within the curriculum.

Historic Places

 John Albert Johnson (1861–1909), governor of Minnesota between 1905 and 1909 and the likely Democratic nominee for president in 1912 before his death in 1909 in his third term as governor, was born near St. Peter. In front of the Nicollet County Courthouse (597-931-6800) stands his statue. The **John Albert Johnson House**, at 418 N. Third Street, is now a private residence. Johnson's grave is in the southeast quadrant of Klein Cemetery off Sunrise Drive. The highway leading into St. Peter from the north is identified as John A. Johnson Memorial Highway.

In 1855 several Swedish families bought land twelve miles northwest of St. Peter, now on State Highway 22, and called the place Scandian Grove. Three years later, the Reverend P. A. Cederstam from Chisago Lake presided at the organizing of the **Scandian Grove Lutheran Church**, 42869 County Road 52 (507-246-5195). A sanctuary built in 1888 was preserved for ninety years, but a fire destroyed it in 1978. A new church has been built on the same site. In the sanctuary is the old baptismal font, and in the library are two walls made from bricks of the former church, some of which bear marks from the fire.

In the adjacent church park is the log house built in 1855 by Andrew Thorson, a leader of the Scandian Grove community who was instrumental in persuading Lutheran church leaders to relocate Gustavus Adolphus College to St. Peter. It was in his house that the Scandian Grove Lutheran congregation was organized. The cabin was moved to the park in 1952. In the nearby cemetery are the graves of five church pastors.

Millersburg

 Christdala Evangelical Swedish Lutheran Church, 4695 Millersburg Road, two miles west of Millersburg on Rice County Road 1, was constructed in 1878, one year after the congregation of thirteen families formed. It is late Gothic Revival in design and constructed of oak, elm, and maple hardwoods from the area's forest, called the "Great Woods" by Swedish settlers. The 24 by 54 foot white-clapboard sanctuary is mostly original, including a handcrafted altar and pulpit constructed in 1880. Swedes first arrived in Rice County in the early 1870s, initially settling in Vasa to the east. Many journeyed fifteen miles to worship with Norwegian settlers, until in September 1876 a tragedy led the Swedes to organize their own church. Nicholas Gustafson, an original settler with limited knowledge of English, was accidentally shot during an attempted bank robbery in Northfield because he did not understand the gang members' commands. The congregation reached a peak of 207 members in the early twentieth century and eventually disbanded. The sanctuary and cemetery are maintained by a preservation association.

Bernadotte

The red-brick, Gothic-style **Bernadotte Lutheran Church**, on County Road 10 five miles east and one mile north of Lafayette (507-228-8680), was built in 1897 for a congregation organized in 1866. In front is a plaque giving the church history and the origin of the name Bernadotte, taken in honor of the Swedish ruling house. Jean-Baptiste Bernadotte (1763–1844), one of Napoleon Bonaparte's field marshals, after election as crown prince by the Riksdag, adopted the Lutheran faith and became known as Karl XIV Johan.

In the church basement is a framed telegram from King Gustav VI Adolf and a letter from the king's secretary on the 100th anniversary of the congregation's founding. In a glass case is a leather-bound book about the life of Gustav V presented in 1933 on the visit of Count Folke Bernadotte (1895–1948), leader of the Swedish

Red Cross and a diplomat. During his appointment by the United Nations to help mediate the Palestinian conflict, he was assassinated in Jerusalem.

Gibbon

Organized in 1871, the **Clear Lake Lutheran** congregation built a Gothic-style, white-frame place of worship in 1890. About four years later, this group merged with the Augustana Lutheran Church, 730 Cedar, Gibbon (507-834-6108), about five miles to the north. The old sanctuary now belongs to the Clear Lake Cemetery Association and is used for an occasional summer service. To the west is the **Clear Lake Baptist Church**, also founded in 1871. Its sanctuary formerly belonged to a German Methodist congregation and was moved here in 1934.

New Ulm

John Lind (1854–1930), born in southern Småland, came to the United States in 1868 with his parents. He was the first man of Swedish birth to be elected to the U.S. Congress (three terms between 1887 and 1893), and he was governor of Minnesota from 1899 to 1901. In 1902 he was elected to a fourth term in Congress, where he served two more terms until 1905. The **John Lind House**, 622 Center Street at N. State, is a Queen Anne–style house constructed primarily of local red brick in 1887 and now owned by the Lind House Association.

Lake Benton

In this southwestern Minnesota community is the **Ernest Osbeck House**, 106 S. Fremont. Osbeck, born in Alvesta, Sweden, in 1859, arrived in Lake Benton in 1884 and helped organize the Lake Benton Co-op Creamery Association, the local bank, and the Lake Benton Opera House. His home, built in 1887 in the Queen Anne style, remains a private residence.

Central Minnesota

The area's first Swedes traveled up the Minnesota River by flatboat in 1854. They founded King Oscar's Settlement in southeastern Carver County, which later divided into the East Union and West Union settlements. The following summer, a party of sixteen from central Västergötland arrived. In 1858 a Lutheran congregation was founded that divided in the same year into the East Union and West Union parishes. In northern Carver County, two miles south of Watertown and directly west of the Twin Cities, a group of Swedes named their community Götaholm. In between these northern and southern sites, Swedish Baptists from Burlington, Iowa, and Galesburg, Illinois, settled around Lake Waconia in 1855 in a colony called Scandia.

Swedish settlements west of the Twin Cities in Wright, Meeker, Kandiyohi, and Swift Counties began in the 1850s and 1860s. Most of the early settlers who arrived in Wright County in 1862 came from parishes in western Värmland. The Reverend John S. Nilson of the Götaholm (Watertown) congregation organized the earliest Swedish Lutheran churches in this county, including Stockholm Lutheran in 1866; Carlslund (now the Zion Lutheran Church, Buffalo) in late 1866; and Swedesburg (which later merged with Zion in Buffalo) in 1873.

Swedes began arriving in Meeker County, west of Wright County, in 1856. Both Erik Norelius and Peter Magnus Johnson, a Methodist minister, preached in the area in 1861. After 1869, the year the St. Paul and Pacific Railroad was built through Meeker County, Swedish congregations were established near the tracks in several communities, including Dassel, Swan Lake, Beckville, Ostmark, Litchfield, and Grove City (formerly Swede Grove).

The railroad meant not only that people and goods could come in but that an employer, the railroad, was at hand. Hans Mattson, who had helped settle Vasa, promoted immigration for Minnesota, and served as railroad land agent. He was instrumental in bringing Swedes to these Minnesota counties.

Carver

East Union Lutheran Church (852-448-3450) and Parish Hall, 15180 County Road 40, about three and one-half miles southwest of Carver, make an attractive site that is listed on the National Register of Historic Places as **King Oscar's Settlement.** The brick church, with its central steeple and Gothic-style windows, was built in 1866, though the congregation was organized eight years earlier. A stone plaque over the front door bears a Swedish inscription. The sanctuary has a raised canopied pulpit, and in the narthex are portraits of the former pastors, including founder Pehr Carlson. The Salem Lutheran congregation, which once thrived in downtown Carver but dissolved in 1952, placed the bell from its church in front of East Union. A cemetery is near the church.

The cream-colored, clapboard **East Union Parish Hall** has a sign over the front door noting that it was the pioneer building of the Union Settlement Church (1856–1866) and St. Ansgar's Academy (1863–1876), forerunner of Gustavus Adolphus College. The East Union congregation purchased the St. Ansgar school property in 1883 and renovated the old building into a parish hall. It is probably the oldest building of the Minnesota Conference of the former Augustana Synod, dating to the pre–Civil War period.

Nine miles west of Carver is the **West Union Lutheran Church** (952-466-5678), founded about six months after East Union so that worshipers would not have to travel so far. The church stands at 15820 Market Avenue at County Road 50. Take County Road 40 south out of Carver and go west at County Road 50.

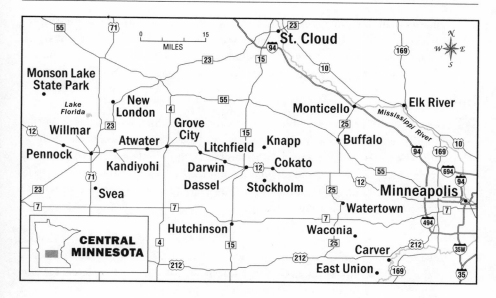

The church's cemetery is on a wooded rise above the cornfields. To the right of a path leading to the church is the original parish hall, built in 1904. A new parish hall was constructed in 1960. The sanctuary was built in 1868, and the spire was added in 1871. The church was remodeled in 1973, its ceiling and walls being covered with light wood, which gives the effect of an inverted ship's hull. Graves in the cemetery date from 1858.

Waconia

 Andrew (Anders) Peterson (1818–1898) was one of the first settlers at Scandia on the northeast shore of Lake Waconia, near present-day Waconia. By 1860 there were some thirty families, most of whom came from Iowa. Peterson, a careful horticulturist and researcher, had a farm, now identified as the **Andrew Peterson (Rock Isle) Farmstead.** Swedes at Scandia organized a Baptist congregation in 1855 in Peterson's log house and built a log church in 1857. In 1973 the building was moved to Bethel University and Seminary near St. Paul. The Scandia Baptist Cemetery, where Peterson is buried, sits directly across the road from the former site of the Scandia Baptist Church, now part of the Island View Country Club.

Watertown

The community at Swede Lake was for many years called Götaholm. The settlers organized a Lutheran congregation in late 1858 and built a small church in 1859. It was used until 1870, when a new sanctuary was constructed in Watertown two and one-half miles north. A third church was built in 1890 and the present struc-ture in 1950. In 1948 the church's name was changed to **Trinity Lutheran**, 513 SE Madison Street (952-955-1891). A monument on County Road 10 marks the site of the original church. Behind the marker are a few gravestones.

Buffalo

 Near Buffalo is the **Marysville "Swedesburg" Lutheran Church**. The red-brick building with Gothic-style clear windows and a dark-wood steeple was built in 1891. The congregation merged with Zion Lutheran in Buffalo at 1200 S. Highway 25 (763-682-1245; www.zionbuffalo.org), and the last regular Sunday service was held in 1950. During the summer, Monday evening services are held in the old church, as are baptisms and weddings.

Knapp

Five miles north of Cokato and one and one-half miles west of County Road 3 is the **North Crow River Lutheran Church**, 45 SW Quinnell Avenue, Cokato (320-286-2354). With Gothic-style windows and a central bell tower, the church bears the inscription, "Sw. Ev. Luth. Church North Crow River 1903." The con-gregation was organized thirty-three years earlier. In the adjacent cemetery is a granite stone with an inscription to the settlers. In nearby South Haven is **Grace Lutheran Church**, 17872 NW Thirty-fifth Street (320-286-2354), and a Swedish cemetery, founded in 1890, at County Roads 37 and 2.

Cokato

The **Cokato Museum** is at Fourth and Millard (320-286-2427). Exhibits feature immigrant memorabilia and Cokato's early years. In the museum is a restored 18 by 24 foot log cabin built by Nils Lans, who had been an officer in the Swedish army. He fought in the Civil War and homesteaded south of Cokato. This cabin was moved in 1940 to Peterson Park across the street from the museum, where it served as a winter warming house. When the museum was built in 1976, the cabin was moved to its present location. The fourth side of the cabin is open for viewing artifacts.

 . Also owned by the Cokato Historical Society and adjacent to the Cokato Museum is the **August Akerlund Photography Studio**, 390 Broadway Avenue at Fourth. This simple, single-story, wood-frame building constructed in 1905 combined a photography studio and residence and remains relatively unaltered. Swedish-born August Akerlund arrived in Cokato in 1902, purchased a photog-raphy studio, and went into business.

Stockholm

About four miles southwest of Cokato is the **Stockholm Lutheran Church**, 16133 SW County Road 30 (320-286-2807), and cemetery. Originally called Mooers Prairie, the area was settled in 1862 by Swedes, who began arriving from Kandiyohi County following the U.S.–Dakota (Sioux) conflict of that year.

The Stockholm Lutheran congregation organized the first church in the county in 1866. A township named Stockholm followed in 1868. The brick-faced church built in 1876 has been modernized in the interior. On the steeple is the inscription, "Sw. Ev. Lutheran." To the west of the church is a Swedish cemetery; another one sits across the road.

Dassel

Gethsemane Lutheran Church (formerly First Lutheran), 221 E. Atlantic Avenue (320-275-3852), was organized in 1873, and the present Gothic-style brick church with bell tower was built in 1886. The sanctuary has a raised canopied pulpit. A three-crown motif has been stenciled near the ceiling.

Seven and one-half miles north of Dassel is the small white-frame Swan Lutheran Church, built in 1899 by a congregation organized in 1873. Although the sanctuary was sold in the mid-1980s to a Finnish congregation, the old cemetery is owned by Gethsemane Lutheran in Dassel.

Darwin

North of Darwin is the **Ostmark Lutheran Church**, 32721-680th Avenue, Watkins (320-693-8450). The congregation was organized in 1894 and a white-clapboard church built in 1911. About five miles south of Darwin is **Lake Jennie Covenant Church**, 8531-705th Avenue, Dassel (321-275-3233) and cemetery. The congregation was organized in 1886 and the white-frame church built in 1921.

Litchfield

 Trinity Episcopal Church at N. Sibley Avenue and Fourth Street (320-693-6035) was built of vertical board-and-batten construction in 1871 as an American Episcopal church. Its second rector became interested in the community's Swedish people and learned Swedish in order to hold services for them. He organized a separate Swedish Mission, later known as Emmanuel Church. In 1929, the two parishes merged. The old altar in Trinity Episcopal is from the former Emmanuel Church. Nearby is the **Meeker County Historical Society**, 308 N. Marshall Avenue (320-693-8911), which displays historical artifacts. One mile south of town on State Highway 22 is the Litchfield Cemetery.

Also seven miles south of Litchfield, at 2052-600th Avenue, is **Brookville Lutheran Church** and cemetery (320-693-2519). This white-frame church with a bell tower, built in 1901, is on a gravel road reached by going south from Litchfield on State Highway 22 for two and one-half miles and then turning north on the gravel road. The congregation was organized in 1869. Bishop Herbert Chilstrom, who was baptized in this church, was the first national bishop of the Evangelical Lutheran Church in America, formed in 1988 by the merger of the American Lutheran Church, the Lutheran Church in America, and the Association of Evangelical Lutheran Churches. Bishop Chilstrom, born in 1931 in Litchfield, is a third-generation Swedish American.

Grove City

Originally called Swede Grove, Grove City is home to **Trinity Lutheran Church** at 54384 E. U.S. Highway 12 (320-857-2001). The church has the date 1922 on its cornerstone. Formerly called First Evangelical Lutheran, Trinity was formed from a merger of Immanuel and Amdahl Lutheran Churches.

Atwater

Immanuel Lutheran Church, at 300 S. Third Street (320-974-8695; www.immanuel atwater.com), was organized in 1868. The white-frame church, which dates from 1876, has Gothic-style windows and a central steeple.

Kandiyohi

Two and one-half miles south of Kandiyohi stands **Tripolis Evangelical Lutheran Church** and cemetery, 3429 SE County Road 8 (320-382-6264). This white-frame church, built in 1881, has a central steeple and Gothic-style windows. This congregation was organized in 1868. In the town of Kandiyohi is **Ebenezer Evangelical Lutheran Church**, 610 W. Atlantic Avenue (320-382-6264), a white-frame structure built in 1907.

    The **Andreas and Johanna Broman and Frank E. and Anna Broman Farmstead**, off Kandiyohi County Road 8, Kandiyohi Township, is a nineteenth-century farmstead settled by Swedes.

Willmar

One-half mile north of downtown Willmar, at 610 NE U.S. Highway 71, is the **Kandiyohi County Historical Society** (320-235-1881). Its museum contains a large collection of artifacts portraying life on the prairie among the county's predominantly Norwegian and Swedish immigrants.

Svea

Another old Swedish congregation is **Svea Lutheran**, 12651 SE 153rd Street (320-995-6500), about eight miles south of Willmar. Organized in 1870, the congregation built its present sanctuary in 1920. Adjacent to the church is an old cemetery.

Pennock

Old Mamrelund Lutheran Church (owned by Mamrelund Lutheran Church)—217 Dakota Avenue (320-599-4548).

This church is considered perhaps the best-preserved rural "Swedish" church in Kandiyohi County. In 1868 Johan Gillberg and John Rådman homesteaded here, and the following year they helped found Mamrelund Church. Rådman apparently named the church while reading the Genesis account of an angel appearing to Abraham at the oaks of Mamre near Hebron.

Two structures preceded the present church, which was built in 1883 at a cost of $1,452.04. The small, 30 by 42 foot, white-clapboard church with its central steeple and Gothic-style clear-glass windows stands in a peaceful grove of oak trees; a nicely maintained cemetery is at the rear of the church.

The sanctuary in this wonderful church still has the original elaborate wall stenciling. Behind the altar is a painted reredos in Gothic style depicting the empty cross draped in white cloth. Above the cross is a deep blue starry sky, and below the cross is the inscription, *Se Guds Lam* (Behold the Lamb of God). Other Swedish inscriptions are stenciled on the walls. In 1989 the congregation had English translations painted on the walls.

The church has an embossed-tin ceiling and wainscoting; walls are fully stenciled with Gothic motifs, including pointed arches just below the ceiling line. There are also various Christian symbols, such as palm branches, the budding cross, the anchor, and the Latin cross. The walls behind the pulpit and the organ have painted drapery with floral motifs. Original objects in the church include old hymnals, a reed organ, a hymn board with carefully cut tin numbers, an elevated wood carved pulpit and altar rail, and beautiful gas lights and oil lamps. The sanctuary contains tightly spaced movable old pews.

In 1915 the congregation built a church in town but also decided to maintain the country church, which has no electricity, running water, telephone, or central heating. During the summer, several services are held here, as are two candle-lit Christmas Eve services. In August an "old time" ladies aid meeting is attended by women in period costume. To reach the church, drive west on U.S. Highway 12 out of Pennock, turn north on County Road 1 (there is a sign at this intersection for the church), go about three and one-half miles, turn east on Seventy-fifth Avenue, a gravel road, go one-half mile, and turn south onto a narrow gravel road.

Historic Lundy Covenant Cemetery and Salem Covenant Church—7811 NW 135th Street (320-599-4574; www.salemcovepennock.org).

In the early 1880s, two early founders of the Mamrelund Church were attracted to the Pietist movement and they joined other settlers at the nearby Lundby Swedish Mission Church. John Rådman became its pastor. Eventually that congregation merged with Salem Covenant Church. About three miles northeast of Mamrelund Lutheran Church is Lundby Covenant Cemetery. Go north on County Road 1 to County Road 27, turn east on County Road 27, travel two miles, and then turn north on a gravel road one-half mile to the cemetery.

Salem Covenant is the oldest existing congregation of the Evangelical Covenant Church of America in Minnesota. Although the congregation worships in a red-brick church built in 1968, the cornerstone notes that the congregation dates from 1871. It formerly met in a building that stood next to the Lundby Covenant Cemetery. In front of the church is a brick monument erected on the congregation's centennial anniversary in 1971. The church is five miles northwest of Pennock on State Highway 104.

Lake Florida Covenant Church.

Lake Florida Covenant Church was organized in 1870 as a Lutheran congregation known as the Swedish Evangelical Lutheran Church of Norway Lake. The tiny white-frame building, located off County Road 29, one and one-half miles east of County Road 5 or twelve miles east of the present Salem Covenant Church, was built in 1873. In 1879, the congregation voted to leave the Augustana Synod and affiliate with the Mission Friends, becoming one of the earliest Covenant parishes in Minnesota. It served as a parish church until 1955 but now is owned and maintained by an association. The nicely restored interior contains many old furnishings. From 1890 to 1907, the Reverend Nils Frykman, also known as a hymn writer, served as pastor to this church and three other central Minnesota congregations.

New London

Louis Larson, a Swedish immigrant, saw the falls on the Crow River in 1860 and in the following year built a cabin nearby. In 1862 he erected a dam and sawmill. This event is noted on a plaque located on SW First Avenue just off Main Street on the banks of the mill pond. The plaque notes that "on August 17, 1862, the Dakota Indian War broke out. Larson and all the settlers in the area were forced to flee for safety and did not return until 1865. Larson and Samuel Stone returned to find the dam washed out. They rebuilt the dam and sawmill and added a gristmill. Settlers came from miles around for lumber, flour, and other needs. Larson named the town New London after New London, Wisconsin. By

1868 New London had grown to forty people, three stores and a blacksmith shop. It was the county seat of Monongalia County from 1866 to 1870, when it merged with Kandiyohi County."

The former Lebanon Lutheran Church was the oldest congregation in Kandiyohi County, having been established in 1859 as the New Sweden congregation in a log cabin of an early Swedish settler. In 1865 this congregation, known as the

Lake Florida Covenant Church, Pennock

Nest Lake Church, was reorganized after the fighting against the Dakota (Sioux) Indians had ended. In 1896 the name of the congregation was changed to Lebanon. The third church building of the congregation, which presently houses the **Monongalia Historical Society and Museum**, 220 SW Norwood Street (320-354-2990), was constructed in 1873. It is a white-frame neo-Gothic building. Next to the museum is a nineteenth-century log cabin.

In the former church sanctuary is a 1901 altar painting by Olof Grafström (1885–1933) portraying Christ with outstretched arms surrounded by followers. Also displayed are various furnishings of the old church. In the balcony are

Massacre marker, Peace Lutheran Church Cemetery, New London

memorabilia from the former Trinity Lutheran Church, New London. This was a Norwegian congregation that merged with Lebanon Lutheran to form the present **Peace Lutheran Church** (320-354-2774), located on the other side of the adjoining Peace Lutheran Church Cemetery.

The West Lake Massacre Historical Inclosure at Peace Lutheran Church Cemetery includes the memorial markers to the victims of the 1862 U.S.–Dakota Conflict. Visitors first notice the tall metal Broberg-Lundborg State Monument listing the thirteen people, all members of the New Sweden Church, who were killed near West Lake on their way home from a religious meeting at the home of Andreas Lundborg. The monument was approved by the Minnesota legislature and dedicated August 20, 1891. The remains of the settlers were removed from West Lake (today called Monson Lake) in June 1891 and now rest where this memorial is erected. This inclosure contains plaques describing the tragic event based on the eyewitness story of Anna Stina Broberg, the lone survivor.

Monson Lake State Park

Two historic markers note the location where members of the Anders P. and Daniel P. Broberg and Andreas L. Lundborg families were killed during the 1862 U.S.–Dakota Conflict. Beyond one stone marker are two depressions where the original settlers' dugouts were located.

A pamphlet titled "Historical Sites of Kandiyohi County" from the Kandiyohi County Historical Society in Willmar lists, locates, and explains additional markers in the county relating to the events of August 1862. Many Norwegians and Swedes experienced the war.

North-Central Minnesota

North-central Minnesota's Morrison County attracted numerous Swedes who settled down to farming and lumbering. The most famous name was Lindbergh.

West of Morrison County is Douglas County, where land seekers began arriving in 1863 after enactment of the Homestead Act. In 1878 the first railroad came to Alexandria, the county seat. Some Swedish settlements prospered in the county, particularly in the Holmes City–Lake Oscar area. The county has declared itself the "Birthplace of America," referring to the 1898 discovery of the Kensington Runestone on the farm of Olof Ohman, an early Swedish settler in the area. The authenticity of this "Viking" artifact is discounted by most scholars.

Otter Tail County was established in 1858, and Swedish immigrants began arriving in the 1870s when the railroad was built. Swedish Lutheran churches were established in Fergus Falls, Christine Lake, Battle Lake, Henning, Eagle Lake, and Parkers Prairie. A Swedish Baptist congregation was organized in Fergus Falls.

Little Falls

Charles A. Lindbergh House—1620 S. Lindbergh Drive (320-616-5421).
The house built by Charles Lindbergh Sr. sits near the banks of the Mississippi River on more than one hundred acres of land bought in 1898. It replaced his three-story, thirteen-room house lost in a fire in 1905. Though simpler in style than the first, the present house rests on the same foundations. Used primarily as a summer home, it was where Charles Lindbergh Jr. spent his boyhood summers. After 1924, the Lindbergh family rarely used the house, and in 1931 it was donated to the state of Minnesota, which designated the site a state park. The Minnesota Historical Society has restored the house and constructed a visitor center to tell the story of the younger Lindbergh's life.

Dedicated in 1973, the visitor center was completely remodeled in 2002 on the occasion of Charles Lindbergh Jr.'s centennial and the 75th anniversary of his epochal flight to Paris in 1927. New exhibits cover the famous aviator's entire life, from his boyhood in Little Falls to his death in Hawaii in 1974, at the age of 72. A film on Lindbergh's life is shown in a ground floor auditorium, and the visitor center also includes a gift shop.

Charles A. Lindbergh House, Little Falls

Ola Månsson (1808–1893), grandfather of Charles Lindbergh Jr., had a farm near Simrishamn, Skåne. He also was a member of the Riksdag before he emigrated from Sweden in 1860. The family homesteaded near Melrose, Minnesota, and Månsson began identifying himself as August Lindbergh, the surname having been previously adopted by a brother in Sweden. Månsson's son, Charles August Lindbergh (1858–1924), attended the University of Michigan Law School and practiced law in Little Falls. He was a Republican member of the U.S. Congress from 1907 to 1917 and was nominated for governor of Minnesota on the Farmer-Labor ticket in 1924, but he died during the campaign. He requested that no grave marker be erected in his memory.

Charles A. Lindbergh Jr. (1902–1974) attended high school in Little Falls, graduating in 1918. He spent two years running his father's farm and then went on to the University of Wisconsin to study civil engineering. Dropping out during his sophomore year, he entered a flying school in Lincoln, Nebraska. As a pilot for an airmail line, Lindbergh decided to try for the $25,000 Orteig Prize for the first nonstop New York–Paris flight. Financed by a group of St. Louis businessmen, Lindbergh helped design the plane, the *Spirit of St. Louis,* used in his historic transatlantic flight on May 20–21, 1927.

 The **Charles A. Lindbergh State Park** off County Road 52, in memory of Charles Lindbergh Jr.'s father, is on the National Register of Historic Places. Members of the Lindbergh family donated the land.

Nisswa

The Nisswa Historical Society's Pioneer Village Museum and Depot, at the north end of Main Street (218-963-3570), houses twelve buildings, including one identified as a Swedish cabin built in the late nineteenth century from Monticello, Minnesota. Its logs had been sheathed with siding, thereby requiring fewer repairs than other buildings in the village. The Pioneer Village, which also includes Norwegian and German immigrant log cabins, began in the mid-1990s around the town's former railway depot. Nearly all the buildings have late-nineteenth- and early twentieth-century furniture and other artifacts.

During the second weekend in June, the popular Nisswa-Stämmen is held in the Pioneer Village. This Nordic folk festival celebrates Scandinavian and Scandinavian American music and features artists from both the United States and Scandinavia.

Nelson

Fahlun Lutheran Church, at NE County Road 74, three miles north and one mile east of Nelson (320-765-9500), is a white frame building with a tall, three-tiered steeple. On stained glass-windows above the main door is the inscription *Sv. Ev.*

Fahlun Lutheran Church, Nelson

Luth. Fahlun Kyrka. A sign in front of the church summarizes the history of the congregation, organized in 1871. The present church was constructed in 1885. The sanctuary has an altar painting (1909) by Grafström and symbolic Gothic-style stained-glass windows with Swedish inscriptions; the windows were added in 1912. A large cemetery with several Swedish inscriptions is adjacent to this lovely rural Minnesota church.

Alexandria

In front of the Douglas County Courthouse is a plaque honoring Theodore A. Erickson (1871–1963), Douglas County superintendent of schools from 1907 to 1915 and founder of the 4-H movement in Minnesota.

Another plaque outside the **Calvary Lutheran Church**, at 605 Douglas (320-767-5178), commemorates the 100th anniversary of the founding of the Svea Swedish Evangelical Lutheran congregation by six Swedish couples. Although the church's current building dates from the 1950s, a stained-glass window from the first church built in the 1880s is displayed in the church library's lounge. The altar and baptismal font from the 1909 church are in the chapel. The church changed its name in 1948.

The **Runestone Museum**, 206 Broadway (320-763-3160; www.runestonemuseum .org), houses the Kensington Runestone. Above the display is a map showing the alleged route taken by visiting Scandinavians in 1362. Other displays include memorabilia that have been excavated, including a battle-ax found near Mora in 1933. One mile east of the Runestone Museum on State Highway 27 is a large replica of the Kensington Runestone, erected in 1951 by the local Kiwanis Club. Near the museum is a twenty-eight-foot Viking statue, weighing 12,000 pounds, which the town considers to be the world's largest Viking statue. The claim that Nordic people visited Minnesota in the fourteenth century is highly controversial.

Fourteen miles west of Alexandria in Runestone Park (Ohman Farm), just south of State Highway 27, is a plaque identifying the site where the runestone was found in 1898. In the park one can see Ohman's white-frame farmhouse as well as a barn displaying pictures of Ohman and various newspaper clippings describing the discovery. The park was dedicated in 1973. The road from Fergus Falls to Sauk Centre is identified as the Viking Trail.

Spruce Hill Township, Douglas County

In the late nineteenth century, over half of the township's population was of Swedish descent. **Spruce Hill Lutheran** congregation was organized in 1876 and a log church built four year later. It was replaced in 1902 by the existing structure, a simple white-clapboard building. In 1967 that congregation merged with Faith Lutheran of Miltona, and in 1994 the Douglas County Historical Society took responsibility for care of the old church. A unique feature of the Spruce Hill Church is a beautifully carved pulpit with biblical scenes crafted by Pehr Christianson in the 1890s. Christianson, who had emigrated from Sweden in 1880, received eighteen dollars for his work on the pulpit. The former church also contains an ornate altar with a 1906 painting of Jesus the Good Shepherd by Olof Grafström. The Spruce Hill Church is reached by driving north from Alexandria on State Highway 29 to County Road 5, then east for five miles to County Road 66.

Holmes City

In the small village of Holmes City is the former Swedish Baptist Church building (future uncertain) and a mill. The congregation of **Trinity Lutheran Church**, 5966 SW County Road 4W (320-886-5678), was organized in 1875. The town cemetery is on the north side of State Highway 27.

Oscar Lake

About four miles west of Holmes City is **Oscar Lake Lutheran Church**, 14044 SW County Road 26, Farwell (320-283-5568), located near the lake honoring King Oscar II. The congregation was organized in 1866, making it the oldest Swedish Lutheran church in the Red River Valley. The sanctuary has been modernized, but some of the old furnishings have been retained. A cemetery south of the church contains graves with Swedish inscriptions from some early settlers who came in the 1860s. To reach the church, take Douglas County Road 7 off State Highway 27 for about three miles. A sign on the right side of the road before reaching the church indicates a nearby historic site: drive down the gravel road for one-half mile; on the left is a wooded path to a ten-foot granite monument erected in 1921 "in loving memory of about 200 of the first settlers [1866] that are laid at rest here." The inscription concludes with Psalms 108:6 in Swedish.

Hoffman

The Elk Lake Pioneer Cemetery, dating from 1870, was one of the first pioneer burial grounds in Grant County. A plaque in the small cemetery explains that residents of Elk Lake Township built a schoolhouse in 1872, and the following year the Reverend Laurits Carlson organized Grant County's first congregation.

Fergus Falls

In 1900 Swedish Lutherans founded Northwestern College. A two-year academy and business school, it closed in 1932 for financial reasons. Some 1,500 individuals attended Northwestern during its existence. Today, an apartment house known as Northwestern Manor, at 418 E. Alcott Avenue, owned by and adjacent to the Broen Memorial Home for the elderly, uses the former school building.

Other Swedish Lutheran educational academies existed in northwestern Minnesota. The Red River Valley Conference of the Augustana Lutheran Church was not only involved with Northwestern College, but also North Star College in Warren, about 140 miles north of Fergus Falls in Marshall County. Swedish Lutheran pastor S. J. Kronberg organized the Lund Academy at rural Christine Lake in Otter Tail County in 1898, but it closed in 1901. Hope Academy in Moorhead was founded in 1888.

Detroit Lakes

Although the Detroit Lakes area was more heavily settled by Norwegians, Swedes organized in 1871 and built the white-frame **Upsala Lutheran Church** in 1876 in an attractive rural setting. The church was closed in 1964, but a Midsummer service is held every year. In the trees to the east is the church cemetery.

Ten miles northeast of Detroit Lakes is **Lund Lutheran Church**, Route 2 (218-847-9662), constructed in 1903, and its cemetery. The congregation was founded in 1884. The attractive red-brick **Eksjo Lutheran Church** (218-238-5762), four miles west of Lake Park, has a cornerstone noting "Sw. Ev. Luth. Church of Eksjo Ad 1901." There is an adjacent cemetery.

Moorhead

 The **Bergquist Pioneer Cabin**, 719 N. Tenth Avenue, is identified as the oldest house in Moorhead on its original site. John Gustav Bergquist, born in Småland, built a one-story log cabin in 1870, two years after coming to America. In 1873 his brother, Peter, joined him and they added a second floor. John worked on the railroad, farmed, and developed a brick manufacturing business while Peter started a grocery store. After Hank Peterson, a later resident, added many rooms to the log structure, the original was lost to view but protected from the weather. In 1976, Peterson, a prominent Clay County farmer, donated the building and lot to the Bergquist Pioneer Cabin Society. Restoration commenced, and fifteen years later that group donated it to the Clay County Historical Society (218-299-5520), which maintains a museum and archives in the Hjemkomst Center. To reach the Bergquist cabin, drive west on N. Eleventh Avenue toward the Red River. Between N. Seventh and N. Eighth Streets in a modern housing subdivision, turn south. The cabin sits in a wooded area adjacent to the Red River.

Bergquist Pioneer Cabin, Moorhead

The **Hjemkomst Center** ("Homecoming"), 202 N. First Avenue (218-299-5511), features a 76-foot replica Viking ship (modeled after the Gokstad burial ship) constructed in 1980 in nearby Hawley under the leadership of Robert Asp. In 1982, a crew of twelve sailed the *Hjemkomst* from Duluth to Bergen, Norway. The museum also features a replica of the Hopperstad Stave Church in Vik, Norway. During the last weekend in June, an annual Scandinavian festival is held at the center.

Bethesda Lutheran Church, 401 S. Fortieth Avenue (218-236-1420), occupies a building constructed in 1971. This congregation, founded in 1880, was responsible for funding Hope Academy in Moorhead between 1888 and 1896.

Northwest Minnesota

Kittson, Marshall, and Roseau Counties are in the extreme northwest corner of Minnesota. The oldest Lutheran church in Kittson County is **Red River Lutheran Church**, twelve miles southwest of Hallock (218-843-3665), organized in 1881. Its first services were held in the log house of Len Mattson, brother of Hans Mattson. The community is called Mattson. Several other townships and communities in Kittson County have Swedish names: Skane, Tegner, and Karlstad. Bethel Lutheran, 206 S. First Street, Karlstad (218-754-2491), and Maria Lutheran in Kennedy (218-674-4311) are of Swedish origin. Settlers in Kittson County were more likely to be Swedish than any other nationality.

In Warren, seat of Marshall County, the Reverend E. O. Chelgren established North Star College in 1908; it served students until 1936. Swedish Lutheran churches in the county include Bethesda at Anderson and Third Streets, Strandquist (218-597-2641); First Lutheran, 105 S. Sixth Street, Warren (218-745-4221); and Immanuel Lutheran, Luna Road, Route 1, Vega Township, Warren (218-745-4221). In Roseau County, First Lutheran, 101 SW Third Avenue (218-463-1392) and Bethel, 37484-250th Street (also 218-463-1392), in Roseau were Augustana Lutheran congregations.

THE SOUTH

With the exception of Texas, the South attracted relatively few Swedish immigrants. Small, organized colonies sprang up in Florida (New Upsala, Pierson, and Hallandale) and in Alabama (Silverhill and Thorsby), but there are few landmarks in Georgia, Louisiana, the Carolinas, and Virginia.

The largest southern concentration of Swedes is in Texas, particularly around the state capital of Austin and in other central areas of the state. The first Swedes arrived there in the late 1840s under the leadership of Swen Magnus Swenson, from the Jönköping area.

VIRGINIA

Falls Church

Swedish-born Carl Milles (1875–1955) labored twelve years to complete the monumental sculpture *The Fountain of Faith* at National Memorial Park, a private cemetery on Lee Highway (703-560-4400). The sculpture was dedicated in 1952 in the presence of 25,000 people. Milles, who became an American citizen in 1945, sculpted twenty-nine figures in this work to portray his joyful reunion after death with people he has known in the United States, Sweden, and France. The bronze figures were cast in an art foundry in Stockholm. Also located in the National Memorial Park is Milles's *The Sun Singer.* A second casting of this work is in Allerton Park, near Champaign, Illinois.

Richmond

Carl Milles's *Small Triton Fountain* in front of the Virginia Museum of Fine Arts, 2500 Grove Avenue (804-340-1400), shows Triton seated on waves and holding a conch shell to his lips.

Newport News

The **Mariners' Museum**, 100 Museum Drive (800-581-7245; www.mariner.org), holds a sizable collection of engineer John Ericsson memorabilia, most of which relates to the Civil War battle between the *Monitor* and the *Merrimack* on March 9, 1862. Ericsson (1803–1889), a contributor to the invention of the propeller, designed the USS *Monitor.* When the Union's *Monitor* defeated the South's *Merrimack,* it marked not only a significant day in Civil War naval history but also

277

a new era in warship design and construction. Swedish-born Ericsson served in the Swedish army before working in London for twelve years. In 1839 he brought his expertise to the United States, where he lived for the next fifty years.

On December 31, 1862, the *Monitor* sank in a storm sixteen miles off the coast of Cape Hatteras, North Carolina. In 1973 the wreck was discovered lying upside down in 235 feet of water. Two years later, the site was designated the Monitor National Marine Sanctuary. On the 125th anniversary of the battle, the Mariners' Museum became the principal museum for the Monitor National Marine Sanctuary, managed by the National Oceanic and Atmospheric Administration (NOAA).

The museum cares for artifacts recovered from the *Monitor* site. On view is the anchor, the first large metal piece recovered in 1983. The most impressive item yet recovered is the turret. Other items on view include an Ericsson portrait, a *Monitor* model, the reversing wheel, an iron plate, the thermometer from the engine room, and parts from the ship's lantern. The museum contains copies of Ericsson's drawings.

Dahlgren

Dahlgren, the site of the Naval Weapons Laboratory and the Naval Weapons Factory, is named in honor of American-born Rear Admiral John Dahlgren (1809–1870). He was the son of a Swedish merchant who arrived in New York in 1806 and eventually served as Swedish consul at Philadelphia.

NORTH CAROLINA

Flat Rock

Writer Carl Sandburg, the son of Swedish immigrants, spent his final twenty-two years (1945–1967) at Connemara Farm. Connemara ("country estate" in Gaelic) is now the **Carl Sandburg Home National Historic Site**, 81 Carl Sandburg Lane (828-693-4178; www.nps.gov/carl). The twenty-two-room house was built about 1838 by Christopher Gustavus Memminger of Charleston, South Carolina, who in 1861 became the first secretary of the treasury of the Confederacy. The 240-acre farm consists of the main house and a number of outbuildings. When the Sandburgs moved to Flat Rock in 1945, three daughters and two grandchildren accompanied them, along with a library of 10,000 books and Mrs. Sandburg's Chikaming goat herd. At Connemara, Sandburg wrote his only novel, *Remembrance Rock* (1948), and published his autobiography, *Always the Young Strangers* (1953).

CBS reporter Edward R. Murrow once interviewed Sandburg at Connemara, and viewing a short film clip of this conversation is an option for house visitors. The house is said to be unchanged from the time the Sandburgs lived there.

Carl Sandburg Home, Flat Rock

On the wall of the music room is a photo of Sandburg with his Swedish tulip-shaped guitar. The downstairs study includes many of the family's books and a life mask. Sandburg's study on the second floor is a small, cluttered room where his typewriter sits on a fruit crate. Across the street is the Flat Rock Playhouse, where the Vagabond Players present *The World of Carl Sandburg* and Sandburg's *Rootabaga Stories*.

SOUTH CAROLINA

Murrells Inlet

An important work by Swedish sculptor Carl Milles, widely considered to be one of the twentieth century's finest sculptors of fountain groups, is *The Fountain of the Muses* (1949–1954). This fifteen-piece group is at Brookgreen Gardens on U.S. Highway 17, midway between Georgetown and Myrtle Beach (800-849-1931; www.brookgreen.org). The work was relocated in 1984 from New York's Metropolitan Museum of Art. Milles chose as the subject for his final major work the mythological story of the sacred fountain of the muses, source of creative inspiration for all who drink its waters. In addition to the muses, four male figures—a poet, a musician, an architect, and a painter—hold symbols of their art. The lone human figure represents Milles reaching for his artistic vision.

Carl Milles's *The Fountain of the Muses*, Murrells Inlet

GEORGIA

Americus

North of Americus on State Highway 49 is a state historic marker indicating the site where Charles Lindbergh Jr., Swedish American pilot famous for the first transatlantic flight in 1927, first flew solo. In 1923 the young aviator came to Souther Field, a World War I training center, and purchased a Curtiss JN-4 "Jenny" to begin his barnstorming career. With less than twenty hours' instruction, Lindbergh soloed for the first time and then spent a week at the field practicing his aviation skills. His record-setting nonstop solo transatlantic flight from New York to Paris was still four years away.

At Souther Field a twelve-foot monument by University of Georgia sculptor William Thompson depicts Lindbergh as a youthful wing walker in his early barnstorming days.

FLORIDA

Many retired Swedish Americans in recent years have settled in Florida, and they have organized a number of churches. The Evangelical Covenant Church of America has a large retirement center called Covenant Village of Florida, 9201 W. Broward Boulevard, Plantation (954-472-2860; www.covenantretirement.com), near Fort Lauderdale.

Earlier, there were several Swedish settlements in the state, the first and largest being New Upsala near Sanford. Swedes were also drawn to Pierson in Volusia County in the 1880s, Hallandale in Broward County, and Vero Beach, beginning in 1904. The Evangelical Mission Covenant Church of Vero Beach was organized in 1942, although the church is currently First Covenant Church, 1955 Twentieth Avenue (772-562-5948).

New Upsala and Sanford

New Upsala, an agricultural settlement north of Orlando, near Sanford in east-central Florida, was founded in 1870 by the Reverend William Henschen (1842–1925), his brother Esaias, and friends. It was named for Uppsala, Sweden, from where the Henschens came. General Henry Shelton Sanford, a wealthy entrepreneur, purchased 12,000 acres of land here, having been advised by Reverend Henschen that many Swedes would be eager to work the land if they had the means to pay for the transatlantic voyage. Sanford agreed to pay the cost in return for labor in the citrus groves.

Another brother, Josef Henschen, recruited the first laborers and led a group to Florida in 1871. He became a large citrus grower and landowner himself, and he is probably responsible for having the former Pinellas Point on the west coast renamed St. Petersburg in honor of a Russian business associate. In 1880 he founded Forest City in Seminole County, now part of the greater Orlando area.

In 1875 Sanford donated one and one-half acres of land for a Swedish church and cemetery. It was served by Swedish Baptist and Presbyterian ministers until 1892, when it became a Lutheran congregation. The church disbanded in 1946 and the sanctuary was torn down. A bronze tablet marks its former location.

Nearby is the Swedish cemetery amid giant live oaks draped with Spanish moss. Also at the site is a Seminole County Historical marker entitled "Upsala Swedish Community." It notes that "this site was the center of the earliest and largest Swedish community in Florida. Located here were the Scandinavian Society Lutheran Church; its cemetery; and a meeting house, which also served as a school until 1904. In May 1871 thirty-three Swedish immigrants (twenty-six men and seven women) arrived under the sponsorship of Henry S. Sanford for the purpose of developing his citrus groves. . . . General Sanford's initial cost was $75 per person ($65 for transportation and $10 to a recruiting agent). He also agreed to give each immigrant free rations and living quarters for one year, after which each would be given a parcel of land. In November 1871, twenty additional Swedes arrived and joined the original immigrants to form the Upsala community. Many descendants of these early immigrants still live in the Sanford area."

This site is located on Upsala Road not far from the **Presbyterian Church of Upsala**, a white-clapboard structure (at Twenty-fifth Street). In front of the church is a Seminole County historical marker with the following inscription: "In October 1890, the younger generation of Swedish immigrants, whose parents had been persuaded to settle here by Henry Sanford, organized a Swedish Presbyterian congregation along American lines. . . . The original structure was erected in 1892, and was used continuously until . . . the new building was constructed in 1985. The first pastor of the Upsala Church was the Reverend John Fredrick Sundell, who also organized the Lake Mary Church, two miles south of here."

At the entrance to the **Henry Shelton Sanford Memorial Library and Museum**, 520 E. First Street, Sanford (407-302-1000), there is a bronze plaque that notes that "much of the labor in the groves was performed by Swedish immigrants who settled in nearby New Upsala." A street where many early Swedes lived is named Upsala Avenue, and many homes in historic downtown Sanford were built by Swedish carpenters. The museum displays artifacts from the early Swedish community, including photos of Nels Julius Stenstrom, who established the first dairy in central Florida in the 1870s and who married Josephine Jacobs, a teacher of English to the Swedes of New Upsala. The **Museum of Seminole County History**, 300 Bush Boulevard (407-665-2489; www.co.seminole.fl.us), exhibits a number of early photographs of the county and sells books of historic interest.

In the Windchase subdivision outside Sanford is the Belair historical marker, which identifies a 400-acre portion of the original 12,000-acre grant acquired by General Sanford in 1870. Part of this land became an experimental station for various citrus fruits. Swedes were involved with these experiments.

In nearby Lake Mary in front of the Lake Mary Historical Museum is a plaque showing the community's historic sites. Many houses and other structures have Swedish connections. The town may have been named for Reverend Sundell's wife, Mary Amelia. A prominent resident was merchant and entrepreneur Axel Evald Sjoblom, who formally platted the town as a resort. First Presbyterian Church, at 128 W. Wilbur Avenue, was organized in 1894 by Reverend Sundell, minister of Upsala Presbyterian Church.

Presbyterian Church of Upsala, Sanford

Oviedo

Behind the First Baptist Church at the corner of Broadway Street and Central Avenue is a Seminole County historic marker reading: "In the late 1860's Confederate veterans and freed slaves from the war-devastated South began to move into the settlement called 'the Lake Jesup Community,' to be joined later by others from northern states and from Sweden. One of the Swedish immigrants, Andrew Aulin, appointed postmaster in 1871, named the new post office Oviedo after the city in northern Spain." Ahlin's house at 401 S. Central Avenue (State Highway 434) is privately owned.

Pierson

Pierson, in Volusia County northwest of De Land, was named for Peter Pierson (Per Persson, 1857–1926), who arrived in 1876 with his brother Anders Nils. Another brother was a horticulturist in Cromwell, Connecticut. In the mid-1880s, the Pierson Colonization Society was organized to induce Swedes to relocate in Florida. **Ebenezer Lutheran Church**, 139 S. Volusia Avenue (904-749-2676), was founded in 1884, and the congregation erected a sanctuary in 1894 that was enlarged three years later. The 1894 sanctuary has been remodeled.

Vero Beach

 The Indian River Historical Society owns the **Hallstrom Farmstead Home**, 1723 Old Dixie Highway. The house was built by Axel Hallstrom, a banker and plantation owner. The two-and-one-half-story, red-brick structure with a central dormer is being restored.

In the **Vero Beach Museum of Art**, 3001 Riverside Park Drive (772-331-0707; www.vbmuseum.org), is the Agnes and Magnus Wahlstrom Sculpture Garden that includes a bronze by Carl Milles entitled *Sunglitter*.

Fort Lauderdale

According to art critic Todd Wilkinson, *Sailfish in Three Stages Ascending* is the largest wildlife sculpture in the world. Created by Swedish-born sculptor Kent Ullberg, this amazing fountain sculpture sits outside the Broward County Convention Center. The work is enormous; the black-granite wave foundation is 150 by 125 feet, six feet high on one end, sloping two feet below ground level on the other. The focal point is a bronze sailfish that rises thirty-six feet above the pool and appears to be supported by a spray of water. Ullberg's innovative sequenced use of the water creates an illusion of forward movement. Ullberg describes his art as "a three-dimensional paradigm of the Florida marine environment.

Hallstrom Farmstead Home, Vero Beach

Conceptually, it appears as though a wedge has been cut from the ocean and lifted onto land." (For additional information on Ullberg, see Corpus Christi, Texas.)

Hallandale

Hallandale in Broward County was founded in the late nineteenth century as a daughter colony of the Halland Settlement of Stanton in southwest Iowa. It was named for Lutheran pastor Bengt Magnus Halland, who established the Iowa colony. **Bethlehem Lutheran Church**, 300 W. Beach Boulevard (954-454-2954), was organized by the Swedish settlers.

ALABAMA

Silverhill

In 1890, the Svea Land Company was organized in Chicago for the purpose of establishing a Swedish colony. After research, it was decided that the settlement would be located in Baldwin County in southern Alabama. During the economic depression of 1893, five men, including Oscar Johnson of the Svea Land Company, went to look over the land. The first family arrived in Silverhill before the end of 1896.

The early years here were extremely difficult. Insects and disease killed more than 11,000 new peach trees. The settlers then turned to raising dairy cattle, establishing the first creamery in Alabama. Dr. Oscar Winberg, a veterinarian and horticulturist originally from Västergötland, introduced modern farming methods, became a recognized authority on orange cultivation, and developed a sweet variety of kumquat and the satsuma orange. Gradually the area began to prosper.

The **Svea Land Company Office**, at 21961 S. Sixth Street, was established in 1896. Also used for a period of time as a school and church, it is now the **Oscar Johnson Memorial Library** in honor of the first manager of Silverhill. The local park is also named for Oscar Johnson.

Like the Land Company Office, the **People's Supply Company**, 21950 Broad Street (currently United Bank), dates from the 1890s. Oscar Johnson's brother Theodore founded the People's Supply Company, and his white-clapboard, two-story house is located at the corner of Broad Street and E. South Boulevard.

The **State Bank of Silverhill** is on the National Register for its commercial and architectural significance.

Zion Lutheran Church, initially known as Swedish Lutheran Zion Church, was built in 1916; the congregation organized in 1905. The church is a white-clapboard, Gothic-style structure on the corner of Seventh Street and Fourth Avenue (251-945-5209). Across the street is the former schoolhouse, now a private residence.

In 1902 the Covenant congregation was organized as the *Svenska Evangeliska Mission Församling*, or the Swedish Evangelical Mission Congregation. The Silverhill Land Company soon gave the congregation two lots on which to build. The new church was a small, white-frame building with a steeple. In 1957 the congregation offered the old building to Blakely Historic Park, about twenty-six miles north in Spanish Fort. A plan was made to move the church building in four parts—remove and airlift the steeple and then cut the sanctuary into three sections and truck them to the new site. The airlift was accomplished in 1978, but the part of the sanctuary that survived the move was destroyed by a hurricane. The steeple has been placed on top of the park pavilion, dedicated as the Church Pavilion in 1982. The present **Evangelical Covenant Church** is at 16094 State Highway 104 (251-945-5143).

A **Baptist congregation** was founded in 1899. The original building has been incorporated into the present brick church, constructed in 1970 on the corner of Silverhill Avenue and Seventh Street (251-945-1000).

Silverhill Cemetery, on County Road 49 one mile north of State Highway 104, contains numerous Swedish graves. Silverhill is delightful to visit in March, when the azaleas, wisteria, and dogwood are in full bloom.

Oscar Johnson Memorial Library, Silverhill

Thorsby

Thorsby lies between Montgomery and Birmingham off Interstate 65 in Chilton County. In 1895 three men (including T. T. Thorson) from Indiana and Iowa arrived in the area searching for a suitable place to start a community. Impressed by the quality of the land, they decided to form the Concordia Land and Improvement Association. Scandinavians subsequently were attracted to the town. In the late 1890s a Norwegian Lutheran congregation was formed, and in 1902 it erected the first church building in Thorsby. A building erected by Swedish Lutherans that year no longer exists. In 1916 the membership of both churches had dwindled and members decided to form a single congregation. They worshipped in the Norwegian sanctuary, which was eventually sold to a Congregational church. In 1957 this group disbanded, and the building was sold to the Masons, who later gave the property to the town. In 1998 the church was restored and became known as the **Helen Jenkins Chapel.** It is now the Museum of Thorsby History. The white-clapboard church with Gothic detail, including a large stained-glass window and a steeple with a bell tower, is on Concordia Avenue close to U.S. Highway 31. Nearby on Alabama Avenue is the Scandinavian cemetery.

The town contains a number of houses built by early Swedes and Norwegians, including the T. T. Thorson House, a large, three-story, white Victorian structure with a wraparound front porch that is on Jones Street between Iowa and Michigan Avenues. The oldest house in town was built by Nels Johnson on Wisconsin Avenue. It is a light-blue clapboard house with a front porch and a stained-glass window. The Hedberg House, a two-and-one-half-story, white-clapboard structure, is on Jones Street. Details and locations of these houses, all privately owned, and of other sites can be found in a brochure available at the town hall on U.S. Highway 31.

The Swedish heritage of Thorsby is still apparent on the badges worn by the local police officers, which feature American and Swedish flags surrounding a peach, the main crop grown in the region. On the third Saturday in September, Thorsby holds an annual Swedish festival.

LOUISIANA

Hammond

The graves of Peter Hammond (1789–1870), members of his family, and an "unnamed slave boy" are on the south side of the 500 block of E. Charles Street between N. Holly and N. Olive Streets in Hammond. Sited under an enormous live oak, the graves are marked with a historic plaque. Hammond, from Hammerdal parish in Jämtland, arrived in Louisiana about 1815 and founded this town in Tangipahoa Parish, sixty miles northwest of New Orleans. The official plaques near his grave note that the town was founded by Hammond about 1818 to 1820. He purchased a considerable amount of timberland from the government and thereafter produced pitch, turpentine, tar, and masts for ships. In 1830 he married a cousin of Mrs. Ralph Waldo Emerson. During the Civil War, the family lost most of its wealth.

One of the plaques placed in memory of Hammond by descendants states that he "launched a tar and forest products industry, pioneered shipping these products from Springfield and Wadesboro to New Orleans, ran a commissary supplying staples for the people, gave right-of-way between Hammond and Pass Manchac for the construction of the railroad."

The city of Hammond became a shoe-making center for the Confederacy during the Civil War. By the early twentieth century, it was known as the "Strawberry Capital of America."

TEXAS

The early history of Swedish immigration to Texas revolves around Swen Magnus Swenson, born near Jönköping in 1816. Swenson emigrated to New York, made his way to Texas in 1838, and at twenty-five became overseer of a large cotton plantation near Richmond, southwest of Houston. With his uncle, Swante Palm, Swenson became involved in a mercantile business in La Grange. In 1848 Swenson married the Richmond plantation owner's widow and made a fortune in cotton, commerce, and real estate. He became one of the richest men in Texas, owning large tracts of land in Travis, Williamson, and Jones Counties.

In the 1840s, Swenson made two visits to Sweden to encourage people to immigrate to Texas, working with a brother in Småland and with Swante Palm. In 1848 twenty-five of Swenson's relatives, as well as farm laborers and single women, left Småland for Texas, their way paid by Swenson. They worked for him until their debts were paid. Often after one year, the young Swedes were able to buy their own land. They then turned to cotton production and became prosperous farmers. Two-thirds of the Swedes came from the Jönköping area and generally settled in central Texas's Travis and Williamson Counties, though some also went farther west to Brady in McCulloch County and Stamford in Jones County and to the coastal areas of Willacy County, as well as Galveston and Houston. In Austin, Swedes settled around Swede Hill, which today is bisected by Interstate 35.

Swenson was a convinced Unionist opposed to slavery and secession. He found his life and the lives of his family endangered, and they were forced to flee to Mexico during the Civil War. He next settled in New Orleans as a cotton exporter, and in 1867 relocated to New York City, where he established a banking firm and lived until his death in 1896. Swenson's sons and daughters continued to run the Texas ranches, and their descendants still own tens of thousands of acres.

Texas is second only to Minnesota in the number of historical markers dedicated to Swedish American history.

San Antonio

University of Texas Institute of Texan Cultures—
801 S. Bowie Street, at Durango Boulevard on HemisFair Plaza
(210-458-2300; www.texancultures.utsa.edu).
Swedish displays in the museum examine Swedish achievements in Texas and include early settler artifacts and memorabilia from the Palm Valley Lutheran Church in Round Rock. A large wall board notes the more important events and people in the history of Swedish immigration to Texas.

Swedish settlers established two institutions of higher learning: Trinity Lutheran College in Round Rock and Texas Wesleyan College in Austin, but neither exists today. From 1896 to 1982, the *Texas-Post* was the leading Swedish newspaper. A number of Texas place-names are attributed to Swedes, including Govalle, Palm Valley, Lund, Ericksdahl, and New Sweden. Some 160,000 Texans claim Swedish ancestry.

Austin

Historic Places

Swedish Log Cabin—Zilker Park, 2220 Barton Springs Road (512-477-8672;
www.ci.austin.tx.us/zilker).

S. M. Swenson bought a large tract of land east of Austin in 1850 and named his ranch Govalle, a shortened form of a Swedish word meaning "good pasture." Gustaf Palm, Swante Palm's brother and S. M. Swenson's uncle, arrived with his family in 1848 and lived in a log cabin, which had been built on the land around 1840. After the Civil War, when Gustaf's family built a home in Austin at Fourteenth and San Jacinto Streets, he moved the log cabin there and used it as a wash house. Relocated to Round Rock in nearby Williamson County, the restored log cabin was moved again to Zilker Park in 1965. The cabin, which holds a number of artifacts associated with early Swedes, is maintained by the Austin Parks and Recreation Department and the Texas Swedish Pioneers Association. **Zilker Park Historic District** is included on the National Register of Historic Places.

Old Bakery and Emporium—1006 Congress Avenue, one block south of the
State Capitol (512-477-5961).

In 1863 Charles Lundberg emigrated from Sweden to the United States, and nine years later he moved to Austin. A journeyman baker, he soon bought out his employer's business and, according to his newspaper obituary, "from that day on he conducted the largest and most successful bakery in Austin." The building served as a bakery from 1876 to 1936.

Swedish Log Cabin, Zilker Park, Austin

Rescued from deterioration, the two-story brick bakery is owned by the city of Austin. It houses a lunchroom, and its shop sells handicrafts and baked goods made by senior citizens. Lundberg's seventeen-foot bakery paddle still hangs on the wall, and his name, carved in stone, is visible near the roof line.

C. E. Johnson Home—2201½ Lake Austin Boulevard at Highway 1 (MoPac Expressway).

Erected in 1858 by Sam Houston's friend Charles Johnson, a Swedish immigrant, this home was built by fellow Swedes out of native stone from Johnson's quarries. The long porch and six Ionic columns were added later. In 1924 it became the home of the Travis County American Legion.

Deep Eddy Bathing Beach—401 Deep Eddy Avenue.

In 1902 two of Charles Johnson's children, Mary and Henry, opened the Deep Eddy Resort near Johnson's home. A Texas Historical Commission plaque notes that "the Johnsons named the park for a deep hole in the limestone bed of the Colorado River at this site." Mary Johnson sold the park in 1915, and the new owner built a concrete swimming pool and renamed the resort Deep Eddy Bathing Beach. In 1935 the city of Austin purchased the park, which it maintains.

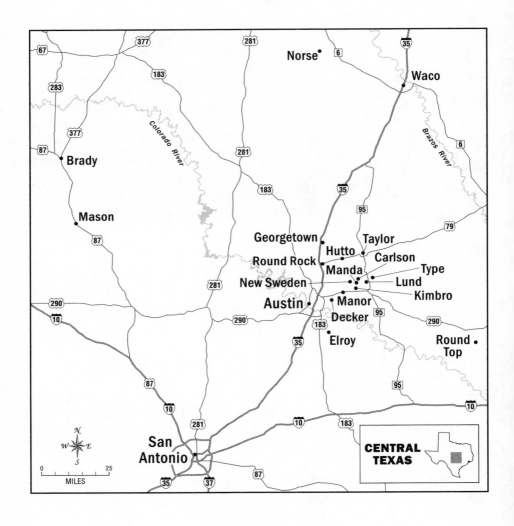

CENTRAL
TEXAS

Swedish Hill (Svenska Kullen) Historic District, bounded by Red River, Fourteenth, Eighteenth, and Navasota.

In the 1870s Swedish Hill was home to immigrants who erected houses and churches in the area. It is now divided by Interstate 35 yet tied together by neighborhood, government, and university interests. Swedish Hill Historic District includes the 900 and 1000 blocks of E. Fourteenth Street and 900 block of E. Fifteenth Street. At 907 E. Fourteenth Street is Swede Hill Park, supervised by the Austin Parks and Recreation Department.

Palm School—100 N. Interstate 35, at E. Cesar Chavez Street.

The tan, stucco building is named for Swante Palm, Sweden's former consul to Texas, prominent Austin resident, and University of Texas benefactor. At the main entrance are photographs and plaques describing the school's history. Completed in 1892, it was one of the first schools in Austin. It closed in 1976, and is now the Travis County Health and Human Services Building.

Churches

Gethsemane Lutheran Church—1510 Congress, three blocks north of the State Capitol.

Gethsemane Lutheran Church, dedicated in November 1883, served its congregation as a place of worship until purchased by the state of Texas and transformed into a state historic site in 1965. The light tan, brick building with central bell tower has Gothic Revival decorative elements, stained-glass windows, and rural Swedish-church architectural elements such as a curved, hood-shaped base for the cupola. Stone retrieved from the 1852 Texas Capitol that burned in 1881 and doors from the Old Main Building at the University of Texas found new use in this structure.

In 1868 the first Swedish Lutheran service was held in Austin. A congregation then formed, making Gethsemane the second-oldest Lutheran church in Texas (Germans formed the first). Swante Palm chaired this organizational meeting. In 1875 the congregation officially joined the Augustana Synod. In 1950, when Gethsemane found itself becoming engulfed by the expanding state offices, church leaders purchased property at 200 W. Anderson Lane on the north side of Austin. A new sanctuary was dedicated in 1963. The 1883 church was designated a Texas historic landmark, acquired by the state, and restored in 1970 and 1971. A plaque recounting its history is to the right of the front door. Still visible are the lovely stained-glass windows. The Bergstrom family donated a few of them, along with the natural-wood Gothic altar and steeple bell. The pulpit, altar painting, and baptismal font are noteworthy. Adjacent to the church is Luther Hall, the former parish hall that now serves as office space for the Texas Historical Commission (512-463-6100; www.thc.state.tx.us).

The new sanctuary of the Gethsemane Lutheran congregation, 200 W. Anderson Lane at Purnell Drive (512-836-8560), has a contemporary design with impressive modern stained-glass windows. In the narthex is the original cornerstone from the downtown church's steeple.

Near the old Gethsemane Lutheran Church were two other Swedish congregations, a Methodist and an Evangelical Free. As the government complex

Former Gethsemane Lutheran Church, Austin

expanded in the 1950s, both church sanctuaries were sold and torn down. The congregations moved elsewhere in Austin, and state historic plaques mark the original locations.

Swedish Central Methodist Church plaque—W. Fourteenth Street and Congress.

The Swedish Central Methodist Church congregation was organized in 1873 by the Reverend Carl J. Charnquist, a minister from Michigan. His preaching initiated revivals, resulting in the formation of several Methodist congregations in the Austin area. From 1896 to 1900, the congregation's pastor was O. E. Olander, who later organized Texas Wesleyan Academy and served in the Texas state legislature. During his pastorate, a Gothic church building was acquired at the corner of Thirteenth and Colorado. The congregation worshipped here until the building was sold to the state in 1956 and a new church was built at 6100 Berkman (512-452-5796). The new church has the bell, organ, and stained-glass windows from the first church.

Swedish Evangelical Free Church plaque—W. Fifteenth and Colorado Streets.

The first Evangelical Free church in the Austin area was organized in 1891 in Decker, in eastern Travis County. In southeast Travis County at Elroy, another Evangelical Free church was founded thirteen years later. To serve the children of the early immigrants, who had begun moving into Austin, a church was built in 1925 at the corner of W. Fifteenth and Colorado Streets. Swedish was spoken in the services into the 1930s. In 1952 "First" replaced "Swedish" in the name as a result of a merger with a Norwegian group. When a new sanctuary was completed in 1962 at 4425 Red River, the former sanctuary was torn down.

St. David's Episcopal Church—304 E. Seventh Street (512-472-1196).

S. M. Swenson, a member of this parish in the late 1850s and early 1860s, was senior warden from 1859 to 1863 and chairman of the building committee. The main entrance was given in his memory by his grandchildren.

Schools

University of Texas at Austin—(512-471-3434).

The University of Texas at Austin is the largest university in the South. On the fifth floor of the Geology Building are a plaque and photo of Johan August Udden (1859–1932). After teaching natural science at Bethany College in Lindsborg, Kansas, and Augustana College in Rock Island, Illinois, Udden arrived in Texas in 1903, and he became director of the Bureau of Economic Geology from 1911 to

1932. He conducted oil explorations, and his success greatly improved the financial position of the university. In the basement of the Geology Building is the Sedimentation Research Laboratory, named in his honor.

Swante Palm (1815–1899), a Renaissance gentleman of the Southwest, served as vice consul for Sweden and Norway from 1866 until his death. A justice of the peace, alderman, postmaster, and bibliographer, Palm gathered the largest private book collection in nineteenth-century Texas. In the 1850s, Palm built a small house on Ash Street (now Ninth near Congress Avenue), which served as the Swedish consulate. His growing book collection forced him to enlarge the structure. Palm donated most of his 12,000-volume collection to the University of Texas in 1897. The remainder went to the university on permanent loan in 1953. On campus, an oil portrait of Palm hangs in the Harry Ransom Humanities Research Center, and a bust is displayed in the Eugene C. Barker Texas History Center. His 3,000-volume collection of books in Swedish has been described as a "private public library" because it encompassed a broad range of subjects and genres. He chose the University of Texas rather than a Swedish American institution as his collection's depository because "Texas is my second fatherland." In 1990 a historical marker was added to his restored grave site in Oakwood Cemetery, and in 1991 the state of Texas dedicated an official historical marker on W. Ninth Street where Palm's home once stood.

In 1912 the Texas Wesleyan College/Academy, organized by O. E. Olander, opened. It operated until 1936, when the twenty-one-acre campus was sold to the University of Texas. Renamed Wesleyan Hall, the building survived until the late 1970s, when it was torn down to make way for a new building. A plaque near the site at Twenty-sixth Street near the entrance to the University of Texas Law School commemorates the Swedish Methodist school.

Swante Palm Elementary School—7601 Dixie Drive (512-414-2545).

This elementary school was dedicated in Palm's honor in 1987. Other schools in Austin honoring Swedish Americans are the Carl T. Widén Elementary School, at 5605 Nuckols Crossing, and the Linder Elementary School, at 2800 Metcalf. Widén was a leader in the Texas Swedish community for many years before his death in 1986 at the age of 101.

Other Points of Interest

Oakwood Cemetery—bounded by Navasota, Martin Luther King Jr. and Bob Harrison.

Near the corner of E. Sixteenth and Navasota is a state marker describing the history of this noteworthy cemetery where Swante Palm, Johan August Udden, and O. E. Olander are buried. At Swante Palm's grave, a Texas marker highlights his life's contributions.

Lester E. Palmer Auditorium and Convention Center—400 S. First Street (Barton Springs Road and Riverside Drive).

This civic building was named for Lester E. Palmer, mayor of Austin in the 1960s and a second-generation Swedish American.

Seaholm Water Works—E. First near North Lamar.

The installation is named for Walter Seaholm (Sjöholm), former superintendent of Austin's water department, whose father emigrated from Sweden.

Austin Bergstrom International Airport—State Highway 71.

Formerly Del Valle Air Base, the facility was renamed in 1942 to honor Capt. John August Earl Bergstrom, believed to have been Austin's first World War II casualty. Bergstrom, whose father and mother were of Swedish ancestry, was born in Austin in 1907. He lost his life in an air attack in the Philippines.

Round Rock

 Round Rock was originally settled by Swedes. The 100 and 200 blocks of E. Main Street have been designated the **Round Rock Commercial Historic District.**

Historic Places

Andrew J. Palm House Museum and Visitor Center—212 E. Main Street (512-255-5805).

This museum, a Texas historic landmark since 1978, is a one-story clapboard house built around 1873. Andrew Palm, the fourth son of Anna Palm, was a farmer and rancher who arranged for other Swedish families to settle in Central Texas's Palm Valley. The house was originally one mile from the Palm Valley Lutheran Church on land first owned by S. M. Swenson. In 1976 the structure was moved to its present location and restored. The interior features a central hall, a large, high-ceilinged Victorian parlor, and a pioneer kitchen.

J. A. Nelson and Company—201 E. Main Street.

This early commercial building, erected in 1900, served a variety of businesses, among them J. A. Nelson's lumber, hardware, and agricultural implements establishment. This building is architecturally important for its façade of cast iron and pressed tin and ornamented pilasters. The building, which is a Texas historic landmark, has been restored and is used by several businesses.

Andrew J. Palm House Museum, Round Rock

Plaques on lampposts in the business district commemorate former business people and community leaders, many of whom had Swedish backgrounds.

Nelson–Crier House (Woodbine Mansion)—405 E. Main Street, at Burnet Street.

The large brick house with six Ionic columns, which is an official state historic site, has three floors, as well as a basement, attic, and widow's walk. The Arvid Nelson family arrived in Texas in 1854 and settled in Williamson County, where they first rented land from S. M. Swenson. Eventually they purchased their own farm. The Nelson's oldest son, Andrew or A. J., was an entrepreneur who developed a thriving business hauling flour and cotton to Gulf ports and returning with supplies. During the Civil War his younger brother August served in the Confederate army while A. J. continued his transport business. After the war, A. J. developed extensive farming enterprises in Williamson County. When he died in 1895, his widow, sons, and daughters started the construction of this impressive residence that took five years to build using material from Austin homes that were being dismantled. Several generations of Nelsons resided there until it was sold in 1960. It remains a private residence.

A. J. and Carolina Anderson House—602 Liberty Avenue, at W. Stone Street.
This privately owned two-story, cream-colored house is a Texas Historic Landmark. A plaque notes that the house was "built in 1908–09 for the family of Swedish immigrant Anders Johan Anderson (1858–1929) just after the death of his first wife, Edla Maria (1859–1906). . . . The house remained in the Anderson family until 1963. The Folk Victorian structure, with details including fishscale shingles and classical columns, reflects Round Rock's prosperity and status as a mercantile center for Swedes in the early 20th century."

Olson House—808 E. Main Street.
This Queen Anne–style house featuring a two-story wrap-around porch with Tuscan columns and fishscale shingles is a Texas Historic Landmark. The house was built in 1908 for Swedish immigrant Johanna Olson (1835–1914) after she returned to Round Rock upon the death of her husband, Johannes. Johanna and her daughters took in boarders from nearby Trinity College. The family remained in the house until 1945. The house is a private residence.

Israelson Telander Heritage House—off U.S. Highway 79, east of Palm Valley Lutheran Church.
The two-room house, built in 1885 of limestone, was one of the first homes in the area. It remains a private residence.

Palm Mansion—3300 Palm Valley Boulevard, U.S. Highway 79 at Old Settlers' Park (512-246-9033).
This two-story, white-frame house with a double porch was carefully restored and dedicated in 2003. Owned by the Old Settlers' Association, it is used for weddings, parties, meetings, and reunions and as a bed and breakfast.

The first floor has a wide central entrance hall flanked by double parlors, pocket doors, and a formal dining room, all furnished in modified period style. The mantels in the parlors and wood floors are original. Beautifully carved balustrades on the front and rear staircases open onto the wide second-floor hallway. The upstairs bedrooms have been furnished in period style.

T. E. Nelson Homestead—four miles north of U.S. Highway 79 on Farm Road 1460.
The large house built by Andrew J. Nelson has walls that are two feet thick. Nelson brought Swedish families to the area, and in return for their passage, they worked on his ranch. T. E. Nelson was his son. The house is marked by a state medallion—"Home of A. J. Nelson, rancher-banker from Sweden. Swedish masons, paying voyage costs, built this house, 1860."

Church

Palm Valley Lutheran Church—2500 Palm Valley Boulevard, east of Interstate 35 on U.S. Highway 79 (512-255-3322; www.palmvalleylutheranchurch.org).

This area was originally called Brushy Creek, but it was renamed Palm Valley in honor of the Palm family. Swedes arrived in the Brushy Creek district as early as the 1850s. Among the first was Anna Palm, who arrived along with her husband, Anders Andersson Palm, and their six sons. She had been encouraged to settle here in 1853 by Swante Palm, her brother-in-law, and S. M. Swenson, her nephew. After only a few months in Texas, her husband died, and in 1863 Henning, her youngest son, succumbed to pneumonia. She requested that the land where Henning was buried be designated a cemetery. Henning was the first to be buried in what became the Palm Valley Lutheran Cemetery.

The congregation was organized in 1870 and a wooden church built to replace a log church. Under Pastor Gustaf Berglund's leadership, the decision was made in 1894 to construct a new sanctuary. The present church is a red-brick, Gothic-style structure with a high steeple. The sanctuary has twelve outstanding stained-glass windows. One is dedicated to the Palm family and another to the early pioneers. A glass case in the main hallway outside the Palm Room contains Bibles from the Sellstrom family, a model of the second church, and the communion wine jug that was regularly carried to the Palm Valley railway station and then to San Antonio to be filled with wine. The bell from Trinity Lutheran College in Round Rock is located outside the main entrance. In the center of the west end of the large cemetery are the oldest graves, some with Swedish inscriptions on the markers. A quarter of the congregation is of Swedish ancestry, and they annually celebrate Santa Lucia Day.

School

Trinity Lutheran College—1000 E. Main Street at College Street.

This college was founded in 1906, with Dr. J. A. Stamline serving as its first president. When financial problems forced its closing in 1929, it merged with Evangelical Lutheran College and became known as Texas Lutheran College, which was located in Seguin. A state plaque marks the site of the college. In 1929 the Lutheran Welfare Society opened Trinity Lutheran Home, presently called the Trinity Campus of Care. It is no longer a Lutheran institution.

Georgetown

 As early as 1871, Swedish settlers near Union Hill, south of Georgetown, began holding Methodist worship meetings in homes. Through 1880, the Reverend

Carl Charnquist served as a circuit preacher. In 1883 a church was built, one year after the Swedish Methodist Episcopal Brushy Church congregation was officially organized. As the years passed, Swedes bought land east and north of Georgetown, making the distance to and from the country church inconvenient. In 1906 the congregation elected to move to Georgetown, and the present white-limestone, Gothic-style **St. John's United Methodist Church** was built at 311 E. University Avenue (512-863-5886) by Swedish carpenters. In the rear of the sanctuary are twelve pews and lighting fixtures, originally kerosene, from the old Brushy church. The congregation has a Swedish Heritage Sunday in mid-April, Lucia Fest in December, and a *julotta* Christmas service, in which part of the service is conducted in Swedish.

The small St. John's Cemetery (Swedish Methodist) is five miles north of U.S. Highway 79 on the west side of Farm Road 1460. It contains the graves of early Swedish pioneers of the Union Hill area. Brushy Methodist Church was adjacent to the cemetery.

The former Brushy **Evangelical Free Church** is presently located at 1323 E. University Avenue. The marker notes that "Swedish immigrant settlers in Williamson County met together in homes for worship services as early as 1884. In 1891 this congregation was organized in the home of Mr. and Mrs. Sven Peterson by 21 charter members. Known as Brushy Evangelical Free Church, the congregation built a sanctuary in 1892 on land southeast of Georgetown donated by C. J. Gustafson. [The present] Georgetown site was acquired in 1960 and a new sanctuary was dedicated in 1963." Outside of Georgetown, four and one-half miles north of U.S. Highway 79 on County Road 110, is the Evangelical Free Church cemetery.

Hutto

Incorporated in 1911, Hutto prospered when Swedish immigrants made cotton production a major agricultural enterprise. A historical marker is on U.S. Highway 79, east of the intersection with Farm Road 1660.

Hutto United Methodist Church, 605 East Street, at Liberty Street (512-759-1707), was founded when Swedish Methodists organized the congregation in private homes in 1892. Nineteen years later they dedicated the present sanctuary. In 1938 this congregation merged with an American Methodist group, but they continued to use the old building. The interior features a pressed-metal ceiling painted in white and gold. In front of the church is an official Texas Historical Commission marker.

The white-clapboard **Hutto Evangelical Lutheran Church**, 402 Church Street, at Live Oak Street (512-759-2064), was organized in 1892. The Texas Historical Commission marker notes that "Lutheran Church services in Hutto can be traced to 1890, when ministers M. Noyd and Gustav Berglund of the Palm Valley

Lutheran Church . . . conducted occasional services for the area's rapidly growing Swedish population. In 1892 August Swenson led a successful effort to organize the Hutto Evangelical Lutheran Church. The first church structure (1893) was destroyed by a tornado and replaced in 1894. In 1902 a third church building was constructed at this site. . . . Church services were conducted in the Swedish language until 1940."

The farming community of Monodale was located five miles north of Hutto. Today only a few scattered farmhouses mark the site. A Texas Historical Commission marker five miles north of County Road 132 at County Road 100 reads: "The people of Monodale community were cotton farmers, chiefly Swedish and Czechoslovakian immigrants."

Taylor

Tenth Street United Methodist Church (512-352-2244), originally called the Swedish Methodist Episcopal Church North, was founded by the Reverend Carl Charnquist in 1900. The white-frame church building at 410 W. Tenth, at Hackberry Street, was formerly owned by a disbanded Presbyterian congregation. In 1911 the Methodists moved the building to its present location, where a marker notes its significance. Swedish was used in the worship service until 1935.

Type

In a rural setting on County Road 466 six miles east of Coupland in Williamson County is the **Type Church and Cemetery.** An official Texas marker for the Type Cemetery states that "Swedish and Danish immigrants arrived in the 1890s. Swedish-born August Smith owned a store which straddled the line between Bastrop and Williamson Counties. Smith opened the Type Post Office in that store in 1902, probably naming the community for the printing machine owned by his friend, Jonas Sunvison. The Type Cemetery was established on land conveyed by Peder and Christine Nygaard when the Swedish Free Mission Church was founded in May 1908." The cemetery contains graves of Scandinavians as well as several Mexicans. The nearby Evangelical Free Church contains beautiful stained-glass windows obtained from a disbanded Polish Roman Catholic Church.

Manor

The impressive white-clapboard **New Sweden Evangelical Lutheran Church,** 12809 New Sweden Church Road (512-281-0056), has the highest steeple—104 feet—in eastern Travis County. Set four and one-half miles north of Austin on U.S. Highway 290, two miles northeast of Farm Road 973, the church and nearby New Sweden Lutheran Cemetery, two miles southwest on New Sweden Church Road, near its intersection with Farm Road 973, are all that remain from a Swedish settlement. It had been developed by a group of young men sponsored by S. M. Swenson. The church organized in 1876 as the Swedish Evangelical Lutheran Congregation of Manor. In 1879 the first church was completed. The present edifice was constructed in 1921 and 1922. It is traditional for the Easter service to be held at the cemetery. The congregation also hosts a *julotta* service every Christmas (*see frontispiece*).

Manda, Carlson, and Kimbro

The Swedish presence in Manda, Carlson, and Kimbro, small communities northeast of Manor, is recorded on official historical markers. Manda was founded by Swedish immigrants in the 1880s and named for Amanda Bengston Gustafson, sister of the town's postmaster. Organized in 1892, the Manda Swedish Methodist congregation was active until 1962. A Methodist cemetery located at Wells School Road and Wells Lane serves as a reminder of the early settlement. A Lutheran chapel was built in 1896. The Manda historical marker rests on Wells School Road near Manda-Carlson Road. Of the original Manda structures, the school building survives, now serving as a community center. This building on Manda-Carlson Road and the nearby marker are about one mile east of the New Sweden Lutheran Church.

At the intersection of Felder Lane with Manda-Carlson Road (go 1.2 miles east of Manor on U.S. Highway 290, then 8.7 miles north on Farm Road 973, and then east on Felder Lane to Manda-Carlson Road), a marker for Carlson notes that Swedish brothers Pete and John Carlson came to the United States in 1869 and settled in the community in 1881. Pete opened the community's first store, and John operated the local cotton gin.

Kimbro, another nearby community, was settled in the 1870s by Swedes, Danes, and Germans. A Swedish Evangelical Free church in Kimbro was moved to nearby Elgin in 1954. Kimbro's marker stands on Manda Road at the Free Church's cemetery: from Manor go four and one-half miles east on U.S. Highway 290, three miles north on Farm Road 1100, then left on Manda Road.

A Texas Historical Commission marker identifies the site of the Willow Ranch School, established in 1898. The plaque notes that "most of those who attended were the children of Swedish immigrant farmers; some sharecropped the P. C. Wells Land [he donated land in 1894] for the school." The school closed in 1938. This marker is located across the road from the Manda Methodist Cemetery at Wells School Road and Wells Lane.

Lund

The small settlement of Lund, five and one-half miles northeast of Elgin (go four miles north from Elgin on State Highway 95, then one and one-half miles east on Lund Road), includes a few houses, a water tower, a church, and a cemetery. On the Monday after Easter in 1980, the old Bethlehem Lutheran Church, twelve miles east of the New Sweden Lutheran Cemetery, was destroyed by a tornado, and the present light-colored brick structure was constructed the following year. This small Lutheran church contains items saved from the former sanctuary, including stained-glass windows, the altar painting, and pews. A separate structure was built for the old church bell. The congregation was organized in 1897 and the first church built across the road near the cemetery in 1898.

Elroy

In Elroy, southeast of Austin, a Texas historical marker in front of the library notes that Swedish and German immigrants settled the area in the 1890s. Three Swedish churches served the settlers.

Decker

The white-clapboard **Decker United Methodist Church**, 8304 Decker Lane (former Farm Road 3177), two miles south of U.S. Highway 290 (512-272-5371), is the congregation's second sanctuary. It dates to the turn of the twentieth century. Early Swedish Methodist immigrants in Decker attended church in Austin in the late 1860s and early 1870s before they erected their first church in 1879. The sanctuary is noted for its dark wood paneling and beamed ceiling. The interior is essentially unaltered. The church cemetery is nearby.

On Decker Road near its intersection with U.S. Highway 290 is the cemetery of the former Decker Swedish Evangelical Free Church. An official Texas plaque notes that "among the Swedish immigrants who settled in Decker in the 1880s were many seeking freedom from the Swedish State Church. The immigrants held meetings in homes and school houses, and organized the Decker Swedish Evangelical Free Church." Land was deeded in 1892 to the congregation on which a church building was erected and a cemetery was established. "Drought and crop failures forced many members to leave the area and the churches in Decker and Elroy disbanded. The church building located here was later torn down. In 1923 the Swedish Evangelical Free Church was formed in Austin; it was renamed the Evangelical Free Church of Austin in 1952."

Waco

 In front of the Victorian **Forsgard Homestead**, 1122 N. Fourth Street, is a Texas historic plaque informing the visitor that "Samuel Johan Forsgard (d. 1912) came to Texas from Sweden in 1855. Two years later he married Mary C. Johnson (or Jonsson; d. 1897) and moved to Waco. Their son, Edward Ferdinant 'Fuzzy' (1870–1941), married Anna Marie Weaver (1877–1963), and he and his father designed this home, which was built by Swedish carpenters and completed in 1908. . . . Samuel and Edward were both special Texas Rangers, and Edward held the 1908 world title in trapshooting. He and his father were also inventors. Anna, also known as Annie, or 'Queenie' to the doctors she assisted, dedicated her life to sharing, giving food and drink to many at the back door. . . . The main house is a modified Ell, designed in the Queen Anne style with classical columns and decorative shingling at the roof gable end. The porch, modified in 1930, features a low, solid wall, reportedly added to hide the legs of women and girls as they sat on the porch. Today, the house remains an architectural landmark of Waco's history."

Samuel Johan Forsgard is buried in Waco's First Street Cemetery. An official Texas historic marker near his grave states that he was born in Klockergarden, Forserum, Sweden, in 1828. In Waco he established a bakery, restaurant, and confectionary business, but he also found time to invent and patent farming equipment and to establish Ambold's Sporting Goods Company.

A plaque near Edward Ferdinant Forsgard's grave in Oakwood Cemetery notes that Edward toured the country as a marksman and trapshooter: "At the outset of World War I, he became a shooting instructor for the military, working at Rich Field in Waco. He also later served as a special Texas Ranger and as a game and fish warden for McLennan County. In addition to his skill with a gun, another trait Edward shared with his father was his love of inventing, patenting an automatic dishwasher for restaurants and a chemical and sawdust floor sweep designed to absorb dirt and moisture."

Norse

Norse is a small community about 100 miles north of Austin where a number of Norwegians settled, beginning in 1854. In the cemetery of Our Savior's Lutheran Church, at the junction of Farm Roads 219 and 4150, Clifton (254-675-3962), is the grave of Gustaf W. Belfrage (1834–1882), a Swedish American naturalist noted for his work on insects. Belfrage arrived in Waco in 1868, and Samuel J. Forsgard (see Waco), a prominent merchant born in Sweden, took him into his home. Belfrage then moved to Norse. Between 1868 and 1873, he sent valuable collections of insect specimens to educational institutions in New England, Sweden, England, and Russia. Belfrage lived a reclusive life and was buried in an unmarked grave in this cemetery. Later students from Southern Methodist University, Texas A&M University, and Baylor University honored Belfrage with a special grave marker, which may be found at the rear center of the cemetery.

This historic cemetery is particularly significant for Norwegian Americans. Cleng Peerson (1782–1865), pioneer of Norwegian immigration to the United States, who landed in America in 1821, is buried here. A large monument was erected by Texas Norwegians, and in 1982, King Olav V of Norway visited his grave. Also here are graves of early local Norwegian settlers, many inscribed in Norwegian. At the entrance to the cemetery is an impressive monument dedicated to the first seventeen Norwegian settlers of Bosque County, who arrived in 1854. The adjacent red-brick, Gothic-style church, begun by Norwegian pioneers in 1875 and completed and dedicated in 1885, is beautifully maintained. Originally wooden, in 1907 the church was enlarged and veneered with brick. The interior and chancel furniture are unchanged. The congregation was formally organized in 1869 with 230 charter members. In 1962 the church was awarded the Texas Historical Building Medallion.

Six miles from this church is another lovely, well-maintained Norwegian church known as St. Olaf Lutheran Church or The Rock Church, with its adjacent cemetery. It was built in 1886 of native stone by Norwegian architects for members of Our Savior's Lutheran Church of Norse. By 1902 the community had grown sufficiently to warrant organizing St. Olaf as a separate congregation. Fifteen years later, a new sanctuary was erected in nearby Cranfills Gap. The Rock Church is now used only for special services.

Mason

 The three-story Victorian **Reynolds-Seaquist House**, 400 Broad Street, was constructed of sandstone in the 1880s for a wealthy banker and completed by Oscar Seaquist (Oscar Edward Johnson Sjökvist), who purchased it in 1919. Seaquist, born in Oslo, emigrated at the turn of the century and developed a successful boot-making business in Mason.

The twenty-two-room house with fifteen fireplaces features a third-floor ballroom, exterior galleries surrounding the entire first and second floors, and small balconies on the third floor. On top are a profusion of gables, turrets, and chimneys. The house, still owned and occupied by Seaquist's heirs, has five indoor stairways. In 1972 and 1973, the house was totally restored; it is not open to the public.

Brady

The first Swedes came to Brady, 110 miles northwest of Austin, in the 1880s and 1890s. Carl Hurd, a cousin of S. M. Swenson, had emigrated earlier in the century. In 1885 four young Swedes, including Dan and Lee Hurd, sons of Carl Hurd, arrived in McCulloch County, and each bought one-half section of land five miles east of Brady. Shortly thereafter other Swedish families arrived, and the settlement was named East Sweden. A schoolhouse and church followed. Since the first minister was Presbyterian, the **East Sweden Church** was identified with that denomination. A marker, five and one-half miles northeast of Brady on U.S.

East Sweden Church, Brady

Highway 190 and just east on a county road, officially commemorates East Sweden Presbyterian Church. The marker indicates that the original Swedish settlers at first established homes in Williamson County, but by 1889 twelve families had relocated here. "Most of the settlers were Lutherans, and they held worship services in their homes. In 1890 a traveling Presbyterian minister, the Reverend J. A. Irvine, came to East Sweden and conducted worship services. The settlers agreed to become Presbyterians. . . . A sanctuary was built on this site in 1892, and continued to serve the congregation until it was destroyed in a windstorm in 1916. The church members met in the schoolhouse until this structure (the extant church) was built in 1921. Exhibiting handsome features and quality craftsmanship, the East Sweden Presbyterian Church has become a local landmark. Outstanding features of the vernacular church structure include its hip-on-hip wooden shingled roof, Gothic-arched windows, boxed eaves, and projecting portico with boxed columns." Joyce and Bobbye Hurd restored the church in 1999. Across the road is the East Sweden Cemetery.

A second migration of Swedish settlers took place here between 1900 and 1908. The Reverend E. Severin became a land agent and brought parties from Williamson and Travis Counties to an area seven miles west of Brady. Sixteen families settled there in 1905 and 1906 and called it West Sweden. The only visible sign of the West Sweden community is the cemetery and marker on the David Dahlberg farm eight miles west of Melvin on U.S. Highway 87. The West Sweden Lutheran Church, built in 1912, was located next to the cemetery and closed in the early 1950s. The sanctuary was destroyed by fire.

A third group of Swedish families moved to Melvin, seventeen miles west of Brady. Many of these families made their living from the land, but others brought skills in carpentry, stonemasonry, and blacksmithing. In front of the **Evangelical Free Church of Melvin** is a state historic plaque describing the history of the Swedish Free Mission Church: "Swedes began settling in the western part of McCulloch County in 1907. A Sunday School was begun that year, and the families met for worship in homes. A church congregation was formally organized in 1910 with fifteen charter members. A ladies aid society was formed in 1911. By 1915 a church building had been completed. Worship services were conducted in the Swedish language until the 1940s. The congregation's name was changed to the Evangelical Free Church in the 1940s." Outside of Melvin is the town cemetery with numerous Swedish graves.

The ninety-five early Swedish families who helped populate McCulloch County between 1886 and 1912 in East and West Sweden and Melvin are honored on a thirteen-foot stone obelisk at the **East Sweden Community Center**, which was once the schoolhouse. The building serves as a meeting place for those interested in preserving the area's history.

In Brady at White and Grant Streets is the former Swedish Trinity Methodist Church. The red-brick structure is presently the Cara Care Center for children.

April is an ideal time to visit Central Texas because the wildflowers are in full bloom. Many roadsides and fields in the hill country are carpeted with Indian paintbrush and Texas bluebonnets.

Abilene

 Built in 1910 for Swen Magnus Swenson's great-nephew William Gary Swenson and his wife, Shirley McCollum Swenson, the **Swenson House**, 1726 Swenson (915-676-3750), reflects the Prairie and Mission styles popular during the early twentieth century. The house is distinctive for its split staircase, oval dining room, and well-preserved woodwork. Swenson was the founder of Citizens National Bank of Abilene, and he also held financial interests and leadership positions in railroad, utility, real estate, and oil enterprises. The Abilene Preservation League (915-676-3775), which owns the property, hosts the Festive Swedish Smörgåsbord in June.

Avoca

Avoca is 200 miles northwest of Austin, near Stamford. The Ericksdahl Community, about four miles northeast of Avoca, was organized between 1905 and 1909 primarily by Swedes and their descendants from Travis and Williamson Counties. The area's first Swedes, however, were S. M. Swenson and his sons, who as early as 1854 had secured 100,000 acres. After 1900 he authorized his sons, under

Bethel Lutheran Church, Avoca

the name of the S. M. Swenson Land and Cattle Company, to sell land to settlers of Swedish descent.

In 1906, Pastor J. A. Stamline formally organized **Bethel Lutheran Church**, 10625 N. Farm Road 600 (915-773-2878). This Ericksdahl congregation held worship services in private homes until the "Little White Church on the Hill" was completed in the fall of 1907 on land previously part of the Swenson ranch. The present impressive Gothic-style stone church with a high steeple, which is visible for miles above the flat farmland, was completed in 1941 to replace the older one. Its Heritage Room in the sanctuary balcony has a model of the previous sanctuary as well as numerous photographs. In front of Bethel Lutheran Church is a state historic marker honoring the Swedes who settled the Ericksdahl community. Adjacent to the church is the large, well-maintained Bethel Lutheran Cemetery.

Stamford

In Stamford several historic plaques and structures focus on S. M. Swenson. West of downtown on McHarg Avenue, in a park where the annual Texas Cowboy Reunion is held the first week in July, a Texas historical marker notes that "Swedish native, Swante Magnus Swenson and his two sons, Eric Pierson and Swen

Albin Swenson, came to Texas in 1882 to establish the SMS ranches. In 1899, Eric P. and Swen A. Swenson donated a large section of land for a townsite on an extension of the Texas Central Railway. . . . Business, churches and utilities soon were established. The booming town was incorporated in January, 1901. . . . Stamford relied primarily on agriculture for its economy. Cotton, Swenson's Herefords, and other area livestock brought substantial income."

One-half block from the city's central square is the **Swenson Land and Cattle Company Headquarters** at 210 E. McHarg Avenue. The Texas marker in front of its headquarters notes, "Businessman Swen (Swante) Magnus Swenson (1816–1896), first Swedish settler in Texas, is closely associated with Sam Houston and his effort to keep Texas in the Union prior to the Civil War. In 1854 Swenson purchased large land tracts here, which he greatly expanded by the mid-1880s with school tracts and railroad scrips. As a result of new state taxes on land, Swenson leased his west Texas land to his sons Eric Pierson and Swen Albin in 1882. Eric and Swen formed the Swenson brothers' partnership and by 1885 their ranching operations consisted of 1800 shorthorn and 180 Indiana pure crossbred Hereford-short horn cows bearing a distinctive reversed (SMS) cattle brand still in use today. . . . The Swenson family holdings were . . . one of the largest ranches in Texas with over five hundred thousand acres. Swenson Land & Cattle Co., incorporated in 1926, established its headquarters here in 1927. It is noted for its introduction of an innovative mail-order system for selling cattle, brush management programs, and integrated ranching operations. The ranch was divided into four separate family-owned corporations in 1978." Across the street one can see the remains of the hotel where early settlers and ranchers stayed. This building is in grave danger.

At 200 S. Swenson Avenue is the former **Swenson Ranch Commissary**. A plaque states that "the Texas Central Railroad and the SMS Ranch collaborated to create the town of Stamford in the late 1890s. Built about 1900, this building was strategically located to serve as the central supply storage facility for the four extensive Swenson ranches in west Texas. . . . The utilitarian structure was constructed of Lueders Stone, and located adjacent to the Railroad tracks. Supplies were offloaded from the trains and stored until the various ranch foremen could come into town to collect their supplies and exchange news."

The **A. J. Swenson House** at 305 E. Oliver was built in 1905. Across the street from 111 N. Swenson Avenue is a large wall mural featuring scenes from the lives of cattlemen. Clearly visible is the Swenson reversed-SMS brand.

Breckenridge

The **Swenson House** was built in 1908 by Peter Swenson, a Swedish immigrant to America in 1864 who settled first in Minnesota and, in 1881, came to Stevens

County, Texas. The house, which is ten miles east of Breckenridge off U.S. Highway 180, was considered the best and most expensive residence in the county. Swenson's son, Selmar, a sheep farmer, was one of the first to use barbed-wire fences. Oil was discovered on his land during the local oil boom of 1918–1920. The Swenson Cemetery is also located east of Breckenridge, Texas.

A local Breckenridge museum at 116 W. Walker is named the Swenson Museum (254-559-8471). The building was formerly a bank.

Dallas

The **Dallas Museum of Art**, 1717 N. Harwood (214-922-1200; www.dm-art.org), holds Claes Oldenburg and Coosje van Bruggen's sculpture *Stake Hitch* (1984) in its collection. It is often impressively displayed at one end of the Barrel Vault and Quadrant Galleries; the work measures over fifty-three feet in height.

Dayton

Brought by the railroad and land agents, Swedish immigrants helped settle the community of Stilson, which is commemorated by an official historical marker two and one-half miles west of Dayton, on the south side of the U.S. Highway 90 right-of-way. Dayton is located in Liberty County, northwest of Houston.

The plaque notes: "The community of Stilson traces its origins to the arrival in the 1890s of the Texas and New Orleans Railroad. Out-of-state developers O. H. Stilson and Rodney Hill bought land in 1896 and immediately began planning a town. They advertised the new community to farmers in Iowa, and a number of families came here to begin new lives. Among those who came to build homes and establish farms were many Swedish immigrants, including C. F. Seaberg and C. D. Nelson. By the late 1890s the town boasted a fourteen-room hotel, a general store, a gin, a blacksmith shop, a rice mill, a warehouse, a barber shop, a post office, a railroad depot, and a school. . . . Stilson began to decline when the population gradually shifted to nearby Dayton." Stilson is now a ghost town.

Houston

Swedish-born architect Olle J. Lorehn (1864–1939) came to Houston to design buildings. **Houston Fire Station No. 7** at 2403 Milam Street near downtown has a plaque reading: "Houston's oldest fire house . . . was designed by Olle J. Lorehn and was completed in January, 1899. The two-story brick structure features rusticated stone details, a five-bay front with central arched entry flanked by two apparatus bay entries, and unique parapet details. Updated in the 1920s to change from horse-drawn to motorized equipment, the station remained in active service until 1968." Today it is the **Houston Fire Museum** (713-524-2526; www.houstonfiremuseum.org).

Lorehn was most known for the Binz Building, 513–519 Main, reportedly Houston's first office building, completed in 1895 and demolished in 1950. Lorehn also designed the Sacred Heart Co-Cathedral, 1111 Pierce Avenue, a cruciform, neo-Gothic church in buff brick and limestone dedicated in 1912. It is threatened with demolition.

Lorehn also designed the **James Bute Company Warehouse**, 711 William Street, listed on the National Register of Historic Places, as well as several Houston homes, including at least one in the **Courtlandt Place Historic District** on the National Register of Historic Places.

Another local architect of Swedish background was **Gustaf M. Borgstrom**. His Queen Anne–style house at 1401 Cortlandt Street is on the National Register.

Galveston

The **Texas Seaport Museum**, Harborside Drive at Twenty-first Street, Pier 21 (409-763-1877; www.tsm-elissa.org), contains the 1877 tall ship *Elissa*, one of the world's oldest surviving sailing ships. In the late 1800s, she carried Texas cotton from Galveston to the mills of Europe. In 1911 she was sold to a Swedish owner, who renamed it *Gustaf*, and in 1959 she passed to Greek ownership. The museum features a theater presentation entitled *Passage to Galveston—The Story of Elissa*. The Texas Seaport Museum also features an immigration database for immigrants to Galveston.

Round Top

Swedish nobleman Anders Oxehufwud and his wife, Josephine, emigrated to the United States in 1923 and settled in Los Angeles. The family belongings were stored in Stockholm until 1949, when part of the estate went into Nordiska Museet (Nordic Museum) and the remainder were shipped to the United States. Oxehufwud was an engineer with AT&T, and in 1964 the couple retired to La Grange, Texas. They willed their collection to the **International Festival-Institute in Round Top** after his death in 1987. The institute's beautiful, dark-wood paneled Anders Gustaf Fredric and Josephine Oxehufwud Museum Room opened in 1993, and the permanent collection includes more than one hundred works of art, furniture, paintings, ceramics, glass, silver, textiles, books, photographs, and other items from the seventeenth to the twentieth century. The black cabinet made in the early seventeenth century is perhaps one of the most valuable items in the collection.

The International Festival-Institute in Round Top (979-249-3129) is a place where international musicians gather to study and perform.

Olivia

Along the Texas coast across Lavaca Bay from Port Lavaca is Olivia, named for the wife of the Reverend Carl J. E. Haterius of Galesburg, Illinois, who in 1892 acquired the land for the town. Swedes established a cemetery and church, later called the Eden Lutheran Church, but Hurricane Carla destroyed much of the small community in 1961. A historic marker for the early settlement and cemetery is located at State Highway 172 and County Road 317.

Corpus Christi

Swedish native Kent Ullberg is a sculptor whose works are found around the world. He has a home on North Padre Island. In 1982 the *Corpus Christi Caller Times* commissioned Ullberg to create a monumental sculpture on the city's bayfront. The resulting work, *Wind in the Sails,* consists of two leaping bronze sailfish on a red-granite foundation. The sculpture is twenty-three feet tall. Most of Ullberg's work in and around Corpus Christi celebrates wildlife. These include the twenty-four-foot *Leaping Marlin* commissioned by the Coastal Bend Community Foundation, which is located on the John F. Kennedy Memorial Causeway approaching North Padre Island; an eight-foot bronze great blue heron on stone entitled *Spring Plumage* and two entwined river otters cast in bronze in an octagonal fountain entitled *Ring of Bright Waters,* both on the grounds of the Texas State Aquarium; and *Water Music,* two leaping dolphins cast in stainless steel, a technique pioneered by Ullberg, located in the lobby between two banks on Water Street in the 600 block.

One Ullberg sculpture in Corpus Christi is a significant departure from his wildlife monuments: a fifteen-and-one-half-foot-tall Christ stilling the waters entitled *It Is I.* Christ is depicted with uplifted arms, standing in the bow of a boat in rough waters. The sculpture rests on an eight-foot granite base facing Corpus Christi Bay at the entrance to First United Methodist Church, 900 South Shoreline.

Other examples of Ullberg's works in the United States include a two-thousand-pound ram at Kenan Football Center, Chapel Hill, North Carolina; *American Eagle,* a twenty-one-foot bronze on granite at the American Re-Insurance International Headquarters, Princeton, New Jersey; *Whooping Cranes–Conservation Fountain* at the National Wildlife Federation Headquarters, Washington, D.C.; and *Waiting for Sockeye,* a six by ten foot grizzly bear at the National Museum of Wildlife Art, Jackson Hole, Wyoming. His works also appear in the Museum of the Southwest, Midland, Texas (915-683-2882). (See Fort Lauderdale, Florida; Omaha, Nebraska; and Philadelphia for additional Ullberg works.)

Monte Alto

Stockholm Cemetery, the only reminder of a Swedish community promoted by the Wallin, Johnson & Matson Land Company of Minnesota, lies northwest of McAllen and Edinburg between Monte Alto and Lyford in the Rio Grande Valley in the southernmost part of Texas. On Farm Road 491 about one mile west of Farm Road 1425 and six miles east of Monte Alto, the cemetery holds the graves of some of these early settlers.

About three hundred feet from the cemetery is a Texas Historical Commission marker with these words: "The Swedes, who settled here between 1912 and 1914, were attracted by the area's abundance of inexpensive, fertile farmland. They formed a farm club to share information and problems, and raised cotton, grain, and corn. Some were dairy farmers. Stockholm, also known as Turner Tract, had churches, a school, grocery store, and cotton gin. Near this site is the Stockholm Cemetery, one of the few physical reminders of the ghost town."

THE WEST

NEW MEXICO

Clayton

Eklund Hotel, Dining Room, and Saloon—15 Main Street (877-355-8631; www.theeklund.com).

Only a handful of Swedes migrated to the American Southwest, attracted by mining and farming opportunities. Among them was Carl Eklund (1866–1956), who arrived in the United States from Sweden in 1885 aboard the same ship that brought parts of the Statue of Liberty to New York. He made his way to Longmont, Colorado, where he worked for a farmer for three years to repay his transportation debt. He then moved to Folsom, New Mexico, for a job with the railroad being built from Fort Worth to Denver. Eventually, he arrived in Clayton, where he discovered a two-story rock building in which he opened a bar and lunch counter. Seeking a wife, Eklund returned to the Swedish settlement of Ryssby near Longmont, Colorado, where he met and married Gerda Magnie. The couple returned to Clayton, and in 1897 they purchased the rock building. Eklund added an elaborately carved bar (still in use) and a lunch counter. The building was enlarged to include a third floor and "opera balcony." The Eklund Hotel, Dining Room, and Saloon was recognized by travelers as the fanciest hotel between Fort Worth and Denver.

Eklund, an adventurous man with a free spirit suited to the West, was at various times a cattleman, farmer, sheep man, saloon keeper, stonemason, miner, railroader, civic leader, and hotel operator. He ultimately owned about 150,000 acres of ranch land north of the city, which he called the JE Ranch, after his father, Johannes Eklund. Prominent in politics, Eklund was well known throughout New Mexico.

The hotel was sold to the history-minded Eklund Association and reopened in 1992 as the Eklund Dining Room and Saloon.

Santa Fe

Museum of International Folk Art—Camino Lejo, off Old Santa Fe Trail (505-476-1200; www.moifa.org).

Florence Dibell Bartlett founded this museum more than fifty years ago. It houses the thousands of folk art objects she collected from more than thirty countries.

Bartlett had a particular interest in folk art from Sweden, and Swedish folk art objects are frequently on display.

ARIZONA

Willcox

Faraway Ranch—Chiricahua National Monument (520-824-3560; www.desertusa.com/chi).

Chiricahua National Monument is about 120 miles east of Tucson. In the park is Bonita Canyon, settled by Swedish immigrants Neil and Emma Erickson. Emma Sophia Peterson was nineteen years old when she emigrated from Sweden in 1873. She joined her brother in Chicago and first found employment as a cook's assistant with a wealthy family residing on Michigan Avenue. An independent woman, she occasionally took positions to see a different part of the country, and in 1883 she moved to Fort Craig, New Mexico Territory, as housekeeper for the post commander. By 1885 Emma Peterson was managing a boardinghouse in Fort Bowie, Arizona Territory. When a vacant two-room cabin in Bonita Canyon became available, she bought it.

Neil Erickson was born in the province of Skåne. His father had emigrated to the United States in the early 1870s but was killed during an Indian attack while working on the railroad in New Mexico Territory. In 1879 Neil himself succumbed to "America fever" and arrived in Boston. Two years later, he joined the army and was assigned to New Mexico Territory, where he met Emma Peterson.

They married, and Neil filed a claim for the 160-acre homestead adjacent to Emma's Bonita Canyon cabin. As their family grew, the Ericksons continued to enlarge their house. By 1915, the original cabin had been razed and the main house made of stone became the U. S. Forest Service Headquarters. Neil Erickson was the first ranger of the Chiricahua Forest Reserve. In 1917 when he was transferred to northern Arizona, the couple left the ranch in the hands of daughters Hildegarde and Lillian, who began to develop it into a guest ranch named Faraway Ranch. When Hildegarde married, Lillian took over the management. She married Ed Riggs in 1923, and the couple was instrumental in the establishment of Chiricahua National Monument in 1924.

In 1979 **Faraway Ranch** was sold to the National Park Service, and it became a historic district within the monument. The house is furnished with historic artifacts. Architecturally the ranch house is significant because it shows the evolution from a relatively primitive American frontier cabin of the late nineteenth century into a modest stone house and finally into a mid-twentieth century adobe structure. In 1988 the restored ranch house was opened to the public.

COLORADO

Swedes initially came to Colorado to search for minerals, particularly gold, and to claim free land under the Homestead Act of 1862. They worked in the lead and silver mines around Leadville and in forestry. By 1890 almost 10,000 Swedes lived in Colorado, the state's fourth-largest foreign-born nationality. The Scandinavian heritage is preserved at the popular Scandinavian Midsummer Festival held the last weekend in June in Estes Park.

Longmont

In 1869 Swedes founded Ryssby, named after a parish in Småland, near the present city of Longmont. Sven Johan Johnson, leader of the first Ryssby settlers, arrived in 1869 with his brother and five other young men, who were followed by their families. They built one-room cabins from logs cut in the foothills of the Rocky Mountains, some eight miles to the west. Working first as hired men on other farms, as lumberjacks, and as miners, they gradually acquired about 2,000 acres. Other settlers arrived, and in 1875 a schoolhouse was built.

In early 1878, the Reverend Frederick Lagerman, fresh from the Augustana Theological Seminary in Rock Island, Illinois, helped to organize in Boulder County the **Swedish Evangelical Lutheran Church–Ryssby**. Although Lagerman left shortly, plans went ahead to build a church, and in 1881 Pastor Johannes

Swedish Evangelical Lutheran Church–Ryssby, Longmont

Telleen of Denver laid the cornerstone. Ryssby Church, on Sixty-third Street, one mile south of Nelson Road, sits on a knoll in rolling farm country near the foothills of the Rockies. Modeled after a church in Ryssby, Småland, it is a simple structure of sandstone. Beautifully maintained, the church has an entryway surmounted by a short steeple constructed in 1924 after the original steeple was hit by lightning. The simple interior has a fir floor, hard-backed pews (six are original), ornate chandeliers, a pot-bellied stove, and the original pump organ. Above the altar is the Swedish inscription, *Ära vare Gud i höjden* (Glory be to God on high). The church completed an extensive interior restoration in 1992.

By 1900 booming employment opportunities were making Longmont into an important regional municipality, and young people began leaving Ryssby. The church's last regular service was held in 1906, and eight years later the congregation merged with the Elim Lutheran Church of Longmont. Two pastors from Longmont and Loveland determinedly preserved the legacy of the Ryssby church by reinstituting a Midsummer service in 1924. Also popular are annual candlelight services on the second weekend in December. More than 1,500 people attend these services, which feature seasonal music and a Bible reading in Swedish.

Outside the church, large locust, elm, and maple trees planted by the original settlers still shade the grounds. To the east is the cemetery, where the oldest graves are in the southeast corner.

The congregation of **First Lutheran Church**, 803 W. Third Avenue at Terry (303-776-2704; www.firstluth.org), in Longmont was originally called Elim Lutheran and was organized in the late 1880s. In 1902 the old Methodist church on Terry between Third and Fourth Avenues was purchased and was used by the Lutheran congregation for about thirty-five years. Today the building is a funeral home. After Ryssby and Elim became a "joint parish," the name was changed to First Lutheran Church. Later, the present Gothic-style church made of red sandstone was dedicated. The architect was Hugo Hansen, also responsible for designing Mount Olivet Lutheran Church in Minneapolis, the largest Lutheran congregation in the country.

Adjacent to the main sanctuary is the Ryssby Chapel with a painting of the Ryssby Church. In the church library is a glass case containing memorabilia, including the original door knob and lock as well as old Bibles and hymn books.

Denver

Institutes and Museums

Swedish Medical Center—501 E. Hampden Avenue, Englewood (303-788-5000; www.swedishhospital.com).

The most outstanding name among Swedes in Denver related to health care in the early twentieth century was Dr. Charles A. Bundsen (1872–1956), originally from Holma, a village near Lysekil, Bohuslän. As a young man, Bundsen went to sea, eventually landing in Canada and the United States. After serving with the Medical Corps in Manila during the Spanish-American War, Bundsen attended medical school in Denver. One night, as the story goes, Bundsen dreamed of founding a sanatorium where Swedish people could be treated for tuberculosis. (Colorado's high altitude, low humidity, and considerable sunshine were regarded as ideal for treating tuberculosis.) A plan for establishing such an institution was presented to a group of Denver businessmen, who in 1905 agreed to its incorporation as the Swedish Consumptive Sanatorium (changed in 1909 to Swedish National Sanatorium), with Bundsen to be its chairman. The Swedish Ladies Consumptive Aid Society was formed in 1905 to promote the idea of a sanatorium, and in 1906 a committee was authorized to purchase five acres of land in nearby Englewood. The first building was begun the following year, and twenty-five patient cottages and an administration building soon went up. Five Swedish denominations and five fraternal organizations joined forces in supporting the project.

In 1921 the board decided to expand the facilities further and adopted the "mayflower" program. Considerable funds for the fight against tuberculosis had been raised in Sweden since 1907 through the sale of artificial *majblomman,* and after a visit to Sweden in 1921 by Bundsen and John Osterberg, a Rhode Island businessman, the mayflower idea was brought to the United States, with proceeds going exclusively to the Swedish National Sanatorium. In 1923 and 1924, three additional buildings were completed, as well as an iron fence with donor plaques. In 1927 Sweden's Prince Wilhelm visited the sanatorium, which greatly encouraged further expansion. In the mid-1940s, Bundsen resigned as medical director, and in 1952 a new wing of the Mayflower Building, known as the Bundsen Addition, was completed. Today, two other hospitals have joined forces with the sanatorium, and the complex is known as the Swedish Medical Center, one of Denver's largest hospitals.

Historic Places

Colorado State Capitol—Broadway and E. Colfax Avenue (303-866-2604).
Near the main rotunda, in a niche to the right of the main stairway, is a bronze bust of Edwin Carl Johnson (1884–1970), a Colorado governor (1933–1937, 1955–1957) and U.S. senator (1937–1955) of Swedish ancestry. (George A. Carlson, Colorado governor, 1915–1920, was also of Swedish background.) Johnson was born on a farm near Scandia, Kansas, and later moved to Colorado to improve his health. Initially a supporter of Franklin D. Roosevelt, Johnson became a critic and was considered a party maverick.

Goosetown Tavern—3242 E. Colfax Avenue.
The red-brick building with unique architectural details was originally located near Golden Gate Canyon State Park west of Denver and was moved to its present location. Proprietress Mary Wikstrom, the daughter of Swedish immigrants Lars and Martha Wikstrom who homesteaded in 1873 at the junction of Betty and Dry Creeks, married Nels Dahlberg, a prominent figure in Golden's Swedish community who purchased the Goosetown Tavern. When Nels died, Mary and her son ran the tavern.

Churches

Augustana Lutheran Church—5000 E. Alameda Avenue (303-388-4678; www.augustanadenver.org).
This congregation was organized in 1878, and two years later, Dr. Johannes Telleen took charge. From a group of eleven, the congregation has grown to become one of the largest Lutheran churches in the United States with over 2,000 baptized members. In 1881 the first service was conducted in a sanctuary on Broadway, Welton, and Nineteenth Streets. Telleen remained with the congregation until 1884, serving also as Swedish vice-consul in Denver. He then went to the West Coast and established congregations in California. In 1889 a new sanctuary was built at Twenty-third and Court Place. Augustana grew rapidly in the 1920s and 1930s. During the pastorate of Dr. Paul H. A. Noren in the 1950s, five and one-half acres were purchased and the present strikingly modern sanctuary constructed.

In the patio is the first building's cornerstone. An Archives Room contains memorabilia. The impressive church is on high ground with good views of parts of Denver and the Rockies, including Mount Evans and Pikes Peak.

Bethany Swedish Evangelical Lutheran Church—1625 Martin Luther King Jr. Boulevard, at Gilpin Street.
This 1910 red-brick building with its prominent corner bell tower is an example of Gothic Revival architecture. Adjacent to the church is the 1913 brick parsonage, a craftsman-style bungalow. Since 1957 it has been the Denver Gospel Church.

Golden

At the **Golden Pioneer Museum**, 923 Tenth Street (303-278-7151; www.golden pioneermuseum.com), visitors can purchase a walking-tour guide identifying various historic buildings in the **Golden Historic District**, bounded by Eleventh, Thirteenth, Maple, and Arapahoe Streets. Many homes in this district had Swedish connections. Turn-of-the-century builder Oscar Nolin designed houses in bungalow style at 1119 Eleventh Street (constructed in 1908 and known as the Elmer Bengsen residence), 1102 and 1106 Cheyenne Street, 1100 and 1101 Illinois

Street, and 1006 Thirteenth Street. Nolin also updated the house at 1220 Cheyenne Street. The Bengson/Goetz residence (1869) at 1107 Eleventh Street was originally the home of Swedish immigrant Nels Bengson, a tailor by trade. Golden's small community of Swedes established a Swedish Lutheran Church on Washington Avenue, but that building no longer exists. Swante Bergstrom, an officer of the Swedish Lutheran Church, lived at 1100 Ninth Street. A number of Swedish Americans are buried in the Golden Cemetery on Ulysses Street.

Tallman Ranch in Forgotten Valley—Golden Gate Canyon State Park (303-582-3707; www.parks.state.co.us).

Anders Tallman arrived in the United States from Sweden in 1869 looking for a new home for the family he left behind. When able, he sent for his wife and three children, but his wife did not survive the voyage. Tallman chose land along Nott Creek, an area identified today as Forgotten Valley, because it reminded him of Sweden. He and his children began homesteading in 1876 and immediately constructed a log cabin. That same year Anders remarried; his new wife was Christina (Steena) Bengson, daughter of a new Swedish family in the area. When Tallman found an unused one-room schoolhouse, he moved it to the ranch, adding three rooms and a front porch for the family's home.

In 1891 Tallman suffered an incapacitating stroke, but his wife kept the ranch going. One account relates that Steena Tallman regularly drove an oxcart to Black Hawk, where she traded her produce, eggs, and milk for staples. Despite the fact that the trip took seven hours each way at the ox's pace of two miles per hour, she made the round-trip in a single day. In 1898, after Anders Tallman's death, their married daughter, Anna Bengson, inherited the homestead, which eventually would total some four hundred acres. The family maintained it until 1955. Forty years later, the Tallman Ranch was added to the Colorado State Register of Historic Properties and was incorporated into the Golden Gate Canyon State Park, Colorado's second-largest state park. In 1996 a grant from the Colorado State Historic Fund enabled plans to be prepared for preserving the buildings, which include the old schoolhouse and several farm buildings. This preservation project is ongoing.

To reach the park, take State Highway 93 north from Golden one and one-half miles to Golden Gate Canyon Road; turn left and continue for thirteen miles to the park. Visitors take a one and one-half mile hiking trail of moderate difficulty to reach the Tallman Ranch.

Idaho Springs

Gold strikes brought Swedes to Idaho Springs, some thirty-five miles west of Denver. At the eastern end of town is the small Gothic-style **Zion Lutheran**

Church, 1921 Virginia (303-567-4378; www.clearcreeklutherans.org). The congregation was organized and the church built in 1896, and in the 1940s the frame church building was renovated. Several new stained-glass windows produced by members of the congregation depict the church's history.

Gypsum

At one time, Swedes, Norwegians, and Finns made up three-fourths of Gypsum Valley's population. **First Lutheran Church** on Eagle Street (970-524-7919) was most likely built in the 1890s by the local Nordic settlers. Across the street is the former Upper Gypsum School, originally three miles south of town and probably built by immigrants. Area farmers raise grain, potatoes, and livestock. Old Swedish congregations in other towns include Trinity Lutheran Church in Loveland, Mount Calvary Lutheran Church in Boulder, and Tabor Lutheran Church in Pueblo.

Colorado Springs

At the 14,110-foot summit of Pikes Peak near Colorado Springs, a plaque commemorates Swedish American artist Carl Gustafson Lotave, born in Jönköping in 1872. He studied under Swedish artist Anders Zorn, spent time in Paris, and in the 1890s accepted a position in the art department at Bethany College, Lindsborg, Kansas, where he was an associate of Birger Sandzén. Later Lotave moved to Colorado Springs, where he became noted for his landscapes, portraits, and frescoes.

Lotave reportedly wanted his ashes deposited on Pikes Peak while Richard Wagner's "The Ride of the Valkyries" played on a phonograph. One story has it that while on his deathbed, someone played the music, and Lotave staggered to attention until it was finished. His friend J. Alden Brett was so moved by the scene that he scribbled an ode to the painter, the last words of which were, "Farewell, O soul on starlit seas adrift"; this ode appears on the Pikes Peak plaque. Five hundred people attended the ceremony when Lotave's ashes were brought to the summit after his death in 1925. **Colorado Springs Pioneers Museum**, at 215 S. Tejon Street (719-385-5990), has several of Lotave's paintings, including *The Riding Master,* in its collections.

An early Colorado Springs church, **Bethany Lutheran**, at 1401 S. Eighth (719-632-9017), was organized in 1897.

Peterson Air Force Base southeast of Colorado Springs was constructed in 1942 and named for Lieutenant Edward J. Peterson Jr., who lost his life at the airfield during that summer. He was born in 1917 on a farm in Nebraska, his grandfather having emigrated from Blekinge.

Victor

Many Swedish miners were attracted to such places as Victor, Leadville, and Cripple Creek. Victor's former **Swedish Lutheran Church** (1905) is at Second Street and Portland Avenue across from Our Lady of the Mountain Roman Catholic Church. It is constructed of red brick with a gray-shingled gable and short bell tower. At the northwest end of town is the large cemetery with the graves of persons from many ethnic groups, including Swedes, who were attracted by Victor's mining opportunities.

Telluride

This southwest Colorado community was one of many late-century boom towns. Finnish and Swedish immigrants (mainly Swede-Finns) came to work as miners, blacksmiths, or boardinghouse employees. Telluride's east side was known as Finn Town, and there Finns and Swede-Finns each formed their own tight-knit communities with their own social halls. Finn Hall, built in 1896, served the town's five hundred Finns and also held Lutheran church services through the 1920s.

The **Swede-Finn Hall**, 472 W. Pacific at Townsend, was built in 1898 near Finn Hall. In the early decades of the century it bustled with activity, and among its users was the Order of Runeberg, a national Swede-Finn lodge focused on temperance and benevolent aid. During the Depression, the building fell into disuse. Ironically, Swede-Finn Hall served as a bar and restaurant; it has been owned by the Elks Lodge since 2002. Telluride is now a popular year-round resort.

Lafayette

Columbine Mine Massacre Monument—Lafayette Cemetery.

On November 21, 1927, state police fired into a 500-person rally during a strike, killing six miners and injuring sixty. The Industrial Workers of the World (IWW), also known as Wobblies, organized the strike. Five of the six miners are buried in this cemetery, and in the late 1980s, the Columbine Mine Masssacre Monument was dedicated. At the unveiling, the ashes of Joe Hill were scattered over the grave site.

Joe Hill, born Joel Emanuel Hagglund in Gävle in 1879, was an active member of the IWW. In 1902 he emigrated to the United States and changed his name to Joseph Hillstrom. In California he joined the IWW and began writing stirring labor songs. In 1913 he was briefly jailed for a crime that was not proved. While in Salt Lake City the following year, he was charged with the murder of a former police chief and his son, tried, and convicted. Hill was executed there on November 19, 1915, although he maintained his innocence. Many people believe he was framed because of his commitment to the labor movement. Some 30,000 people attended his funeral in Chicago. Although no specific monuments commemorate Hill, his songs live on in this country's musical heritage.

UTAH

Between 1850 and 1905, about 30,000 Nordic immigrants, converts to the Church of Jesus Christ of Latter-Day Saints (LDS), arrived in Utah. Danes were the most numerous, but over a third were Swedish, the largest contingents coming from the Skåne and Stockholm areas. By 1900 Scandinavians formed about a third of Utah's foreign-born population. The earliest known Swedish Mormon was John Eric Forsgren (1816–1890) from Gävle. After serving in the Mormon Battalion in California during the Mexican War, Forsgren arrived in Salt Lake City in 1847, three months after Brigham Young. Three years later, Forsgren was sent to Sweden as a missionary. In Gävle, his brother, Peter, accepted Mormonism, becoming what is believed to be the first baptized LDS convert in Scandinavia. Eventually Peter settled in Brigham City, Utah, where he became a patriarch in the church. Banished from Gävle, John and other LDS missionaries successfully proselytized in Denmark and nearby Skåne.

Brigham Young advised the first large party of 300 Nordic immigrants (one-third of whom were Swedish) who arrived in Salt Lake in October 1853 to settle in the Sanpete Valley west of the Wasatch Mountains and south of Salt Lake City. Swedish immigrants subsequently populated communities including Mount Pleasant and Spring City. Other Swedes settled in Salt Lake City (which by 1885 had a "Swede Town") and in Cache County, north of Salt Lake City, particularly in Brigham City and Logan. Scandinavian farmers helped make Sanpete and Cache Counties the granaries of Utah.

The Mormon leadership pushed immigrants to learn English quickly and put away their European culture. Despite rapid assimilation, Nordic meeting groups did exist. Resenting Danish domination, Otto Rydman advocated Swedish meetings within the church and became editor of *Utah Korrespondenten*, founded in 1890. Swedish Lutherans arrived after the Mormons, but Lutheran congregations were largely confined to the larger urban areas.

Salt Lake City

On the grounds west of the **State Capitol**, 350 N. Main, is a plaque honoring the 86,000 settlers who peopled the valleys of the Rocky Mountains between 1847 and 1869. Västergötland-born Hilda Anderson Erickson, recognized at her death in 1968 (age 108) as the last of the early Utah pioneers, arrived in Utah at age six on foot and by oxcart from Nebraska with her mother and two brothers.

On the grounds east of the Capitol is a plaque honoring the Mormon Battalion that served during the Mexican War. John Eric Forsgren was a private in the battalion's Company D, and his name is listed on a plaque near the monument.

The large **Daughters of Utah Pioneers Memorial Museum**, 300 N. Maine, across from the State Capitol (801-538-1050), is dedicated to the memory of the LDS pioneers. The museum contains a considerable variety of memorabilia, with numerous ones belonging to early Swedish Mormons. Names of Nordic pioneers are found throughout the museum.

In the early years, the Mormon Church maintained a works program in Salt Lake City to help the immigrants find employment and to take advantage of their skills. Nordic carpenters and builders were involved in the construction of such structures as the Mormon Temple, the Mormon Tabernacle, and Brigham Young's Beehive House.

In July 1882, the Reverend Johannes Telleen of Denver with five charter members organized the **Zion Lutheran Church**, the first one in Utah. Leaders of the Augustana Synod believed that Swedes nominally converted to the Latter-Day Saints would be willing to rejoin a Lutheran church, but despite much zeal, Lutheran success was limited. The Zion Lutheran congregation constructed its first church in 1885. Six years later a second structure was built; it remained the sanctuary until 1956, when the present building at 1970 Foothill Drive (801-582-2321; www.zelc.org) was completed. At the northwest corner of S. Second and E. Fourth is a plaque noting the location of the earlier churches.

Brigham City

In Brigham City Cemetery are buried a number of Swedes, including John Eric Forsgren (1816–1890); his father, John O. Forsgren (1793–1880); and other family members. The cemetery's entrance is on E. Third near S. Fourth.

Ogden

The second-oldest Lutheran congregation in Utah is Ogden's **Elim Lutheran Church**, 575 Twenty-third (801-394-5543), organized in 1888. The Reverend F. A. Linder, its founder, met with some hostility from Mormons who did not welcome his missionary efforts. The first church was constructed in 1889–1890, but the present sanctuary dates from 1948.

Mount Pleasant

 The oldest building in the **Mount Pleasant Commercial Historic District** is **Liberal Hall** at 51 W. Main Street, constructed in 1874–1875. In the 1870s this stucco building with a gable roof was a meeting place for locals disenchanted with the authoritarian style of the local Mormon leadership or the ban on Swedish in church services. In 1875 a Presbyterian minister from Illinois established a Presbyterian church and mission school in Mount Pleasant. In 1881 the Presbyterian Board of Home Missions purchased the building; since then it has changed hands several times. Although Presbyterian schools never drew many people away from the LDS church, they were important in stimulating the growth of a public education system throughout the state of Utah.

 Two other nineteenth-century buildings, the **N. S. Nielson House** at 179 W. Main Street and the **Sanpete County Cooperative Store** at 160 W. Main Street, were built in whole or in part by Swede N. S. Nielson (1884–1925), who arrived in Mount Pleasant in 1869 after converting to the LDS church. Becoming disenchanted with the faith, Nielson and his two brothers joined other disaffected Mormons as stockholders in the Sanpete County Cooperative Store, which was known as the "Swedish" or "Gentile" store. Until the Depression, the store was one of Sanpete Valley's most prominent establishments. N. S. Nielson was a successful banker, sheep man, and entrepreneur who served as mayor in 1896 and 1897. The N. S. Nielson House, constructed in the early 1890s, is an example of Victorian eclecticism combining Second Empire, Queen Anne, and Beaux Arts classical external motifs. Listed on the National Register of Historic Places, the house reflects the prosperity that a growing livestock industry brought to Mount Pleasant.

Ephraim

 Nordic Mormons, particularly Danes, settled in this Sanpete County community. The small, square **Niels Ole Anderson House**, 308 S. 100 East, with Federal-style and Greek Revival detailing was constructed by Swedes in two stages. The oldest is two rooms built of fired brick in the late 1860s. Owners expanded the house with a two-room adobe addition in the early 1880s. Since then the house, typical of the area's pioneer architecture and craftsmanship, has remained relatively unaltered. Anderson, part owner of a sawmill and active in church and community life, had emigrated as a boy to Utah from Sweden in the mid-1850s. Arriving with his family, which had converted to the LDS faith, he kept a journal of pioneer life and his Indian encounters and became known as a folklorist and an expert craftsman. He returned to Sweden between 1880 and 1882 as a Mormon missionary.

The **Johnson-Nielson House**, 351 N. Main Street, is a large Victorian-style home, also built by early Swedes. Scandinavian Americans made homes in other communities in Sanpete County, including Spring City, in the late nineteenth century. Many are built in the style described by Swedish folklife scholar Sigurd Erixon as a "pair house," which features a large central unit flanked by a single room on each side.

WYOMING

As early as the 1870s, Nordic Mormons also helped settle Wyoming as well as Arizona, Colorado, Idaho, Nevada, and New Mexico. In Wyoming, three Swedish Lutheran congregations were organized: St. Lukes in Buffalo, at 614 N. Burritt Avenue (307-684-7892); St. Paul in Cheyenne, at 218 E. Nineteenth (307-632-9212); and Trinity in Sheridan, at 135 Crescent Drive (307-672-2411).

MONTANA

Most Swedish settlers in Montana engaged in mining and cattle ranching in the state's western mountain regions. Several Lutheran congregations were established before World War I, including St. John's (1895) in Helena, at 1000 Helena Avenue (406-442-6270); Immanuel (1898) in Missoula, at 830 NW South Avenue (406-549-0736; www.imluchurch.org); and Emanuel (1898, later renamed Gloria Dei) in Butte, at 2300 Florence Avenue (406-723-9182). After the war, two Augustana Lutheran churches were started in Great Falls: Bethel, 1009 SW Eighteenth Avenue (406-761-1543); and First English Evangelical Lutheran, 112 N. Eighth Street (406-453-9551).

Three Montana governors have been of Swedish ancestry: J. Hugo Aronson (born at Gällstad in Älvsborg), John G. Erickson, and Forrest H. Anderson. (Neighboring Idaho has had one: Donald W. Samuelson.) **Malmstrom Air Force Base** (www.malmstrom.af.mil) in Great Falls is one of three U.S. Air Force bases named for pilots of Swedish ancestry. Colonel Einar Axel Malmstrom, born of Swedish parents in Chicago, died in an air disaster in 1954 near Great Falls.

IDAHO

Although Swedes never came in large numbers to Idaho, there was one significant settlement named New Sweden near Idaho Falls. Important church landmarks are found in Boise and near Moscow. In 1905 Idaho's Swedish Lutherans organized a college—Coeur d'Alene—in northwestern Idaho, but it closed fifteen years later.

Idaho Falls

In the 1890s, Chicago's Swedish Land Company encouraged a number of Swedes, mainly from the Oakland area of northeast Nebraska, to homestead in the Upper Snake River Valley west of Idaho Falls. Later, settlers from Småland were attracted to the region. By digging irrigation canals, they transformed the sagebrush valley into a rich agricultural land for growing potatoes and grains, including barley and oats.

New Sweden Mission Church was organized in 1894 and a sanctuary built the following year. Failing to sustain membership, the church lost the building in 1928. Only the parsonage and graves of the early Swedes in the well-maintained **New Sweden Cemetery** remain. Facing the cemetery on a monument of flat lava is a historical marker reading: "In loving memory . . . for their many hardships to give us our proud heritage in this thriving and prosperous community." The cemetery is on Pioneer (Thirty-third) Road near its intersection with New Sweden School Road, northwest of exit 113 on Interstate 15.

The **Alliance Covenant Church**, now at 557 South Boulevard, dates from the 1929 merger of the New Sweden and Idaho Falls (organized in 1899 as the Swedish Evangelical Mission Church of Idaho Falls) congregations. First called the Mission Covenant Church, the church now belongs to the Christian Missionary Alliance denomination.

In April 1898 the Scandinavian Evangelical Lutheran Gustaf Adolphus Church was organized. The congregation adopted the name **First Evangelical Lutheran Church** in 1939 and began constructing the present red-brick sanctuary at 455 W. Sunnyside Road (208-522-9301; www.firstlc.com). The Gothic-style lanterns in the sanctuary, obtained from a Boise bank, are made of Swedish iron, and the stained-glass windows are in memory of former Swedish congregants. The altar painting is by Gustav Nathanael Malm (1869–1928), a student of Olof Grafström.

Boise

 In Boise the **Immanuel Evangelical Lutheran Church**, at 707 W. Fort, three blocks north of the State Capitol (208-344-3011, www.ilcboise.org), was organized in 1908. In 1913 a sandstone Gothic-style sanctuary known as the Augustana Chapel was erected. Architect Charles F. Hummel was also involved in constructing the State Capitol. The chapel's features include a cruciform plan with an off-center tower. It has its original wooden pews, chancel rail, baptismal font, pulpit, and gold-trimmed white Gothic-style altar. Augustana Chapel is still used by the congregation for early morning Sunday worship service. In the foyer of a new church built in 1980 is the old pump organ.

Moscow

In Moscow's city cemetery are the graves of the Reverend and Mrs. Peter Carlson. During his ministry, Carlson, the first pioneer Swedish Lutheran pastor in the Pacific Northwest, established Lutheran congregations throughout Idaho, Oregon, and Washington. Carlson, born in Småland in 1822, emigrated in 1854, was ordained in 1859, and initiated his pioneer ministry in 1879. In 1884 he organized **First Lutheran Church**, a Swedish congregation that built a white-clapboard sanctuary in 1906, at Second and Van Buren. In 1961, First Lutheran and a Norwegian congregation merged to form **Emmanuel Lutheran,** 1036 W. A Street (208-882-3915). The current sanctuary was dedicated in 1968. The Van Buren building was sold in 1966 for a senior center and in 1984 was purchased by a Unitarian congregation.

Cordelia Swedish Evangelical Lutheran Church, organized by Carlson in 1880, built a sanctuary in 1883. The first Swedish congregation in the state and the oldest Lutheran building in Idaho, Cordelia Lutheran also claims to be the site of the first Lutheran confirmation in the West. Southeast of Moscow, Cordelia is one mile east of Genesee Troy Road, between its intersection with Enid and Lenville Roads.

Originally known as "The Swedish Evangelical Lutheran Congregation, Cordelia, Nez Perce County, Idaho Territory," the church persevered until 1913, when the congregation merged with a forerunner of Moscow's Emmanuel Lutheran Church. The church, a modest 18 by 24 foot structure that must have suited the eighteen founding members, lay dormant until 1948, when some restoration was undertaken. More restoration followed in the early 1990s. Behind the church is a small cemetery with some Swedish gravestone inscriptions. In the cemetery is a granite stone with a reference to Reverend Carlson.

Cordelia Swedish Evangelical Lutheran Church, Moscow

Troy

Carlson organized the Westdala Lutheran Church in 1886, and its members built a sanctuary in 1891. In 1902 the building was moved to Main Street and Third, where members remodeled it several times. In 1949 the church was renamed **Troy Lutheran Church** (208-835-3641).

Coeur d'Alene

The Swedish Lutheran Coeur d'Alene College was founded in 1905 by J. Jesperson, a former business manager at Augustana College in Rock Island, Illinois. The Reverend Carl J. Renhard (1870–1946), pastor of Immanuel Lutheran Church in Portland, Oregon, and founder of Emanuel Hospital there, was chosen as the college's second president. Several buildings, including dormitories and a gymnasium, were constructed between 1905 and 1920. In 1908 this coeducational institution had 120 students, but the Swedish American Lutheran constituency in Idaho was not large enough to support it, and it was forced to close. Norwegian Lutherans converted it into a home for the aged. Today it is the interdenominational Coeur d'Alene Homes at 704 W. Walnut Street. The original buildings no longer exist.

WASHINGTON

The Pacific Northwest, particularly Washington, attracted numerous Swedes, the first sizable group arriving in the 1880s. The majority were attracted to the Puget Sound area by opportunities in farming, fishing, and lumbering. By the turn of the century, businessmen, builders, mechanics, and engineers joined the influx. Larger communities with significant Swedish American populations exist in Seattle (particularly the Ballard section), Tacoma, Everett, and Bellingham. Smaller western Washington towns with many Swedes include La Conner, Hockinson, Mount Vernon, and Enumclaw. Hoquiam and Aberdeen had many Swede-Finns. Swedes and Swede-Finns also settled in other parts of the state, including Selah in the Yakima Valley and Spokane.

Ferndale

 In Hovander Homestead Park, 5299 Nielsen Road south of Ferndale off Hovander Road (360-384-3444), stands the **Hovander Homestead**, a fine example of turn-of-the-century Swedish immigrant domestic architecture. A frame structure, the Hovander House was erected between 1901 and 1903 by Håkan Hovander (originally named Håkan Olsson Håvander), an architect. In 1969 the Hovander Homestead was purchased by Whatcom County.

Hovander was born in 1841 in Sallerup, Skåne. As a teenager, he came to the United States, where he worked as a mason's helper and bricklayer. He returned to Sweden, marrying in 1879 in Stockholm. Failing health prompted him to move on, first to New Zealand but then to the West Coast, first San Francisco and then Seattle. In 1898 Hovander purchased 100 acres of homestead land and three years later began the house, for which he himself laid the brick foundation. A high peaked roof with many gables tops the lovely home, which is accented with a white scalloped trim. The large rooms with high ceilings contain many pieces of the Hovander family's furniture brought to Washington around Cape Horn. In the parlor and along the hallway are portraits of King Oscar II. In the Architect's Room (formerly Hovander's sons' bedroom) are some of his plans, including drawings of a building in Stockholm. The second floor is an incomplete storage area.

In addition to the main house are several other structures, including a large red barn, milk house, and water tower. In the 1911 barn are pieces of farm equipment and an old stagecoach. The nearby water tower was constructed in 1916. The restored milk house is furnished with equipment for making butter and cheese. The farm became almost totally self-sufficient, producing meat, eggs,

Hovander Homestead, Ferndale

dairy products, fruit, and grains. After Hovander died in 1915, his wife continued to live on the farm, and their son Otis, one of seven children, oversaw the farm until Whatcom County purchased it in 1969.

Mount Vernon

The **Salem Lutheran Church**, 2529 N. LaVentura Road (306-336-3600), was organized in 1913 by the merger of several congregations, including the Swedish Finnish Evangelical Bethesda congregation of Cedardale. The Bethsaida congregation of Pleasant Ridge joined in 1925. The light-colored brick sanctuary was constructed in 1916. In the Fireside Room on the second floor of the education building is a 1918 Olof Grafström painting of the Last Supper.

An early home is the **Magnus Anderson House** at 2018 Dike Road. At 1775 Dike Road stands another hand-built reminder of earlier times, a windmill constructed by Axel E. Carlson in 1906. Windmills with elevated tanks were a common sight on Skagit County farms.

Pleasant Ridge

In this community near La Conner is the old **Bethsaida Lutheran Church parsonage**, at 1745 Chilberg Road, and the adjacent church cemetery. Bethsaida, begun in 1881, was the first Swedish Lutheran congregation in Washington. In 1892 a sanctuary was built (it burned in the late 1960s), and in 1925 the congregation merged with Salem Lutheran Church of Mount Vernon. Also noteworthy among the buildings of Pleasant Ridge is the historical home of Peter Downey, at 1880 Chilberg Road.

In the Pleasant Ridge Cemetery on Valentine Road is the reddish-granite stone of Magnus Anderson (1836–1926) and his wife and son. Anderson was an 1869 settler, and a cabin he built still stands in La Conner. On the grave of Charles Willam Rosenquist (1857–1920) is the inscription, "Here rests a woodman of the world."

La Conner

Many Swedes, Norwegians, and Swede-Finns were attracted to the rich Skagit Valley, noted for its dairy and vegetable farms. To the east are the Cascade Mountains, including Mount Baker. The town of La Conner is situated on the east bank of Swinomish Channel. This picturesque community, the oldest in northwest Washington, has a number of well-preserved buildings from the 1870s to 1910, some with Swedish connections. Started as a trading center in 1867, La Conner became an important fishing town, and fish canneries and vegetable-processing plants are common sites. The **La Conner Historic District** is roughly bounded by Second, Morris, and Commercial Streets and the Swinomish Channel.

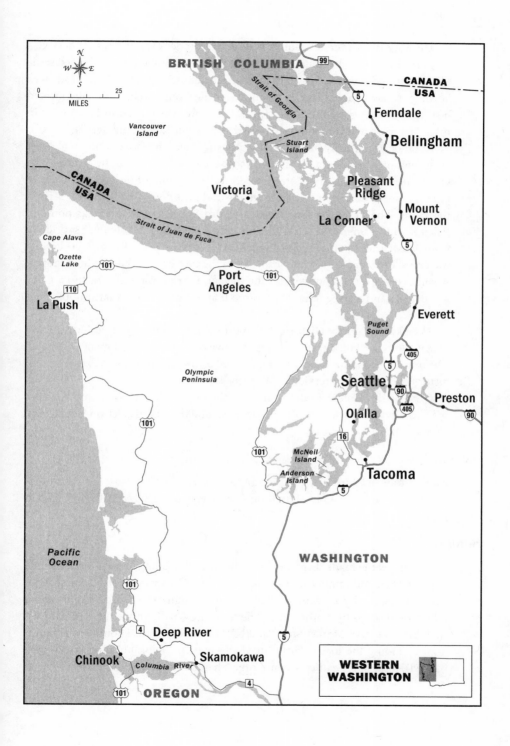

The **Magnus Anderson cabin** stands as a reminder of early days. Anderson, a Swedish ship's carpenter, built the one-story, 12 by 20 foot cabin and helped settle Pleasant Ridge after arriving in the area in the 1860s. The cabin, built of squared hewn logs, has a gabled roof extending over the front porch. Originally located near the north fork of the Skagit River, the cabin was moved to La Conner in 1952. Anderson and his family are buried at Pleasant Ridge Cemetery.

Another noteworthy building is the **Nelson-Pierson Grocery** on First Street at the end of Washington. Erected in 1908, the grocery was run by Swedes. The **Ole Wingren House**, 212 Morris Street, was the home of an early La Conner photographer and stationer, whose shop stood next door. The house dates from the 1890s. The **Perry Polson House** at Third Street and Benton was home to Polson, who immigrated with his father, Olof Polson (or Pålsson; 1833–1903), from Sweden. The Polsons, along with Carl John Kilberg (Chilberg), were among the first settlers, many of whom came from the province of Halland in the 1870s. A surveyor, construction worker, and farmer, Perry Polson moved to La Conner in 1884 and started a hardware store that expanded into a farm implement business.

The **Skagit County Historical Museum**, 501 S. Fourth (360-466-3365; www .skagitcounty/net/museum), has pamphlets that outline a walking tour of La Conner. The museum contains numerous items used by Swedes and has an extensive oral history collection of interviews with early settlers.

Other early homes of interest include the Olof Polson House, on Fir Island, the Nels Larson House, 1895 Bradshaw Road, and the Charlie Nelson House, 1836 Chilberg Road.

Everett

Zion Lutheran Church, 47th Street and Alger Avenue (425-252-1429), was organized in 1900, but the old church building has been replaced with one built in 1963.

Seattle

Swedes in Seattle made their way in medicine and retailing and the steel, fishing, construction, and lumber industries. The city has a strong Nordic connection, which is especially evident in Ballard, where signs proclaim *Velkommen til Ballard* and shops fly Nordic flags. The four-block Ballard Avenue Historic District, between NW Market Street and NW Dock, has typical commercial buildings, including the former Scandinavian-American Bank building (5300–5304 Ballard), for a time Seattle's second-largest bank.

Institutes and Museums

Nordic Heritage Museum—3014 NW Sixty-seventh Street (206-789-5707; www.nordicmuseum.org).
Housed in a 1907 public school that served children of Nordic immigrants, the Nordic Heritage Museum is the largest ethnic museum in the Pacific Northwest. An effort by the Heritage Museum Foundation, founded in 1979, the museum features collections from five Nordic countries. Exhibits focus on the immigrants' struggles in the old and new countries and the development of Ballard.

Heritage Rooms highlight the material culture of the five Nordic countries, including folk costumes, chests and cupboards, looms and textiles, painted utensils, and Saami artifacts. There is also a library and a gift shop. The Swedish Room includes exhibits on the Swedish Hospital in Seattle, entrepreneurial enterprises, church and domestic life, maritime occupations, and fraternal organizations, especially the Vasa and International Good Templars Orders.

The 51,000-square-foot museum hosts international exhibits and offers a large library reading area and facilities for language and rosemaling instruction. The museum recreates Scandinavian cultural events at Christmas and holds an annual summer festival. More than 65,000 patrons visit the museum each year.

Swedish Hospital Medical Center—747 Broadway Avenue (206-386-6000).
Opened in 1910, Swedish Hospital was founded in 1908 by a group of Seattle's Swedish residents under the leadership of Dr. Nils August Johansson (1872–1946). Born in Lund but despairing of limited opportunities to become a physician, Johansson arrived in 1893 in Boston. After working in the Colorado mines, Johansson studied medicine at the University of Denver and then moved on to Washington. Working at St. Luke's Hospital in Denver, he resolved that someday he would start his own hospital. This became a reality in Seattle when ten Swedish men promised him $1,000 each. When the founder of a private hospital at Summit and Columbia was killed in a car accident in 1912, Johansson was able to buy this facility.

As a result of Johansson's interest in cancer research in the early 1930s, the hospital opened a tumor institute. On the second floor of the Arnold Medical Pavilion are several plaques, including one honoring the institute. In the main lobby of the hospital is a portrait of Johansson. The hospital's library is named in his honor and the Katherine Brown Johansson Chapel for his wife. The Swedish colors are in evidence in the hospital's flag and the hospital's color scheme. In 1980 two of Seattle's hospitals, Doctors and Seattle General, merged with Swedish, making it the largest private hospital in the Pacific Northwest.

Churches

Ballard is dotted with churches, several of which began as Swedish congregations. Though their ownership has sometimes shifted, several sanctuaries constructed shortly after the turn of the century still survive. These include the Free Swedish Evangelical Mission Covenant Church, 1723 NW Sixty-first Street, and Swedish Bethel Lutheran Church, 2052 NW Sixty-fourth Street, both now used by other congregations. **Ballard Baptist Church** was founded in 1893 by eight Swedes. Its two early locations were at 1719 NW Fifty-seventh Street and at the corner of NW Twentieth Avenue and NW Sixty-first Street. In 1916 the present church at 2004 NW Sixty-third Street (206-784-1554) was dedicated. This is a daughter congregation of First Baptist, which became known as Central Baptist, Seattle. Originally known as First Scandinavian Baptist and then First Swedish Baptist Church, the Central congregation was organized in 1883. It had its roots in the pioneer work of Olaus Okerson, who arrived in Portland, Oregon, in 1869. Central Baptist no longer exists, but its building was located at Ninth and Pine. Artifacts from that church are at First Baptist Church of Seattle at Seneca and Harvard. Another daughter congregation of First Baptist (Central Baptist) is **Elim Baptist** at 2410 N. Fifty-sixth Street in the Sunnyside section of Seattle (206-632-4354). The congregation of Elim Baptist constructed its building in 1913.

First Covenant Church—400 E. Pike (at Bellevue; 206-322-7411; www.seattlefirstcovenant.org).
Built in 1910 and 1911, the large sandstone edifice, constructed in the classical style, is the third for this congregation, which was organized in 1889. The building is one of the Reverend Erik August Skogsbergh's tabernacles that still survives. Skogsbergh (1850–1939), a Minneapolis pastor recognized for outstanding preaching, worked for several years in Seattle and built monumental auditoriums in both cities. First Covenant was dedicated in 1911 and originally seated 2,500. Renovations, including the addition of a sizable lobby, have reduced the number of seats. Nonetheless, the oval high-domed auditorium remains impressive, its balcony encircling three-fourths of the sanctuary. Stained-glass windows depicting lilies grace the building throughout. Though the words "Swedish Tabernacle" formerly appeared on the Pike Street pediment, "First Covenant Church" has replaced it.

Gethsemane Lutheran—911 Stewart Street, at Ninth Avenue (206-682-3620).
A daughter church of First Lutheran in Tacoma, Gethsemane was established in 1885 by the Reverend Peter Carlson. Its modern sanctuary was completed in 1961.

First Covenant Church, Seattle

Columbia Lutheran Home—4700 N. Phinney Avenue (206-632-7584).

Formerly Columbia Conference Home for the Aged, Columbia Lutheran Home was founded in 1920 by Dr. C. R. Swanson as a home for indigent Swedes. Gradually the home's purpose changed, and today it is a skilled-care nursing home operated by the Pacific Northwest Synod of the Evangelical Lutheran Church in America. A new building replaced the old one in 1980.

Emmaus Lutheran Church—169 NW Sixty-fifth Street.

A Swedish congregation, organized in 1906, built the frame structure with Gothic-style windows between 1910 and 1915.

Schools

University of Washington—(campus operator 206-543-2100; www.washington.edu).

The impressive Alfred H. Anderson Hall, a nineteenth-century Gothic-style building, honors Alfred H. Anderson (1854–1914), the son of a Swedish immigrant who became a prominent lumberman, a member of the Washington State legislature, and a leader in establishing the university campus. Another building, the Warren G. Magnuson Health Sciences Center, is named in honor of the former U.S. senator who was born in Minnesota and reared in a Swedish-Norwegian family. One of the largest in the United States, the Department of Scandinavian Studies (206-543-0645; www.depts.washington.edu/scand), established in 1909, saw unprecedented growth under the chairmanship of Professor Walter Johnson in the late 1960s and early 1970s. At Suzzallo and Allen Library, the front façade on the Suzzallo entrance bears emblems of various European universities, including one from Uppsala University.

Adelphia College—2400 E. Eleventh Avenue.

In 1905 the Swedish Baptist school known as Adelphia College was organized by Dr. Emmanuel Schmidt (1868–1921) from Hälsingland. A number of its graduates became missionaries in China. Financial problems during World War I forced the school to close. The red-brick Adelphia Hall, built in 1905, continues to be identified by that name. It is owned by the Seattle Preparatory School–Matteo Ricci College (206-577-2102), a Jesuit school, which has added a gymnasium in front of the building.

Other Points of Interest

Nordstrom—500 Pine Street, at Fifth Avenue (206-628-2111).

Nordstrom began in 1901 as a shoe store in downtown Seattle, and John W. Nordstrom and two sons expanded the business. Although the original store at Fourth and Pike no longer stands, Nordstrom has grown into a nationwide department store chain. A third generation of Nordstrom family members holds executive management positions.

Founder John Nordstrom (1871–1962) was born in Luleå, Sweden. At age sixteen, he left his native land, first working in the iron mines in Michigan's Upper Peninsula. In 1889 he headed west, arriving in San Francisco. After trying logging in the redwoods, Nordstrom went on to the Klondike in Alaska in 1897, where he struck it rich. He and a partner opened a shoe store in Seattle. The present main store and corporate headquarters at Fifth and Pine was built in 1938. Its colored terrazzo skin hides the old structure except near the top of the southernmost end.

Frederick and Nelson Department Store—Fifth and Pine.
One of the original partners of Frederick and Nelson was Nels B. Nelson (born Nils B. Nilsson in Kristianstad, Skåne, in 1854). After emigrating, he went to Colorado, where he farmed and mined for gold. In 1891 he headed to Seattle, where he became partners with Frederick (a Dane) in the department store business. Nelson died in 1907, and the business was sold in the 1930s to Marshall Field's. Today Nordstrom owns the building.

Lake View Cemetery—1554 E. Fifteenth (206-322-1582).
Seattle's earliest Swedish settlers are buried in this cemetery.

Nils A. Johansson House—2800 E. Broadway, near E. Hamlin Street.
The Swiss chalet–style Nils A. Johansson House, in the North Capitol Hill area, was built in 1909.

Swedish Cultural Center (formerly known as the Swedish Club)—1928 N. Dexter Avenue (206-283-1090; www.swedishculturalcenter.org).
The Swedish Club was founded in 1892 by Nels B. Nelson. At first the group assembled in various halls and private homes. In 1902 the Swedish Club began meeting at its own clubhouse on Eighth Avenue. For almost sixty years that location remained its home, while its members banded together to improve opportunities for Swedes. The Dexter Avenue facilities, acquired in 1960, feature a members' restaurant on the upper floor overlooking Lake Union as well as meeting rooms and classrooms. Originally open only to men, the club expanded to include women in 1989.

In the building lobby, remodeled in 2002, one can view Swedish glass and Swedish dolls in provincial folk costumes from the internationally known doll and folk dress factory of Charlotte Weibull in Åkarp, Skåne. The collection is owned by the Swedish Cultural Society of Seattle. Two nineteenth-century Mora clocks are also on view. The second-floor bar features portraits of the Swedish monarchs, beginning with Gustav Vasa.

A block of iron ore from Sweden, displayed at the 1962 Seattle World's Fair, stands in front of the center near where an inscription on the Memorial Fountain greets visitors with the saying: "Happy is the house which shelters friends and treasures their memories."

Currently the Swedish Cultural Center offers Swedish-language instruction, sponsors scholarships and lecture series, and makes facilities available for Scandinavian cultural events.

Sculpture

At the Shilshoe Bay Marina, 7001 NW Seaview (206-728-3006), the Leif Eriksson statue erected in 1962 commands an impressive view of the Olympic Mountain range in the distance and a large marina to the east.

Preston

In 1888 a group of Swedish Baptists from Minnesota arrived in Washington to work in lumber camps and mills near Snoqualmie Pass, east of Seattle. In 1892 they bought a shingle mill near Lower Preston, which began to flourish under the leadership of Värmland's August Lovegren (1861–1917), one of the original owners. Later, an additional shingle mill and sawmill in Lower Preston attracted additional Swedish Baptist immigrants.

Swedish Lutherans from Jämtland settled in nearby Upper Preston. They held services in the Vasa Hall, founded in 1902. The lodge was built in 1948.

In Lower Preston in 1900, twenty people including Lovegren donated a plot of land, and in 1902 the present white-frame Preston Baptist Church was built. In 1954 the sanctuary was remodeled.

Lovegren built a planing mill on a site next to the general store. His three-story, white-frame house with blue trim still stands. In the cemetery are buried many early Swedish settlers, but Lovegren and his wife, Hilma (1863–1954), are buried in nearby Fall City Cemetery.

Olalla

Across from Vashon Island in Olalla is the **Charles F. Nelson House**, built in 1913 as the home of Swede merchant Charles F. Nelson. The large two-and-one-half-story, late-Victorian frame house at Nelson and Crescent Valley Roads, still a private residence, has a five-sided steeple. With a long veranda across the front, the house sits on a knoll overlooking Puget Sound's Colvos Passage. During the Alaska gold rush, Nelson traveled to the Yukon where he operated a store. In 1904 he returned to Olalla, opened a store, and soon became the town's principal merchant.

Olympic Peninsula

In the spring of 1888, K. O. Erickson, a legendary Swede of the Pacific Northwest, became an Olympic Peninsula fur trader. He learned the local Indian language and was made an honorary chief. His earliest trading post was near La Push and the Quilleute Indian Reservation on the Olympic coast at a site he named Mora after his home in Dalarna. Erickson also had a store farther north at Lake Ozette near the Makah Reservation. He founded a savings and loan association at Port Angeles as well and gave money for the construction of a park across from the Zorn Museum in Mora, Dalarna, and to the Swedish Boy and Girl Scouts. Author, newspaperman, and merchant Svante Lofgren recorded Erickson's life in his book *Vita Björnen* (The White Bear). Lofgren lived on Washington's Stuart Island, the most northwesterly island in the continental United States.

Another settler on the Olympic Peninsula was Lars Ahlström, who home-steaded at Ahlström's Prairie near Lake Ozette. The University of Washington's Dr. Brian Magnusson reports that a three-mile plank trail from the Pacific Ocean to Lake Ozette, a forest walk used by thousands of tourists every year, was origi-nally an Indian trail and that the path was improved by Ozette's Scandinavian settlers in the late nineteenth century. The cedar planking is said to have been laid by Lars Ahlström, whose use of parallel planks with crosswise puncheons represents a long tradition in northern Sweden and Finland. Magnusson notes that Ahlström's neighbor was Swede Peter Roose and that both Hälsingland-born men came to the Lake Ozette area in the early 1900s. In the 1890s, Lake Ozette had several hundred Scandinavians, the majority from Norway, but many Danes, Finns, and Swedes as well. By far the finest house was the Anders Nylund home, and nearby was the August Palmquist homestead. Only the Roose homestead survives partially intact.

Port Angeles

Displayed in the old Clallam County Courthouse, currently the **Clallam County Historical Society**, 223 E. Fourth Street (360-417-2364), is a painting entitled *Ediz Spit and Port Angeles* by Count Johan Gustaf Kalling, whom Dr. Brian Magnusson has identified as the first Swedish-born fine arts painter to portray the Pacific Northwest. It was exhibited at the 1893 World Columbian Exposition in Chicago in the Washington State Pavilion.

Tacoma

Nicholas Delin (Nikolaus Dalin) may have been the first white man to settle within the present city limits of Tacoma. In 1852 the Gotland native built a water-powered sawmill. A city street is named in his honor. Another street bears the name of Swedish king Karl XIV Johan, who reigned from 1818 to 1844.

Because Tacoma was at the westernmost terminus of the Northern Pacific Railroad, thousands of Scandinavians poured into the area from the Midwest, and the city became known as "the Scandinavian city on the West Coast." Between 1900 and 1910, Tacoma's Scandinavians established more than a dozen churches and numerous social organizations.

The **Washington State History Museum**, 1911 Pacific Avenue (888-238-4373; www.washingtonhistory.org), opened in 1996. The museum holds a Swedish corner cupboard from an early settler. The Washington State Historical Society Research Center Library, 315 N. Stadium Way (253-798-5914), is affiliated with the museum.

First Lutheran Church, 524 S. I Street, at S. Sixth, across from Wright Park (253-272-1538), was one of the city's earliest churches, organized in 1882 by Pastor Peter Carlson. The following year, a small sanctuary was completed. Norwegians worshiped with the Swedes until 1887, when they organized their own congregation.

In 1889 a second church building, at S. Eighth and I Streets, was constructed by well-known Tacoma contractor Edward Young, a recent Bohuslän emigrant to the United States. Pastor Johannes Telleen, Columbia Conference president of the Augustana Lutheran Synod and present at the dedication, called it the "Swedish Lutheran Cathedral of the West Coast," but a 1924 fire destroyed it. Three years later the church dedicated the red-brick Gothic building in which it still worships. Young was also responsible for the construction of the classical-featured First Church of Christ, Scientist, 902 Division, and Lincoln High School, 701 S. Thirty-seventh Street.

Two former Swedish churches are the red-brick Covenant Church, at the corner of S. I and S. Tenth Streets, with the date 1909 on its cornerstone, and First Swedish Baptist Church, at the southeast corner of S. Twelfth and S. I Streets. First Swedish Baptist was organized in 1893 by Olaus Okerson, and the Gothic-style, white-frame building was dedicated in 1902. The current congregation, known as **Central Baptist Church**, meets at 5000 W. Sixty-seventh Avenue (253-565-6500).

The oldest Swedish lodge west of the Mississippi and the first Swedish secular organization in the Pacific Northwest was the Swedish Order of Valhalla, first called Freya Lodge, organized in Tacoma in 1884. The **Valhalla Building** is at 1216 Martin Luther King Jr. Way. The three-story building, constructed in 1906, held many turn-of-the-century furnishings; on the second floor was an auditorium with a curved balcony and on the third a dining room. This building with its Neo-Renaissance façade is portrayed in a large exterior history mural at Ninth and Martin Luther King Jr. Way. The building was sold in 1998. The current address of the Swedish Order of Valhalla is 608 S. Stevens Street (253-383-5701).

 The **Sandberg-Schoenfeld Building**, 1411–1423 Pacific Avenue in downtown Tacoma, was described by Brian Magnusson as "a beautifully restored skyscraper erected in 1907–1908, and quite possibly the oldest structure in the 'Chicago Style' in the Pacific Northwest." It was one of the first skyscrapers on the West Coast constructed of steel-reinforced concrete. Former owner Peter Sandberg, for whom the ten-story building was named, retained architect Frederick Heath to design the building; Heath later designed Stadium High School in Tacoma.

Mural including the Valhalla Building, Tacoma

Sandberg was born at Tröskefors bruk, Värmland, in 1866 and trained as a carpenter. He emigrated to the United States in 1888 and Washington State the following year. An entrepreneur, he acquired much real estate in Tacoma and a large pub that brought him considerable negative publicity (he was labeled Tacoma's "vice king"). Sandberg also contributed to the construction of the Valhalla Hall and supported *Tacoma-Posten,* the city's Swedish-language newspaper. The flamboyant Swedish American fell on hard times during World War I, and the Sandberg Building was sold to the Schoenfelds Furniture Company in 1922. In 1996 the furniture store went out of business, and the building remained vacant until its recent restoration and conversion into an office building. Peter Sandberg's name is sculpted at the building's top, and the renovation is considered important to the revival of Tacoma's downtown commercial district.

Pacific Lutheran University, S. 122nd Street at S. Park Avenue (253-531-6900; www.plu.edu), founded by Norwegian Lutherans in 1890, opened its doors to thirty students in 1894 as Pacific Lutheran Academy and Business College. With the demise of Coeur d'Alene College in Idaho in 1920, Swedish and Norwegian Lutherans in the Pacific Northwest gradually became convinced that cooperation was necessary. The college became known as Pacific Lutheran College.

On the campus is the Scandinavian Cultural Center, 34 S. Park Avenue (253-535-7532; www.plu.edu/~scancntr). In 1992, a twenty-five-foot-tall Viking ship prow, weighing 2,200 pounds, was placed in front of the Cultural Center. It was designed and built by Paul Schweiss of Anacortes, Washington. The Cultural

Sandberg-Schoenfeld Building, Tacoma

Center offers a wide variety of exhibits and events centered on the Scandinavian cultural traditions. The school also houses one of the largest Scandinavian archival collections in the Pacific Northwest.

The largest cemetery in the city, **Tacoma Cemetery**, at S. Tacoma Way and S. Forty-eighth Street, is also the final resting place of many early Swedish settlers.

Southwest of Tacoma and accessible by ferry from Steilacoom are Anderson and McNeil Islands. In 1896 twenty-one Swedish adults and their children organized the Swedish Evangelical Lutheran Sunne Congregation of Anderson and

McNeil Islands. A small frame church was built near the south coast of McNeil Island; nearby was a cemetery. The congregation no longer exists, and there is now a federal penitentiary on McNeil, making it off-limits to tourists. Many descendants of early Swedish settlers live on Anderson as well as Fox Island, where houses and farm buildings displaying Scandinavian architectural features may be seen.

Selah

East of the Cascade Range and north of Yakima is Selah. Today, descendants of the five Swedish families who arrived in 1908 as second-wave immigrants from Sioux City, Iowa, own and operate large orchards and fruit-processing plants in the Yakima Valley. Swedish immigrants soon organized the **Swedish Mission Covenant Church**, 193 N. First (509-697-6116), and by 1910 they had built a church where many community functions were held, simply because it was the city's largest public auditorium. Until 1928 services were conducted in Swedish. The church still stands, although it has been altered over the years.

Skamokawa

 The rural community of Skamokawa in southwest Washington is on the north side of the Columbia River estuary, some thirty miles from the Pacific Ocean. Swedes and Norwegians began coming to the area in the late 1860s and 1870s, attracted by fishing, farming, and logging opportunities. The part of Skamokawa known as "Swede Town," the **Skamokawa Historic District**, has several frame houses dating from the 1880s and 1890s. In 1887 the Swedish Evangelical Lutheran Bethany congregation was organized in Skamokawa; it has disbanded.

 Further west along the north side of the Columbia River, in Deep River, the Finns organized the **Deep River Pioneer (Finnish Holy Trinity Evangelical) Lutheran Church.** The white-frame Gothic Revival structure was constructed in 1898, four years after the congregation was organized. Although it is no longer used for regular worship, summer Sunday concerts have been held in the sanctuary because of its excellent acoustics. Restoration work continues on the building, which is two miles north of the Deep River Bridge at State Highway 4 between Naselle and Rosburg. Nearby cemeteries have a number of Swedish names on the markers. Both Swedes and Finns were attracted to the area because of the economic opportunities in logging and salmon fishing.

Chinook

The fishing community of Chinook near the mouth of the Columbia River attracted Scandinavians after it was established in the late 1870s. At the turn of the century, the congregation, which was more Norwegian than Swedish, organized the

Evangelical Lutheran Church, on Main Street opposite the post office (360-777-8416). The church was designed by a carpenter from nearby Astoria, Oregon, and built by local Scandinavians. On occasion, Swedish pastors from Astoria came across the wide Columbia River to serve the congregation. The white-frame church with a central steeple has Gothic-style windows and a barrel-vault wood ceiling.

Spokane

In 1888 the Reverend Peter Carlson organized the **Salem Lutheran** congregation, 1428 W. Broadway (509-328-6280). The following year, the church constructed a brick-veneer building at Broadway and Walnut. In 1949 during work on an adjoining building and gymnasium, a spark from a cutting torch ignited a disastrous fire, but many of the stained-glass windows, most of the pipe organ, and the Olof Grafström 1924 painting of the Good Shepherd were saved. The windows were incorporated into the new sanctuary. Other notable churches in town include the former **Swedish Baptist Church**, 212 S. Division Street (509-747-2818), whose new building houses in its narthex the cornerstone of the former Covenant Tabernacle (*Svenska Tabernaklet*).

OREGON

As in Washington, Swedes first arrived in Oregon in significant numbers during the 1880s. The 1905 Lewis and Clark Exposition in Portland and the work of the Oregon State Commission of Immigration attracted many more Swedes, so that by 1910 the state hosted about 10,000 Swedish-born residents, representing nearly 10 percent of all foreign-born. Swedes were largely "second stage" immigrants, having settled first in other states.

The largest contingent of Swedes lived in Portland, where they were frequently builders, carpenters, or sawmill employees. The oldest Swedish Lutheran congregation in the Pacific Northwest was organized in Portland by missionary Peter Carlson. The first important Swedish settlement in the state was Powell Valley, fourteen miles east of Portland. Swedes also lived in considerable numbers in Astoria, Warren, Colton, The Dalles, Ione (north-central Oregon), and along the Pacific Coast, particularly around Coos Bay.

Astoria

Salmon fishing and lumbering opportunities first attracted Swedes (and even more Finns) to Astoria. A Midsummer festival draws them back annually.

Several of Astoria's outstanding historic homes have Swedish connections, including the Captain Eric Johnson House at 960 Franklin Avenue, Albin W. Norblad House at 1625 Grand, Benjamin Young House and Carriage House at 3652 Duane

Street, and Dr. Toivo Forsstrom House at 726 Seventh Street. Norblad was first elected governor of Oregon in 1929, and his son Walter served as a congressman from 1946 to 1965. Young was one of the leading salmon packers on the lower Columbia, and he further expanded by opening canneries in Alaska and on the Fraser River in British Columbia. For a complete description of these homes, many of which are built on steep slopes near the wide mouth of the Columbia River and all of which are privately owned, consult the brochure, *Walking Tour of Astoria,* which may be purchased at the 1885 Victorian-style home of Captain George Flavel, 441 Eighth Street (503-325-2203) or at the Clatsop County Heritage Museum, 1618 Exchange (503-325-2203).

Swedish Lutherans in Astoria organized the First Swedish Evangelical Lutheran Church in 1880 under the guidance of the Reverend Peter Carlson, making it the second-oldest congregation of the former Columbia Conference of the Augustana Lutheran Church. In 1929 this congregation merged with a neighboring German church. The new Trinity Lutheran congregation disposed of the old properties and in 1930 built a sanctuary on the corner of Sixteenth and Franklin. This edifice is now the Performing Arts Center of Clatsop Community College. The old organ and stained-glass windows remain in the building.

In 1974 Trinity Lutheran consolidated with Zion Lutheran, a Finnish congregation, to form **Peace Lutheran Church**, 565 Twelfth Street (503-325-3871). This congregation used the former Zion Lutheran sanctuary, built in 1947 and later modernized. In the narthex is a stained-glass window from the Trinity church. Also in the narthex are two glass cases with memorabilia from the two congregations—one with Finnish items, the other with Swedish.

In 1919 plans began for what would eventually become **Columbia Memorial Hospital**, which involved many Swedes over the years. Two years after the Astoria Finnish Brotherhood began to consider providing a hospital for Astoria, the Fraternal Hospital Association, composed of numerous Astoria fraternal organizations, was organized. It eventually sought and won support for its hospital proposal from the Columbia Conference of the Augustana Lutheran Church, and groundbreaking took place in 1927. Today that structure is a nursing home, and the hospital serves the community in a 1978 building at 2111 Exchange Street (502-325-4321; www.columbiamemorial.org).

Mist

Swedes began arriving in this wooded hill country in 1877. A Swedish Lutheran congregation was organized in 1886, but neither the colony nor the church flourished. The little white-frame church is at least ninety years old, and since the early 1960s has been owned by the Community Church of nearby Birkenfeld. On U.S. Highway 30, near the turnoff for Mist, is a sign noting Swedetown Road.

Warren

Bethany Lutheran Church, 34721 Church Road (503-397-2050), was constructed in 1908, a year after the congregation organized. The white-frame church with a central steeple and twentieth-century, Gothic-style windows features a painting of Christ in Gethsemane, one of approximately two hundred altar paintings by Olof Grafström. The building has been modernized. North of it is the Bethany Memorial Cemetery. Mount St. Helens is visible to the northeast. Nearby on U.S. Highway 30 is the Warren Baptist Church (503-397-1005), also organized by Swedes.

Portland

Churches

Three active churches in Portland have Swedish roots. **First Immanuel Lutheran Church** may be called the mother church of the former Columbia Conference of the Augustana Lutheran Synod. Established in 1879 as the Scandinavian Evangelical Lutheran Church, it immediately became the Swedish Evangelical Lutheran Immanuel Congregation. The Reverend Peter Carlson, its founder and first pastor, was born in Småland in 1822 and emigrated in 1854, first residing in St. Charles, Illinois. Five years later he was ordained a minister.

Immanuel Lutheran's first sanctuary was erected in 1882 at Burnside and Tenth. The Columbia Conference of the Augustana Lutheran Church was organized there in 1895. During the Reverend Carl J. Renhard's pastorate (1904–1910), the present sanctuary was built at 1816 NW Irving Street, at NW Nineteenth Avenue (503-226-3659; www.firstimmanuelluth.org) and dedicated in September 1905. The early twentieth-century church in the Gothic style features a tall off-center spire. The sanctuary's stained-glass windows represent a number of Christian symbols in memory of various former members of the congregation and include numerous Swedish inscriptions. Adjacent to the church is the old parsonage. The multiethnic congregation continues to celebrate Lucia Fest and *julotta* traditions and hosts an annual Nord Fest in September.

The mother church of the Pacific Northwest's Swedish Baptists is **Temple Baptist Church**, 1219 NE Seventh, opposite Lloyd Center (502-233-5953; www.temple-baptist.com). Baptists began meeting in 1875, but 1884 is the official founding year of the First Scandinavian Baptist Church of Portland. In 1878 the Reverend Olaus Okerson, born in Skåne and the early leader of Swedish Baptists in the Northwest, had spoken to the group. The sanctuary, built in the classical style and featuring exterior Ionic columns, was dedicated in 1927 and renovated in 1973.

The former **Swedish Tabernacle**, 1624 NW Glisan Street (at NW Seventeenth Avenue), grew from a congregation formed in 1887 as the Swedish Mission Church. Built in 1912, the two-story, red-brick, Gothic-style rectangular tabernacle features an auditorium with a U-shaped balcony, its face decorated with a repeating motif of plaster rosettes. In 1953 the congregation sold the tabernacle, which was eventually called the Swedish Evangelical Mission Covenant Church, and now meets as First Covenant at 107 NE Forty-fifth Avenue (503-238-5950; www.firstcov.com). The tabernacle has been a theater and a union hall; currently it is a theater pub.

Other Points of Interest

Immanuel Lutheran's minister Carl J. Renhard (1870–1946) was the moving spirit in the founding of Emanuel Hospital and Health Center, 2801 N. Gantenbein Avenue (503-413-2200), one of the largest health facilities in the Pacific Northwest. The hospital is now **Legacy Emanuel Hospital and Health Center**. Renhard was born in Småland and immigrated to the United States at the age of ten. He grew up in Nebraska, was confirmed at the Swede Home Church near Stromsburg, and was trained at Augustana Theological Seminary. In 1909, he gathered nine Swedish men (shortly increased to twelve) and formed the Swedish Lutheran Hospital Board. Three years later, Emanuel Hospital purchased a three-story residence at 209 SW Taylor Street on the southwest side of Portland.

In 1916 the first building at the hospital's present location on the northeast side of the Willamette River, at N. Stanton Street and Vancouver Avenue, was opened (this structure was razed in 1952 for a 128-bed addition). In 1918 the Nurses Home was opened to serve the Emanuel Hospital School of Nursing, which taught nurses for more than fifty-five years. In 1926 the main hospital was erected at Commercial Avenue and Graham Street, and six years later two more additions were constructed. In 1977 President Gerald Ford dedicated the patient tower, and in 1980 the complex expanded further. The surrounding neighborhood was once known as Swede Hill. At the corner of Rodney and Stanton is the former **Augustana Lutheran Church**, but since the 1940s the congregation has met at 2710 NE Fourteenth Avenue (503-288-6174; www.augustana.org).

Two blocks west of Immanuel Lutheran Church is **Linnea Hall**, 2066 NW Irving Street, now a mixed-use building. Linnea was one of the oldest Swedish societies in the Pacific Northwest and the only independent Swedish lodge in Portland. Organized in 1888 as *Svenska Bröderna* (The Swedish Brothers), the group changed the name to *Svenska Sällskapet Linnéa,* the name on the 1910 cornerstone. On top of the two-and-one-half-story frame building are a curvilinear gable and square-domed corner pavilions. Wooden pilasters with Corinthian capitals flank a deeply recessed central entrance with double-leaf doors. Above the entrance are two stained-glass windows and a painted wood carving of the Swedish national emblem. The rear two-story dance hall was destroyed by fire in 1929.

Playing an important role in the cultural and historical development of Swedish heritage in Portland, the society sponsored picnics and parties at which Swedish was spoken, Swedish food prepared, and Swedish folk traditions observed. Though the membership reached 500 in the early 1920s, it declined in the 1930s. By 1946 it had shrunk to 125, and in 1979 the hall was sold. In 1980 the building was named a Portland historical landmark.

Fogelbo is a private residence at 8740 SW Oleson Road, currently owned by Ross A. Fogelquist, honorary Swedish vice-consul for Oregon and a leader of the Portland Swedish community. The log home was built between 1938 and 1940 for Mr. and Mrs. Oscar Olson by Henry Steiner, one of the chief carpenters of the historic Timberline Lodge on Mount Hood. In 1952 the Charles Fogelquist family purchased the house. It has been the location for numerous Scandinavian festivals.

One thousand feet above the city of Portland in Pittock Acres Park is the **Henry L. Pittock Mansion**, 3229 NW Pittock Drive (503-823-3627; www.pittockmansion .com). This twenty-two-room mansion was built in the French Renaissance style between 1909 and 1914 by the founder of Portland's *The Daily Oregonian* (later called *The Oregonian*). It showcases fine examples of Swedish craftsmanship. In the first-floor library is an intricate wood carving above the fireplace depicting the family crest, hand executed by William G. Klingenberg, one of Portland's Swedish craftsmen. On the second floor is ornate hand-carved Victorian walnut furniture made in the 1880s by Daniel Wennerberg, a Swedish cabinet maker. Mrs. Edward Atiyeh, an Oregon governor's wife and granddaughter of Wennerberg, gave the furniture to the mansion.

Gresham

Swedes came to Gresham and Powell Valley as early as 1875, and a larger number followed in the 1890s. The congregation of **Trinity Lutheran Church**, 507 W. Powell Boulevard (503-665-3197; www.trinitylutherangresham.org), organized in 1899, was originally known as the Swedish Evangelical Lutheran Saron Church of Powell Valley. The building constructed that year no longer exists. A new sanctuary containing the altar painting from the former church was erected in 1932.

Colton

In 1906 the Reverend Carl J. Renhard, the Portland minister who spearheaded the founding of Portland's Emanuel Hospital, established the Oregon Swedish Colonization Company in an attempt to encourage Scandinavian Lutherans to move to the Pacific Northwest. Renhard sought people who were Swedish, Lutheran, and Republican. Most original settlers came from Nebraska, particularly Oakland, Wakefield, and Omaha. Among the arrivals were the Hults from the Swede Home Lutheran Church near Stromsburg, Nebraska. Nels P. Hult became a successful lumberman after building the first lumber mill in the area. Two thousand acres of land were purchased to be made available to the settlers. In 1907 the Swedish Evangelical Lutheran Carlsborg congregation was formally organized in Hult's home. During the following years, the white-frame church was built. In 1945 the congregation changed its name from Carlsborg Evangelical Lutheran to **Colton Lutheran** (503-824-3425). The church stands on the south side of State Highway 211 next to the high school. In nearby Colton Cemetery are the graves of Renhard (1870–1947); his wife, Anna (1874–1945), who was Hult's daughter; and other members of the Hult family.

On Hult Road west of town is the Lutheran Pioneer Home, a nursing home begun by the Hults. The Luther Cornay Chapel has the original pews and altar curtain of the Colton Lutheran Church. The Hults also contributed to Oregon charities and the arts, including the Hult Center for the Performing Arts between Sixth and Seventh on Willamette in Eugene (541-687-5000; www.hultctr.org).

The Dalles

The **Fort Dalles Historical Museum** at Fifteenth and Garrison Streets (541-296-4547) features three late-nineteenth-century log structures on the National Register—the **Lewis Anderson house, barn, and granary**. A Swede built the house for Anderson, a fellow Swede. This noteworthy complex of Scandinavian vernacular buildings was originally on Anderson's homestead on Pleasant Ridge south of The Dalles, overlooking Mount Hood to the west and the rolling Columbia River plateau to the north. The museum commission serving both Wasco County and The Dalles began dismantling the structures in 1972 and moving them to the historical museum.

Made of hewn yellow-pine logs with dovetailed corners, the rectangular, 34 by 24 foot one-and-one-half-story house rested (as did the other farm buildings) on a fieldstone foundation. On the first floor were a parlor, pantry, small bedroom, kitchen, and front bedroom. Stairs led up to a sleeping area. The small hip-roofed shelter for the front entry was added later. The period furnishings include a pump organ and a loom.

The 30 by 30 foot barn was on a slope at its original location; thus, it has an upper and lower level (hayloft and threshing floor above, central double row of mangers below). Builders used 50-foot hewn tamarack (evergreen) logs in 1890 for its construction. The granary was built between 1885 and 1890 at a homestead at Rock Prairie. Anderson had it dismantled and moved to his property about 1898.

Born in northern Sweden in 1862, Anderson went to sea on an English vessel at age fourteen. After he returned in 1881 to Sweden, he left almost immediately to accompany his sister and a group of settlers to the United States. Marrying in Wisconsin, Anderson next went to Minneapolis but then pushed on to Pleasant Ridge in 1885. Although he persuaded other Swedes to follow, Pleasant Ridge's lack of water was a shortcoming few could overlook. Most would-be settlers moved on, but Anderson and his family persevered. Finally, after his four children divided the land, he moved to The Dalles and worked in the construction trade.

Ione

Ione is located in a sparsely populated area of north-central Oregon where the wheat farms are 2,000–4,000 acres in size and where Swedes found some of the last land available for homesteading in the lower forty-eight states. Swedes arrived here in 1883 and worked as sheepherders.

The Reverend Erik Norelius, an emigrant from Hälsingland who helped found and lead the Augustana Synod of the Swedish American Lutheran Church, visited this isolated community, then known as Gooseberry, in 1886. In April

Valby Lutheran Church (before remodeling), Ione

he conducted the first Lutheran church service and organized the congregation. Called **Valby Lutheran**, 60492 Valby Road (541-676-9970), the small white-frame building with its short steeple was dedicated in 1897.

Junction City

For many years an annual Nordic festival has been held in mid-August in Junction City. Danes, Finns, Norwegians, and Swedes each have a special day during this four-day festival.

Florence

 Heceta Head Lighthouse on U.S. Highway 101 twelve miles north of Florence is the most powerful beacon along the Oregon coast. A crew of Swedish-born carpenters, including A. G. Linn (see McPherson County Courthouse, McPherson, Kansas), built the lighthouse and keeper's quarters between 1892 and 1894. This is probably Oregon's most-photographed coastal lighthouse. Although fully automated today, Swedes formerly operated and maintained this lighthouse, as they did many lighthouses along Oregon's coast.

Coos Bay

In North Bend near Coos Bay, formerly called Marshfield, Scandinavian immigrants who worked in the sawmills and logging camps of Coos County built the First Lutheran Evangelical Church of North Bend at 777 Florida in 1908. Many were Swedish-speaking men and women born in Finland. In 1958 First Lutheran and Trinity Lutheran, a Swedish congregation organized in 1884, merged to form **Gloria Dei Lutheran** (541-267-2347) and constructed a new building at 1290 W. Thompson Road that was dedicated in 1960. Trinity Lutheran's sanctuary at Third and Commercial was torn down.

 Coos Bay historic homes owned by or built by Swedes include three still in private hands. The three-story, white-frame **Hjalte Nerdrum House**, 955 S. Fifth, constructed 1911–1912, is considered one of the finest homes in the Coos Bay area. Nerdrum emigrated from Finland and was employed by native Swede C. A. Smith at his lumber company. Nerdrum pioneered a new technique for making pulp with salt water from the bay.

 The Italianate **Nasburg-Lockhart House**, 687 N. Third, was constructed in 1884 by Andrew Nasburg, who in the early 1860s owned and operated the first general store in Marshfield (Coos Bay). A second-stage immigrant who had first settled in Illinois, Nasburg came to Oregon in 1859.

The **Myren-Hillstrom House**, 353 S. Fifth, was built about 1889 by Norwegian Robert Myren. His daughter Rose married into the Hillstrom family, who were Swedish-speaking Finns.

The two-story Queen Anne–style **Patrick Hughes House,** built in 1898, stands in Cape Blanco State Park. Designed and constructed by Swede Peter John (Per Johan) Lindberg (1851–1920), a Port Orford building contractor, the house was home to pioneer rancher and dairy farmer Patrick Hughes.

CALIFORNIA

The first Swedes in large numbers came in the 1870s, although gold seekers, fishermen, sailors, traders, and adventurers had arrived as early as the 1840s. A Swedish-Norwegian consulate was established in San Francisco in 1850. This city and Los Angeles became the main centers of the Swedish community in the state, attracting almost half of the Swedish-born settlers. The two most important rural settlements, both in the San Joaquin Valley, are Kingsburg and Turlock. The former has become known as the Swedish village of California, in somewhat the same way that Solvang, near Santa Barbara, is identified with the Danes, although the latter has been more fully developed as a tourist attraction. Swedes settled throughout the northern, central, and coastal parts of the state and in the southern cities of San Diego and Pasadena. By 1970 this most populous state claimed more Swedish-born residents than any other state, followed by Illinois, New York, and Minnesota.

San Francisco

Churches

Ebenezer Lutheran Church—678 Portola Drive (415-681-5400).
The Reverend Johannes Telleen organized the church in 1882. Telleen, born in Sweden in 1846, had emigrated to the United States as a boy of seven and settled with his parents in Moline, Illinois. Ordained as a Lutheran pastor in 1878, Telleen subsequently held several pastorates, including one in Denver, before coming to San Francisco. Telleen was important to San Francisco Swedes because he was responsible for the Ebenezer church bulletin, which in 1887 became *Vestkusten* (The West Coast), a Swedish weekly still published in San Francisco.

In 1885 the first church, on Mission Street between Eighth and Ninth, was dedicated, but in 1903 it was sold to the Salvation Army and destroyed in the 1906 earthquake. The congregation constructed a new church at 208 Dolores that escaped considerable interior damage during the quake, thanks to a bucket brigade. Parishioners carried water up ladders to the steeple and poured it on the many small fires that broke out on the roof from flying sparks. Unfortunately, fire destroyed the building in 1993, and the present church on Portola Drive was built shortly thereafter.

Outside the former chapel, now a photo and art gallery, are two historical plaques honoring Telleen and Jonas Auslund, a Swedish Lutheran missionary in California in the 1870s. The 1909 bell that came around Cape Horn is currently on the sidewalk near the church entrance. The congregation also owns an 1893 altar painting by Olof Grafström.

St. Mark's Lutheran Church—1111 O'Farrell, between Franklin and Gough (415-928-7770; www.stmarks.sf.org).

In Ross Hardy Pioneer Plaza in front of this German Lutheran church, built in 1894, are eight historical plaques commemorating early Lutherans in America and California and historic San Francisco congregations of different faiths. St. Mark's congregation, which was founded in 1849, claims to be the oldest Lutheran church in California. Included among the plaques is one honoring the Reverends Johannes Telleen and Lars Paul Esbjörn; the latter was a Lutheran emissary of Sweden's state church in the Midwest for fourteen years.

First Covenant (Dolores Park) Church—455 Dolores, between Seventeenth and Eighteenth (415-431-8755).

In 1877 First Covenant Church was established as the Swedish Evangelical Mission Church of San Francisco. Its first sanctuary was a former German church on Jessie Street. In 1893 the Swedes built a church on the same site, but it was destroyed in the 1906 earthquake. The present tabernacle-style church was completed in 1907. In the 1950s both the exterior and interior were modernized and the "gingerbread" removed. Off the balcony is a well-organized heritage room containing historical photographs and documents of the congregation.

Occasional Swedish services are still conducted at the Norwegian Seamen's Church—3454 Hyde Street (451-775-6566).

Other Points of Interest

William Matson Residence—1950–1960 Jackson Street, between Gough and Octavia.

This brick, Georgian-style structure, which has served envoys of both Sweden and Germany, overlooks the Golden Gate Bridge and Marin County. Built by Swede William Matson (1849–1917), the U-shaped mansion partly encloses a beautiful garden. Matson was born in Lysekil, Bohuslän; by 1867 he was a sailor in San Francisco. In 1901 he organized the Matson Navigation Company, and his Pacific cargo-ship line thrived. Matson earned respect as an innovator in shipping; his ships used wireless telegraphy and a gyro pilot and compass before any others on the Pacific. Operating both cruise and cargo lines, he developed commercial trade with Hawaii and expanded his line's routes eastward as far as the Indian Ocean.

For a time, Matson was president of the San Francisco Chamber of Commerce and honorary Swedish consul general in San Francisco. In the mid-1940s the Swedish government bought his mansion for use as a consular office and residence. In 1985 it was sold to the German government, and it continues to be used as that country's Consulate General in San Francisco.

The **Matson Building and Annex**, 215 Market Street, was placed on the National Register of Historic Places in 1995 for its architectural and commercial significance for transportation development.

Swedish American Hall—2174 Market (415-861-5016; www.swedishamericanhall.com; www.scandinavius.com).

The Swedish Society, founded in 1875 mainly as a group to benefit the sick, met in various locations until Scandia Hall was built. Fire destroyed it in 1906. In 1907 and 1908 the society constructed this hall, with the financial assistance of Erik O. Lindblom, one of three Swedes credited with discovering gold in Nome, Alaska. Lindblom also founded a Swedish bank in San Francisco and built the Claremont Resort Hotel, a gleaming, palace-like hostelry across San Francisco Bay in the Oakland hills. The four-story Swedish American Hall, one of some 300 San Francisco buildings designed by Swedish architect August Nordin, has several recently restored meeting rooms including the Freja Hall and a collection of books in Swedish. The building's exterior has scalloped trim protruding from the gable. The Café Du Nord, a well-known nightclub, is on the basement level.

Vestkusten office—30 Sharon Street, between Fifteenth and Sixteenth Streets.

Begun in 1886 as a bulletin of the Ebenezer Lutheran Church, *Veskusten* soon became a secular weekly. In 1890 Alexander Olsson from the province of Halland began working on it, and four years later he and Ernst Skarstedt, a well-known writer and chronicler of Swedish people in the West, purchased the paper. Skarstedt withdrew and the paper became Olsson's. When he died in 1952, his son, Hugo Olsson, took over, and thirteen years later, Karin W. Person, a journalist from Blekinge, bought the paper. In the early 1990s she sold it to Barbro Sachs-Osher, who continues its publication (415-381-5149; www.vestkusten.com). Barbro Sachs-Osher currently is Sweden's general consul in San Francisco and is a philanthropist along with her husband. (The new de Young Museum in Golden Gate Park includes the Bernard and Barbro Osher Wing, and a work by Oldenburg and van Bruggen entitled "Corridor Pin, Blue" (1999), a gift of Osher and the Pro Suecia Foundation.) The former Vestkusten office on Sharon Street is a highly ornate, three-story San Francisco townhouse.

Alexander Olsson was also one of the five founders of **Sveadal**, now a 110-acre recreation park at 8220 Croy Road, Morgan Hill (www.sveadal.org), in the

Swedish American Hall, San Francisco

Santa Cruz Mountains south of San Jose. Since 1926, when the Swedish-American Patriotic League purchased the park, it has been the traditional meeting place for northern California Swedes. Swedes first met in Golden Gate Park at the Midwinter Fair and Exhibition in 1894, but now they meet in Sveadal at the Midsummer Festival, which includes the ritual of raising and dancing round the maypole, the naming of a queen, and a parade.

Raoul Wallenberg Traditional High School—40 Vega (415-749-3469).

In 1981, World War II hero Raoul Wallenberg was made an honorary citizen of the United States, an honor formerly accorded only to the Marquis de LaFayette and Sir Winston Churchill. Wallenberg had personally saved the lives of thousands of Hungarian Jews. His incarceration and death in a Russian prison stirred an international controversy.

Wallenberg Traditional High School, whose 600 students specialize in high academics, opened in 1981. It was the only educational institution in the United States named in honor of the Swedish hero at the time.

Swedenborgian Church of the New Jerusalem—3200 Washington Street at Lyon Street (415-346-6466; www.sfswedenborgian.org).
This church, constructed in 1895, was planned by theologian and architectural critic Joseph Worcester. It combines Italian and California architectural styles. The interior evokes a rustic forest lodge, with wood beams and a prominent fireplace. The church is a popular wedding site.

Woodside

Five miles north of Woodside on Cañada Road is the **Filoli Estate** (650-364-8300; www.filoli.org), built in 1915 and acquired in 1937 by Lurline and William P. Roth, shipper William Matson's daughter and son-in-law. The mansion provided the set used for the popular television program *Dynasty*. The estate is known for its magnificent mansion and spectacular gardens.

Oakland

St. Paul Lutheran Church, organized in 1887, was first located at Ninth and Clay. The second church was built in 1901 at Tenth and Grove. The congregation now worships in a sanctuary at 1658 Excelsior Avenue, constructed in 1946 (510-530-6333; www.stpaul-lutheran.com). The **Salem Lutheran Home**, 2361 Twenty-ninth Street (501-261-1406; www.salemlutheranhome.com), was organized at St. Paul Lutheran Church in 1924. Through the years it has maintained a close link with this congregation. The 1971 church of the **First Covenant** congregation, organized by Swedes in 1887, is at 4000 Redwood Road (510-531-5244).

Berkeley

Founded in 1897 as a Sunday school in a rented hall, **Berkeley Covenant Church**, 1632 Hopkins (510-516-8775), enjoys a long history of religious service and fellowship that grew from a handful of Swedish-speaking families. Not until 1903 was the church officially chartered by sixteen members as *Svenska Missionen*, or the Swedish Mission Church. The members incorporated in 1906, built the first church in 1907, and navigated the rough waters of periodic closings between 1917 and 1922, when growth resumed under the pastorate of the Reverend David Sandstrom. Congregants were reluctant to adopt English, and until 1934 pastors conducted services in Swedish. In the 1950s the church celebrated its fiftieth anniversary with a groundbreaking ceremony for new construction.

The former **Framåt Lodge 405**, located at 1900 Addison Way, was built in 1927 as the local chapter of the Vasa Order. Five years later the Depression forced the Vasa Order to sell the building, whose attractive brick façade with terra cotta trim is in the Classical Revival style. In 1997 the substantial building was designated a Berkeley landmark. A historic plaque notes that "on November 8, 1927, Prince William of Sweden laid the cornerstone, proclaiming, 'Through the magic of the melting pot you are becoming Americans, and I can only admonish you to be good Swedes but even better Americans.'"

The **Judah L. Magnes Memorial Museum** (the Jewish Museum of the West), 2911 Russell Street (510-549-6950), awards the Raoul Wallenberg Holocaust Hero Medal, named in honor of the selfless efforts of Wallenberg during World War II to rescue Jews from the Holocaust. Per Anger, Swedish consul general in San Francisco in the 1950s, was an attaché in the Swedish Embassy in Budapest during World War II. He assisted Wallenberg in saving Hungarian Jews.

Sacramento

On the second floor of the **State Capitol** (916-324-0333) at the double-door entrance to the senate chamber is a portrait of Earl Warren (1891–1974), governor of California and chief justice of the U.S. Supreme Court (1953–1969). Warren's mother, Christine Hernlund, was born near Sundsvall, Hälsingland, in Sweden and his father, Matt, in Haugesund, Norway. His wife, Nina Elisabeth (1893–1993), also Swedish, was the daughter of the Reverend Nils Peter Palmquist, an early minister of the Swedish Baptist Church in San Diego.

Lake Tahoe

Vikingsholm, a thirty-eight-room mansion built between 1929 and 1935 and now in Emerald Bay State Park (530-525-7232), resembles by plan an ancient Norse fortress and chieftain's castle. Designed by Swede Lennart Palme, the two-story stone structure has on each end a tower, one three stories high and the other two. Palme, trained in civil engineering at the Royal Technical University in Stockholm, was born in Stockholm in 1881 and was a first cousin of the father of Swedish prime minister Olof Palme (1927–1986). An enclosed balcony on the second floor is highly ornamented by carvings, and the house features Swedish antique furnishings. The living room offers a panoramic view of Emerald Bay. Also in the Nordic style is a caretaker's log house with wood carvings, a roof overlaid with split logs, and a chimney reminiscent of those in Dalarna.

Although now owned by the California Department of Parks and Recreation and open seasonally for tours, the house was built for Lora J. Knight, widow of a

Chicago multimillionaire, who lived in the house until her death in 1945. From a parking lot on State Highway 89, visitors reach Vikingsholm via a steep one-mile trail. The grounds are also accessible by boat.

Turlock

Located in the San Joaquin Valley and famous for its melons, Turlock was founded largely by Swedish Mission Friends from Youngstown, Ohio. Probably the most prominent land agent was Nels O. Hultberg from Torrlösa, Skåne. After working in Illinois, he was sent in 1893 by the United States government and the Mission Friends to Alaska, where he maintained a mission church and carried out tasks for the government. After staking a claim, he struck gold in 1898 on the Seward Peninsula. That same year, John Brynteson, Erik Lindblom, and Jafet Lindeberg also struck gold, thus initiating the turn-of-the-century rush that brought almost 20,000 prospectors to Nome.

In 1902 Hultberg settled in Turlock where he sold land, opened the first dairy, participated in other commercial enterprises, and developed a fruit orchard. He drew many Swedes to the area with advertisements in Swedish-language religious periodicals in the United States and Sweden.

Turlock Covenant Church, 316 S. Laurel Street, at Laurel and High Streets (209-667-1191), was organized in 1902 as Beulah Covenant and built its first sanctuary, now gone, at W. Main and Lander. With growth, the congregation decided in 1923 to purchase the high school on Laurel and High Streets. The pastor named the area Beulah Park because of the beauty of the tall palm trees and flowering shrubs on the grounds. In 1927 and 1928 the church built the Beulah Tabernacle on the site, hanging in it the old church's bell, which had been cast in New York and transported by ship around Cape Horn to California in 1888. Into the 1930s, the church was known locally as the Swedish Mission Church.

Emanuel Medical Center, 825 Delbon (209-634-9151; www.emanuelmedical center.org), opened in 1917 under the name Emanuel Hospital at 1318 Canal. Brothers Eric and Albert Julien, both doctors, founded the hospital and, along with the Reverend A. G. Delbon, pastor of the Turlock Covenant Church, and the Reverend E. N. Train, pastor of Covenant Church in Hilmar, promoted it in the early years. A highly respected Covenant-owned institution, Emanuel Medical Center encompasses the hospital itself, Brandel Manor Convalescent Hospital, and the residential retirement community of Covenant Village.

Another Turlock landmark is **Nazareth Lutheran Church**, 125 Orange Street, at Columbia (209-668-2228). It was organized in 1912 and its sanctuary constructed in 1927. At the corner of Columbia and Locust is the former Swedish Baptist Church, constructed in 1937 after the congregation was organized in

1908. Turlock Memorial Park, 575 N. Soderquist Road (209-632-1018), is a city cemetery with numerous Swedish graves.

Hilmar

The farming community of Hilmar, south of Turlock, was founded in 1917 when the Tidewater Southern Railway extended its track southeasterly to Lander Avenue. The town took its name from the Hilmar Colony, a settlement area of 17,000 acres promoted by Nels O. Hultberg and Andrew Hallner, minister, author, and journalist. Begun in 1902, the colony was named for Hultberg's oldest son. Hultberg and Hallner advertised for settlers in Swedish periodicals, principally in the Midwest. Within eight weeks of the first advertisements, twenty-two families had arrived in Turlock. More followed. Grasshoppers, rabbits, and sandstorms tested the colonists, but irrigation sustained farming, and almond and walnut orchards, along with dairy farms and cheese factories, predominate today.

Two early congregations built churches and cemeteries on Tegner Road in the colony. The Covenant congregation was organized in 1902, making it slightly older than Beulah Covenant in Turlock. In 1921 the **Hilmar Covenant** congregation constructed a sanctuary at 8515 N. Lander Avenue (209-668-0400; www. hilmarcovenant.org). The cornerstone has a Swedish inscription with the dates 1903–1921. The **Berea Lutheran Church**, currently at 2001 SW Bloss (209-634-3010), was organized in 1906. In 1948 this congregation moved its small 1910 sanctuary from a site near Berea Lutheran Cemetery on Tegner Road two miles west to its present location. In the cemetery is a monument to the memory of the Reverend and Mrs. Edward Nelander by the Angelica Swedish Lutheran Church of Los Angeles. Nelander had been president of Bethany College, Lindsborg, Kansas, and between 1905 and 1915 was pastor in Los Angeles.

Kingsburg

The San Joaquin Valley town of Kingsburg, home of Sun Maid Raisin Growers, the world's largest raisin production facility, prides itself on being California's Swedish village. Early settlers were predominantly Swedish; in 1921 more than 90 percent of the people in the immediate vicinity were identified as Swedish. Beginning in 1886 Frank D. Rosendahl of Närke and Andrew Erikson from Ishpeming, Michigan, worked to recruit Swedish settlers. The following year the first Swedish Lutheran church in the San Joaquin Valley was founded, and others followed in Kingsburg.

The business district attempts a Swedish look with steeply peaked shingled roofs, windows in gables and dormers, and side paneling with cross boards and used bricks. The Dala horse and Swedish flags appear on light poles, and the water tower is shaped like a Swedish coffee pot. Many buildings contain shields with the coat of arms of the various Swedish provinces. On the Marion Street side of the Kingsburg branch of the Fresno County Library is a historic mural including a group of Kingsburg's Swedes with a proverb in Swedish emphasizing the importance of reading. On the third weekend of May the town hosts a Swedish Festival, including the crowning of a queen, a ten-kilometer "Dalahorse trot," and a parade ending with the erecting of a Maypole. The town celebrates St. Lucia Day the first Saturday of December. In Memorial Park at the end of Draper Street is a three-crown fountain, monuments commemorating former Swedish residents, and a cedar tree from the town's sister city of Sunne, Sweden.

Institutes and Museums

Kingsburg Historical Park—east of Kingsburg at 2321 E. Sierra Street between Madsen and Twenty-second avenues.

Historic structures moved to the park give a sense of early life in the community. Typical is the three-room Clay Elementary School, built in 1913 at Saginaw and Smith and moved to the park in 1975. The Peter Olson House (also known as the Olson-Ball House) was constructed in 1908 by Swedish immigrant Peter Olson, born in Ängelholm, Skåne, in 1857. Olson arrived in Chicago in 1880 but continued on to Minnesota, where he worked as a logger and learned the carpenter's

Kingsburg Historical Park, Kingsburg

trade. Twelve years later, he moved to Kingsburg, where he took up farming and ranching and grew fruit, especially grapes. An old barn containing handmade agricultural tools, a water tank house, and the Olson Bros. Implements and Bottle Shop suggest the agricultural ingenuity of the community. Other buildings that are historically significant to the Swedish community are Rieffel's Grocery Store, the medical-pharmacy building, and a firehouse. The Kingsburg Chamber of Commerce is at 1475 Draper Street (559-897-1111).

Churches

The oldest congregation in town, **Concordia Evangelical Lutheran Church**, 1800 Sierra Street at Eighteenth (559-897-2165; www.concordiakingsburg.com), was organized in 1887. Six years later the California Conference of the Augustana Evangelical Lutheran Church was founded in Kingsburg. In the narthex of the 1917 Gothic, red-brick building is the original communion service set and other memorabilia significant in the congregation's history. Organized by the Reverend Telleen, who was prompted to action by correspondence from Andrew Erikson, the congregation built its first sanctuary in 1888 on Lincoln, just off Sierra. The structure, though now owned by another congregation, still stands.

The **First Baptist Church**, 1615 Draper Street (559-897-3310), is a reddish-brick, Romanesque-style building with a cornerstone inscribed, "Swedish Baptist Church A.D. 1920." The **Evangelical Covenant Church**, 1490 Lincoln Street (559-897-3031), was organized in 1907. In 1917 the congregation decided to erect a Romanesque building on the same site as the old one, built in 1907. **Colony Covenant**, 11474 South Zediker Avenue at E. Rose Avenue (559-897-3854), five miles from Kingsburg's Memorial Park, was organized in 1891 as the first Covenant church in the area, and was built halfway between Kingsburg and Reedley in the midst of peach orchards and vineyards. The Kingsburg Town Cemetery, S. Academy Avenue and E. Clarkson Avenue, has in its northeast section graves with Swedish inscriptions.

Templeton

Templeton, a small rural community six miles south of Paso Robles, is home to probably the oldest Swedish church building in California still serving its original congregation. **Bethel Lutheran Church**, at Third and Crocker Streets, was organized by the Reverend Telleen in 1887 and the sanctuary completed in 1891. This attractive brick church has nineteenth-century windows in the Gothic style and a central wood steeple, a later addition. The sanctuary retains the original pulpit, semicircular altar rail, and wooden pews. The original altar is in Fellowship Hall, having been moved there after the December 2003 earthquake. The church still owns original wooden offertory plates.

In another part of town is the church's attractive cemetery, which has a lovely rose garden display at its center. Underscoring the community's Swedish heritage is the multitude of gravestones with Swedish names and inscriptions. Early settlers were attracted by the region's lumbering opportunities. Several wooden markers, including that of Anders Anderson, bear Swedish inscriptions.

Santa Barbara

At the north end of the city are the Earl Warren Showgrounds, at Las Positas Road and U.S. Highway 101. The Covenant Church's Samarkand Retirement Center, 2550 Treasure Drive (805-687-0701), is also located here. About one hour northwest of Santa Barbara is the attractive community of Solvang, a Danish-oriented tourist town.

Pasadena

The **Messiah Lutheran** congregation, 570 E. Orange Grove Boulevard (626-795-7748), was founded in 1912; its twentieth-century, Gothic-style sanctuary was constructed in 1924. The 1921 altar painting is by Olof Grafström. The **Pasadena Covenant Church,** 539 N. Lake Avenue, was organized in 1912 and erected its sanctuary in 1947.

Los Angeles

Swedish landmarks in Los Angeles include noteworthy churches and locations of commercial and entertainment-industry interest. The mother church for Southern California Swedish Lutherans is **Angelica Lutheran Church**, 1345 Burlington Avenue at Fourteenth (213-382-6378). Two years after organization by the Reverend Telleen in 1888, the first church at Tenth and Grand was dedicated. Twelve years later a second sanctuary was built at Seventeenth and Hope. The Burlington sanctuary was completed in 1925. A large landscape painting by Christian von Schneidau depicting an idyllic, romanticized Los Angeles, including the two former Angelica sanctuaries, is currently undergoing restoration.

Roger Dahlhjelm (1881–1950) and Howard F. Ahmanson (1906–1968), whose grandfathers emigrated from Sweden, were influential in Los Angeles commercial development. Dahlhjelm's paternal grandfather, Claes Dahlhjelm, arrived in the United States from Östergötland in the early 1850s and became one of the first settlers in Minnesota's Chisago Lake area. In 1934 Dahlhjelm founded the **Farmers Market**, 6333 W. Third Street at Fairfax Avenue (323-933-9211; www.farmersmarketla.com), visited by thousands of people every day. When the Farmers Market opened in 1934, there were eighteen stalls. Today the sprawling market has dozens of stalls, stores, and restaurants. Above Gate 1 is the former office and space where Dahlhjelm lived. He remained the market's manager until 1949.

Ahmanson, who was the grandson of Jönköping immigrant Johan August Åhmanson, developed the successful Los Angeles–based Home Savings and Loan Association. Out of that enterprise grew the Ahmanson Foundation, which provides financial encouragement and assistance in education, the arts, and medical research. Named in his honor are the Ahmanson Building in the Los Angeles County Museum of Art, 5905 Wilshire (323-857-6000; www.lacma.org); the Ahmanson Center for Biological Research at the University of Southern California; and the Ahmanson Theatre, 125 N. Grand Avenue (323-972-7401), near the Walt Disney Concert Hall. Two blocks away is the Cathedral of Our Lady of the Angeles, which contains a series of John Nava's tapestries, including St. Bridget of Sweden located on the north wall.

On the sidewalk at **Mann Chinese Theatre**, 6925 Hollywood Boulevard (323-464-8111), are the signatures and the handprints and footprints of famous actors and actresses. Included are Gloria Swanson, whose father was of Swedish parentage; Swedish film and stage star Viveca Lindfors; and Swedish American actress and singer Ann-Margret, whose family (the Olssons) came from Valsjöbyn. Swedish actress Ingrid Bergman received an Academy Award for best actress in 1944 *(Gaslight)* and 1956 *(Anastasia)* and for best supporting actress in 1964 *(Murder on the Orient Express)*. Famed actress Greta Garbo is honored with a star embedded in the sidewalk near the Mann Chinese Theatre.

Claes Oldenburg and Coosje van Bruggen's *Toppling Ladder with Spilling Paint* (1986) is located at 919 S. Alban Street at the Loyola Law School. Oldenburg's *Giant Binoculars* is on Main Street in Venice, and his *Hats* is in Salinas.

Claremont

The **Nordic Collections, Honnold/Mudd Library of the Claremont Colleges**, 800 Dartmouth Avenue (909-607-3977; www.libraries.claremont.edu), began with the donation of the private library and residual estate of Waldemar Westergaard, a professor at Pomona College, 1916–1925, and the University of California–Los Angeles, 1925–1950. Westergaard and his colleague David Bjork frequently traveled to Scandinavia, acquiring books, pamphlets, and microfilms. A significant amount of their microfilm is also stored in UCLA's Library. Other Scandinavian scholars, including former director Franklin Scott and Columbia University professor John H. Wuorinen, have contributed additional works to the Honnold/Mudd Library.

Thousand Oaks

The campus of California Lutheran University, 60 W. Olsen Road (www.clu.edu), is located on the former Pederson Ranch. In 1959 Richard Pederson, child of Scandinavian immigrants, donated to the university his scenic ranch, which forms the heart of the 225-acre campus.

The **Scandinavian Cultural Center** near campus has recently obtained a house at 26 Faculty Road (805-241-0391). It sponsors a well-attended April Scandinavian festival. The center also sponsors symposia on historical topics related to Scandinavia.

Riverside

The **Eden Lutheran Church**, 4725 Brockton Avenue (909-684-3336; www.eden lutheran.org), dates from 1888 as the Scandinavian Evangelical Eden Church. The building was constructed in twentieth-century Romanesque style in 1952.

Rancho Palos Verdes

The all-glass **Wayfarers' Chapel**, 5755 S. Palos Verdes Drive (310-377-7919; www .wayfarerschapel.org), stands as a national memorial to Emanuel Swedenborg; it is owned by the Swedenborgian Church. The cornerstone was laid in 1949 and the chapel dedicated two years later. A favorite site for weddings, the chapel was designed by Lloyd Wright, son of architect Frank Lloyd Wright. The chapel looks out on the Pacific Ocean and Catalina Island on the horizon. Surrounding the chapel is a lovely garden. A visitor's center contains exhibits and literature about the Swedenborgian faith, including one about Johnny Appleseed (John Chapman), a Swedenborgian missionary on the American frontier.

Nearby in Rolling Hills Estates is the **Rolling Hills Covenant Church**, 2222 N. Palos Verdes Drive (310-519-9406), a huge modern complex with perhaps the largest membership of any Covenant church in the United States.

In San Pedro a Swedish service is held monthly at the Norwegian Seamen's Church, 1035 S. Beacon Street (310-832-6800), which was built in 1951.

San Diego

In San Diego several landmarks focus on Charles A. Lindbergh Jr., who flew the first nonstop solo transatlantic flight. Lindbergh, a twenty-five-year-old aviator at the time of his 1927 flight, was the son of a Stockholm-born immigrant who became a well-known, five-term Republican congressman from Minnesota. At the **San Diego Aerospace Museum**, 2001 Pan American Plaza in Balboa Park (619-234-8291; www.aerospacemuseum.org), a reproduction of Lindbergh's *Spirit of St. Louis* is featured along with other Lindbergh memorabilia. At Solar Turbines, Inc., 2200 Pacific Highway at Juniper Street, is a historical plaque identifying the site where Lindbergh supervised the airplane's construction. In the lobby of the East Terminal at Lindbergh Field is a bust of the flier sculpted by Paul Fjelde. At the west end of Terminal 2 West is another sculpture, *Charles A. Lindbergh: The Boy and the Man,* by Minnesota sculptor Paul Granlund. Lindbergh is depicted

Wayfarers' Chapel, Rancho Palos Verdes

in two images—a small boy playfully pretending to fly and the young solo aviator who flew nonstop from New York to Paris.

Other San Diego sites of Swedish interest include the House of Sweden in **Balboa Park.** Coffee and refreshments are served Sunday afternoons in the stucco building that is part of the complex known as the House of Pacific Relations (619-234-0739; www.balboapark.org/museums.html).

Noteworthy churches include a congregation formed in 1891 that built a Swedish Baptist chapel at Nineteenth and H (Market). Six years later, its new pastor was the Reverend Nils Peter Palmquist from South Bend, Indiana, whose daughter later wed Earl Warren, U.S. Supreme Court chief justice from 1953 to 1969. Although Palmquist left for Oakland at the turn of the century and the church closed shortly thereafter, the congregation reemerged in 1907 under the name Bethel Baptist Church and met at Sixteenth and E Streets. Today that congregation is the **College Avenue Baptist Church** (619-582-7222), located since 1940 at the corner of College and Adams. Also currently in the city are two former Augustana Lutheran congregations: Ascension, 5106 Zion Avenue (618-582-2636); and Calvary, 3060 Fifty-fourth Street (619-582-5581).

ALASKA

As the nineteenth century gave way to the twentieth, Swedes were drawn to Alaska's vastness mainly by gold; by employment opportunities in forestry, minerals, and fishing; and by mission work. Prospectors included John Brynteson, Erik Lindblom, and Jafet Lindeberg, known as the "Three Lucky Swedes," who discovered gold in Alaska at Anvil Creek near Nome on September 22, 1898. Statues honoring the three men stand in Anvil City Square, Nome. Two Swedes, Charles John Anderson, who made a fortune in Alaska and lost it in the San Francisco 1906 earthquake, and John Erikson, who found gold and became a Seattle newspaper publisher and banker, are also well-known players in the gold rush drama.

Sitka

Before 1867, when Alaska was still part of Russia, the Russian American Company employed Finns and Swede-Finns, as well as Baltic Germans, Estonians, and Latvians, as officers, clerks, carpenters, shipwrights, sailors, and sea captains in New Archangel, the Russian name for the principal port of Sitka. There Captain Arvid Adolph Etholén, governor from 1840 to 1845, held Alaska's first Lutheran service, perhaps the first on the North American West Coast, in the governor's residence in 1840. A Lutheran church was dedicated on Lincoln Street in 1843, the first Protestant church in Alaska. Services were conducted in Finnish and Swedish, and occasionally in German. When Alaska came under United States control, many members returned to Europe, and the congregation was left without a pastor. The building deteriorated until 1888, when it was torn down. A small group of Lutherans continued to worship in homes between 1888 and 1942, when a new church was constructed on the old site. A fire claimed the building in 1966, and in 1993 the third sanctuary was also destroyed by fire. But the **Sitka Lutheran Church** congregation, 224 Lincoln Street (907-747-3338; www.sitkalutheran.org), again rebuilt the church in 1995. A Kessler organ built in Estonia in 1844 and shipped to Sitka in 1846, thought to be the first one on the West Coast, was damaged in the 1993 fire, but it has been restored. The altar painting, *The Transfiguration of Christ,* was rendered by Finnish artist Berndt Abraham Godenhjelm (1799–1881). Buried in the small Lutheran cemetery is Edvard Etholén, son of the early governor.

Anchorage

 The small, 20 by 40 foot **Oscar Anderson House**, 420 M Street (907-274-2336), may be the oldest wooden house in Anchorage. Overlooking the Knik Arm of Cook Inlet, it was built by a Swedish immigrant in 1915. Anderson first settled in Seattle in 1905 and owned a restaurant. A sign in the adjacent park says he arrived in Alaska in 1915 and was later joined by his wife, Elizabeth (another Swedish immigrant), and their three children. For several months they lived in a tent on the bluff overlooking the house under construction. A friend once remarked, "Anderson provided the two things Anchorage needed most in its beginning—food and fuel." Shortly after his arrival he went into the cold-storage business with another man, and their firm became the region's primary meat packer. In 1915 Anderson built the Ship Creek Meat Market on Fourth Avenue. He became co-owner of the Evans Jones Coal Company and then its president and general manager. He was also involved in an airline and on the board of the former *Anchorage Times.* He lived in the house until 1969, and in 1976 his widow donated it to the city, which restored it to a near-original state. In the front room are photos of family members and a player piano bought in Seattle. The kitchen contains Anderson's butcher table from Fourth Avenue and his mother's china brought from Sweden. During December the house features a Swedish Christmas.

Delta Junction

 The site of **Rika's Roadhouse and Landing**, ten miles northwest of Delta Junction, in Big Delta State Historical Park (907-895-4201; www.rikas.com), near the Tanana River, holds the large log roadhouse, an historic barn, and several other small log buildings.

Rika Wallen operated this roadhouse from 1918 through the early 1960s. In local historian Judy Ferguson's book *Parallel Destinies,* she writes that Wallen was born Lovisa Erika Jakobson in 1874 on a farm near Örebro, Sweden. Rika joined her brother Carl in Minneapolis in 1891, where they changed their names to Wallen. Following his accidental death, she and her sister moved to San Francisco, where Rika cooked for the Hills Brothers coffee family until the 1906 earthquake. In 1916 Rika booked passage for Valdez, in part because she thought Alaska would be like Sweden. Eventually she was employed by John Hajdukovich as a cook at his roadhouse on the Tanana River. Wallen worked for a year without pay, and in 1918 Hajdukovich deeded the property to her in payment for back wages. Later she applied for a homestead patent and enlarged the property to 320 acres.

Oscar Anderson House, Anchorage

Rika's Roadhouse and Landing barn, Delta Junction

Wallen was a natural farmer who designed and built the barn with a unique ventilation system for wintering cows, sheep, oxen, mules, and poultry. The park service refers to the roadhouse as "the oldest non-refurbished historic building in Alaska."

HAWAII

Honolulu

 At Pier Seven in Honolulu is *Falls of Clyde*, a restored ship owned and operated by the Matson Navigation Company headquartered in San Francisco. William Matson was born in Sweden.

Hana

Aviation pioneer Charles Lindbergh Jr. (1902–1974) spent the last six years of his life in the community of Kipahulu near the eastern tip of Maui, about nine miles from Hana. Lindbergh's grave is in the cemetery of the Palapala Hoomau Congregational Church. (Visitors should not confuse the Hoomau Church, located off the main road at the end of a dirt drive, with the peach-colored St. Paul's Church.) On Lindbergh's simple grave is an inscription from Psalms: "If I take the wings of the morning, and dwell in the uttermost parts of the sea." The graveyard is near the edge of a high cliff overlooking the Pacific Ocean; the island of Hawaii is visible to the south. To reach this remote location, visitors drive what may be the most spectacular Hawaiian coastal road, State Highway 360, known as the Hana Highway. The road's 600 sharp turns and fifty-four bridges carry visitors alongside waterfalls and through thick tropical rain forests.

Appendix A

Swedish American Sites Listed on the National Register of Historic Places

THE NORTHEAST

Delaware

Fort Christina State Park–Wilmington
Holy Trinity (Old Swedes) Church–Wilmington
Swedish Blockhouse–Claymont

New Jersey

Trinity Episcopal (Old Swedes) Church–Swedesboro
C. A. Nothnagle Log House–Gibbstown
Swedish Granary–Greenwich

Pennsylvania

Governor Printz Park–Philadelphia
Lower Swedish Cabin–Philadelphia
Morton Homestead–Philadelphia
Gloria Dei (Old Swedes) Episcopal Church National Historic Site–Philadelphia
St. Gabriel's Church and Cemetery–Douglasville
Mouns Jones House–Douglasville
Hopewell Village National Historic Site–Birdsboro

New York

Governor Reuben Fenton Mansion–Jamestown

Connecticut

Barnum Museum–Bridgeport

Rhode Island

Gloria Dei Evangelical Lutheran Church–Providence

Maine

Swedish Lutheran Church–Monson
Larsson-Noak Historic District (including Noak Blacksmith and Woodworking
    Shop, and Larson-Ostlund log house)–New Sweden
Gustaf Adolf Lutheran Church–New Sweden
Anders and Johanna Olsson Farm–New Sweden (Westmanland)

Timmerhuset–New Sweden
Anderson Brothers Store (Lewis Anderson Hardware)–Stockholm

THE EASTERN MIDWEST

Illinois

Old Main, North Park University–Chicago
Swedish Club of Chicago–Chicago
East Rockford Historic District–Rockford
Lake-Peterson Home–Rockford
Old Main, Augustana College–Rock Island
Jenny Lind Chapel–Andover
Bishop Hill–Bishop Hill
Olof Johnson House–Galva

Indiana

Chesterton Commercial Historic District–Chesterton
Oldfields-Lilly House and Gardens–Indianapolis

Michigan

Carl Sandburg House–Harbert
Our Saviour's Historical Museum Church–Manistee
Charles Paulson House–Au Train

Wisconsin

Polk County Museum (Courthouse)–Balsam Lake
Albin Johnson Log House–Spirit

THE WESTERN MIDWEST

Iowa

New Sweden Chapel–Lockridge
Swedesburg Historic Commercial District–Swedesburg
Charles E. Hult House–Swedesburg
John Hultquist House–Swedesburg
Swedesburg Evangelical Lutheran Church–Swedesburg
Red Ball Garage–Swedesburg
Carl and Ulrika Dalander Cassel House–Madrid
Charles John Alfred Ericson Memorial Public Library–Boone
State Bank of Stratford–Stratford

Oklahoma

Oscar Brousse Jacobson House–Norman

Kansas

Swedish Pavilion and Old Mill–Lindsborg
Lindsborg Post Office–Lindsborg
Daniel J. Johnson House–Lindsborg
Hans Hanson House (Hanson-Lindfors Mansion) and Cabin–Marquette

Nebraska

Howard Hanson House–Wahoo
Peter Peterson Farmstead–Waverly
Stockholm Lutheran Church and Swedish Cemetery–Shickley
Hanson-Downing House–Kearney
Salem Methodist Episcopal Church–Axtell
Ernest A. Calling House–Gothenburg

South Dakota

Forest Avenue Historic District–Vermillion
Olof Erickson (Solomon Anderson) Farm–Alsen
Tabor Lutheran Church–Strandburg
Augustana Lutheran Church–Claremont
Peter Norbeck Visitor Center–Hermosa

MINNESOTA

Twin Cities

American Swedish Institute (Swan J. Turnblad Mansion)–Minneapolis
Milwaukee Avenue Historic District–Minneapolis
Floyd B. Olson House–Minneapolis
Grace Evangelical Lutheran Church–Minneapolis
Fredrika Bremer School–Minneapolis

East Central

Marine on St. Croix Historic District–Marine on St. Croix
Hay Lake School and Johannes Erickson Log House–Hay Lake
Franconia Historic District–Franconia
Munch-Roos House–Taylors Falls
Summit Avenue Historic District–Center City
Gustaf Anderson House–Lindstrom
C. A. Victor House–Lindstrom
Frank A. Larson House (Fridhem)–Lindstrom
J. C. Carlson House–Rush City
Our Saviour's (Swedish) Evangelical Lutheran Church of Ham Lake–East Bethel
Linden Barn–Isanti
Erickson Farmstead–Isanti

West Riverside Museum School–Cambridge
Oscar Olson House–Braham
South Maple Ridge Covenant Church–Maple Ridge

Northeast

Louis Hultgren House–Kerrick
Bethlehem Lutheran Church–Aitkin
Andrew G. Anderson House–Hibbing

Southeast

Vasa Historic District–Vasa
Welch (Cross of Christ) Lutheran Church–Welch
Swedish Evangelical Lutheran Church–Millville

South

Vista Lutheran Church–New Richland
Adolph Olson Eberhart House–Mankato
Old Main–Gustavus Adolphus College–St. Peter
John Albert Johnson House–St. Peter
Christdala Evangelical Swedish Lutheran Church–Millersburg
John Lind House–New Ulm
Christdala Evangelical Swedish Lutheran Church–Millersburg
Ernest Osbeck House–Lake Benton

Central

East Union Lutheran Church (King Oscar's Settlement)–Carver
West Union Lutheran Church–Carver
Andrew Peterson (Rock Isle) Farmstead–Waconia
Marysville "Swedesburg" Lutheran Church–Buffalo
August Akerlund Photography Studio–Cokato
Trinity Episcopal Church–Litchfield
Andreas and Johann Broman and Frank E. and Anna Broman
    Farmstead–Kandiyohi County

North Central

Charles A. Lindbergh Lindbergh State Park–Little Falls
Bergquist Pioneer Cabin–Moorhead

THE SOUTH

Florida

Hallstrom Farmstead Home–Vero Beach

Alabama

Svea Land Company Office (Oscar Johnson Memorial Library)–Silverhill
People's Supply Company (now United Bank)–Silverhill
State Bank of Silverhill–Silverhill

Texas

Zilker Park Historic District (including Swedish Log Cabin)–Austin
Old Bakery and Emporium–Austin
C. E. Johnson Home–Austin
Deep Eddy Bathing Beach–Austin
Swedish Hill Historic District–Austin
Gethsemane Lutheran Church (Texas Historical Commission)–Austin
St. David's Episcopal Church–Austin
Round Rock Commercial Historic District–Round Rock
St. John's United Methodist Church–Georgetown
Forsgard Homestead–Waco
Reynolds-Seaquist House–Mason
Swenson House–Abilene
Swenson Land and Cattle Company Headquarters–Stamford
A. J. Swenson House–Stamford
Houston Fire Station No. 7 (Houston Fire Museum)–Houston
James Bute Company Warehouse–Houston
Courtlandt Place Historic District–Houston
Gustaf M. Borgstrom House–Houston

THE WEST

New Mexico

Eklund Hotel–Clayton

Arizona

Faraway Ranch, Chiricahua National Monument–Willcox

Colorado

Swedish Evangelical Lutheran Church, Ryssby–Longmont
Bethany Swedish Evangelical Lutheran Church (Denver Gospel Church)–Denver
Golden Historic District–Golden

Utah

Mount Pleasant Commercial Historic District–Mount Pleasant
N. S. Nielson House–Mount Pleasant
Niels Ole Anderson House–Ephraim
Johnson-Nielson House–Ephraim

Idaho

Immanuel Evangelical Lutheran Church (Augustana Chapel)–Boise
Swedish Evangelical Lutheran Church, Cordelia–Moscow

Washington

Hovander Homestead–Ferndale
Bethsaida Lutheran Church Parsonage–Pleasant Ridge
La Conner Historic District–La Conner
Charles F. Nelson House–Olalla
Sandberg-Schoenfeld Building–Tacoma
Skamokawa Historic District–Skamokawa
Deep River Pioneer (Finnish Holy Trinity Evangelical) Lutheran
    Church–Skamokawa

Oregon

Swedish Tabernacle–Portland
Linnea Hall–Portland
Pittock Mansion–Portland
Lewis Anderson House, Barn, and Granary–The Dalles
Heceta Head Lighthouse–Florence
Hjalte Nerdrum House–Coos Bay
Nasburg-Lockhart House–Coos Bay
Patrick Hughes House–Coos Bay

California

Matson Building and Annex–San Francisco
Balboa Park–San Diego

Alaska

Oscar Anderson House–Anchorage
Rika's Roadhouse and Landing–Delta Junction

Hawaii

Falls of Clyde–Honolulu

Appendix B

Swedish American Sites with Other Significant National and State Designations

THE NORTHEAST

Delaware

Holy Trinity (Old Swedes) Church National Historic Landmark–Wilmington

Pennsylvania

Gloria Dei (Old Swedes) Episcopal Church National Historic Site–Philadelphia
Hopewell Village National Historic Site–Birdsboro

New York

Ellis Island National Monument and Statue of Liberty National Monument–
New York City
Castle Clinton National Monument–New York City

THE MIDWEST–EAST OF THE MISSISSIPPI RIVER

Illinois

Bishop Hill State Historic Site–Bishop Hill
Carl Sandburg Birthplace–Galesburg

Indiana

Chellberg Farm, Indiana Dunes National Lakeshore–Porter

Michigan

Paulson House, Hiawatha National Forest–Au Train

MINNESOTA

Charles A. Lindbergh House National Historic Landmark–Little Falls

THE SOUTH

North Carolina

Carl Sandburg Home National Historic Site Flat Rock

THE WEST

Arizona

Faraway Ranch, Chiricahua National Monument–Willcox

Colorado

Tallman Ranch, Golden Gate Canyon State Park–Golden
Carl Lotave plaque–Pikes Peak, Colorado Springs

California

Vikingsholm, Emerald Bay State Park–Lake Tahoe

Swedish Crosses Cemetery, Gothenburg, Nebraska

Index